THE CIA
INTELLIGENCE
ANALYST

Other Titles of Interest from Georgetown University Press

Analyzing Intelligence: National Security Practitioners' Perspectives, Second Edition
Roger Z. George and James B. Bruce, Editors

To Catch a Spy: The Art of Counterintelligence
James M. Olson

Intelligence in the National Security Enterprise: An Introduction
Roger Z. George

The National Security Enterprise: Navigating the Labyrinth
Roger Z. George and Harvey Rishikof, Editors

Thwarting Enemies at Home and Abroad: How to Be a Counterintelligence Officer
William R. Johnson

THE CIA INTELLIGENCE ANALYST

VIEWS FROM THE INSIDE

ROGER Z. GEORGE AND ROBERT LEVINE

EDITORS

GEORGETOWN UNIVERSITY PRESS / WASHINGTON, DC

The publisher is not responsible for third-party websites or their content. URL links were active at time of publication.

All statements of fact, opinion, or analysis expressed in this book are those of the authors and do not reflect the official positions or views of the Central Intelligence Agency or any other US government agency. Nothing in the contents should be construed as asserting or implying US government authentication of information or endorsement of the authors' views. This material has been reviewed solely for classification.

Library of Congress Cataloging-in-Publication Data

Names: George, Roger Z., 1949- editor. | Levine, Robert (Military analyst), editor.
Title: The CIA intelligence analyst : views from the inside / Roger Z George and
    Robert Levine, editors.
Other titles: Central Intelligence Agency intelligence analyst
Description: Washington, DC : Georgetown University Press, 2024. | Includes
    bibliographical references and index.
Identifiers: LCCN 2023057180 (print) | LCCN 2023057181 (ebook) |
    ISBN 9781647124694 (hardcover) | ISBN 9781647124700 (paperback) |
    ISBN 9781647124717 (ebook)
Subjects: LCSH: United States. Central Intelligence Agency. | Intelligence
    service—United States.
Classification: LCC JK468.I6 C5 2024 (print) | LCC JK468.I6 (ebook) |
    DDC 327.1273—dc23/eng/20240325
LC record available at https://lccn.loc.gov/2023057180
LC ebook record available at https://lccn.loc.gov/2023057181

25 24   9 8 7 6 5 4 3 2 First printing

Cover design by Jim Keller
Interior design by BookComp, Inc.

To Robert Jervis—a renowned scholar whose research, insights, and constructive criticism of intelligence analysis bridged the academic and intelligence worlds.

Contents

Illustrations

FIGURE

TABLES

Foreword

Long overdue, this book on the CIA's analytic work fills a significant gap in the intelligence literature, most of which focuses on espionage and special operations. In part, this gap stems from the stereotypical image of a lone, deskbound analyst. That image is misleading in its implicit slighting of how analysts drive and participate in intelligence collection, work collaboratively to interpret incomplete and often inconsistent information, and support the nation's most senior civilian and military decision-makers.

As this book demonstrates, there is much to understand about the complexity of the CIA's analytic operations. There is a danger in overgeneralizing about intelligence analysis, given the wide range of disciplines needed to provide a complete picture of an issue, the unique types of analytic challenges inherent in those disciplines, and the fact that analysts practice their craft for a wide range of customers in Washington and around the world. (The Agency refers to those who use analytic products as "customers" or "consumers.") Analytic support for Ukraine and the alliance that backs it displays political, military, economic, technical, and other disciplines in the most serious type of international engagement.

Some observers describe the CIA's analytic directorate as a kind of university whose "faculty" covers the full range of disciplines. The size, academic qualifications, and subject matter expertise of this analytic cadre support the claim that it could staff a major university. But there are important distinctions. Each discipline has its subject matter experts who must respond quickly and briefly to a select audience of senior civilian and military leaders who wrestle with momentous decisions on US national security. Each expert conducts varying types of analysis using tailored methodologies and multiple sources of information, including sensitive—and sometimes very limited access—classified intelligence reporting. Moreover, CIA experts often must attempt to bound the range of uncertainty facing decision-makers. While some officials are themselves foreign policy specialists and experts in their own fields, many are generalists who must rely on the CIA and other intelligence community analysts to understand the intricacies of foreign weapons developments, the internal political dynamics of closed societies, or the broader downstream consequences of technological or economic developments.

As a senior reviewer of products going to the president and his senior advisers, I could cite many examples that highlight the critical importance of integrating deep substantive knowledge and insights of analysts from distinct disciplines. One memorable case involved an unusual construction site in Syria. Our nuclear and weapons technical experts assessed this was clandestine construction of a nuclear reactor—discussed in chapter 5 of this book—that ultimately could alter the region's military balance. Included in the assessment was the analysis by political analysts on Syrian president Assad's likely calculations in undertaking a program whose discovery risked strong international reactions—first and foremost, from Israel. Rigorous editing and review helped to prepare CIA senior leaders who briefed the key elements of this assessment to the senior US decision-makers; that briefing proved critical to the White House's decision on this issue.

The contributing authors of this book shine a much-needed spotlight on the nuts and bolts of the Agency's daily analytic work. They are among the finest senior analysts that I had the privilege of working with during my own Agency career. As a former deputy director of intelligence for analytic programs, briefer for the President's Daily Brief, and deputy director of one of the CIA's Mission Centers, I saw their products and their impact. Their review of the analytic process and challenges underlying the Agency's analytic work also helps explain why the Directorate of Analysis continues to play a vital role. The expertise and analytic rigor provided by Agency and intelligence community analysts are even more critical in a digital age when misinformation and disinformation reach global audiences.

Whether scholars of intelligence studies, teachers of intelligence analysis, or students curious about the nature of analytic careers inside the intelligence community, readers of this volume will gain a unique, inside look at the CIA's world of analysis.

Peter Clement
Columbia University, School of International and Public Affairs
Former Deputy Director for Intelligence for Analytic Programs, CIA

Preface

This book, like many, has its origins in the editors' previous professional careers. Both of us were CIA intelligence analysts with doctorates in international relations or policy analysis, and we had common experiences in teaching intelligence. We first met as Bob handed off to Roger the position of the CIA's faculty representative to the National War College in the summer of 2001. At a senior military service college, there was never sufficient reading material for sophisticated officers to help them understand, at a very practical level, how intelligence analysis operated within the US national security enterprise. Stories of espionage and technological wizardry were abundant. However, we needed to explain the nexus between intelligence assessments and national decision-making.

Since then, we have observed that classification and the rare practitioner writing about analysis has kept that bookshelf nearly empty. Surveys of national intelligence tended to lump all "analysis" together, as if they covered it at all. Few textbooks mention the various analytic disciplines, and none explained how discipline-specific analysts did their work or why that mattered. (The contributors have provided essays on suggested reading in appendix A.)

If anyone needed an illustration of how important these disciplines can be, we would point to the war in Ukraine that was occurring as this book was written. A full range of analytic disciplines is on display. At the outset, no doubt some political and warning analysts at the CIA were reporting on the Kremlin's plans and demands, while others were probably assessing how the Ukrainian government, neighboring states, and others farther afield would react. Military analysts, of course, would be describing Russian force preparations (mobilizations and deployments); assessing the two sides' perceptions, intentions, and capabilities; and tracking and assessing the two sides' operations and strategies, focusing on their strengths and vulnerabilities. Leadership analysts were likely attempting to describe Vladimir Putin's state of mind, past behaviors, and the origin of his twisted narrative about Ukraine never having been a nation. Volodymyr Zelensky's potential for leadership success or failure as a wartime president was surely addressed. As the West responded with sanctions, CIA economic analysts would be assessing the impact of those on a wide range of Russian financial and commercial operations, like oil production, not to mention the collateral impact on European economies dependent on Russian energy exports, and others dependent on wheat exports. Less obvious would be the role of the CIA's counterintelligence and cyber analysts, who would be watching for Moscow's security services' use of social media and cyber weapons to spread chaos within Ukraine, aimed especially at its economy and defenses, and to weaken resolve among Western allies. Finally, Putin's hints about using tactical nuclear weapons would send US officials asking the CIA's science, technology, and weapons analysts about the Russian nuclear capabilities and about warning indicators of such weapons movements or other readiness measures. The pros, cons, and means of expanded intelligence sharing with Ukraine and the United States–led coalition of allies also required in-depth analysis.

The Ukrainian crisis resurfaced the need for analytic work on areas that may have received less attention in the past but clearly called for renewed attention. Political and economic analysts would have examined how much of the Ukrainian population would lose access to electricity, safe water, and heating; what would be the number of refugees; how they would leave threatened areas; and where they would go (with what support and imposing what burden). Science, technology, and weapons analysts would focus on threats to nuclear reactors subject to attack or isolation and their safe maintenance. Other technical analysts would concentrate on other industrial facilities that could pose environmental threats, such as the unintended release of chemicals.

Such examples of discipline-specific work are merely the most obvious ones. A full inventory of possible intelligence questions that the disciplines at the CIA might address in just this one conflict are too numerous to list. However, it underlines the importance of distinguishing among the different types of analysis as well as acknowledging that there must be collaboration across them to produce the best picture of a complex international crisis.

Moreover, close attention to these discrete analytic disciplines will also illustrate *how* analysis is conducted in each and reveal similarities and differences in methodologies and tradecraft that analysts use in the different disciplines. The editors hope that this volume will begin to fill that bookshelf with useful descriptions of the range of analytic disciplines, and the conduct of analysis in each, that are essential if the CIA is to continue providing comprehensive coverage of major global events that have implications for US national security.

This volume is possible only because of the enthusiastic cooperation of our colleagues from the CIA's Directorate of Analysis, who participated in this effort. Obviously, each of the contributors is a subject matter expert. Far more than that, each has the combination of skills, knowledge, and experience that made them respected senior analysts. While some have retired after decades in the business, others continue to make contributions that remain unsung, at least for the time being. We want to thank other colleagues who offered valuable advice, discussed issues with us, and reviewed some of the chapters. Among these, special thanks to Peter Clement for writing the foreword to this book and for his analytic leadership and collegiality over many decades.

As mentioned above, the paucity of books on analytic disciplines and their techniques is partly the result of the necessary classification of sensitive CIA publications and operations. However, this project was possible only because of the diligent work of the CIA's Pre-publication Clearance Review Board. This board's staff reviewed draft materials and worked with the contributing authors to ensure that these chapters could be published without the inadvertent exposure of sensitive sources and methods.

1

INTRODUCTION:
BUILDING ANALYTIC DISCIPLINES

Roger Z. George and Robert Levine

The Central Intelligence Agency (CIA) has been portrayed—in mind-bending contradictions—as sinner and saint, omnipotent and incompetent, the nexus of national security and irrelevant. The Agency has carried out clandestine operations that penetrated foreign powers' most closely held secrets, has engaged in covert actions that upheld or overthrew distant regimes, and has developed breakthrough technologies that met Isaac Asimov's third law, proclaiming that any sufficiently advanced technology is indistinguishable from magic. It has also failed on more than one occasion to carry out its most important mission: to warn national decision-makers about critical threats and persuade them to take preventive or ameliorative action.

The literature on the CIA's activities, both popular and academic, understandably has focused on such dramatic developments, events, and outsize personalities. Often, former CIA directors or senior clandestine officers craft gripping "I was there" narratives.[1] The stories are captivating. But they are far from complete. Behind the scenes, a large cadre of analysts, who are experienced subject matter experts, play a critical, seldom discussed, and poorly understood role in piecing together incomplete and contradictory information. A singular revelatory clandestine report makes for a great movie scene. But reality is a far more complex landscape.

What is often overlooked is that when President Harry Truman established the CIA in the late 1940s, he was primarily interested in getting a comprehensive set of intelligence assessments from a single agency rather than being inundated with separate reports coming from all parts of the government.[2] Hence, the concept of the "central" intelligence agency was born. This was intended to emphasize this first task of compiling reports from military officers, diplomats, and spies and distilling them into a single assessment that a busy president and his closest advisers could read.

Attention to analysis, however, remains little understood or appreciated. Few readers have any idea how analysts sift through voluminous reports, meet with sources or foreign intelligence officials, or brief presidents and Cabinet officials on urgent events around the world. This book is designed to begin filling this gap. As such, it introduces the reader to the world of analysis and its many disciplines, as seen from those inside the CIA's Headquarters in Langley, Virginia.

Of course, there is a rich intelligence studies literature on the intelligence–policy relationship and numerous scholarly works on past intelligence failures, which involved poor collection and/or analysis.[3] This is not that kind of book. Instead, this volume demystifies how analysts do their jobs and operate with other colleagues in the CIA and the broader intelligence community. The book examines how they form partnerships with those who collect the unclassified and classified information upon which they depend. Importantly, it also provides more real-world examples of the roles that analysts play in conveying their assessments to policymakers. The contributors to this book also illustrate to the outside reader the unique organizational culture that motivates CIA analysts and how it interacts with the separate cultures found in other parts of the Agency, the larger intelligence community, and the policymakers whom they serve.[4]

ANALYSTS AS ENABLERS

One of the contributing authors to this volume has written elsewhere that the analyst is the connector between the collection of raw intelligence reports and the policymakers who need to get the vital information and insight that is contained in them.[5] This role makes the analyst essential in several ways. First, analysts must assess an individual report to determine its veracity—including whether the information is from a credible source and is correct, timely, and relevant to US national security policy. Second, analysts must combine those individual raw (unevaluated) reports into a more complete description and assessment of the issue; that is, they produce what is called "finished intelligence" that can enable policymakers to reach informed decisions on an important policy issue. Third, analysts must simultaneously be asking those collecting information to seek out additional data to fill in gaps in the analysts' understanding of a target country or issue. While evaluating this information, they will often meet with outside experts as well. As analysts interact with policymakers to get their feedback on finished intelligence reports, they will get additional questions, or "tasking," that will generate new "requirements" (requests for information) for collectors. In other words, the analyst is also the essential enabler to get policymakers' need for information satisfied by the collectors.

This sounds simple. However, we can assure you it is not. Obviously, analysts must serve a wide set of decision-makers. The policymaking community is far larger than simply the president and his closest advisers; to be sure, what distinguishes the CIA

from other parts of the intelligence community is its special focus on serving the president and the National Security Council (NSC), which is written into US law. However,
the CIA also considers itself the one agency that must provide global coverage to all
the major national security agencies. Thus, its mission is to support the work of those
serving in the departments of State, Defense, Homeland Security, Justice, Treasury,
Commerce, and many other federal agencies.

The CIA's customers may be the secretary of defense, an NSC staff member, a
military commander, or an ambassador serving overseas. Necessarily, their intelligence requirements or needs will be very different from each other. So, CIA analysts
writing on any given topic will find that each customer will need more tailored forms
of analysis. The chapters in this book provide individual analysts' perspectives on
what it is like to work with both collectors and policymakers, and they highlight the
rewards and challenges such relationships can offer analysts. However, to make this
comprehensible, we first briefly describe the intelligence community, in particular
the collection environment where analysts operate, as well as the policymaker's world
that they strive to support.

WORKING INSIDE THE INTELLIGENCE COMMUNITY

The CIA has the distinction of being the only intelligence agency of the more than
a dozen that is not part of or responsible to a single government department. This
fact also contributes to its own self-image as being unique as well as both central
and autonomous compared with other intelligence units within large departments
such as the Department of State or Department of Defense. The CIA's role is also
more multifaceted than most other intelligence community agencies. It is the principal collector of human intelligence (HUMINT), and it contains the largest cadre of
national, all-source analysts.[6] In addition to these two core missions, the CIA is the
executive agent for managing the Open Source Enterprise, which is the major collector of unclassified open source intelligence (OSINT). The CIA also is responsible
for detecting foreign counterintelligence (CI) threats to the US government.[7] Finally,
but in the forefront of many movies and novels, the president has given the CIA the
primary responsibility for conducting covert action in support of his or her foreign
policies. What is critical to understand is that CIA analysts can be involved directly or
indirectly in all these missions, be it HUMINT, OSINT, CI, or covert action.

CIA analysts are part of a large organization in which there are multiple directorates, Mission Centers, and subgroups within those. The four key directorates are
the Directorate of Analysis (DA), the Directorate of Operations (DO), the Directorate
of Science and Technology (DST), and the Directorate of Digital Innovation (DDI).[8]
(An additional component, the Directorate of Support, provides critical financial,

logistical, technical, and other assistance to operations and analysis.) Each director-ate has its own leadership, recruitment and promotion system, and, accordingly, orga-nizational culture.[9] Most analysts serve in the DA, where the organizational culture is driven by the need to produce exceptionally rigorous analytical work and serve the senior-most policymakers like the president and NSC advisers.[10] Part of becoming an all-source analyst involves learning the analytic "tradecraft" (i.e., analytical methods and writing style) that is taught and practiced throughout the DA.[11]

The Directorate of Operations is typically described as the "heart" and most pow-erful part of the Agency.[12] It operates far-flung overseas stations that are responsible for some of the most sensitive intelligence gathered by the intelligence community; in the field the chiefs of station (COS) are the equivalent of an ambassador or mil-itary commander in directing the activities of all those serving in his or her sta-tion. Those station chiefs are also considered the senior (in-country) intelligence official among all other US government officials, who is responsible for managing the intelligence relationship with foreign intelligence counterparts. Even though the intelligence business traditionally involves competition with other governments' security services, today the DO must work cooperatively with many foreign intelli-gence services to gather the best information. This principle was established early in World War II, when the United States joined forces with the intelligence services of the United Kingdom, Canada, Australia, and New Zealand. This so-called Five Eyes group has been the model for multilateral intelligence cooperation and continues to this day.[13]

With all these responsibilities for overseas collection, liaison relationships, and covert action, the DO often sees its work as more important than that of other ele-ments of the CIA, including its analysts. Nevertheless, some DA analysts serve in the DO to provide direct support to their operations and to help vet DO sources. One of the most direct functions analysts can play is in supporting the DO's respon-sibilities for managing its overseas relationships with foreign intelligence services. This is known in the intelligence business as "liaison." For analysts, it often means meeting with a foreign government's intelligence analysts as part of formal analyti-cal exchanges, hosted by the DO. This benefits both the analysts and operators: the former get their analysis critiqued and are exposed to alternative views, and the lat-ter earn credibility with the host liaison service in allowing their services to hear the views of the CIA's experts.

Rounding out the list of analytical partners inside the CIA are the DST and DDI. The Directorate of Science and Technology also contains analysts and other techni-cal experts who specialize in both assessing key foreign technology developments but also building unique technical devices—including covert communications and disguises—to aid collection efforts.[14]

Finally, the newest Directorate of Digital Innovation has collected a wide range of skills previously spread among other directorates so that it can concentrate on developing very special digital capabilities for collecting against and countering foreign cyber operations. So, in each directorate, there are analysts of various types working against separate sets of targets. Often there must be collaboration across the directorates when, for example, a technical collection operation run by the DO needs the assistance from analysts found in the DA, DST, and/or DDI. "One agency, one mission" has become the motto of the CIA, even if it is not practiced as often as everyone would hope.

As a CIA analyst, one must understand not only one's own role in the CIA but also how an analyst fits into the broader intelligence community. Therefore, a good analyst will learn how the various collection disciplines operate. How does the US government collect overhead imagery and produce geospatial intelligence? The proficient analyst will know how to put in requirements for tasking satellites and other platforms to collect information on key military, economic, counterterrorism, and many other targets; they will also know the capabilities and limitations of the various types of intelligence, known as "INTs." That analyst would also know the single-source imagery analysts working on these targets at the National Geospatial Intelligence Agency. In a similar fashion, the National Security Agency (NSA) is collecting voluminous electronic signals (SIGINT) in the form of foreign missile test data, telephonic transmissions, satellite communications, and foreign Internet traffic. So, CIA analysts need to know the kinds of information they can expect to receive daily as well as how to task those systems.

Obviously, because the CIA is the principal HUMINT collector, every analyst working on a country or topic would be wise to have a working relationship with collection management officers (CMO) sitting in the CIA's Directorate of Operations (DO). These CMOs—formerly called reports officers—are the ones who receive clandestine HUMINT reports from overseas stations and prepare them for release to all-source analysts within the Directorate of Analysis (DA) and to other intelligence community analysts. For CIA analysts, these CMOs are the ones who can help enlighten them about specific sources, including their strengths and weaknesses and their credibility for reliability and accuracy. In turn, analysts can give a CMO updated collection requirements in hopes that some sources could report on those topics. Finally, it is common knowledge that for most analysts the bulk of the information at his or her disposal will be open source materials in the form of speeches by foreign leaders, scientific reports, or current news items in the foreign press that the Open Source Enterprise must collect, translate, and disseminate to every analyst across the intelligence community. Thus, the typical analyst's electronic inbox will daily include a stack of SIGINT reports on conversations or weapons tests, diplomatic reports as well as clandestine DO HUMINT reports on political developments, or open source news reporting on a country's economic prospects or a recent election. This is the raw reporting, out of which analysts will build a variety of assessments, depending on the topic, its complexity and sensitivity, and time horizon.

Before analysts can even begin to prepare reports, they must assure themselves that the facts and data they must work with are accurate, timely, and relevant. As mentioned above, they must have a good grounding in how human and technical intelligence works and how to evaluate the quality of this intelligence. The editors of this book have both had experiences working with collectors. While there are senior collection managers—called national intelligence collection managers—who operate at the "strategic" level of working on collection strategies and assigning resources, it is the analysts who know the details.[15] As a national intelligence officer, one of this book's editors chaired a regular HUMINT collection meeting, where analysts provided him with a detailed report card on where this kind of source reporting was strong or where there were gaps. National intelligence collection managers now chair those meetings, but they must rely heavily on the analysts who work directly with the reports and know how useful they are. Likewise, this book's other editor had occasion to support the then–CIA deputy director for collection, Charles Allen. It was Allen who admitted that he had to rely heavily on the cadre of analysts as he did not have the time or energy to be knowledgeable on the capabilities and actual use of the intelligence community's many collection platforms. These analysts became experts on collection by serving rotational assignments at the National Security Agency, where they worked side by side with SIGINT analysts; or they had similar assignments in the DO, where they sat next to the collection reports officers. Analysts, thus, remain critical enablers for gathering the best information possible.

ANALYTIC PRODUCTION

Regardless of an analyst's specific discipline, there are four general types of intelligence assessments. The first one that will be familiar to most people is a type that was at one time referred to as current intelligence. Although that term has fallen out of favor in the intelligence community, it captures a critical stream of analytic production. One of the bread-and-butter tasks of analysts is to track developments in their account, their regional or functional area of study. When noteworthy events occur, analysts produce short products that report and explain the events. While DA analytic standards push analysts to do more than merely report events—that is, to explain why they matter and their impact on US national interests—no analyst holds back on straightforward reporting of a major event.

The second general type of assessment is the building-block research study. This product presents fundamental information about foreign organizations or activities through the accumulation, filtering, and organizing of raw reporting. Such a product is light on analysis—for example, it gives lists of people occupying key foreign government positions. Nevertheless, these building-block studies are the critical basis for analyses of trends and forecasts. In the past, the CIA's National Intelligence Surveys recorded political, military, economic, social, and other dimensions of closed societies.[16] Preparing or updating such a survey allowed a junior analyst to develop in-depth knowledge. DA studies such as the "Saudi Arabia Handbook" served a similar set of purposes.[17]

The third general type—intelligence assessments—arguably is the most important work done in the DA. Material in raw reports and building-block studies is aggregated and evaluated to interpret why events or trends are occurring and to give their implications for US national interests. Moreover, each analysis builds on the findings of previous ones. An insightful product on Moscow's behavior in crises, for example, built on previous studies of how the Russians had acted in specific situations. When analysts refer to "analysis," this is most commonly what they mean.

The fourth category—anticipatory or estimative analysis—shares characteristics with the one just discussed but has an additional feature. All analysis is forward-looking, in the sense that even past events are reported and studied because of their bearing on future events or conditions. Not all analysis, however, attempts to anticipate what is likely to happen. Products that estimate or forecast face challenging tasks.[18] Anticipatory assessments are beset by complexity and are highly contingent on the interactions of numerous independent actors (including US actions). The best known of these products are National Intelligence Estimates, though NIEs are hardly the only vehicle for anticipatory analysis. Not all consumers welcome these products, although many find them stimulating and of great value. The best anticipatory products are (1) evidence based, (2) logical and explicit about their logic, and (3) probabilistic, in the sense that assumptions and other uncertainties are considered, and different outcomes are offered. Inductive reasoning, the heart of intelligence analysis, is by its very nature open to different general conclusions—and even more so when peering into the future.

There is not a simple, set correspondence between the general type or category of intelligence assessment and its form, although some patterns are well established (see box 1.1). Current intelligence frequently appears in the President's Daily Brief (PDB) and in Worldwide Intelligence Report (WIRe) articles, but Mission Center serial publications carry it as well. Anticipatory intelligence dominates NIEs, but it can play a major role in intelligence assessments (i.e., long-form publications).

BOX 1.1: EVOLVING ART FORMS OF INTELLIGENCE PRODUCTS

PDB—President's Daily Brief

The PDB is the premier publication of the intelligence community, delivered to the president and a small set (typically about a dozen) of his Cabinet members and senior-most advisers six days a week.[19] Although the Office of the Director of National Intelligence is responsible for the PDB, most of its analytic contents are provided by CIA analysts. While the length has varied, in most years only a handful of articles were included in any issue. Most articles are brief—typically a page or less.[20] It has undergone rapid evolution since the presidency of George W. Bush to satisfy the preferences of the incumbent.[21] It can also be provided electronically.

WIRe—Worldwide Intelligence Review electronic

The CIA, and now the intelligence community,[22] has had a daily (six days a week) publication with broad distribution since the Truman presidency.[23] The form of the vehicle has changed, as has its name. Previously, it was the NID (National Intelligence Daily)[24] and the SEIB (Senior Executive Intelligence Brief).[25] With electronic distribution, there are looser limits on the number and length of analytic pieces. Nevertheless, most WIRe articles are one or two pages long. Moreover, the WIRe is a general delivery vehicle and depository for many products that would not have appeared in earlier daily publications.

Periodic Publications

Historically, the CIA has produced numerous weekly, monthly, and quarterly reviews.[26] They have carried titles like the Western Europe Review,[27] Science and Weapons Review, International Economic & Energy Weekly, the Proliferation Digest, Africa Review, European Review, and USSR Review. Many did not represent a significant event or recent discovery, demanded for current publications, or required longer treatment. Some allowed analysts to develop their craft and provided interested consumers with additional insights.[28] Other short-lived publications were SitReps (Situation Reports) that covered developments in conflicts or crisis situations, such as the Balkan Situation Report, Middle East Situation Report,[29] and the Afghan Situation Report.

Long-Form Publications

Research and analytic products that required space to develop their stories have appeared under a variety of forms—IAs (Intelligence Assessment), IRs (Intelligence Report), IMs (Intelligence Memorandum), and Memoranda.[30] Some distinctions were occasionally drawn between forms (IRs were often longer and more data-rich building blocks than IAs). Unlike WIRe articles of perhaps one to two pages in length, long-form publications can run to dozens of pages and be heavily illustrated with graphs, maps, and images. With the electronic dissemination system of the WIRe, these products ride that vector to make it to consumers.

NIE—National Intelligence Estimate

The intelligence community's products generated under the auspices of national intelligence officers, NIEs provide a broad, intelligence community-wide perspective on an issue.[31] NIEs and related intelligence community products—such as SNIEs (Special National Intelligence Estimate), Memos to Holders of NIEs, and IIM (Interagency Intelligence Memoranda)—typically take weeks or months or sometimes years to create and estimate future conditions. They can forecast developments from a few months to several years, depending on the topic and policymakers' interest.

Analysts use several products for their research and analysis to reach consumers. Traditionally, the predominant forms have been hard copy papers or articles—generally short (one to two pages) for senior consumers and longer products for specialists and advisers—and in-person briefings. The forms are constantly evolving.[32] Some have lineage that is traced through more than seven decades (e.g., the President's Daily Brief), while others come and go. Many have changed names, while their basic structures hardly have altered. Some products are used exclusively by individual disciplines. For example, LPs, or Leadership Profiles, are produced only by leadership analysts; some technical reports are produced only by science, technology, and weapons (ST&W) analysts.

New electronic dissemination systems have expanded presentational options and no doubt will continue to do so, allowing more rapid and broader dissemination and more extensive use of multimedia and interactive products.[33] Secure video conferencing has expanded the types and eased the logistics of "in-person" briefings. With the creation of the Office of the Director of National Intelligence, more of the products are under intelligence community control, vice the CIA's.

ANALYTIC TRADECRAFT

Another feature of intelligence analysis that deserves careful attention is the changing priorities of DA production, largely the results of trying to meet new consumer demands. Consumers and authorities within the CIA have long had concerns about the relative effort put into the production of current intelligence items—mostly brief, factual reports—many seeing that effort as disproportionately heavy.[34] Beginning in about 1990, a combination of events, technologies, and consumer demands pushed the directorate to enrich short products carried in daily publications. For those of us who lived through that period, it was obvious that a "CNN effect" was at work during and after the first Gulf War in 1991.[35] If TV viewers could watch cruise missiles fly by cameras in near real time, what was the value added of intelligence reporting? How could we prove our value?

Some of the first steps involved separating factual reporting from analysis in any given article. Papers, talks, and guidance from influential senior officers, such as Doug MacEachin (named deputy director for intelligence in 1993) and Jack Davis,[36] pushed for greater rigor and thoroughness in analytic thinking and writing.[37] A few years later, the analytic component began a directorate-wide effort to instill those traits through Tradecraft 2000, a short retraining effort, and the creation of the Sherman Kent School for Intelligence Analysis in 2000. The failures associated with 9/11 and Iraqi weapons of mass destruction (WMD) fueled additional self-studies (e.g., as described in chapter 5 below by Jane Fletcher). One area received increased attention—the use of structured analytic techniques (see box 1.2)—originally called alternative analysis.[38] Within several years, the directorate established an analytic quality framework to evaluate products.[39] Each of these initiatives changed the character of analytic products.

According to this quality framework, every item is now expected to go well beyond mere reporting of a foreign event or trend. The main description of an event must explain why it is significant and what risks and opportunities it carries for US decision-makers. Analytic judgments, not merely factual descriptions, are required and must be supported by corroborating evidence logically linked to the judgments. The entire presentation must be clear, consistent, and easily followed.

These are not easy standards to meet. There is constant tension between rigor and the brevity that encourages consumers to find time to read our products in their brutally paced days. Any comparison of analytic products from the 1970s (especially brief articles) and more recent ones, nevertheless, would quickly reveal improvements.

Producing a piece of finished intelligence or an assessment involves initially reviewing all relevant reports and comparing notes with fellow analysts in the CIA as well as other agencies like the DIA or the State Department's Bureau of Intelligence and Research (INR). Daily, the analyst in one of the dozen or so Mission Centers at the CIA[40] will decide if they need to write up a current intelligence item for publication in the PDB[41] or the Worldwide Intelligence Report (WIRe). The PDB is the most exclusive and highly classified daily publication, intended only for the president and a handful of senior officials. Each recipient has an assigned senior analyst, who briefs the PDB's contents and gets feedback and follow-up questions from his or her customer. The WIRe is distributed electronically to a broader set of users in Washington-based agencies but also to overseas embassies and military commands.[42]

A CIA analyst's written product must also go through a process called "coordination"—a euphemism for allowing other analysts to critique and modify a piece of analysis. Only then will it be ready for higher levels of review by the analyst's supervisor, Mission Center leadership, directorates, and even the director or deputy director of the CIA, on rare occasions. More like running the gauntlet, this coordination process is designed to ferret out improper use of reporting, poor argumentation, analytical bias along with faulty grammar. By the time a piece of analysis is ready for publication and transmission to policymakers, it is truly an Agency product and not solely that of the principal drafter of the assessment. In this respect, the CIA is accountable, not just the analyst. This process is an important foundation for the analytic culture at the CIA. There is considerable pride among CIA analysts for producing what they rightly regard as the "gold standard" for analysis. It stems from their relying on all-source intelligence reporting, using well-practiced analytical techniques for vetting source reporting and uncovering hidden analytic biases as well as going through multiple reviews designed for quality control.

This analytical culture can at times seem arrogant. Notions like the "gold standard" can set the teeth of all-source analysts at the State Department's INR and the DIA on edge. It is true that the CIA has the largest cadre of analysts covering the most targets of any analytical element in the intelligence community. Also, it has the distinction of writing most of the PDB items for the president and his key advisers. Still, the DIA is rightly proud of its own assessments of foreign militaries, their weapons systems, and defense institutions. Similarly, the small cadre of analysts at the INR (roughly three hundred) has spent as much time if not more on their respective intelligence accounts and are

BOX 1.2: STRUCTURED ANALYTIC TECHNIQUES

CIA officers have used structured analytic techniques (SATs) for decades. Some approaches came out of think tanks (e.g., RAND's DELPHI technique) and others came from academic and government sources (e.g., war games).[43] A recognition that cognitive biases—innate, unconscious biases or errors in thinking—could lead analysts astray moved SATs to prominence in analytic training. CIA officer Richards Heuer took research by Daniel Kahneman and Amos Tversky to demonstrate how cognitive biases could skew analysis and argued for the use of SATs to expose flawed assumptions and mental models.[44]

Heuer's proof of principle was how analysts could test alternative hypotheses about an event or situation rigorously by examining how individual pieces of evidence were consistent, inconsistent, or not applicable to each hypothesis. Evidence that was inconsistent with—or, even better, disproved—a hypothesis was especially valuable. Heuer demonstrated how this technique he termed an analysis of competing hypotheses helped analysts fight against such traps as the confirmation bias (looking for or valuing evidence that confirmed a belief) and anchoring bias (the tendency of analysts to weigh initial evidence more heavily than subsequent evidence). In addition to an analysis of competing hypotheses, some of the SATs most frequently used are:

- *Structured brainstorming*—a managed group process designed to encourage new ideas and concepts.
- *Key assumptions check*—a review of the key working assumptions on which conventional lines of analysis rest.
- *"What if?" analysis*—assumes that an event has occurred with potential (negative or positive) impact and explains how it might come about.
- *Team A / Team B*—use of separate analytic teams that contrast two (or more) strongly held views or competing hypotheses about a common set of facts.
- *Devil's advocacy*—constructing the case against a conventional line of analysis by proposing alternative assumptions and interpretations of evidence.
- *Alternative futures*—developing a matrix usually of four alternative futures built on combining a limited set of uncertain factors to imagine how the environment might be radically different from the present.

Although the Directorate of Analysis encourages analysts to use SATs and courses at the Sherman Kent School teach them to all analysts, it appears that few are widely used (discounting analysts who merely "check the box" for their use).[45] After nearly two decades, there is only limited research into whether SATs produce better analysis than traditional, unstructured, intuitive analysis.[46]

writing for the secretary of state, whose decisions are nearly as consequential as those coming out of the Oval Office. Hence, when a CIA analyst sends a draft PDB item for "coordination" to one of those other agencies on a topic that they feel is within their area of responsibility, it is almost expected that some changes will be required, or perhaps even a dissenting commentary will need to be added to reflect another agency's analytical views. Such is the complicated intelligence world for CIA analysts.

THE POLICYMAKER'S WORLD

Outsiders may believe that CIA analysts are merely researchers or academics who ply their trade inside classified vaults. If that were the case, the CIA would probably be producing academic studies that no one would ever read. Instead, the first task for today's analyst is to understand what information policymakers need to make important decisions. In its early days, the CIA perhaps did not worry sufficiently about the relevance of its analytic work, as it thought everything it could learn and write about the Soviet Union and its Eastern European satellites was important. More than a few senior officials, like Henry Kissinger, at times described CIA analysts as too content to write what interested them and too passive in not asking him what specific information he needed.[47] Moreover, the CIA in the early Cold War held the view that its analysts should remain "at arm's length" from policymakers, so that its assessments would not be subject to politicization.[48] That perspective never completely insulated analysts from politics. Moreover, the effort to keep analysts detached from their customers was abandoned consciously as the Soviet Union collapsed; the CIA realized it needed to focus more specifically on the precise intelligence needs of policymakers found in many national security agencies. Robert Gates, a former director of the CIA—as well as being deputy national security adviser for President George H. W. Bush—captured this reality when he wrote in the mid-1990s that "relevance" had become more important than ever. Moreover, analysts needed to get "downtown" to find out what information policymakers needed to know for a fast-changing world of new potential threats.[49]

This amounted to a huge change in the business model of the CIA. Instead of lengthy reports on arcane aspects of a foreign political or military development, the CIA strove for brevity and impact in its assessments. As President George W. Bush phrased it, he wanted "actionable intelligence" rather than nice-to-know facts. Hence, CIA analysts churned out short, highly sensitive PDB items for the president's eyes only as well as a series of other short daily publications suited to the mid-level policymakers across Washington who had to formulate policy recommendations for their seniors. Accordingly, analysts needed to know what policies and options the NSC and other key elements of the national security enterprise were considering. Indeed, this did necessitate more analysts going downtown, either to brief officials and obtain their feedback or to take rotational assignments on policy staffs that would acquaint them with the content and process of policymaking within the various federal departments and agencies. In sum, analysts needed feedback on what they had written. At the same time, they were soliciting guidance, or "tasking," on what further information these policymakers required.

Once CIA analysts have had a few briefing sessions in the offices of policymakers, they realize how different the atmosphere and culture are from the quiet hallways at Langley.[50] A senior policymaker has scant time to read, much less think about, the intelligence they are provided. Senior officials are running to and from meetings, greeting and negotiating with foreign dignitaries, traveling abroad, or testifying before congressional committees. They are naturally optimistic about the power and cleverness of their policy initiatives; moreover, they crave certainty about the issues they are attempting to address. However, intelligence analysts—by their very nature—are skeptics who cannot provide many assessments with a high degree of certainty. Instead, they qualify their forecasts with phrases such as "we judge with a moderate degree of confidence that X will occur." Alternatively, analysts might craft forecasts that see a range of outcomes saying that—assuming that no exogenous factors shift—there is a high, medium, or low possibility of various events occurring.

This is inherently frustrating for many, but not all, decision-makers. One can recall, for example, that before the raid on Bin Laden's hideout in Pakistan, the CIA could characterize his presence there as only a 60 to 70 percent certainty.[51] Such is the reality for policymakers who must make tough calls in the absence of complete knowledge of what is occurring or likely to occur. In advance of the withdrawal of US forces from Afghanistan, intelligence analysts forecast that the Kabul government would eventually collapse; however, no one—policymakers included—expected its collapse within weeks.[52]

These examples highlight the inevitable friction in the intelligence–policy relationship. Sometimes, analysts are dealing with policymakers who have been disappointed with their assessments in the past and are either agnostic or hostile toward the value of such efforts. Other times, policymakers—especially those who are less informed about what intelligence can reasonably do—expect complete accuracy, timeliness, and certainty and then also become disenchanted. As the Washington saying goes, however, "there are no policy failures, only intelligence failures."

Lest readers think that analysts are doomed to failure with policymakers, many have developed good working relations with their principal policy interlocutors. Seasoned analysts—such as those featured in this book—have spent considerable time educating decision-makers on how analysis is conducted, what evidence and assumptions it is built on, and what inherent uncertainties or information gaps exist of which the policymaker must be aware. In this fashion, trust can be built. However, it takes devoted time and effort by analysts to prove that they are there to support policy decisions and can provide a unique perspective available nowhere else.

BUILDING ANALYTIC DISCIPLINES

The analysts within the CIA constitute an exceptional cadre of experts with varied talents and experiences. Over past decades, several analytic disciplines have grown up that distinguish the CIA from every other member of the US intelligence community through the sheer number and scope of its disciplines. The Agency's use of the term "disciplines" can be confusing to those used to seeing the word paired with "academic." Academic disciplines or fields are categories of knowledge. They are characterized by specialized journals, associations, and departments within colleges and universities. The number of disciplines continues to grow, resulting in ever-greater academic specialization.

Analytic disciplines in the CIA are considerably fewer in number and are broader than academic disciplines. Thus, individuals slotted into positions as political analysts may work on a country's or region's domestic politics, foreign policies, ethnography or other aspects of anthropology, public opinion, or any number of academic fields. This "big tent" approach to analytic disciplines has its advantages and disadvantages. One of its strengths is the ability to offer internal analytic, discipline-based courses in the DA's Sherman Kent School for Intelligence Analysis. Greater subdivisions would make it difficult to provide learning opportunities to rather small pools of specialists. Conversely, it is misleading to suggest that a science, weapons, and technology analyst is likely to understand conventional, nuclear, chemical, and biological weapons; surface and air-launched missiles; command-and-control networks; and so on. Specialization occurs.

Analytic disciplines provide an intellectual home for personnel. Many of us at the CIA have shifted our work focus from one country or region to another, plying our growing analytic expertise on new issues and problem sets. In courses, conferences, and especially on the job, we build deep ties with other specialists in our disciplines from whom we can tap insights.

No division of intellectual scope or labor is ideal. The CIA has expanded its number of disciplines somewhat over the years, most recently with cyber analysts. Its big tent approach has, to date, displayed greater strengths than weaknesses.

THE VOICES FROM INSIDE THE CIA

By presenting a range of voices from inside the CIA, the reader will get a mosaic of how analysis is conducted and used. The reader will come away with an understanding of the range of types of analysts and what it is like to do their jobs. The authors of the chapters in this volume are among the most accomplished in their respective fields, and they bring a wide range of insights from their work with collectors as well as their dealings with policymakers. (See their biographies in the contributors section near the end of the book.) To introduce them, first it is necessary to understand the range of disciplines that these analysts represent. Within the Directorate of Analysis, these major disciplines are easily recognized:

- *Political analysts* assess the domestic politics and foreign policy goals and actions of key countries and regions, including how these governments are performing and what trends might pose challenges to US foreign policy goals.
- *Military analysts* assess the military plans and programs, weapons capabilities, and operations of foreign militaries and report on changes that could lead to conflicts or direct threats to US interests.
- *Economic analysts* assess both regional and national economic and financial trends, including countries' trade and commercial practices that could have an impact on US economic interests and American commercial competitiveness.

- *Science, technology, and weapons analysts* assess foreign scientific and technological research and weapons performance that would add to foreign military potential, threaten US interests, or change the state of world scientific knowledge.
- *Leadership analysts* assess the characteristics, personalities, and attitudes of key foreign leaders and other influential individuals who might meet with US officials or about whom policymakers wish to know more.
- *Counterintelligence analysts* provide intelligence support to those US decision-makers responsible for identifying, neutralizing, and exploiting the intelligence activities of terrorist groups, foreign powers, or other organizations or entities seeking to harm the United States or its intelligence operations.
- *Counterterrorism analysts* support the monitoring of foreign terrorist groups and cells by assessing their cohesiveness and relationships, capabilities and weaknesses, and plans and objectives.
- *Cyber analysts* identify and characterize foreign electronic threats to critical US computer systems, including those posed by individual actors, criminal groups, or foreign governments.

This volume covers these major disciplines and more. The book begins by examining what might be called the "core" disciplines where the bulk of DA analysts work—political, military, economic, and ST&W. Most assessments to be found in the PDB and other current and estimative intelligence publications are written by analysts in these disciplines. CIA analysts have produced them in various forms from the beginning of the Agency's existence—as well as earlier in the Office of Strategic Services. The authors have been longtime analysts in each discipline and have literally grown up with their particular discipline and seen it evolve. A characteristic of each of these disciplines is their breadth. Adam Wasserman, the author of chapter 2, on political analysis, specializes in examining the potential transitions of states from autocratic or dictatorial status to democracies. He is the first to note that the political analysis field is vast. It ranges from the internal politics of foreign governments to legal systems, to ethnic and religious identities and influences, to class distinctions and conflicts—the list seems never-ending. Wasserman exemplifies the flexibility of analysts, who can move among different topics and regions of the world, serve abroad for expertise building, and take rotational assignments in other government departments to provide direct support to the policymaking process.

The book's coeditor, Robert Levine, also wrote chapter 3, on military analysis. Levine worked on conventional arms and WMD in different regions. His experiences included analysis conducted in several analytic offices of the CIA, as well as in-depth research in Europe and at the Lawrence Livermore National Laboratory, where he produced book-length studies. Like Wasserman, he worked closely with collectors—both technical and human—and wrote "raw intelligence" reports for the National Security Agency, Defense attachés, and the CIA's Directorate of Operations (using information from his debriefings of clandestine sources). Like many senior analysts, Levine taught at the Sherman Kent School for Intelligence Analysis for several years, running its military analytic training program, and taught senior military officers while serving as the CIA's representative teaching at the National War College.

Cindy Barkanic is a deeply experienced economist who wrote chapter 4 on analysis in her discipline. Over her career, she has worked on different topics in several regions, including South Asia and the Middle East. Her analytic production has covered the gamut of products, from short, immediate reports to lengthy, insightful studies. Like the other contributors, she has engaged senior consumers regularly with oral presentations and discussions that have elicited, and met, their requirements. Her mentorship of new economic analysts was critical in developing academically knowledgeable individuals into officers who could see implications for US policy in what might be esoteric data and findings.

The last core discipline chapter—chapter 5, on ST&W—was written by Jane Fletcher, an officer who served as senior scientist in the Weapons Intelligence, Non-Proliferation, and Arms Control Center (now a Mission Center in the CIA). She specialized in monitoring chemical and biological weapons, but her work carried her into many of other technical fields within ST&W analysis. Her career also included serving on various US interagency delegations, advancing tradecraft at the Sherman Kent School for Intelligence Analysis and beyond, and a commitment to mentoring analysts at all phases of their professions. She played a key role in the CIA's assessment of the mistakes and shortfalls associated with our analysis of Iraqi WMD, and her findings informed managers and analysts across the DA and the intelligence community, just to name the most obvious. She has delivered her analytic judgments to the highest levels of the US government, and her expertise has been in great demand.

While much of the work of the CIA's Directorate of Analysis is found in the four core disciplines, two other traditional fields also offer more specialized work that is less well known or understood. Leadership and counterintelligence analysis have histories almost as long as the more traditional ones in the CIA. Chapter 6, on leadership analysis, by Jeff Waggett, is one that highlights a unique role that CIA analysts perform. Over decades, the analytic products on foreign leaders have been among policymakers' best sellers. Even someone as knowledgeable as Henry Kissinger "still had a need for and would welcome tactical information that would allow him to deal better with a particular leader."[53] Waggett has been one of the longest-serving leadership analysts in the Agency, and he was the first analyst to be hired with an advanced degree in this field.

Like leadership analysis, counterintelligence has been practiced since the inception of American espionage. Knowing an enemy's intelligence capabilities to penetrate the US government and its intelligence agencies has been a CIA priority since the KGB became a major opponent. But today, CIA counterintelligence analysts must monitor and assess not only the foreign intelligence services of key adversaries but also those of nonstate actors. What makes CI analysis unique is that this discipline often is most useful to the Directorate of Operations and other intelligence collectors, which foreign intelligence services are often trying to compromise. The authors of chapter 7, James Bruce and Blake Mobley, have worked in the CI field for many years as both analysts and training instructors within the CIA's counterintelligence center. They have assessed the capabilities and intentions of foreign intelligence services targeting the United States, supported the validation of recruited assets, and worked with defectors from other countries and on major "damage assessments" of American spies as well as other highly sensitive CI operations.

The remaining two discipline chapters are relatively more recent compared with many others—namely, counterterrorism and cyber. Both began to emerge in the 1980s and 1990s but now are among the most dynamic and challenging. In chapter 8, Clark Shannon takes the reader through the world of counterterrorism analysis, with special attention to the post-9/11 expansion of the discipline. As he notes, the creation of an entirely new, associated analytic career track of targeting "puts the analyst at the center of efforts to disrupt if not entirely destroy major international terrorist organizations."[54] One of the first analysts to work on al-Qaeda, Shannon lays out the analytic methods and connections to collectors and policymakers. He also warns that counterterrorism has thrust the analyst into a gray area where some threats may partly have domestic roots or connections, which raise legal and perhaps some ethical issues for the CIA.

Chapter 9, on cyber analysis, by Steve Stigall, illustrates how an analytic discipline—and his own career—can emerge from initial interest in how a foreign government might use technology to defeat US military systems to an entirely new domain. Seldom has the rapid development of computer-based technologies offered so many possibilities for human progress but also societal vulnerabilities. Stigall was one of the first analysts at the CIA in the cyber field, and thus he brings a unique perspective. Like counterterrorism, this discipline must deal with complications caused by linkages to Internet systems and events in the United States. In the world of cyber, there is no clear "three-mile limit" to distinguish foreign from domestic matters.

These newer disciplines, in combination with the more traditional ones, provide the reader with insights into the wide world of CIA analysis. Lest it seem exhaustive, the editors readily acknowledge there are other subdisciplines within each major field, along with other specialized types of writing. One significant area is the production of National Intelligence Estimates (NIEs). A volume coeditor, Roger George, explores in chapter 10 the preparation and challenges of NIEs, where analysis meets and sometimes clashes with policy. While the previous chapters illustrate the varied ways analysts have supported policymakers, the authors have carefully avoided overly critical commentary on the difficulty of satisfying every demand that policymakers place on CIA analysts. Politicization was barely mentioned—although, as practitioners, we know it can occur in both blatant and subtle forms. Thus, chapter 10 examines the intelligence–policy relationship and the perils of providing assessments to ambitious and highly confident decision-makers. George has worked closely with senior policymakers at the National Intelligence Council but also as a senior policy planner at the Department of State and Department of Defense. His experiences suggest that politicization is sometimes inevitable when foreign policy interests are high and intelligence analysis is skeptical about a presidential policy's impact.

The conclusion, chapter 11, is the coeditors' attempt to find commonalities and differences among the disciplines and to identify challenging issues that all the disciplines must confront. Both authors served in units that selectively evaluated the quality of analysis and have been involved in numerous so-called product reviews to ascertain where analytical errors or flawed assumptions might have led analysts astray. Most of these challenges have existed for decades and are not amenable to quick or easily identified solutions, or even ones that would not be very disruptive to the current analytical business model. As practitioners, we know there are problems to be addressed, but chapter 11 can only hint at partial fixes. A first step, however, is to acknowledge the problems exist and their costs to higher analytic quality for the future.

Analysts reared in a classified work environment where secrecy is required find that writing an unclassified chapter on their profession is an unnatural act. Moreover, readers must consider how the secret nature of the CIA's work can obscure what analysts can say publicly and what examples or cases they are permitted to use illustrate how analysis is conducted. All CIA employees are bound, as a condition of initial employment, to protect secrets they learn through their work at the Agency. This commitment extends into retirement. All the contributors to this book, including those who are still working with security clearances and those who have completely retired, take this requirement seriously. They have seen the consequences of its breach in losing unique and expensive technical collection and causing the imprisonment or death of human sources.[55]

One feature of this lifelong commitment to secrecy is that all potentially published material must be reviewed by Agency personnel in the Pre-Publications Clearance Review Board (PCRB). The professionals in the PCRB do not prevent criticisms or bury criticisms of a nonsecret nature. They assiduously read submitted drafts and go out of their way to suggest changes or amendments to allow as much as possible to be released. In most cases, the PCRB asks for small changes that obscure a precise location, individual, or system to protect sources and methods. Thus, in this text, when reference is made to "a foreign chief of station" or "the command and control of a WMD capability," the authors are not trying to tease the reader. There are necessary limits to full transparency that leave the core points untouched.

The PCRB is not responsible for the declassification of published and unpublished internal CIA materials—that is the Sisyphean task of another unit that feeds the CIA Freedom of Information Act reading room (https://www.cia.gov/readingroom/) and the National Archives. All the chapters in this book have exploited declassified CIA materials to explain and illustrate. Some CIA materials are not subject to declassification, and those that are reviewed and released are redacted, sometimes heavily, to protect sources and methods. Obviously, it is less risky to release older material, and thus many of the references cited in this chapter and others point to documents that are decades old.

Readers may question if such dated and selective examples, especially broad critiques of behaviors and conditions, have current validity. The contributors to this volume have knowledge of very recent and sensitive matters.[56] They have been allowed to refer generally to some of these, and to use older, declassified, and more detailed materials to show the reader specific examples. For example, we could have asserted without examples that there are tensions and trade-offs between the production of "current" and long-term research. We think it is valuable for the reader to see that many of these issues date back decades, and to read the words of a former national security adviser to the president to support our concerns.

The other related question readers may ask is whether the contributors are too distant from current analytical operations and thus are out of touch. No doubt, changes in the Directorate of Analysis go on all the time.[57] There are three critical points to make. First, some of the contributors still work in the Agency and are aware of the current conditions, and others retired recently. Second, as mentioned above, organizational cultures change slowly. John Brennan, director of central intelligence from 2013 until 2017, said after he looked at some DA publications, "These look just like they did decades ago when I was a young CIA officer!" Both editors of this book believe that changes have indeed been slow and incremental, having served in the product review unit within the DA. The third point may be the most important. This book explains what discipline-specific analysis is: how it is done, how analysts work with collectors, and how they interact with consumers. The contributors were, and indeed are, experts in their fields, and most of them have mentored and taught analysts. While technical means and procedures evolve, and nomenclature shifts, what these contributors discuss will retain its value for many years to come. After reading this volume, we are confident that you will be far better informed about the state of intelligence analysis and its challenges into the future.

NOTES

1. See appendix B for a glossary of intelligence terms.

2. Several intelligence historians have described how Truman wanted the newly created Central Intelligence Group (the precursor to the CIA) to assemble and collate all sources of intelligence into a daily summary. This document later became the President's Daily Brief (PDB). See Christopher Andrew, *For the President's Eyes Only: Secret Intelligence and the American Presidency from Washington to Bush* (New York: Harper Perennial, 1996), 165; Richard Immerman, *The Hidden Hand: A Brief History of the CIA* (New York: Wiley Blackwell, 2014), 14–15; and David Priess, *The President's Book of Secrets: The Untold Story of Intelligence Briefings to America's Presidents* (New York: PublicAffairs, 2017).

3. Readers will find suggested readings by analytic discipline in appendix A.

4. Readers are referred to appendix B for a glossary of terms.

5. Roger Z. George, *Intelligence in the National Security Enterprise: An Introduction* (Washington, DC: Georgetown University Press, 2020), 101.

6. "All-source" refers to analysts who are privy to multiple sources of information, including clandestinely acquired HUMINT reports, signals intelligence intercepts (SIGINT), geospatial intelligence imagery reports (GEOINT), and open source intelligence (OSINT). See appendix B for a complete list of the intelligence terms used in this volume.

7. The Federal Bureau of Investigation (FBI) is responsible for detecting and stopping domestic counterintelligence threats; in practice, the CIA and FBI should be working closely together—e.g., in countering Russian or Chinese counterintelligence operations wherever they are occurring.

8. In 2015, the CIA created its newest Directorate of Digital Innovation, which encompasses the existing Open Source Enterprise, the Information Operations Center, and the Agency-wide IT enterprise as well as other units designed to create new analytical options for CIA analysis and operations. See Sean Lyngaas, "Inside the CIA's New Digital Directorate," *FCW*, October 1, 2015, https://fcw.com/articles/2015/10/02/cia-digital-directorate.aspx.

9. Typically, a fifth Directorate of Support (DS) is not discussed, as it focuses primarily on providing various types of support to analysts and operators regarding financing, logistics, and technical support required to conduct analysis and operations.

10. For more discussion of organizational culture and the intelligence community, see Roger George and James Wirtz, "Strategic Culture of the Intelligence Community," in *Handbook of Strategic Culture*, ed. Kerry M. Kartchner, Briana D. Bowen, and Jeannie L. Johnson (New York: Routledge Press, 2024).

11. At the CIA, the Sherman Kent School for Intelligence Analysis provides every new employee with a multiweek Career Analyst Program (CAP) training course that introduces tradecraft principles as well as inculcates the ethics of analytical objectivity and importance of resisting politicization of their work.

12. In his book, a retired senior operations officer uses the term "heart" to describe the Directorate of Operations, which captured his personal view that "without the directorate of operations," the CIA would "basically be a small think-tank. Without it, the analysts would have nothing out of the ordinary to analyze [and] technical experts would have no one to invent for." See Tyler Drumheller, *On the Brink: An Insider's Account of How the White House Compromised American Intelligence* (New York: Carroll & Graff, 2006), 138.

13. The Five Eyes remains the most important intelligence liaison exchange of sensitive information in the US government. Through it, analysts and collectors trade their views and the most sensitive information about the highest-priority targets. Through it, CIA analysts gain the opportunity to test hypotheses and assumptions as well as vet source reporting with other governments' analysts who may have different perspectives and information.

14. Robert Wallace, H. Keith Melton, and Henry R. Schlesinger, *Spycraft: The Secret History of the CIA's Spytechs, from Communism to Al-Qaeda* (New York: Plume, 2009).

15. National Intelligence Collection Managers are part of the office of the director of national intelligence and sit on the National Intelligence Management Council. It serves as the DNI's principal substantive advisers within and across specific regions and functional issues while conducting individual and collective strategic oversight of the intelligence community by integrating collection, analysis, counterintelligence, and resource programming.

16. "National Intelligence Survey Program," April 17, 1973, declassified from CONFIDENTIAL, https://www.cia.gov/readingroom/docs/CIA-RDP78-05597A000200010004-0.pdf. See an example on Nigerian armed forces, February 1973, declassified from SECRET, https://www.cia.gov/readingroom/docs/CIA-RDP01-00707R000200100001-4.pdf. The National Intelligence Survey is no longer produced, but the "CIA Factbook" fulfills some part of its original purpose.

17. "Saudi Arabia Handbook," December 1972, declassified from SECRET, https://www.cia.gov/readingroom/docs/CIA-RDP79-00891A001300080001-1.pdf.

18. Much of the analytic cadre has taken the findings of Philip Tetlock to heart; see Philip E. Tetlock, *Expert Political Judgment: How Good Is It? How Can We Know?* (Princeton, NJ: Princeton University Press, 2005). Tetlock's study showed that experts were seldom better than nonexperts in predicting future conditions. The predictions Tetlock measured in his research and in more recent intelligence community work share only limited similarities with the forecasts of most classified anticipatory analysis. (Analysts are not asked to predict the price of gold in six months' time.) Nevertheless, his admonitions to consider base rates, offer precision in forecasts, track previous forecasts, and show willingness to update forecasts are all useful. See Philip E. Tetock and Dan Gardner, *Superforecasting: The Art and Science of Prediction* (New York: Crown, 2015).

19. Access an example at https://www.cia.gov/readingroom/docs/DOC_0006004754.pdf. An interesting description of what is needed in the PDB is "Memo from the Office of the Vice President," March 7, 1980, declassified from SECRET, https://www.cia.gov/readingroom/docs/CIA-RDP95M00249R000801110024-5.pdf. The history of the PDB is well covered by David Priess, *The President's Book of Secrets*, repr. ed. (New York: PublicAffairs, 2017). Priess is a former CIA analyst and PDB briefer. What is probably the most famous PDB, "Bin Ladin Determined to Strike in US," August 6, 2001, declassified, https://nsarchive2.gwu.edu/NSAEBB/NSAEBB116/pdb8-6-2001.pdf, is atypical of PDB articles.

20. At the beginning of the Reagan administration, guidance from the White House called for short pieces: "One paragraph for most issues, two-to-three paragraphs at the outside should be the guide for presentation." "Memo from the Office of the Vice President," March 7, 1980, declassified from SECRET, https://www.cia.gov/readingroom/docs/CIA-RDP95M00249R000801110024-5.pdf. One of the authors recalls a PDB he produced exploiting sensitive HUMINT revelations about a foreign power's nuclear command and control—one of the most closely held and important secrets in any country. The PDB editors eliminated confirmatory SIGINT evidence for the sake of brevity.

21. In his final CIA briefing as president-elect, Governor George W. Bush told his briefer, "When I am sworn in, I expect I will be getting the good stuff." This stirred concerns in Langley when it was reported. The CIA had been giving him "the good stuff" all along. John L. Helgerson, Getting to Know the President, 1952–2016 (CIA: Center for the Study of Intelligence, 4th ed., October 2021), 184. https://www.cia.gov/resources/csi/static/Getting-to-Know-the-President-Fourth-Edition-2021-web.pdf

22. No examples of WIRe articles appear to have been declassified.

23. The number of addressees has varied greatly. In 1982 it was pruned to about 150. "Dissemination of Intelligence Information" (Memo from Robert Gates, Deputy Director for Intelligence), February 11, 1982, declassified from SECRET, https://www.cia.gov/readingroom/docs/CIA-RDP83M00914R001800020002-3.pdf.

24. An example is National Intelligence Daily, November 8, 1982, declassified from TOP SECRET, https://www.cia.gov/readingroom/docs/CIA-RDP84T00301R000600010042-5.pdf.

25. An example is "Senior Executive Intelligence Brief, 25 September 2000," declassified from TOP SECRET, https://www.cia.gov/readingroom/docs/DOC_0005445135.pdf. Another publication with very short pieces was the "Current Intelligence Bulletin, 21 March 1953," https://www.cia.gov/readingroom/docs/CIA-RDP79T00975A001000660001-7.pdf.

26. Remarkably, some components offered daily products, such as the *Scientific and Weapons Daily Review*. "Dissemination of Intelligence Information" (Memo from Robert Gates, Deputy Director for Intelligence), February 11, 1982, declassified from SECRET, https://www.cia.gov/readingroom/docs/CIA-RDP83M00914R001800020002-3.pdf. That publication was sent by cable to about a hundred addressees.

27. Examples are Western Europe Review, November 29, 1978, declassified from SECRET, https://www.cia.gov/readingroom/docs/CIA-RDP79T00912A001600010014-7.pdf; Science and Weapons Review, November 26, 1993, declassified from SECRET, https://www.cia.gov/readingroom/docs/DOC_0000832107.pdf; International Economic & Energy Weekly, February 1, 1985, declassified from SECRET, https://www.cia.gov/readingroom/docs/CIA-RDP85-01097R000400110007-1.pdf; Africa Review, November 3, 1978, declassified from SECRET, https://www.cia.gov/readingroom/docs/CIA-RDP79T00912A002700010023-5.pdf; and USSR Review, February 1988, declassified from SECRET, https://www.cia.gov/readingroom/docs/CIA-RDP89T00992R000100080001-7.pdf. A document discussing concerns of the SACEUR notes that 232 copies of the European Review were distributed to addressees outside the CIA, December 10, 1982, declassified from SECRET, https://www.cia.gov/readingroom/docs/CIA-RDP84B00049R001800280006-2.pdf.

28. One of the least formal of these publications were Staff Notes. An example is Staff Notes: Western Europe, Canada, International Organizations, September 19, 1975, declassified from CONFIDENTIAL, https://www.cia.gov/readingroom/docs/CIA-RDP79T00865A001800090002-3.pdf.

29. Examples are "Middle East Situation Report #15 (as of 1100 EST, 16 January 1984)," declassified, https://www.cia.gov/readingroom/docs/CIA-RDP85T00287R001300210001-6.pdf; and "Afghanistan Situation Report, 6 November 1984," declassified from TOP SECRET, https://www.cia.gov/readingroom/docs/CIA-RDP96R01136R001302320005-4.pdf.

30. An example is "The Soviet Attack Submarine Force and Western Sea Lines of Communication, April 1979," declassified from SECRET, https://www.cia.gov/readingroom/docs/DOC_0005499486.pdf.

31. An example is "NIE 15-90, Yugoslavia Transformed, October 1990," declassified from SECRET, at https://www.cia.gov/readingroom/docs/DOC_0000254259.pdf. What is probably the most famous NIE, "Iraq's Continuing Programs for Weapons of Mass Destruction," October 2002, declassified from TOP SECRET, has gone through a few releases. The most complete version can be accessed at https://foreignpolicy.com/2019/05/17/document-of-the -week-the-2002-national-intelligence-estimate-on-wmds-in-iraq/. This flawed product was composed in an atypical, very short time period.

32. A brief description of the production formats in 1964 is "Format for Publications of the Directorate of Intelligence," August 5, 1964, declassified from CONFIDENTIAL, https:// www.cia.gov/readingroom/docs/CIA-RDP84-00951R000400040015-0.pdf. In less than two years, the mix of types changed; see "Publications of the Directorate of Intelligence," April 15, 1966, declassified from SECRET, https://www.cia.gov/readingroom/docs/CIA-RDP84-00951 R000400040016-9.pdf.

33. No examples of CIA multimedia or interactives appear to have been declassified. The kind of subject that lent itself to multimedia presentation was the consequences of the Islamic State (ISIS) damaging dams under its control and flooding the Euphrates Valley. An unclassified video using previously classified material is "Syria's Covert Nuclear Reactor at Al Kibar," https://www.youtube.com/watch?v=yj62GRd0Te8.

34. E.g., see "The Directorate of Intelligence: A Brief Description, Office of the DDI," February 1977, declassified from CONFIDENTIAL, https://www.cia.gov/readingroom/docs/CIA -RDP80-00473A000600100010-8.pdf. Attached to this document is "Analysis in the DDI: Problems and Issues, Memo from the Deputy Director for Intelligence, 25 August 1976."

35. E.g., the presence of TVs tuned to CNN became ubiquitous in senior military leaders' offices. One of the authors traveled to Supreme Headquarters Allied Powers Europe (SHAPE) to brief one of the senior-most officers. After greeting the general, the author went over to switch off the TV. The general's aide literally gasped. The author turned to the aide and said, "I didn't travel almost 4,000 miles to compete with that." The general smiled. A somewhat twisted sense of the interaction of CNN and intelligence occurred in 1991 during the Persian Gulf War. The same author was discussing matters with an NIO at CIA Headquarters when the NIO received a secure telephone call alerting him that the Iraqis had launched another SCUD missile. The NIO quickly switched to watching CNN to try to catch the missile's interception or impact. Although this marriage of information sources worked a couple of times, it is hard to believe the product of this union was very useful (or "intelligent").

36. See "A Compendium of Analytic Tradecraft Notes," February 1997, http://intellit .muskingum.edu/analysis_folder/di_catn_Folder/contents.htm.

37. Useful discussions of analytic tradecraft development are Jim Marchio, "Analytic Tradecraft and the Intelligence Community: Enduring Value, Intermittent Emphasis," *Intelligence and National Security* 29, no. 2 (2014): 159–83, DOI:10.1080/02684527.2012.746415, https:// www.tandfonline.com/doi/pdf/10.1080/02684527.2012.746415?needAccess=true; and Stephen Marrin, "CIA's Kent School: Improving Training for New Analysts," *International Journal of Intelligence and Counterintelligence*, 16 (2003): 609–37, https://www.academia.edu /3695302/CIAs_Kent_School_Improving_Training_for_New_Analysts.

38. CIA, *A Tradecraft Primer: Structured Analytic Techniques for Improving Intelligence Analysis*, March 2009, https://www.stat.berkeley.edu/~aldous/157/Papers/Tradecraft %20Primer-apr09.pdf.

39. Martin Peterson, "What I Learned in 40 Years of Doing Intelligence Analysis for US Foreign Policymakers," *Studies in Intelligence* 55, no. 1 (March 2011): 13–20, https://www .cia.gov/resources/csi/studies-in-intelligence/volume-55-no-1/what-i-learned-in-40-years-of -doing-intelligence-analysis-for-us-foreign-policymakers/. The initial version of the Quality Framework is on p. 16.

40. Mission Centers were established in 2015 as part of a wide-ranging modernization program instituted by CIA director John Brennan. Those centers focus resources across all the directorates (e.g., DO, DA, DST, and DDI) on specific topics or targets such as counterterrorism, counterintelligence, and the Middle East. Recent press reports indicate, e.g., that the CIA is creating a new Mission Center on China to highlight a greater priority on collection and analysis of America's peer rival. See Peter Martin, "CIA Zeros In on Beijing by Creating a China-Focused Mission Center," *Bloomberg News*, October 7, 2021, https://www.bloomberg .com/new/article/2021-10-07/cia-zeros-in-on-beijing-by-creating-a-new-china-mission-center.

41. David Priess, *The President's Book of Secrets: The Untold Story of Intelligence Briefings to America's Presidents* (New York: PublicAffairs, 2017). The author, a former analyst, recounts how the PDB has evolved and has been used by presidents.

42. Previously, this widely distributed classified daily intelligence summary was called the *National Intelligence Daily* (NID).

43. "Report on an Experimental Use of the DELPHI Technique," February 1972, declassified from SECRET, https://www.cia.gov/readingroom/docs/CIA-RDP82M00531R00040020000 2-1.pdf.

44. Richards Heuer, *Psychology of Intelligence Analysis* (Langley, VA: CIA Center for the Study of Intelligence, 1999), https://web.archive.org/web/20120529171949/https://www.cia .gov/library/center-for-the-study-of-intelligence/csi-publications/books-and-monographs /psychology-of-intelligence-analysis/. A short version of the basic points is available from Richards Heuer, "Limits of Intelligence Analysis," *Orbis* 49, no. 1 (Winter 2005): 75–94.

45. In his recent book, Bruce Pease, a former senior CIA officer, says of structured analytic techniques, "I rarely caught an analyst using one on his own initiative." Bruce Pease, *Leading Intelligence Analysis* (Thousand Oaks, CA: Sage, 2020), 65.

46. Some techniques appear to have a positive effect, but others may not, and some were counterproductive as originally taught. Stephen Coulthart, "What Works? An Evidence-Based Assessment of 12 Core Structured Analytic Techniques," *International Journal of Intelligence and CounterIntelligence* 30, no. 2 (2017): 368–91, https://doi.org/10.1080/08850607.2016 .1230706; Stephen Artner, Richard Girven, and James Bruce, *Assessing the Value of Structured Analytic Techniques in the US Intelligence Community* (Santa Monica, CA: RAND, 2016). Brainstorming did not take steps to prevent the ill effects of group dynamics until recast, after taking to heart the work of the University of Texas at Arlington professor Paul Paulus.

47. "Interview of NSC / White House Staff Member, Memorandum from A. W. Marshall, 6 February 1973," declassified from SECRET, https://www.cia.gov/readingroom/docs/CIA -RDP80M01133A000800110012-6.pdf.

48. The internal debate about how close analysts should be to policymakers is referred to as the Kent-Kendall debate in the Agency. Jack Davis, "The Kent-Kendall Debate of 1949," *Studies in Intelligence* 36, no. 5 (1992): 91–103, https://www.cia.gov/static/59d729cb6f0de8a9ab87 b0b04e5342c7/Kent-Kendall-Debate-1949.pdf. For this and related issues, see *Intelligence Community and Policymaker Integration: A Studies in Intelligence Anthology* (Langley, VA: CIA

Center for the Study of Intelligence, 2014), https://www.cia.gov/static/924532c178fe832eac069
ca2359f08f7/Intelligence-Community-Policymaker-Integration.pdf.

49. Robert Gates, *From the Shadows: The Ultimate Insider's Story of Five Presidents and How They Won the Cold War* (New York: Simon & Schuster, 1996), 56.

50. The authors strongly recommend Robert Jervis, "Why Intelligence and Policymakers Clash," *Political Science Quarterly* 125, no. 2 (2010): 185–204.

51. See Garrett Graff, "I've Never Been Involved in Anything as Secret as This," *Politico*, April 30, 2021, https://www.politico.com/new/magazine/2021/04/30/osama-bin-laden-death-white-house-oral-history-484793. This article includes comments from several dozen senior officials who were privy to the decision and expressed concern about whether President Obama could be sure about finding Bin Laden at his Abbottabad hideout.

52. Julian Barnes, "Intelligence Agencies Did Not Predict Imminence of Afghan Collapse, Officials Say," *New York Times*, August 18, 2021, https://www.nytimes.com/2021/08/18/us/politics/afghanistan-intelligence-agencies.html. See also Vivian Salama and Warren P. Strobel, "Four Intelligence Agencies Produced Extensive Reports on Afghanistan, but All Fail to Predict Kabul's Rapid Collapse," *Wall Street Journal*, October 28, 2021.

53. Interview with NSC/White House Staff Members, February 6, 1973, declassified from SECRET, https://www.cia.gov/readingroom/docs/CIA-RDP80M01133A000800110012-6.pdf.

54. There is no separate chapter on targeting as an analytic field, for a simple reason. The nature of the work is classified and rich; unclassified or declassified examples are inadequate.

55. New analysts find the responsibility to protect secrets daunting. One of the authors attended a well-connected Washington wedding with his wife a few months after joining the CIA. They found themselves standing next to a famous national TV news personality. There was no way to avoid a conversation. The newscaster soon asked what the author did. "I work for the US government." He asked, "Which part?" The newscaster's wife elbowed him and said, "_____, you shouldn't ask that! The young man works for the CIA. Or he works for Commerce and wants you to think he works for the CIA."

56. One of the authors was surprised to find that he was "read into" (allowed access to) over 150 separate sensitive compartments of information within the Top Secret classification.

57. E.g., the authors debated how to describe different types of organizations and publications. The Directorate of Analysis has been reorganized and renamed several times. The names of publication types have come and gone—sometimes only to return to earlier labels.

2

POLITICAL ANALYSIS: MAKING SENSE OF A COMPLEX WORLD

Adam Wasserman

During all the dramatic developments in the world's political firmament over the last decades, US national decision-makers and their advisers have looked to political analysts at the CIA to keep them informed and to conduct in-depth analysis and research. An internal proposal in the early 1970s to strengthen the CIA's political analysis defined four general issues:

- The decision-making processes of major countries of interest to the United States.
- The foreign policy, internal politics, and sociological aspects of these countries and their societies.
- The interaction of these factors with economic and military considerations in the formulation of major foreign policies of these countries.
- The effect of these policies on important interests of the United States.[1]

Since this straightforward guidance was written, US national interests have grown to cover a panoply of nonstate actors—international organizations, terrorists, and superempowered individuals, to name only some of the most obvious. National security challenges have expanded to include environmental and demographic threats, such as global warming. However, if the words "foreign actors" are substituted for "countries," this could serve as current guidance for political analysis at the CIA.

Clearly, the scope of political analysis is broad and complex. It calls for expertise and effort—as well as diverse collection activities—in a bewildering number of areas—for example, foreign governmental operations, societal conditions, demographic changes, cultures, and ideologies. Describing these efforts, much less explaining how each is done, is far beyond the bounds of this chapter. What can be accomplished here is to give a sense of how political analysts approach their tasks as well as what is unique about the discipline compared with the others covered in this volume.

It helps to provide coherence to the political analysts' mission to focus on the question of *power*: who rules or has power, what are they doing or intending to do with that power, and what difference does this make for US interests? Analysts examine how power is gained, maintained, transferred, lost, and used. The questions analysts ask include:

- What are the sources of power: force, position, charisma, or performance?
- Does power reside in an individual, a clan, a party, an institution, or a social movement?
- How is power shared or divided between regions, ethnosectarian groups, and administrative units?
- How important are formal rules and laws—for example, constitutions versus informal structures and relations?
- What are the interests of key substate actors—businesses, militaries, churches, unions, nongovernmental organizations, cartels, or the media—and how do they try to influence governments?
- Do international or multilateral organizations—such as the international financial institutions, the UN, and regional military or economic organizations—shape or constrain the exercise of power?
- What is the interplay between a country's foreign policy and domestic politics?
- How are foreign actors trying to influence who holds power?

Policymakers are seldom interested, however, in broad, sweeping assessments of how power is shared among political actors in another country. Rather, their concerns tend to be far more specific and near-term. It is common to receive tasking from senior policymakers asking, "Will the upcoming election in [country X] be free and fair?" Or "What is [country Y] willing to do to aid in US efforts to alleviate a pending hunger disaster, and what will [country Y] ask for, or demand, in return?"

WHO ARE POLITICAL ANALYSTS?

Given the nature of such profound and difficult questions about power, one can easily imagine roles for analysts with backgrounds in foreign area studies, anthropology, history, political science, sociology, demography, and any number of academic fields. Indeed, the CIA recruits from all these fields and more to staff its large cadre of political analysts. Some of my closest colleagues came from academia with degrees in international relations, history, and psychology. Others were drawn from law, business, journalism, and a host of other related fields.

In my case, I had studied Marxism and communist ideology in college and then received an advanced international relations degree with a focus on Soviet foreign and security policy. Before joining the CIA, I served in the Congressional Office of Technology Assessment; hence, I was hired initially as a Soviet military analyst to work on strategic nuclear forces. But like many political analysts, my background was only a starting point for my career. As internal politics in the USSR heated up in the 1980s, I moved from military to political analysis. As the world changed, my assignments changed along with US intelligence priorities. Over the years, I worked with political analysts with very different backgrounds: some, like me, started in different disciplines; others sold appliances overseas, served as missionaries, or had degrees in medieval history.

A good part of my own CIA career was spent studying the transitions of authoritarian governments to democracies, or something short of them. This remains one of the enduring challenges facing US foreign policy. Hence, this chapter looks at this kind of political analysis to better illustrate what political analysts do, how they do it, how they work with collectors, and the challenges of supporting decision-makers who often believe they are their own best analysts.

POLITICAL ANALYSIS OF GOVERNMENTAL TRANSITIONS

Since 1945 at least, US national security policies have supported—in principle, if not always in practice—the transition of dictatorships and other forms of authoritarian states toward democracies. Accordingly, CIA political analysts have spent considerable time assessing the progress or setbacks to democratization in many parts of the world, be it Southeast Asia, Latin America, Eastern Europe, post-Soviet Russia, or the Middle East. For me, this issue came to the fore during the collapse of the USSR, when politics jumped from the secret corridors of the Politburo into the press and the streets, and democracy suddenly became a live option. After the USSR disappeared in 1991, my skill set was still somewhat useful, especially in the newly independent republics of the former Soviet Union (FSU). In the 1990s, democratization became a major Clinton administration focus, and I became accidentally at first, but then more deliberately, a general expert on regime transitions, first in the FSU but later in other regions.

Fortunately, the CIA gives analysts many opportunities to broaden their expertise. I took advantage of an opportunity to do a yearlong research project on changing attitudes and values across the FSU; this involved working with polling experts from the

US Agency for International Development, which had years of survey data on those societies.[2] I consulted with leading experts about earlier cases of democratic transitions, such as occurred in post-1945 West Germany, which helped to make sense of trends emerging in Russia, Ukraine, and other FSU republics. Over time, my experience and knowledge of regime transitions proved useful elsewhere, and I rotated to other assignments related to Southeast Asia and later Iraq. Although not a Middle East specialist, my understanding of democratization and a four-month field experience in Baghdad led to my remaining a political analyst on Iraq for over four years.

One reality in the CIA is that resources are finite. Outsiders see the massive, billion-dollar budgets of the intelligence community and probably conclude that the CIA has the luxury of unlimited numbers of analysts on virtually any topic it chooses. Not true. No matter how large the budget, priorities change, and with them, the amounts of money and people available. While budget figures on CIA analysis and other missions remain classified, comparatively speaking, analysis is not a major dollar figure. It is worth mentioning the resource reality, because when the USSR disappeared, many political analysts who had been following that Cold War target—like myself—had to reinvent themselves. Many moved to higher-priority targets or learned new skills, as I tried to do with democratization. After 9/11, they found themselves following counterterrorism or counterproliferation or became analysts on the Middle East or South Asia. Such priority shifts in accounts likely occur in every analyst's career and across all the disciplines. In my experience, those political analysts who have excellent methodological and writing skills often make those transitions easily.

CHARACTERISTICS OF POLITICAL ANALYSTS

Political analysts share many of the same educational backgrounds and pre-Agency work experiences that are found in other disciplines. However, there are some unique factors. Many have studied political science or international relations and are knowledgeable in the methods and theories of these specialties. Others are area specialists who know languages and cultures; many have spent time abroad working or studying. In addition, some in this discipline have a tendency more than in other disciplines to move among different regions, as I did, because they chose to be generalists as opposed to becoming regional specialists.

Regional Specialization

In-depth knowledge of countries or regions is highly prized. Many political analysts get this from foreign area studies programs found in many universities. These can range from private schools like Harvard and Georgetown to public land-grant colleges such as the University of Nebraska and the University of Hawaii. Or they may have spent considerable time living and working in foreign countries, having grown up in those cultures and learned the local languages. Some were missionaries or worked for humanitarian organizations or other nongovernmental organizations before their government services. No matter in what way they have developed their interest in and knowledge of a region or country, they come to the CIA expecting to remain focused on these targets.

The CIA and the intelligence community also benefit greatly from the multicultural diversity found in the United States, which has produced many second- and third-generation "hyphenated" Americans who still speak the mother tongue and have cultural connections and sensitivity by virtue of being raised by immigrants from every continent. In my own experience, the CIA has benefited from hiring those whose knowledge included Afghanistan, China, India, and Cuba—as well as many other countries.

Of course, these backgrounds would contribute to every analytic discipline, but they are particularly valuable for political analysis. An important part of our job is to see the world "through the eyes" of foreign actors. Analytical judgments about politics often rest on the kind of inside knowledge available only through these kinds of experiences. Hence, political analysts take advantage of opportunities to work overseas, study and maintain foreign languages, and immerse themselves in foreign media, literature, films, and even music.[3]

Political Science Methods and Theories

Political analysts need to be familiar with specialized tools and conceptual frameworks that assist in assessing foreign political systems. For example, analysts should be familiar with opinion polling, quantitative methods, and established theories of international relations. These would include such older approaches as content analysis, decision-making theories, and POLICON. Other, more recent methods would include game theory and war gaming, computer-aided models of political behavior, and futures scenario generation. Even board games have been created and used effectively to understand complex political dynamics. Some analysts come to the Agency with methodological backgrounds, while others learn on the job or in training and educational programs offered by the Agency. Also, the CIA maintains a group of methodologists and statisticians whom analysts often consult regarding their use of modeling, data management, and quantitative methods.

These skills allow some political analysts to supplement academic work with in-house models. For example, more than a decade ago, political analysts created a model of "state power," which integrated indicators of military, economic, cultural, and other forms of power in international relations. This model allowed for cross-cultural comparisons of different states' overall power and for tracking changes over time. Analysts found that existing academic models were obsolete and tracked principally "hard power" measures such as military expenditures. Another example of unique methods used by political analysts was the creation of the Political Instability Task Force, which was made up of outside specialists. This unclassified, multidisciplinary effort began in the 1990s to examine the underlying causes of state instability and failure. These databases are available publicly and have contributed to numerous academic publications. The many task force workshops typically bring together top-flight experts—including outside academics—to review different theories of political instability and address questions relevant to the CIA's political analysis.

The political analysis discipline also is likely the most attuned to international relations theories. While policymakers have shown little interest in the explicit use of such theories in intelligence assessments,[4] the good analyst is aware of these and pays attention to how theory-based assumptions may shape their own worldviews as well as those of policymakers (see box 2.1).[5] Concepts about deterrence, soft power, and democratic peace are among those that a political analyst needs to consider when examining an intelligence problem. For instance, my area of interest, the study of regime change, relied heavily on the theory of "democratic peace." This academic literature suggested that well-established democratic states never went to war against each other; while this theoretical work was heavily caveated, sometimes it was translated into an assumption that "democracies were always peaceful," suggesting that an aggressive US promotion of democratic institutions in such places as Iraq and Afghanistan would stabilize the region. CIA political analysts had to be aware that some senior policymakers may hold to this belief regardless of the unintended consequences.

Generalist versus Specialist

As the discussion above suggests, there can be a tension between an analyst remaining essentially a political scientist, who can apply his or her skills to a variety of intelligence problems, or a specialist in a region or country. For example, the generalist would look at a particular country X and determine if there are similarities with other countries or perhaps other historic patterns; he or she might find an appropriate model into which country X's actions fit. For such analysts, moving among various countries or regions and bringing an understanding of underlying political and other factors adds to the perspective held by regional or country specialists.

The credibility of political analysis often rests on how much policymakers trust the views of the analysts presenting their findings. It is important to have political analysts who can demonstrate that they have worked in the region, speak the language, or have other forms of specialized knowledge. In contrast to generalists, specialists view the political situation in country X as unique to the history, geography, and culture

BOX 2.1: SAMPLE OF THEORIES USED BY POLITICAL ANALYSTS

Among the political theories that are in circulation–both among analysts and decision-makers–many have promised more than they have delivered. Analysts must be conversant in these theories and prepared to defend their use or nonuse. Here is a partial rundown of some of the more popular theories that political analysts have employed.

Realism/Idealism/Constructivism

Classical realists such as George Kennan and Hans Morgenthau wrote in the 1950s that international politics was dominated by state actors seeking to maximize power and that the international system was inherently anarchic. Later idealist theorists countered that international regimes could overcome states' quests for power through international norms and organizations. Further modifications expanded these two opposing groups into neorealists (those accepting that there are some limits on state power), neoliberals (who accepted that there were limits on the strength of international norms), and a new constructivist school that postulated that socially constructed factors like identities and ideas shaped international relations.[6]

Democratic Peace

First mentioned by Immanuel Kant in the eighteenth century, political scientists in the 1960s studied and refined the notion that democracies are less likely to engage in conflict with one another than states with other forms of government.[7] Various refinements have been offered, such as the "geriatric peace," postulating that countries with aging populations are less likely to take risks, including going to war.

Deterrence

Popularized by Thomas Schelling's work in the 1960s, this theory postulated that threats of retaliation (generally punishment but also potentially an element of denial) can cause an actor to withhold an intended action, such as an attack.[8] Extremely sophisticated and mathematically complex game theory models subsequently have been applied to deterrence and to political behavior more generally.

Models of Decision-Making

Graham Allison's classic 1971 work, *The Essence of Decision*, posits that there are three different models of governmental decision-making, and analysts can thus explore decisions by looking at "rational actors," "organizational processes," and "bureaucratic politics."[9] A revised edition came out in 1999, but critics have sharply questioned these models.[10]

Soft Power

In Joseph Nye's 1990 book *Bound to Lead*, he defined "soft power" as the ability to co-opt rather than coerce (via hard power) other actors using the attractive forces of a nation's culture, values, and other positive aspects of its society.[11] In later writings, he further refined this to include the power of example and methods for getting others to "want what we want." Some "realist" political scientists have challenged the influence that soft power has on international politics.

Clash of Civilizations

Samuel Huntington's 1993 claim that the dominant sources of conflict in the world, after the fall of communism, were divisions along cultural and religious fault lines.[12] His arguments have been very influential in East Asia and Russia. Other academics have argued that cultural diversity and indistinct boundaries undercut the concept.

of that society. Such specialists often spend most of their careers focused on a single country or region.

Speaking as a generalist who has examined political theories and methods and has applied them across many countries, we are often the "horizon-scanners" who anticipate regime instability early, having seen it elsewhere in the world. However, both generalists and area experts are essential to forecasting political changes in foreign cultures. Luckily, the CIA encourages both types of analysts. For example, the Senior

Analytic Service was created in the early 2000s to reward analysts in all disciplines for maintaining and deepening their regional, functional, or methodological skills; both generalists known for their analytical skills as well as foreign area specialists have been welcomed into the Senior Analytic Service.

TYPICAL POLITICAL ANALYSIS TASKS

Having laid out what makes the political analytic discipline unique, it is important to focus on the kinds of tasks these analysts are asked to address. Again, relying on the major cases of regime transition I dealt with in my own career, we can explore how different countries and time periods have altered the critical intelligence questions that political analysts must answer. Without delving deeply into the history of the USSR's collapse, the post–Cold War Russian democratic transition, Iraq's post-Saddam political development, or the 2011 Arab Spring, it is possible to draw a few lessons from each. In the case of the USSR, the focus was on how the Gorbachev era reforms would promote or undermine that superpower's stability and views of the West. In the post-1990 former Soviet Union, would Russia democratize and allow its former subjects to go their own ways, or try to reassert control? In the case of Iraq, policymakers believed that democratization would be straightforward and could stabilize the region, which analysts had to examine and question. And the Arab Spring opened possible alternatives to long-existing autocratic regimes. In each case, analysts struggled to present assessments that reflected possible outcomes as well as the uncertainties that surrounded them.

The Collapse of the USSR

The end of the Cold War and disintegration of the USSR came quickly in 1991, and analysts had been tracking its demise. At the time, questions analysts were addressing included whether "glasnost" and "perestroika" would stabilize not only the economy but also the inflexible political system that Mikhail Gorbachev had inherited. Analysts looked for signs that reactionary forces were planning to undermine those reforms and move against him. As the Soviet crisis deepened, the Bush administration was intensely interested in knowing whether Boris Yeltsin—a backer of reforms but also a rival of Gorbachev—was a true "democrat." Political analysts at the CIA debated these questions, as did many senior policymakers.

Without delving into the complicated story of whether the CIA "missed" the Soviet collapse, it is fair to say that analysts closely tracked the deepening economic and political crisis. Multiple assessments of regime instability examined the underlying forces and actors working for and against Soviet reforms. Those assessments included forecasting plausible trajectories that the USSR might take and the kinds of indicators that would point to the most likely outcome. The CIA did not predict the exact hour of the fall, but there is no question that CIA political analysts warned of a coming crisis that was likely to end badly for the USSR.[13]

Post-1990 Democratization

In the 1990s, a period often characterized as a "unipolar moment," when the United States faced no comparable rival, the Clinton administration's focus was on globalization and democratization around the globe. It also worried—after the end of Soviet control in Eastern Europe and support for other authoritarian regimes—about the rise of ethnonationalism in Yugoslavia, the newly independent republics, and elsewhere. Instead of the Cold War question of whether a foreign government sided more with Moscow or Washington, the key question became where a country stood regarding democracy or authoritarianism. Would newly independent states and countries around the world join a Western-based free market system or lapse into strongman regimes? In addition, long-repressed ethnic minorities within the former Soviet Union as well as parts of Eastern Europe and the Middle East were restive and very likely to challenge their autocratic leaders. At the time political analysts were looking at the future of fledgling democracies in Poland and Hungary as well as Yugoslavia; simultaneously, other regional political analysts were monitoring regime stability throughout the Arab and Latin American world once Soviet support for repressive regimes like Iraq, Syria, Cuba, and Nicaragua was gone.

Without a main enemy like the USSR, policymakers were open to new forms of analysis. For example, US policy aimed at opening the global energy market to new states in the former Soviet Union in order to promote development and democratic transitions. Working with an energy analyst and an economic analyst, I produced a major research paper that examined how dependence on oil and gas exports could backfire, reinforcing dictatorship and stifling economic development. In this project, we were able to consult with the best outside experts to incorporate emerging research about the "oil curse" and rise of petrol states as well as describe measures to mitigate those risks; our findings helped to shift the focus of US advice to these new states.

Iraq's Political Future

In the wake of the 9/11 terrorist attacks in 2001, the targets and types of political intelligence tasks shifted again. Very quickly, the core question for political analysts became whether a foreign government was with us or against us in the global war on terrorism. This was especially acute in Middle East and Muslim countries. Analysts had to take into account that even when senior officials in these countries wished to support US efforts, they often faced underlying political and societal grievances that could lead parts of society to support radicals and thereby limit what their governments were willing to do.

Reflecting the new post-2001 realities, much more political analysis had to be conducted on the Middle East and South Asia. Accordingly, the CIA created two entirely new regional offices and moved analysts from other areas or functional accounts to handle the endless sets of questions coming from senior policymakers. Following the US invasion of Iraq, the analytic task was to assess what would take the place of Saddam's regime. Accordingly, political analysts had to examine the role and influence of subnational groups and factions while also looking at the workability of the country's new institutions and constitution. Very soon, the rise of a violent insurgency meant that the CIA faced new requests from civilians and military commanders for more tactical information and analysis on various insurgent groups and their affiliations with Iran, al-Qaeda, and other outside actors. Accordingly, the CIA also deployed more analysts, including myself, to the war zone to provide on-site support and rapidly to report back to CIA Headquarters the field perspective on the insurgency and the state of Iraq's democratic process.

These three cases reflect just how varied and changeable political analysis tasks can be. And these are but a small subset of the full range of questions posed to political analysts throughout the CIA. Looking back on these cases, an important takeaway is that political analysts, like those in other disciplines, need to be aware of dominant mind-sets that can obscure changes occurring in foreign societies. In the Soviet case, political analysts—myself included—at first resisted accepting that Gorbachev was truly a reformer and that he had the power to initiate real reforms. Having watched the Soviet Union muddle through and use the KGB and the communist apparatus to repress change for so long, analysts were not convinced that Gorbachev was serious; partly, it was due to the correct belief that if he did institute real reforms, it might bring on a reactionary movement or the eventual collapse of the system. In the case of post-1990 democratization, political analysis struggled to get a handle on what was occurring inside chaotic FSU republics where new sources of information were still being developed. In some cases, analysts underestimated the difficulties in throwing off the impact of decades of dictatorship, and they overestimated the power of the United States and outside actors to influence change. Likewise, analysis of post-Saddam Iraq suffered initially from an abundance of contradictory information or sometimes fabricated and self-serving reports that exiled opportunists wished to provide to the US government. With the deployment of US forces, of course, our information increased; but so too did the challenge of discounting "rosy" embassy and military reporting on the state of Iraq's democratization and societal conditions.

THE CHALLENGE OF COLLECTION

Political analysts, like those in other disciplines, exploit all forms of raw intelligence reporting, with probably more emphasis on open source, diplomatic reporting, and

SIGINT when it is available. Depending on the target country, the degree of open-
ness, and role of a free press, analysts can study the work of journalists on the ground
and official and unofficial statements by political actors. Of course, for harder targets,
ruled by authoritarian leaders and parties, political analysts need to discount the reliability of official reports or at least read them with an eye to deception and manipulation. In such states, clandestine reporting, SIGINT, and available embassy reporting
are more crucial. In working on regime transitions, my own experience suggests that
analysts need to be creative and figure out new methods of collection to fill intelligence gaps.

Modern American intelligence was created to deal with the USSR, a regime that
tried to hide and classify as secret almost every type of information. This ranged
from military details to basic facts about demography, its economy, and its leadership. Special techniques were used to overcome this "hard target." Under the
heading of "Kremlinology," analysts worked to interpret limited pieces of information—like the order of names in an official party list at a diplomatic reception or
subtle changes (termed "content analysis") of the wording found in official pro-
nouncements in party newspapers. Getting direct access to Politburo decisions or
debates was extremely difficult. Émigrés, defectors, and spies of course were helpful
in piercing the Soviet veil, but our knowledge was far from complete, despite every
effort by all kinds of collectors to contribute good information. As the power of
the Communist Party began to fade in the late 1980s, new avenues of information
became available. It became much easier to travel and to meet openly with dissi-
dents and emerging political actors. Emboldened Soviet citizens began to approach
Americans and Westerners; our Moscow embassy in 1990 received many "walk-
ins," some very valuable, but also many who claimed to have inside information
but only wanted to escape to the West or get paid. Examining and validating these
sources found in emerging noncommunist parties, interest groups, and civil society
organizations was very demanding.

In the post-1990 period, political analysis was hampered in places like Ukraine,
the Caucasus, and Central Asia because of the drop in collection priorities against
the post-Soviet target. The State Department attempted to open new embassies and
consulates in these republics as quickly as possible; however, it took time to develop
reporting on newly independent republics where US officials and journalists had seldom been. At the same time, analysts could travel to meet US diplomats and, where
possible, engage with local politicians and activities. In addition, a growing cadre of
political, economic, and development advisers from the US government as well as
private foundations constituted new sources of information for political analysts.

In post-Saddam Iraq, the presence of a huge embassy and a large military deployment suddenly expanded enormously the collection resources available to political

analysts. A flood of information came in from American diplomats and military intelligence units as well as HUMINT collectors. Yet we knew that deployed forces had much more information than was being reported back through official channels. Hence, in 2016 two analysts and I traveled to key US bases inside Iraq over several months to talk directly with US personnel, attempting to leverage their contacts with Iraqi tribal and regional leaders. This proved so successful that it became the model for a new type of intelligence product that was essentially a field intelligence report.

WORKING WITH POLICYMAKERS

Political analysts find that working with policymakers can be more challenging than perhaps in other disciplines because decision-makers—whether diplomats, politicians, or even military commanders—often consider themselves good analysts of political events. They may accept that they are not experts on a military order-of-battle, international economics, or high-energy physics; but politics is another story. Sometimes unconsciously, decision-makers think all political opinions are of equal value—including theirs—and are largely subjective. In their minds, they are just as good at judging political power as a CIA political analyst.

To be fair, many consumers of political analysis have been excellent politicians who have run successful campaigns and know a lot about local and national American politics, parties, and elections. They have commissioned and used opinion polls, worked in or with the media, and understand leadership. In sum, successful political leaders in America have a high opinion of their own political instincts.

However, the underlying belief is that because they understand American politics and institutions, they can therefore generalize to foreign governments and cultures. Not true. The job of political analysts is to highlight the differences found in those countries and indirectly point out where the American experience and perspective can lead decision-makers astray. Because of this, it is necessary for analysts to connect with where US policymakers are coming from and remind them that things are different overseas. For example, when writing or briefing on the early 2000s Iraqi parliament, it was important to state generally that the Iraqi parliament is still a work in progress, and it does not have the established procedures, rules, or customs that characterize the US Congress or European parliaments. Describing how Iraqi parliamentary sessions often involved name-calling, walk-outs, and threats usually helped to make it clear that American assumptions about the legislative process were probably not apt.

As mentioned above, new policy customers often expect the CIA to have "really good stuff"—that is, better information than is available outside the government. If these expectations are not met, those customers can become skeptical. In addition, in today's networked US government, senior policymakers and their staffs have direct access to a great deal of classified raw reporting that can make them think they know as much as the analyst, even though they rarely have the time or the training of the intelligence specialist.

Typically, customers will expect the political analyst to have deep background in the region or country, possibly having spent time there or learned the language. More experienced policymakers recognize the variability of the intelligence community's insight into foreign governments, depending on whether it is a relatively established democracy or a closed authoritarian regime; they can better appreciate the way a seasoned political analyst can exploit both unclassified and classified sources than a newcomer to the US government. In fact, political analysts—both generalists and specialists—can usually overcome skepticism about the CIA's value by getting to know the consumer and his or her needs. A key method is to develop good relations with one's peers, such as the State Department desk officer, the Pentagon action officer, or National Security Council director, who all know what their senior officials know, care about, and need to learn. Through them, analysts also learn what policy initiatives are under discussion, what are the key policy debates, and what intelligence-related questions are likely to come up.

Making such contacts can occur in a variety of ways. Frequent briefings or attending interagency meetings allows the analyst to build his or her own network. More directly, a political analyst—as well as those in other disciplines—may have the opportunity to do a "policy rotation" outside the CIA. In my career, I had three such opportunities. First, in the early 1990s I spent some months working in a US embassy on internal politics, learning how an embassy operated and developing a good sense of the strengths and weaknesses of diplomatic reporting. Second, I spent several years in the mid-1990s serving at the State Department, where I worked with senior diplomats dealing with the former USSR and could see how intelligence informed US strategy toward that part of the world. Third, in the mid-2000s I served on the National Security Council staff as a director for Iraq. In this capacity, one sees the intelligence that is presented to other senior officials, including the president, and how they react. A director must run interagency meetings at which other national security agencies consider intelligence as well as policy options. Presidential priorities made a huge difference in terms of both intelligence support as well as attention in the interagency process. After President Bush left office, I witnessed the lower priority that President Obama placed on Iraq; our work had to adjust to changing policies and attention spans.

When interacting with senior policymakers, it is critical for political analysts to know what the US policy goals and priorities are. An Agency officer on rotation, or an Agency briefer who deals regularly with the customer, can make sure the analysis is on target and does not make the mistake of telling the customer something they already know; indeed, there is nothing worse than wasting the time of a busy senior official. Good "opportunity analysis" is often highly valued but hard to do; bad or vague suggestions, conversely, can hurt our credibility. And analysts should never be afraid to say "I don't know" or "I'll get back to you." Speculating beyond where the evidence and solid reasoning can take you is not our strength. I have seen papers and briefings fall flat for all these reasons.

Usually, our analysis benefits from the prestige of the CIA "brand" and a reputation for doing high-quality work. But some officials have a negative view of CIA analysis because of a bad experience or because of turf wars or personality clashes. I had to deal with a senior National Security Council staff member who ostentatiously looked at the newspaper while I was briefing him. This comes with the job, and analysts must be prepared for disinterest, criticism, and occasional hostility. Fortunately, such instances are rare. Most customers are eager for anything that helps them achieve their goals and are grateful for the information and insights we provide.

OTHER CHALLENGES FOR POLITICAL ANALYSIS

In addition to the challenge that "every policymaker is an analyst," the discipline is confronted with the necessity of conducting multidisciplinary analysis and also avoiding the peril of "predicting" the future of foreign political developments. A wrong prediction can stick in a policymaker's memory and permanently tarnish the view of our analysis. Analysis has to avoid the twin dangers of being too tied to a single outcome or constantly saying "it depends" without giving a useful bottom line. Walking this line demands attention to best tradecraft practices, which the Directorate of Analysis began to strengthen almost three decades ago. Political analysts must practice these methods if they are to retain the trust of US decision-makers and avoid unrealistic expectations.

Multidisciplinary Analysis

In my opinion, it is almost inevitable that political analysts will need to rely on inputs from other disciplines to gain a complete picture of what is occurring in a foreign government or political system. For example, if there is a coup being plotted, most likely some of the participants reside in the military or security services. Food riots that lead to street protests and challenges to local and national leaders inevitably involve the state of the economy. There are many other examples one could cite. The point is that political analysts must be synthesizers of information that is not exclusively political reporting. Many finished intelligence assessments will fall into categories of "political-military" or "political-economic" analysis as the intelligence judgments in one area depend on factors in other domains. Producing analysis that incorporates the expertise of different disciplines, often from different offices or Mission Centers, is more difficult and time-consuming. But it pays off in deeper insights and less chance for errors and bias, helping to make CIA analysis well regarded downtown. Customers have often complained in the past about receiving separate political, military, and economic analyses of the same issue instead of one integrated assessment.

In terms of its internal organization, the Agency has moved steadily away from offices organized by discipline and has chosen to integrate many of the core disciplines (especially political, economic, military, and leadership) into regional or functional Mission Centers. On the positive side, this can produce synergy and encourage the development of multidisciplinary analysis from the beginning. It can also facilitate faster coordination of a product in many cases by reducing the multiple levels of review that an intelligence piece must pass through before it leaves the CIA.

This approach, however, needs to be joined with other forms of discipline-specific support. If an analyst in any discipline works without regular interaction with other similar specialists in the field, he or she can lose perspective, miss out on new tools and practices, and become stale. Being part of a discipline's "tribe" also strengthens morale as well as analytic and ethical standards. Analysts inside the tribe are more likely to share failures as well as successes to learn from both. When I was an analyst, an important support mechanism for political analysts was the Political Analysis Steering Group. This network is run by political analysts so that they can share experiences, ideas, and methods. It holds regular meetings, where analysts can discuss challenges and exchange best practices; often, analysts will present current projects to their peers to get suggestions. Sometimes outside experts are invited to discuss new approaches to the study of politics. Taking classes in the political program at the Sherman Kent School for Intelligence Analysis is another way political analysts share experiences and learn best practices.

The Perils of Prediction

Many complaints about CIA political analysis, as well as other disciplines, focus on whether the Agency predicted an event or warned of some catastrophe in time for policymakers to react. In truth, too many policymakers believe TV and movie thrillers and assume the CIA is prescient on global events. We are not. Our failures are well known—the Soviet invasion of Afghanistan, the Iranian Revolution, the Yom Kippur War, the 9/11 attacks, and the Iraq weapons of mass destruction National Intelligence Estimate. However, policymakers need to understand that precise forecasts depend on having excellent information on how foreign politics are operating inside those ministries and institutions, on who are the key decision-makers and how they think about the issues in question. It is far easier to forecast the outcome of an election in a typical Western European country with a stable party structure and transparent institutions than in a newly emerging democracy with an untested constitution and newly formed parties.

Even under the best of circumstances, political forecasts can be wrong. Political analysis tries to avoid precise predictions—such as who is going to win an upcoming election, a hard thing to do even here in the United States. Instead, analysts can offer their assessment of the range and significance of different outcomes based on the factors that will make each one more or less likely.

As the discussion above of multidisciplinary analysis suggests, political analysis needs to be informed by other sources of information and different perspectives. The biggest danger that political analysts face is believing that their own mental map of a country and its foreign policy behavior are immutable. As we learn time and time again, they are not. Moreover, foreign leaders miscalculate and often make decisions that seem "illogical" or too risky to American analysts. So, it is incumbent on analysts in all disciplines, but especially those in the political discipline, to practice good tradecraft.

As mentioned in chapter 1 of this volume, the CIA's analytic tradecraft has evolved significantly since the first assessments were being crafted about the challenges that Soviet power presented to the Free World in the late 1940s. In my own experience, the use of structured analytic techniques and experience working inside the CIA's Red Cell deepened my appreciation for the importance of using these methods to challenge old lines of analysis or conventional assumptions about a foreign actor. In my years as a Soviet analyst, it was clear that the analytic lines regarding expected Soviet behavior had been broadly correct for decades but that holding on to those views too long kept us from seeing the true weakness and brittleness of the USSR and Gorbachev's genuine desire for change.

It is especially important during times of dynamic and rapid change in a foreign country to apply these techniques because previous assumptions and expectations may well be proven wrong. For example, there were well-known sources of domestic dissatisfaction in the Middle East before a simple fruit vendor in Tunisia self-immolated and set off the 2011 Arab Spring, but few anticipated the wave of unrest that spread throughout North Africa and the Middle East and eventually engulfed Egypt and Syria. At that time, I was serving in the CIA's Red Cell, whose mission is to question long-established analytic positions and pursue alternative hypotheses using a variety of structured analytic techniques. This allowed the Red Cell analysis—which did not carry the "official" CIA position—to stimulate policymakers' thinking and prepare them to envision alternative futures. At the Red Cell, we conducted devil's advocacy analysis on low-probability events, a Team A / Team B paper on Libya's disintegration, and a multiple futures paper on the Middle East's political unrest. These allowed analysts to explore how the Arab Spring might alter the political landscape in the Middle East by promoting terrorism and Islamic radicalism or by leading to new forms of authoritarian rule.

CONCLUSION

The central political issues of the last several decades—such as democratization, globalization, and Islamic radicalism—are still very much with us, but the focus now is shifting back to great power competition with closed, quasi-totalitarian systems.[14] China's rise and how it would employ its growing power has been a central issue for political analysis for decades. Any hope that China would liberalize at home and integrate peacefully into the global system has been dashed under Xi Jinping's personalistic rule. Putin's Russia is supporting anti-US forces around the globe and reviving fears of conventional and even nuclear conflict with NATO. Today's political analysts must constantly consider where other countries stand between China, Russia, and the United States.

American decision-makers have looked to the CIA's analysis for insights about foreign threats and opportunities for almost seventy years. Over my own career, the range of issues that policymakers wanted political analysts to address always grew larger, never smaller; there is no reason to think this will change. There are more, and more kinds of, influential actors on the political stage than ever before. The nature of conflict is shifting as foreign powers can easily reach across borders to sow discord and spread disinformation. New technologies are making it harder and harder to tell truth from fiction. Authoritarian, nationalist regimes are refining techniques to stay in power and are actively collaborating on ways not just to resist liberal democracy and globalization but even to reverse them. The scope of US national security has expanded to include complex environmental, social, and demographic threats, such as global warming, immigration, and corruption.

The fundamentals of power—how it is gained, maintained, passed on, lost, and used—seem to be permanent. In this old but new world, political analysts can still read Thucydides or Machiavelli or Ibn Khaldun and nod in recognition. But the specifics are always in flux. No doubt, political analysts are brushing up on some of the lessons of the Cold War. Analysts are taught, however, not to be trapped by old paradigms. History may rhyme, but it does not repeat.

NOTES

1. "Proposal for an Office of Political Research" (Memo from the CIA Deputy Director for Intelligence), June 21, 1973, declassified from SECRET, https://www.cia.gov/readingroom/docs/CIA-RDP80B01495R000700080005-5.pdf.

2. The author applied for a "sabbatical year" though the directorate's "Advanced Analyst Program," allowing the individual to develop a research project that would make a significant

contribution to the CIA's analytical knowledge. This allowed the analyst to conduct research both inside and outside the Agency and also meet with other non–US government experts at universities and other research centers.

3. One example of this area expertise is the Agency's incentives program for learning and maintaining foreign languages. A CIA officer can receive a financial award for achieving a level of proficiency in many foreign languages and for maintaining that level throughout their career.

4. See Paul C. Avey and Michael C. Desch, "What Do Policymakers Want from Us? Results of a Survey of Current and Former Senior National Security Decision Makers," *International Studies Quarterly* 58 (2014): 227–46, doi:10.1111/isqu.12111.

5. Glossary of Terms and Techniques for Political Analysis, CIAOCI, https://www.cia .gov/readingroom/docs/CIA-RDP85T00875R001100020002-2.pdf; "The Application of Political Instability Research Methodologies," https://www.cia.gov/readingroom/docs/CIA -RDP83B00851R000300130002-8.pdf; "Policon: A Tool for Systematic Political Analysis: A User's Guide," declassified from SECRET, GI M 86-20184, https://www.cia.gov/readingroom /docs/CIA-RDP86T01017R000201260001-9.pdf; Stanley Feder, "FACTIONS and POLICON: New Ways to Analyze Politics," https://fm.cnbc.com/applications/cnbc.com/resources/editorial files/2021/09/15/Factions_and_Policon_CIA_Report.pdf.

6. A good starting place for the literature is Jack Snyder, "One World, Rival Theories," *Foreign Policy* 145, no. 52 (2004): 52–62.

7. Early research on this is Dean V. Babst, "Elective Governments: A Force for Peace," *Wisconsin Sociologist* 3 (1964): 9–14.

8. Thomas C. Shelling, *Arms and Influence* (New Haven, CT: Yale University Press, 1966). The literature on deterrence is vast. E.g., an early contribution is Bernard Brodie, "The Anatomy of Deterrence," *World Politics* 11, no. 2 (January 1959): 173–91.

9. Graham Allison, *Essence of Decision: Explaining the Cuban Missile Crisis* (Boston: Little, Brown, 1971). Allison first published his theories in "Conceptual Models and the Cuban Missile Crisis," *American Political Science Review* 63 (1969): 689–718.

10. Jonathan Bendor and Thomas H. Hammond, "Rethinking Allison's Models," *American Political Science Review* 86, no. 2 (June 1992): 301–22.

11. Nye has written widely about soft power. In addition to *Bound to Lead: The Changing Nature of American Power* (London: Basic Books, 1990), he developed his concepts in *Soft Power: The Means to Success in World Politics* (New York: PublicAffairs, 2004).

12. Samuel P. Huntington, "The Clash of Civilizations?" *Foreign Affairs* 72, no. 3 (1993): 22–49, https://www.jstor.org/stable/20045621.

13. In a 1989 National Intelligence Estimate, CIA and other intelligence community analysts concluded that Gorbachev would either move ahead with limited reforms and muddle through or a conservative backlash and crackdown could end those reforms. A 1991 CIA assessment also warned that reactionary forces would likely attempt a coup, which later occurred in August 1991.

14. Nomaan Merchant, "One Year after Afghanistan, Agencies Pivot toward China," AP, August 8, 2022, https://apnews.com/article/afghanistan-russia-ukraine-al-qaida-biden-ayman -zawahri-15e3f9282d6eac7b9c793394fff5497c.

3

MILITARY ANALYSIS: PEERING OVER THE HILL

Robert Levine

A BRIEF ADVENTURE ABROAD

One of the perks of serving as a senior military analyst at the Central Intelligence Agency is traveling abroad to brief high-level US and foreign authorities, meet with and support collectors, and gain a firsthand sense of the target areas with orientation trips. These can be rewarding experiences.

Some years ago, I traveled to a country that was part of my account, my focus of study. After a week of work giving briefings to senior US officials, meeting with collectors, and the like, I was invited to attend a party at the embassy of a friendly country. Within minutes of wandering into the embassy courtyard, I was approached by a man I had met a few months before, the relatively new chief of an allied country's intelligence presence in the country—what we refer to as the same allied country's "station." I will refer to him as the allied chief of station (COS). Our conversation was easy and quickly came to a point:

> *Allied COS*: "Hello, we met some months ago in Washington, where you briefed me on X."
>
> *Author*: "Of course, I remember it clearly. I hope you are settling in well."
>
> *Allied COS*: "Tell me, are you still working on [a particular aspect of weapons of mass destruction]?"
>
> *Author*: "Yes, among other topics."
>
> *Allied COS*: "Ever hear of Plan [codename]?"
>
> *Author*: (a bit surprised): "Yes . . . why do you ask?" (And privately thinking, why do you ask here at a party?)
>
> *Allied COS*: "Well, we've got some new information from a source and thought we ought to talk about it."

> *Author*: "Interesting." (not having briefed this allied chief of station on CIA information about the plan months before because the information seemed false—a fabrication that had earned the source unwarranted income.)
>
> *Author*: "I don't mean to probe, but are you confident in this source?"
>
> *Allied COS*: "Well, we paid him a rather large amount of money."
>
> *Allied COS*: "Perhaps you could route your flight back to Washington through [his capital] so you can meet with our experts."
>
> *Author*: "Sounds like an excellent idea—I will check with my superiors."

After several more days in country, I flew back, routed through the allied chief of station's capital. I met with several officials and was provided with the information they had gained.

In short order, their expert and I agreed that the information was not worth the paper it was printed on. There was no discussion about the clandestine operation that generated the information or whether the source had established his bona fides in some way. Rather, an examination of the military feasibility of the alleged plan—the weapons' expected means of delivery, integration into other operations, anticipated effects, and so on—did not fit with what the CIA knew about military operations in general and the particular character of the suspect country's operations. We agreed that their source was probably a fabricator—and suspected that their worthless source was in fact the same as our source.

Several years later, in a classified course attended by a young intelligence officer from the allied country, there was a discussion of liaison relationships. I mentioned that our two services ended up sharing the actual name of the source to avoid future misleading information and wasting both agencies' time and money. The young officer said he had been told about the case in his training and that it was the first time the two services had taken such a step.

It was a fascinating experience, but the reason to describe it is to illustrate the odd turns and breadth of the work of military analysts at the Central Intelligence Agency. While much of the daily work involves sitting in Langley, Virginia, reading and making sense of a torrent of incoming intelligence reports, military analysts brief domestic and foreign policy and intelligence officers, collaborate with collectors, and use their knowledge to vet and mine new sources—and to help eliminate misleading ones.

THE PATH(S) TO LANGLEY

The CIA hires military analysts in large measure based on candidates' educational backgrounds and prior work experience. Over the years, this has contributed to a significant percentage—something like 50 percent—of military analytic hires having served in the US military, and another large group having been hired initially into the US intelligence community as imagery analysts. Both career paths provide new analysts familiarity with military organizations and operations. That said, given the focus of the CIA's military analytic cadre—supporting the country's senior-most policymakers, largely at the level of national security strategy and military strategy[1]—former officers seldom have directly relevant experiences. Most had served as junior officers for perhaps five years.

The other pool of applicants who attract hiring advisers' attention are those who pursue international relations or strategic studies academically. These candidates bring a different kind of familiarity, research skills, and writing skills, but most programs teach students few of the tools of analysis.

Thus, even with a stream of well-educated and experienced new military analytic hires,[2] the CIA invested in creating opportunities for analysts to learn about foreign general purpose forces,[3] the operational employment of weapons of mass destruction, counterinsurgency operations, civil–military relations, and the like. In-house courses, run by the Sherman Kent School for Intelligence Analysis, are not intended to substitute for on-the-job learning and mentoring by senior analysts; but they are essential to the development of broadly informed military analysts. Analysts also have opportunities to take other training courses (e.g., missile operations, nuclear weapons development) through the Department of Defense and Department of Energy, visit military training sites and organizations, participate in military exercises, and, for a limited number, attend US military staff and war college programs.

I was fortunate to meet the CIA's selection criteria. My undergraduate degree from a university in Texas (in history, originally majoring in mathematics) was followed by an MA in war studies at King's College, University of London, and a PhD in public policy analysis at the RAND Graduate Institute. RAND's program involved simultaneous work on major projects for the US government. In my case, this involved gaining security clearances; learning on the job from a number of senior, experienced defense analysts; and becoming familiar with several components of the Department of Defense, the Joint Staff, and other organizations involved in US defense issues. The transition to the CIA seemed like a natural, evolutionary movement.[4]

WHAT ARE THE CORE DUTIES OF MILITARY ANALYSTS?

In the midst of a busy career, it is hard to lift one's gaze and identify one's fundamental purposes. It was only many years after becoming a seasoned military analyst that I could distill the central aspects of the job to explain to younger analysts on the job and in training courses. They can be grouped into three "bins": national-level, all-source analysis; working with collectors to gain and vet information; and providing support to policymakers. Each bin has a number of components and unique features.

National-Level, All-Source Analysis

It does not make for a dramatic movie scene, but most of a military analyst's time and effort is devoted to making sense of incoming reports, which are typically described as a firehose of information. Reports derived from clandestine sources—such as human spies and technical collection systems—combine with those from military, diplomatic, and open sources (Internet-based, broadcast, print) to fill an analyst's computer screen with hours of reading per day. On some of my accounts, I had perhaps three hundred reports to read daily—after filters eliminated some redundancies.[5] Virtually all analysts faced the conundrum of how much to filter and read: the certainty of being overwhelmed by mass versus the risk of missing something truly useful. On accounts where several analysts covered a topic, one might hope that colleagues would catch important information one had missed—but all too often, different analysts focused on particular aspects of an account, and budget-cutting actions reduced what some perceived as redundancy, shrinking what had been something of a safety net.

One of my former intelligence colleagues described the typical analytic process as gathering a bunch of reports, reading them, spreading them out on your desk, and coming up with plausible ways to fit them together. That may be a good description; but if so, it is disturbing.

Military analysts must understand a complex situation well enough to offer decision-makers a coherent and persuasive theory that logically ties together the available evidence. More specifically, there are three targets of inquiry for military analysts assessing foreign militaries:

1. *Foreign perceptions.* Identifying the perceptions of foreign political and military leaders, and the sources of influence, is key to providing credible explanations for what has occurred, is occurring, and might occur in a foreign military's activities. At one point in the mid-1980s, US and liaison intelligence services detected anomalous and disturbing activities among Soviet forces. Without an understanding of why these were occurring—a combination of Soviet perceptions and intentions—any countermeasures taken by the United States and NATO could have exacerbated tensions. Revelations from an in-place source of the British Secret Intelligence Service, KGB colonel Oleg Gordievsky, alerted the CIA to Soviet fears that the United States was contemplating a sudden nuclear attack on the USSR. US actions could have exacerbated Soviet fears, perhaps leading to an unintended but terribly dangerous—and misunderstood—situation (See box 3.1).[6]

BOX 3.1: HOW SLIGHTING US ACTIONS SKEWED
UNDERSTANDING OF THE SOVIET "WAR SCARE"

Ignoring US actions can exacerbate misunderstanding, but the selective use of information can have even greater consequences. A particularly egregious example is the 1984 Special National Intelligence Estimate (SNIE), *Implications of Recent Soviet Military-Political Activities.*[7] That document examined whether the Soviet leadership was genuinely concerned about a potential military threat from the United States and NATO in the early 1980s, or if Soviet activities and public postures had other motivations.

The SNIE appeared to take a prudent and modest position insofar as how much Soviet activities were reactions to US actions: "We are at present uncertain as to what novelty or possible military objectives the Soviets may have read into recent US and NATO exercises and reconnaissance operations because a detailed comparison of simultaneous 'Red' and 'Blue' actions has not been accomplished."

In fact, the SNIE skewed its findings by ignoring significant US political and military activities. It made no mention of the September 1983 Soviet shootdown of a Korean commercial airliner and the US reaction; the March 1983 "Evil Empire" speech by President Reagan to an evangelical audience; dramatic changes in US nuclear planning (Presidential Directive 59); and, most tellingly, the Strategic Defense Initiative. It barely notes and does not assess the impact of the US invasion of Grenada; the massive US investment in new precision, conventional weapons; or the new nuclear-tipped intermediate-range missiles the US was deploying to Europe. (These included 108 Pershing II missiles with perceived short flight times to Moscow and Earth-penetrating warheads that could decapitate the Soviet leadership.)[8]

Declassified CIA documents suggest the SNIE's omissions were not inadvertent. The lead author of the SNIE, Fritz Ermarth (national intelligence officer for the USSR), wrote presentations intended for President Reagan that supported the underlying message that the Soviets were pessimistic about the future but there was no true "war scare."[9] Not all US officials were cavalier about US statements and Soviet reactions. A September 1985 declassified document noted, "They [the Soviets] regard references to the USSR as the 'evil empire' and jokes about declaring the USSR 'illegal' and 'start the bombing in five minutes' as indicative of deeply held feeling."[10]

We discovered later from multiple sources that the SNIE's assessment—curtailed by its selective use of information—was far off the mark. Senior KGB officials and clandestine source described the period as a crisis and specific events as shocking. In the words of Lt. Gen. G. V. Batenin, "I don't recall a period more tense since the Caribbean Crisis in 1962 [the Cuban Missile Crisis]."[11] Selective Soviet forces went on alert and aircraft may have loaded nuclear arms in alert status.[12]

Sometime later, Robert Gates, who was serving in the White House during much of the war scare, stated, "We may have been at the brink of nuclear war and not even known it."[13]

---

2. *Foreign intentions.* Intentions are a product of the interactions of perceptions—fears and perceived opportunities—and desires. As with foreign perceptions, foreign intentions are an essential element for explaining detected activities and estimating future ones. In one meeting with case officers, I joined a group of technical weapons experts to explain what information was of the greatest importance to collect regarding a country developing a nuclear weapons arsenal. The weapons experts prioritized weapons design information, including particular components, assembly, and so on. When it was my turn, I stated that I understood the value of that information. But the most important things to understand were the foreign political, military, and technical authorities' perceptions of their own and opponents' weapons, and intentions concerning the types and numbers of weapons and delivery systems needed to cope

with perceived threats. Military analysts must be as interested in what foreign adversaries intend to build as in their military capability.

3. *Foreign capabilities.* This is the most visible and collectable of the intelligence tasks of military analysts. Whether an analyst is studying friendly foreign forces, neutrals, or potential opponents, gaining a deep and secure understanding of what the forces can accomplish, and what the forces' strengths and weaknesses are, is as important as it is obvious.[14] A number of successful military analysts have developed a set of skills to create detailed orders of battle of foreign militaries, tables of manning, equipment, and organizations that are the building blocks of force capabilities.[15] Other analysts have examined in detail foreign militaries' military doctrine, training, and readiness to answer questions about how quickly those forces might be able to pose a threat (or, conversely, come to the aid of friendly countries). Foreign military capabilities encompass hardware (e.g., weapons), what we might think of as "operational software" such as tactics, and support systems that are essential to carry out operations and maintain forces (e.g., communications and logistics systems).

HOW DO MILITARY ANALYSTS DO THEIR WORK?

The variety of issues military analysts cover often leads to specialization by force type and region.[16] Hence, one might find military analysts focused on Chinese ground forces, and others on North Korean air forces. The need to understand the broader context of a foreign country's military and defense planning, however, encourages a common set of topics that analysts are encouraged to study. Key common areas include the following:[17]

- *Force structure and organization.* How does the foreign country organize forces in peacetime and for war?
- *Personnel policies.* How does the country populate its armed forces? Does it rely on conscription or professional, volunteer forces, or a mixture? What challenges does it face in recruiting and retaining qualified personnel, especially noncommissioned and commissioned officers?
- *Combat and support equipment.* The order of battle of a country includes its personnel organized into units and tables of equipment associated with different units. What systems does it operate, and in what numbers? Where does it base forces? What communications and intelligence systems does it use, and do procedures and culture hinder or empower them?[18]

- *Training.* The most common activity of all militaries, aside from the mundane ones of feeding and caring for personnel and maintaining equipment, is training at individual and unit levels. Nothing is more important in turning recruits into effective fighters. What is the country's training program and cycle, and are adequate resources (trainers, equipment, land and air space, etc.) provided for this critical set of activities? How well are forces able to use their equipment and assimilate new systems?
- *Readiness.* Whether a country harbors adventurist aims or is purely defensive, a key measure of its perceptions, intentions, and capabilities is how quickly it can convert to a wartime footing. The state of training, mobilization of reserve personnel, and availability of equipment all feed into the state of readiness.
- *Sustainability and logistics.* A force that is not provided with a steady stream of "beans, bullets, and BTUs" will not be capable of carrying our military missions effectively.[19] A military's consumption of food, water, fuel, spare parts, and the like are its lifeblood.
- *Doctrine.* How does a country's armed forces intend to conduct operations in various conditions and locations? From the lowest level of tactics up through complex, joint operations, militaries must use consistent, honed procedures. These are generally collated in manuals or regulations; taught in the field, schools, and military academies; and essential to organize concerted efforts and prevent chaos.
- *Civil-military relations.* How does the country strike a balance between civilian and military authorities? How does it handle the inevitable tensions and disagreements?
- *Will, morale, cohesion, and leadership.*[20] Morale and the will to fight are influenced by small-unit cohesion, ideology, immediate leadership behavior, and so on—as well as shifting events on the battlefield. How does the country encourage these through incentives (e.g., honor, plunder), emotive measures (e.g., ideological indoctrination), and coercive measures (e.g., social pressures, blocking forces)?

Each of these subjects could be deconstructed for finer examination. For example, training should be considered in terms of physical fitness, proficiency in weapons and support systems use, basic tactics, combined-arms operations, and assimilation of new (especially foreign) systems (and any number of other components). At the same time, these topics or aspects of military power are interdependent and their mutual influences can be critical (see box 3.2).

Military analysts acquire understanding of these and other areas of interest gradually. The best analysts combine a broad study of these factors through military history

---

BOX 3.2: RUSSIAN MILITARY PERSONNEL IN THE 2022 INVASION OF UKRAINE—A VICIOUS FEEDBACK LOOP

Moscow's attack and Kyiv's response illustrate most, if not all, of the nuts and bolts of conventional military analysis. A quick look at its personnel policies and their interdependencies is especially illustrative.

Russia staffs its armed forces with a mixture of professional officer cadres, personnel who volunteer to serve under contract, and short-period conscripts (drafted for one year). Conscripts should not have taken part in Putin's "special military operation," but did in fact.

To fill out its invasion force, Moscow counted on ethnic Russians in eastern Ukraine (those areas under its control since 2014); contractor-supplied mercenaries (e.g., the Wagner Group);[21] and, as Russian casualties mounted, foreign fighters (from Chechnya and Syria).[22] A desire to bound the conflict for domestic reasons seems to have convinced the Russian leadership to delay large-scale personnel mobilization.[23] (When Russia began a limited mobilization in September 2022, hundreds of thousands of Russian men fled the country and severe civil disturbances occurred in numerous parts of the country.) Substantial financial incentives offered to new volunteers have been paired with loosened restrictions on the age of recruits in a drive to increase the ranks.

High personnel casualties and poor soldiers' discipline (fleeing the battlefield, not to mention plundering, rape, and murder) have led to reliance on deceptive and coercive measures to put and keep manpower at the front. A video shows a "recruitment pitch" by the late Yevgeny Prigozhin, a Russian then close to Putin, creator of the Wagner group, in a Russian prison. Prigozhin tells the prisoners, "After six months [at war] you receive a pardon. . . . Those who arrive [at the front line] and say on Day 1 it's not for them get shot."[24]

Personnel problems are tied strongly to other factors that affect a military's combat power.

- A mixture of poorly prepared soldiers (many did not know they were going to war) and underinvestment in noncommissioned officers—the backbone of most armed forces—exacerbated limited weapons proficiency, poor maintenance of equipment, weak tactics, and heavy personnel and equipment losses.[25]
- Ineffective small-unit leadership has put a premium on more senior officers' intervention at the front. Those commanders' undisciplined use of interceptable cellphones (along with inadequate standard communications) has led to Ukrainian strikes against Russian field headquarters and unusually high casualty rates among generals.
- Firepower-heavy battalion tactical groups (BTGs), intended to provide flexibility for rapid advances, have inherent weaknesses in this invasion related to personnel.[26] Their relative lack of infantry—only some 200 soldiers per BTG (out of 700-900 total)—meant that casualties would quickly whittle away a key component of units' combined-arms combat power. Weakened infantry components meant less support for tanks and hence increased vulnerability to Ukrainian anti-tank teams and reduced means to take and hold terrain (especially built-up areas).[27]

Problems in personnel, equipment maintenance, proficiency in weapons use, tactics, and attrition create a vicious feedback loop or cycle that reinforces itself.

---

with a specialized study of how they manifest themselves in their particular target country. Analysts are strongly encouraged to avoid mirror imaging—assuming others do things the way we do things.[28] At the same time, an understanding of how many countries have tackled personnel challenges, for example, allows analysts to draw comparisons and provide a rich perspective to consumers. Many of us have found that we can make the strongest and clearest arguments by laying out how a foreign power views and deals with a situation, such as ammunition requirements for an offensive, in comparison with how US military forces approach the same issue. An effort that involved many analysts and years of work illustrates the value of such an approach.

Learning from Others Does Not Equal Mirror Imaging

Military analysts charged with studying the peacetime and wartime operations of a foreign country's nuclear weapon arsenal have a particularly challenging task. Not only are these among the best-kept secrets any country has, but the observables are limited and there is no history of actual use since 1945 upon which analysts can draw.

There is a wealth of information, however, about how different countries have moved from creating nuclear weapons to how they secure them, make them available, and prepare and plan to use them in desperate situations. Studying the dilemmas and choices made by different countries—including the United States—can help analysts recognize choices that other nuclear powers have to face.

In the last years of the Soviet Union, the CIA's Directorate of Analysis created the Nuclear Weapons Security Task Force to study and monitor the security of the Soviet nuclear arsenal. This task force drew analysts from three major offices—the Office of Soviet Analysis, the Office of Scientific and Weapons Research, and the Office of Imagery Analysis. Each analyst brought unique knowledge and skills.[29]

The task force had to create a template of the activities and concerns a nuclear power would have and, within those, search for vulnerabilities that could lead to the diversion, accidental damage or detonation, or unauthorized use of Soviet nuclear weapons. Analysts in the past had studied these issues rather narrowly—primarily as warning indicators in a crisis or conflict. The team could build on years of work but had to examine activities through a new, different lens.

The team recognized the danger of mirror-imaging in analyzing the Soviets, but it also appreciated that US experience offered ground truth about necessary activities. Thus, analysts traveled to the US nuclear weapons laboratories; facilities that assembled, disassembled, and serviced nuclear warheads; and bases that controlled and would handle and launch nuclear weapons. The team received detailed briefings on the US nuclear command and control system as well as security protocols and US experiences in assessing the security of the US arsenal. Analysts scoured classified publications, such as a history of permissive action links (devices that prevented the use of nuclear weapons without a release code) for themes and issues. These collective efforts allowed the team to identify many of the challenges faced by any nuclear power and helped focus collection efforts:

1. *Numbers and characteristics of weapons.* Are simple fission weapons sufficient for the purposes of the foreign country, or will it need boosted or even thermonuclear warheads? How does it calculate the minimum and desirable number of weapons?

2. *Basing and delivery systems.* How concerned is the foreign country over the vulnerability of systems, and which delivery systems provide the need for speed, accuracy, and certainty of delivery?

3. *Logistics and infrastructure.* How are nuclear weapons stored, and in what state of readiness? Do they require relatively frequent servicing? How are they moved from central depots that can provide all maintenance to bases and delivery systems?

4. *Technologies and procedures for command and control.* All nuclear powers want to make certain weapons will always be available for use when needed but will never be used without authority. How does the foreign power assure control while reducing the likelihood of accident, diversion, rogue use, or use through miscalculation? Which organizations and individuals have authorization to order use?

5. *Integration into national policies and strategies.* Is the nuclear arsenal an overt capability, or is its existence secret and undeclared? Can its potential use be discussed openly or in any forum less than one that is highly secretive and protected?

6. *Military doctrine and plans.* What are the roles of nuclear weapons—strictly retaliatory and intended only for deterrence, or do they have a coercive role? What types of use should they be capable of, to include preemption, launch on tactical warning, rideout, and so on?

7. *Target selection and acquisition.* What organizations select targets, and what criteria do they use? How are mobile targets acquired? How is poststrike damage assessment conducted to allow for restrikes?

8. *Warning and alert systems.* What are the systems and arrangements to provide warning and confirmation of opponents' attacks against the nuclear arsenal or state?

9. *Defenses against weapons of mass destruction.* Does the foreign country possess, or is it intending to acquire, active defense systems against a nuclear attack (e.g., missile and air defense) or passive systems (e.g., civil defense or elite relocation shelters)?

Learning to Exploit Source Material

One set of skills all military analysts must acquire is the ability to exploit documentary evidence or reports. New analysts handed a copy of clandestinely acquired notes, or a memo for the record, detailing a meeting of senior foreign military officials may be thrown by its combination of bureaucratic jargon, excessive detail in some areas, and absence of information in others. A temptation is to cherry-pick—to look for information that is easy to grasp and use. Analysts must learn to exploit source material deeply.

In one CIA course, analysts were provided pre–World War II formerly classified French army committee meeting notes and a report from a French army-level exercise to test and hone their interpretive skills. Analysts were asked to assume that these documents had been compromised when they were written—what insights could they gain from them?

It was a surprisingly humbling experience. Many analysts failed to understand the reported meeting's and exercise's purpose, the roles of the participants, or their conclusions. After spending some time discussing them, however, analysts learned to ask and answer a series of systematic questions:

1. What kind of document is it? What is its foreign classification?
2. Who authored the document and to whom was it sent?
3. Who are the participants (e.g., if a meeting or exercise)? What are their ranks, roles, and interests?
4. What is the purpose of the document? What was the purpose of the reported meeting or exercise?
5. At what level of war (national, strategic, operational, tactical) are the reported discussions or activities?
6. What are the themes of the document?
7. Does the document (and the meeting or exercise) offer clear questions and answers?
8. If an exercise, what kind of exercise occurred—command post exercise? field training exercise? war game?
9. What does the document tell us about foreign perceptions, intentions, and capabilities? (Look back at the list including force structure and organization, personnel policies, combat and support equipment, etc.)
10. What assumptions do the participants or the document convey?
11. Are there "unspokens"—topics that reasonably should have been mentioned or discussed that are missing? What does that suggest about the "unspokens"?
12. Does the document discuss proposed solutions to problems? Do they actually seem like workable and affordable solutions?

This list can be expanded and focused for different types of source material. These general questions, nevertheless, have proven useful to many military analysts.

WORKING WITH COLLECTORS

There is a common complaint among all analysts: all the good books and movies involve operations, either clandestine collection or covert activities. Who is going to make an action movie featuring a young person staring at a computer screen and writing a report? How about an exciting scene with a manager editing a draft report? Fair enough.

Although analysts do not spot, recruit, and run agents, the roles that analysts can fill in collection are surprisingly diverse, and few spend a career without filling several of those roles. A fundamental requirement of all analysts, and especially military analysts, is to gain a profound understanding of collection systems and to exploit them. There may be nothing that differentiates excellent academics and analysts so much as this knowledge and skill set.

Moreover, military analysts develop a feel for their focus of study that works to the benefit of collectors. In some cases, this boils down to language skills. In far more cases, it leads to well-directed collection requirements, the ability to help make sense of ambiguous reporting, and a mutually beneficial contribution debriefing sources or exploiting technical collection. These examples illustrate such efforts at play:

1. When the Soviet Union was coming to its well-deserved end, there was a glut of Soviet intelligence officers who suddenly realized just how delightful the West, democracy, and capitalism were. Several analysts working in the Office of Soviet Analysis (an analytic office) were asked if they were interested in serving half-time in the Directorate of Operations unit debriefing these sources. Quite simply, the job would be to extract whatever insights and information the sources possessed. A handful of analysts jumped at the chance.

2. Why ask analysts to do this work? Bureaucratically, the answer was easy—not enough operations people were available and analysts were free labor. More seriously, those selected were paired with sources whose knowledge matched the analysts' areas of specialization. Two of the sources I spent a considerable time with were a KGB officer and a GRU (Soviet military intelligence) officer. In each case, detailed knowledge of the field in which they worked allowed me to verify their access and knowledge, probe into areas about which we had clues, and help develop new lines of inquiry. One of the sources, for example, should have been in a position to be aware of, and perhaps work on, the massive Soviet collection effort associated with the War Scare mentioned above. Without revealing what the CIA knew already and contaminate his knowledge, our questions led him to suddenly remark, "Oh, there was VRYAN—the system designed to detect a sudden NATO nuclear attack!"[30] He then provided a firsthand account of the tasking for the Soviet effort, the specific requirements, the sources he ran, and so on. It was a treasure trove. Our knowledge of the war scare sentiment in Moscow helped to guide subsequent detailed questioning.

3. During a period when I was studying a particular foreign military's perceptions of threats it faced, Directorate of Operations (DO) colleagues asked if
I might be interested in meeting with a former senior officer of that country
who had commanded and directed operations that might be related. Over a
span of several hours, this officer provided insights into the breadth of his
service's activities but also, even more important, what their perceptions
and intentions had been—matters about which the CIA had known little
previously. My knowledge of the structure and operations of the forces the
officer had commanded, however, encouraged him to talk about them in
greater detail. If the source had been debriefed only by a case officer with
general knowledge of the subject and broad tasking, less would have been
extracted.

4. On a visit to a station, the trip paid off in one giant windfall. A case officer asked, "Wait! Are you the person who sent this cable providing detailed
tasking about a whole range of interests, in case we came across sources
with access?" He pulled out a slightly stained and wrinkled document. Sure
enough, I had sent it over a year before. The case officer smiled, held it up, and
said, "This has been my Bible!" As we talked in more depth about reporting,
I explained how valuable a particular stream of reporting was and how it had
been and could be used. Maps were especially valuable, but the reproduc-
tions received at CIA Headquarters were of poor quality. Out of a drawer, the
case officer brought perhaps a dozen negative film rolls and handed them
over. They formed the basis for a lengthy, graphics-heavy report I produced
and briefed widely to senior consumers.

5. Working with technical collectors, of signals intelligence and satellite imagery, was no less rewarding. At one point, the CIA received a report that personnel associated with a foreign country's weapons of mass destruction were in
dire circumstances. The report sent shock waves through the intelligence and
policy communities. Something, however, seemed fishy about the report. I contacted the collector, with whom I had worked and established mutual trust and
respect. As we discussed the nature of the raw material—how it was collected
and who was describing the dire circumstances—contextual information and
understanding of the subject organizations led to a benign conclusion. It was
more likely that the collectors had swept up the plaintive claim of someone
who may have been dodging personal responsibilities. That was hardly the
basis for the extensive, hyped claims made by some recipients of the report.

For all the instances where analysts can speak of deep, productive relationships
with collectors, there is no denying the inconsistency and lack of systematic sharing of operational information between collectors and analysts.[31] Cooperative work is

dependent on personalities, and occasionally on senior direction. It took the intervention of the director of central intelligence to prod the DO to share relevant information with analytic counterparts after September 11, 2001. I was involved in a research effort involving foreign nuclear command and control that required the deputy director of the CIA to order that all attendees be cleared "for everything, bar none."

One trend I observed was a greater willingness to cooperate in the field, by case officers, than at Headquarters. Part of this may be the product of bureaucratic hierarchy in Langley. Collection management officers (CMOs, previously called reports officers) do not have the cachet or clout of operations officers in the DO. CMOs are the most common interface between operations and analysts, and it seems that their secondary DO status may manifest itself in keeping "real secrets" (e.g., information on sources and their access) from analysts.

SUPPORTING POLICYMAKERS

A characteristic that differentiates military analysts at the CIA from other analysts boils down to our intended consumers and what we offer them. We work with counterparts in other agencies that are home to experienced, insightful analysts (e.g., at the Defense Intelligence Agency and the individual service intelligence agencies). Those analysts serve the interests of their departmental or service chiefs (e.g., the State Department's Bureau of Intelligence and Research supports the secretary of state and senior State officials). CIA military analysts' primary consumers are the senior-most policymakers in the US government—the president and Cabinet members, subcabinet officials, the staff of the National Security Council, and senior officers at the Department of Defense, Department of State, and the US military. Because CIA analysts do not belong to any one department, they have a degree of independence. Historically, that has been valued by senior policymakers (see box 3.3).[32]

Military analytic products feature prominently in the electronically and hard copy disseminated stream of analysis produced by the CIA. Many of these products make innovative use of maps, illustrations (e.g., diagrams of weapons systems), and annotated images as well as multimedia displays.

As vital as the written word is, military analysts have a much greater impact when they engage directly with consumers. Because of the nature of the material, its urgency, and the fact that many consumers do not have a deep understanding of military matters, face-to-face presentations are common. These briefings are two-way conversations in which the consumers can fill in gaps in their knowledge and guide the conversation to best address their needs. Experienced analysts build trust and rapport with their consumers.

Let me illustrate the impact of such relationships. One of my accounts led to frequent contact with the assistant secretary of state for the region and that person's

---

BOX 3.3: WHAT KINDS OF QUESTIONS DO
CIA MILITARY ANALYSTS TRY TO ANSWER?

Policymakers have interests and concerns that cover a vast range of military analytic topics. Some focus on procurement—what weapons are potential opponents acquiring and what should we acquire in response? Others concentrate on force employment—how might opponents use forces, and how can we counter them? Yet others are
concerned with political-military questions that touch on allied and opponent intentions and the stability of military
balances. These are generalized versions of some of the types of questions military analysts try to answer:

- How do potential belligerents see the military balance they face? Are arms acquisitions, new alliances,
  or other events, trends, or situations altering the perceived balance?
- How active are insurgents and counterinsurgents, how do they operate, and how are they evolving?
- How stable is a foreign regime, what are the threats to stability (including potential military coups), and
  what measures does the regime take to counter perceived threats?
- Does the foreign military provide effective support for civil authorities in areas such as counternarcot-
  ics, civil engineering, or emergency response?
- How much can our allies help us in fighting or deterring common foes?
- What are the strengths and weaknesses of a foreign military power that we can bolster or undercut?
- What factors are shaping future foreign strategic forces?
- What are the implications of new arms control initiatives?
- What is the risk of theft, diversion, accident, or unsanctioned use of weapons of mass destruction?
- What are the indicators that would provide warning of war, and how confident in them are we? Warning
  is a complex topic that deserves a much fuller treatment than can be offered here. It is vital to note,
  however, that warning of a tactical nature (e.g., providing intelligence and assessment of an imminent
  attack) differs greatly from strategic warning (which might not warn of an anticipated attack but could
  explain how long enemy preparations for hostilities might require countermeasures and what indicators
  we would anticipate).[33] Analysts could provide operational warning, an intermediate level, as well. For
  example, in the weeks before the Pearl Harbor attack, military commanders were warned that Japanese
  aggression could occur soon, and they were advised to take precautionary measures. Nevertheless, that
  warning did not specify the location, time, or form of a likely Japanese attack.[34]

---

deputy and senior staff. Whenever the CIA finished a study and sent it to the assistant secretary, the CIA offered an oral briefing and discussion—an offer that was frequently accepted. The United States had a major diplomatic initiative concerning the focus of this account that involved the cooperation of several allies. The foreign minister of one friendly country was coming to Washington for talks, and the assistant secretary asked the CIA to brief the foreign minister. The substantive briefing went smoothly. Moreover, I tied an explanation of the intelligence situation to the policy initiative and gave credit to the foreign minister's own intelligence colleagues (both analysts and collector). This may have contributed to later cooperation with that country on rather sensitive HUMINT collection efforts.

In addition to the provision of analytic insights, in written or oral form, analysts contribute to policy support through opportunity analysis and influence operations. Intelligence analysts are mandated to bear in mind how identified events, trends, or conditions in foreign countries affect US national interests. CIA analysts are encour-aged to identify and sometimes are even asked how to exploit such opportunities. All too often, analysts proffer impractical or vacuous options: "The foreign country prob-ably would be willing to accept US financial or technical assistance." Few countries would of course reject such offers, but more creative options often elude analysts, who perhaps do not fully understand policymakers' tool kits or how such tools are even employed. Military analysts fall into the trap of trivializing opportunities as much as analysts in other disciplines. There are exceptions that shine a bright light on how much thorough, original military analysis can enhance US interests:

- Studies of the Soviet military years before the collapse of the Soviet Union revealed a deep, growing pessimism in Moscow about the military balance vis-à-vis NATO. A combination of increasing respect for NATO's general purpose forces, a belief that a war would require substantially more divisions forward-deployed before Warsaw Pact offensive operations could commence, very high anticipated losses, and much higher requirements for ammunition supply meant the Soviets believed they would need additional weeks to ready forces in a crisis.[35] That meant, in turn, that NATO had the opportunity to bol-ster its defensive and deterrent capabilities. NATO could plan on fast sealift to deploy forces that, in previous scenarios, would not have arrived in time. Soviet logistics (especially ammunition supply) became a much richer target for planned strikes, threatening to starve massive Soviet forces of necessary supplies in a conflict. Actions by NATO to exploit both of these newly identi-fied opportunities would compound the Soviets' sense of pessimism.
- A body of innovative analysis, based in part on sensitive technical collection, turned around the United States' fears of Soviet attacks against our sea lines of communication in the event of a war.[36] Before these studies were done, the received wisdom was that large numbers of Soviet attack submarines could inflict severe losses on US ships bringing reinforcements to NATO in a war. Careful studies revealed that US ship losses would be considerably smaller than feared in any number of scenarios. As with the studies cited above, these bolstered US and NATO confidence and enhanced deterrence.

Military analysts who study the perceptions, intentions, and capabilities of for-eign militaries may be uniquely positioned to play a useful role in designing influ-ence operations. If, for example, a foreign power has an inflated view of its strengths, military analysts can suggest a combination of policies, signals communicated by maneuvers, and diplomatic initiatives that can deflate that overconfidence. In one instance, for example, we suggested that an unclassified US study could be placed to encourage a foreign power to increase the security of sensitive arms from accident, theft, or use through miscalculation.

It may seem apparent that analysts supporting policymakers need a good sense of US government positions, agendas, and initiatives. It is a sobering fact that this piece is sometimes missing. Thanks to their participation in briefings and discussions, military exercises and planning, and work with the civilian components of the Department of Defense, military analysts have opportunities to gain a good understanding of what our government is doing and why. Regular engagements with counterparts and consumers in the policymaking bodies is essential to keep that knowledge fresh and relatively complete.

As noted earlier in the chapter, on working with collectors, not all policymaker-analyst relationships and engagements work smoothly, and personalities matter greatly. In addition, analytic findings that run counter to strongly held political views can meet with a cold or hostile reception by senior officers or consumers. A painful example illustrates what can happen.

In the mid- to late-1980s, I undertook a lengthy study of Soviet perceptions of how a war could start in Europe. US and NATO wargames and planning documents traditionally posited versions of a Warsaw Pact attack arising from a deep political-military crisis in Central or Eastern Europe. The new study was intended to look at how the Soviets saw war potentially occurring.

Months of research using a surprisingly rich array of sources—classified Soviet and Warsaw Pact documents, extensive reporting from signals intercepts, debriefings of defectors—yielded a picture that was not consistent with US and NATO planning scenarios. Soviet planners were cautious, risk averse, and fearful of a conflict occurring and what its course might be. The draft paper moved through the internal office coordination and review process relatively smoothly. When it reached one of the national intelligence officers (NIOs), it triggered the most vitriolic response I ever encountered.

The NIO stated that the study "called into question the credibility and the very existence of the Office of Soviet Analysis." His argument was not based on contrary evidence or logic, but on ideology. As he put it, "These [Soviets] are people who beat up old ladies; who shoot down innocent airliners!" [The Korean KAL flight shot down by the Soviets on September 1, 1983.][37]

The NIO's reaction sent shivers of fear through the management of the Office of Soviet Analysis. As my division chief said, handing the draft paper back after another review, "It's a great paper; but it would get me fired." The paper never made it out of the building.

CHALLENGES TO MILITARY ANALYSIS

There are three broad aspects of military analysis that bear careful, cautionary attention. The first is the strong temptation to pay greater attention to features that can be measured—or, more specifically, counted—than other components of military strength. In the words of the famous mathematician Lord Kelvin, "I often say that when you can measure what you are speaking about, and express it in numbers, you know something about it; but when you cannot measure it, when you cannot express it in numbers, your knowledge is of a meager and unsatisfactory kind."[38]

No one who has studied military history, however, would discount the critical nature of forces' morale, cohesion, experience, leadership, or combat skills—none of which are easily measured or counted. The course of the conflict in Ukraine cannot be explained without attention to these "soft factors" as they manifested themselves in Russian and Ukrainian forces. US intelligence officials have admitted to incorrectly forecasting a rapid Russian seizure of Kyiv and possibly a short war, and are studying how the intelligence community analyzes foreign powers' will to fight and the like.[39]

The second temptation is the allure of predicting combat outcomes. The political scientist Jeffrey Friedman offers a sweeping judgment that all analysts should bear in mind: "No known methodology can reliably predict the outbreak of wars, forecast economic recessions, project the results of military operations, anticipate terrorist attacks, or estimate the chances of countless other kinds of events that shape foreign policy decisions."[40]

War is simply too complex a process, involving the competing wills and activities of desperate opponents fighting in a world of uncertainty and friction, to lend itself to accurate predictions of casualties, the extent of loss or gain of terrain, and the rapidity of outcomes. Examples abound of how misleading counts have been and the difficulty of predictions.

The 2021 collapse of Afghanistan's national security forces when the United States withdrew is a recent, vivid example both of the need to look beyond numbers and the unpredictability of combat. Afghanistan's government forces outnumbered its Taliban opponents by as much as four-to-one, and in terms of military equipment the government's numerical and qualitative superiority was yet greater (e.g., 22,000 Humvees [a light military utility vehicle], 8,000 trucks, over 100 helicopters, and over 150 armored personnel carriers). Within days, not the months predicted previously by US military authorities, the Taliban was in control of the country. (On a more positive note, Ukrainian armed forces performed much better than anticipated by the intelligence community against the February 2022 Russian invasion—for all of the community's success in forecasting the Russian attack.)

Accurate predictions of combat outcomes depend critically on foresight into what wars could occur and when. Yet, as Secretary of Defense Robert Gates told West Point cadets in 2011, "When it comes to predicting the nature and location of our next military engagements, since Vietnam, our record has been perfect. We have never once gotten it right."[41]

The third temptation is to avoid the challenging task of understanding what we are doing that influences foreign powers. The Soviet "war scare" highlights how foreign powers study our military plans, practices, exercises, weapons purchases, and so on—and how ignoring our actions is risky. But there is much more to this issue.

We had studied Soviet perceptions of US and NATO military plans,[42] based on extensive documentary evidence (acquired by assets who had risked, and sometimes lost, their lives).[43] But there were some Soviet perceptions we simply could not explain—how they saw British and French nuclear arms, when and how escalation could occur, and so on.

The answers could not be found in our collection. Rather, it required an examination of how the United States and NATO actually planned, prepared, and exercised forces. We had an incomplete jigsaw puzzle, and the missing pieces could be found in the NATO archives.

A yearlong study of NATO's high-level military exercises surfaced the missing pieces of the puzzle. The specifics remain classified. But the central finding is clear. A key to understanding our adversaries' perceptions is to study what we do. Anything short of that leaves us with a partial, perhaps misleading picture.

Although my study of NATO exercises was self-initiated, the need for it was not unprecedented. A declassified 1971 memo to Henry Kissinger (then national security adviser) noted, "It is quite plausible to me that the [Warsaw] Pact has a better understanding of our doctrine revealed in exercises, procedures, etc. than is possible to obtain in Washington." Kissinger endorsed the idea of studying NATO exercises, albeit seventeen years before we undertook the study.[44]

Readers should ask why we assume adversaries have access to our secrets. The regrettable answer is that they have demonstrated such capabilities far too many times. It is also preferable to err in giving adversaries more credit rather than to arrogantly assume they fail in such critical pursuits.

FOCUSING ON THE BIG PICTURE

Returning to the analyst who was gathering a bunch of reports, reading them, spreading them out, and trying to fit them together, one can ask, is there any more to it? If military analysts drive and support collection, exploit source material thoroughly, identify key information, and study the components of military power and effectiveness, what approaches can they use to produce analysis senior policymakers will value? One option is derived from the business writer Michael Porter. His article in the *Harvard Business Review*—"What Is Strategy?"—makes a case for seeing strategy as a matter of "fit."

> What is strategy? . . . Strategy is creating fit among a company's activities. The success of a strategy depends on doing many things well—not just a

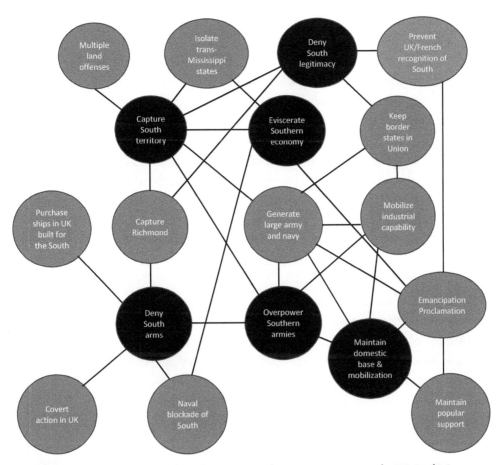

FIGURE 3.1 Activity Diagram of the Union's National Security Strategy in the US Civil War.
Source: Robert Levine.

few—and integrating among them. If there is no fit among activities, there is no distinctive strategy and little sustainability. Management reverts to the simpler task of overseeing independent functions, and operational effectiveness determines an organization's relative performance.[45]

This notion of fit—consistent integration—is the essence of how two military historians and theorists define military effectiveness.[46] What Porter does that captured the CIA's attention was to propose the use of activity system diagrams to depict corporate strategies. Countries' national security strategies (or, indeed, their military strategies, or their approach to the operational level of war) can be depicted with similar activity system diagrams.

Figure 3.1 illustrates how activity diagrams could be used to examine and explain the Union's national security strategy in the US Civil War. A limited number of higher order themes (the darker ovals) reflects the country's fundamental choices about its strategy. The lighter circles represent activities that support those themes.

Activity diagrams can take this one step further. The *most important thing in studying a foreign military is identifying where there is a lack of fit.* Identifying instances of lack of fit, and specific mismatches, can provide policymakers with leverage in dealing with allies (suggesting steps to remedy the mismatches, or at least developing compensating measures) and opponents (mismatches often are like zero-day exploits in cyberattacks—exploitable vulnerabilities that opponents do not even know they have). For all the foreign powers we study, mismatches help identify situations in which events may break oddly and suddenly, producing outcomes not otherwise contemplated.

FINAL THOUGHTS

No description of an analytic discipline can sweep in all its variants. There are military analysts working on weaponry, force employment, economics, diplomacy, and any number of other subfields. Some analysts have specialized in supporting and coordinating with the US military in counterinsurgency operations. Others find their principal consumers in the State Department or National Security Council.

Given the limited size of the military analytic cadre and the need to surge during crises to staff shifts on task forces, the CIA encourages analysts to be flexible and march to the sound of the clattering keyboards (if not the cannons). Possessing common vocabularies, gaining a similar basic understanding of how militaries operate, and displaying skill in exploiting clandestine collection and driving collection efforts are all qualities military analysts are encouraged to keep at the ready. In any career of several years' length, the Agency will call for their employment.

NOTES

1. Military analysis can focus on different *levels of war*. The most complex and comprehensive level is that of *national security strategy*, typically run by a country's senior civilian and military officers. It is concerned with achieving national interests using all the levers of national power (including corporations, societal groups, etc., as well as military power). A second level, *military strategy*, falls more in the purview of senior officers in command positions such as the Supreme Allied Commander Europe (SACEUR) for NATO. It generally involves the coordination of all the armed services as well as allies and select civilian organizations. A third, *operational level of war* typically focuses on military campaigns conducted jointly with extant forces in a theater of operations. The fourth level is that of *tactics*, which runs the gamut from small-unit actions to substantial engagements. Tactics are generally associated with battles, engagements limited in time and space.

2. About three-quarters of new analysts have advanced degrees (mostly master's degrees) and the other quarter has bachelor's degrees.

3. General purpose forces include those that can carry out both conventional and nuclear operations, such as many fighters-bombers.

4. I took advantage of many course offerings and found that other analysts with considerable military experience and advanced degrees enriched these experiences. Later, I taught and was in charge of the military analytic training program at the Kent School and was the CIA's representative to the National War College.

5. The CIA's software system allows analysts to filter reports by using key search terms and Boolean logic on the contents and sources of the reports. Without filters, analysts would be buried by incoming reports.

6. The war scare has been extensively documented. See the following endnotes for sources.

7. *Implications of Recent Soviet Military-Political Activities*, Special National Intelligence Estimate, SNIE 11-10-84/JX, May 18, 1984, declassified from TOP SECRET, www.cia.gov /readingroom/docs/19840518.pdf.

8. These are explained in Ben B. Fischer, *A Cold War Conundrum: The 1983 Soviet War Scare* (Langley, VA: CIA Center for the Study of Intelligence, 1997), www.cia.gov/reading room/docs/19970901.pdf. Weaknesses in the analysis are covered in President's Foreign Intelligence Advisory Board, The Soviet "War Scare," February 15, 1990. declassified from TOP SECRET, www.archives.gov/files/declassification/iscap/pdf/2013-015-doc1.pdf. The PFIAB study refers to a CIA Intelligence Assessment that has not been declassified, "Warsaw Pact Military Perceptions of NATO Nuclear Initiation." That was my first major published paper at the CIA. Readers can see copies of actual Soviet intelligence requirements indicating their concerns in this book: Christopher Andrew and Oleg Gordievsky, *Instructions from the Centre: Top Secret Files on KGB Foreign Operations, 1975–1985* (London: Hodder & Stoughton, 1991). The War Scare has been extensively documented. A comprehensive site for information is the National Security Archive of George Washington University, at https://nsarchive.gwu.edu/project/able-archer-83-sourcebook.

9. Fritz W. Ermath, "Paper on Soviet Strategic Thought for the President, 18 October 1985," declassified from SECRET, https://www.cia.gov/readingroom/docs/CIA-RDP89T0 1156R000100100019-2.pdf; and Fritz W. Ermath, The "Ogarkov Line" and US Strategy, 11 July 1986, declassified from SECRET, https://www.cia.gov/readingroom/docs/CIA-RDP05 S00365R000100330001-8.pdf.

10. "Moscow's View of the Reagan Administration," September 9, 1985, declassified from SECRET, https://www.cia.gov/readingroom/docs/19850909A.pdf.

11. John G. Hines, December 18, 1990 to December 9, 1994, in *Soviet Intentions, 1965–1985: Volume II, Soviet Post–Cold War Testimonial Evidence*, edited by John G. Hines and Ellis M. Mishulovich, BDM Federal, Inc., for the Department of Defense, Office of Net Assessment (December 9, 1994), https://nsarchive.gwu.edu/document/17326-document-25 -series-five-interviews.

12. *Implications of Recent Soviet Military-Political Activities*, Special National Intelligence Estimate, SNIE 11-10-84/JX, 18 May 1984, declassified from TOP SECRET, https://www.cia.gov/readingroom/docs/19840518.pdf.

13. "Able Archer 1983: The Brink of Apocalypse," https://www.youtube.com/watch?v =2EI3_jCIkkA (1:21.25 running time). Gates was referring to events during the NATO exercise and the Soviet reaction.

14. For an example of why and how the US Intelligence Community studies allied powers, see NI IIM 88-10006, *The Military Balance between Greece and Turkey: How It Stands—Where*

It Is Headed—What It Means, June 1988, declassified from SECRET, https://www.cia.gov/readingroom/docs/CIA-RDP93T00837R000400040002-4.pdf.

15. Counting and categorizing the equipment, personnel, and units of forteign militaries is sometimes disparagingly called "bean counting." The implicit criticism is unwarranted. More sophisticated estimates of foreign military capabilities and future operations rely on good counts and understanding force structure. An excellent example is given by David Kenyon, *Bletchley Park and D-Day: The Untold Story of How the Battle for Normandy Was Won* (New Haven, CT: Yale University Press, 2019); see, e.g., the section starting on p. 99.

16. Some readers will be familiar with terms such as "analysis of warning" or "readiness." These are aggregate areas of study. Readiness, for example, combines the study of personnel (recruitment and service cycles), their training, military equipment (its storage and maintenance), sustainability and logistics (availability of fuel and ammunition), and so on. Warning in turn combines the study of readiness, doctrine, perceptions, intentions, and so on. The factors in this section are closer to the true building blocks of military power. E.g., see CIA, National Intelligence Estimate, NIE 4-1-84, "Warning of War in Europe: Changing Warsaw Pact Planning and Forces," September 1989, declassified from SECRET, https://www.cia.gov/readingroom/docs/CIA-RDP94T00754R000200160012-0.pdf.; and "Warning of War in Europe," June 27, 1984, declassified from SECRET, https://www.cia.gov/readingroom/docs/DOC_0001486834.pdf. For a study of readiness, see Interagency Intelligence Memorandum, NI IIM 82-10012, November 1982, "The Readiness of Soviet Ground Forces," declassified from SECRET, https://www.cia.gov/readingroom/docs/CIA-RDP85T00176R001600060007-7.pdf. For a broader look at intelligence analysis that applies to military analysis, see Dr. Robert Levine, "Basic Principles of Intelligence Analysis: One (Former) Analyst's View," *Studies in Intelligence* 65, no. 4, December 2021: 1–7, https://www.cia.gov/resources/csi/studies-in-intelligence/volume-65-no-4-december-2021/voice-of-experience-principles-of-intelligence-analysis/.

17. Each of these could be illustrated by drawing examples from the Russian-Ukrainian conflict in 2022. E.g., sustainability and logistics, and personnel issues, are discussed by Isabelle Khurshudyan and Paul Sonne, "Russia Targeted Ukrainian Ammunition to Weaken Kyiv on the Battlefield," *Washington Post*, June 24, 2022, https://www.washingtonpost.com/world/2022/06/24/ukraine-ammunition-russian-sabotage-artillery/; and Mary Ilyushina, "Russian Army Ramps Up Recruitment as Steep Casualties Thin the Ranks," *Washington Post*, June 16, 2022, https://www.washingtonpost.com/world/2022/06/16/russia-military-army-soldiers-recruitment/.

18. Most of these factors require qualitative assessment, but some have a quantitative aspect. Lawrence Freedman notes, "By the late 2010s, at 400 staff officers, a typical American divisional headquarters was ten times the size of a 1940s headquarters, and at least four times the size of its Cold War equivalent." He notes that a quarter of the 800-person headquarters of the British commander in and around Kandahar City in 2009–10 were on the intelligence side—coping with the volume of incoming information. Lawrence Freedman, *Command: The Politics of Military Operations from Korea to Ukraine* (New York: Oxford University Press, 2022), 494–95.

19. By weight, the heaviest logistic burden due to consumables (not equipment) are fuel, ammunition, water, and food. BTUs (British Thermal Units) is alliterative shorthand for fuel supplies.

20. As vital as these are to assess, they are difficult to gauge and mercurial. At one point, one of the authors had a long conversation with the national intelligence officer in overall

charge of studying foreign militaries (conventional military issues). Inevitably, we drifted onto the topic of how well we tackled so-called soft factors of foreign militaries, such as the quality of service members, morale, and leadership. When pressed about our relative neglect of these in favor of "hard factors" like counts of weapons systems and their physical capabilities (range, rate of fire, etc.), the national intelligence officer shrugged and responded that, yes, we need to examine those "soft factors" better, but "we just can't count and measure them."

21. Mary Ilyushina, "In Ukraine, a Russian Mercenary Group Steps out of the Shadows," *Washington Post*, August 18, 2022, www.washingtonpost.com/world/2022/08/17/ukraine -russia-wagner-group-mercenaries/.

22. "Russia Uses Conscript Soldiers for War in Ukraine," US Embassy in Georgia, April 27, 2022, https://ge.usembassy.gov/russia-uses-conscript-soldiers-for-war-in-ukraine/.

23. Lawrence Freedman, "Constantly Operating Factors," August 24, 2022, https://samf .substack.com/p/constantly-operating-factors.

24. Mary Ilyushina, "Short of Soldiers to Send to War, Russia's Mercenaries Recruit in Prisons," *Washington Post*, September 15, 2022, https://www.washingtonpost.com/world/2022 /09/15/russia-war-mercenaries-prisons-recruit/. The world later witnessed the bizarre turn of events for Prigozhin and Wagner as well as increased prisoner recruitment.

25. Max Z. Margulies and Laura Resnick Samotin, "Why Russian Conscripts Can't Sub- due Ukraine," *Wall Street Journal*, May 5, 2022, https://www.wsj.com/articles/why-russian -conscripts-cant-subdue-ukraine-war-army-volunteers-morale-invasion-military-putin-victory -11651784177?mod=hp_opin_pos_4#cxrecs_s; Dara Massicot, "The Russian Military's People Problem," *Foreign Affairs*, May 18, 2022, https://www.foreignaffairs.com/articles/russian -federation/2022-05-18/russian-militarys-people-problem; Mary Ilyushina, "Russian Army Ramps Up Recruitment as Steep Casualties Thin the Ranks," *Washington Post*, June 16, 2022, https://www.washingtonpost.com/world/2022/06/16/russia-military-army-soldiers -recruitment/; Thomas Grove and Stephen Fidler, "How Russia's Revamped Military Fumbled the Invasion of Ukraine," *Wall Street Journal*, March 17, 2022, https://www.wsj.com/articles /russia-putin-revamped-military-ukraine-invasion-11647469602; Phillips Payson O'Brien, "How the West Got Russia's Military So, So Wrong," *Atlantic*, March 31, 2022, https://www.the atlantic.com/ideas/archive/2022/03/russia-ukraine-invasion-military-predictions/629418/.

26. Lester W. Grau and Charles K. Bartles, "Getting to Know the Russian Battalion Tacti- cal Group," *RUSI Journal*, April 14, 2022, https://rusi.org/explore-our-research/publications /commentary/getting-know-russian-battalion-tactical-group.

27. Henry Foy and Ian Bott, "How Is Ukraine Using Western Weapons to Exploit Russian Weaknesses?" *Financial Times*, March 16, 2022, https://www.ft.com/content/f5fb2996-f816 -4011-a440-30350fa48831. The potential vulnerabilities caused by losses of infantry was ana- lyzed decades ago. See CIA/DI, *The Cutting Edge: Soviet Mechanized Infantry in Combined Arms Operations,* August 1987, declassified from TOP SECRET, https://www.cia.gov/reading room/docs/CIA-RDP89T00296R000400390001-3.pdf.

28. This admonition had been violated in the past with adverse consequences. In the 1960s Sherman Kent, seen by many as a founding father of intelligence analysis, defended a National Intelligence Estimate that predicted the Soviets would *not* put nuclear missiles into Cuba. Kent argued that the Soviet move was illogical and shifted the blame for our intelligence failure onto Khrushchev. "No estimating process," he [Kent] concludes, "can be expected to divine exactly when the enemy is about to make a dramatically wrong decision." The quotation is cited by

Amy Zegart, "The Cuban Missile Crisis as Intelligence Failure," *Policy Review*, Hoover Institution, October 2, 2012, https://www.hoover.org/research/cuban-missile-crisis-intelligence-failure.

29. Drawing analysts from multiple offices achieved another key objective—it mitigated potential interoffice disagreements. Interoffice coordination of analytic findings can be contentious, both for good and questionable reasons. A yearlong study the author conducted at Lawrence Livermore National Laboratory faced blowback from the CIA's Office of Science and Weapons Technology as a product "not invented here." The fight over bureaucratic turf rather than substance reminded the author of a saying attributed to a weapons designer at Livermore characterizing counterparts at the "other" nuclear lab (at Los Alamos): "Remember, the Soviets are the competition. Los Alamos is the enemy."

30. VRYAN is an acronym for *Vnezapnoye Raketno-Yadernoye Napadenie*, "sudden nuclear missile attack." Most sources referred to it as RYAN.

31. The CIA has tried to address this issue by collocating DO and DA components, and by setting up electronic systems to share some operational information.

32. The Central Intelligence Agency often is depicted as a massive organization with vast resources, including a large stable of analysts specializing in different disciplines (military, economic, political, etc.) and regions. Budgetary and personnel restrictions, not to mention desk and parking spaces, in fact impose far greater restraints than most people would assume. Several years ago, I was tasked with identifying all military analysts in the CIA's Directorate of Analysis (previously called the Directorate of Intelligence) and surveying them to determine their professional characteristics (education, training, prior military service, overseas work, etc.). Every manager briefed on the results was surprised at the small size of the cadre. The size and composition of analytic units at CIA remain classified. But to cite one example that no longer carries any risk, when Saddam Hussein's Iraq invaded Kuwait in 1990, the analytic component covering the issue was understaffed and some personnel lacked experience.

33. See Central Intelligence Agency, National Intelligence Estimate, NIE 4-1-84, "Warning of War in Europe: Changing Warsaw Pact Planning and Forces," September 1989, declassified from SECRET, https://www.cia.gov/readingroom/docs/CIA-RDP94T00754R00020016 0012-0.pdf.

34. Hamas's terrorist incursion into Israel on October 7, 2023, illustrates Israeli failures in strategic, operational, and tactical warning. News reports suggest that these failures occurred in large measure because intelligence on Hamas's preparations and actions did not trigger adequate preattack Israeli countermeasures. See, e.g., Ronen Bergman and Adam Goldman, "Israel Knew Hamas's Attack Plan More Than a Year Ago," *New York Times*, November 30, 2023, https://www.nytimes.com/2023/11/30/world/middleeast/israel-hamas-attack-intelligence.html.

35. CIA/DI, *Warsaw Pact Ammunition Logistics: Sustainability for Offensive Operations*, June 1989, declassified from TOP SECRET, https://www.cia.gov/readingroom/docs/1989-06-01.pdf; NIC, *Warning of War in Europe: Changing Warsaw Pact Planning and Forces*, September 1989, declassified from SECRET, https://www.cia.gov/readingroom/docs/CIA-RDP94T00754R000200160012-0.pdf.

36. See NFAC, *The Role of Interdiction at Sea in Soviet Naval Strategy and Operations*, May 1978, declassified from TOP SECRET, https://www.cia.gov/readingroom/docs/DOC_0005530564.pdf; and NFAC, *The Soviet Attack Submarine Force and Western Sea Lines of*

Communications, April 1979, declassified from SECRET, https://www.cia.gov/readingroom /docs/DOC_0005499486.pdf.

37. In a moment of pique, I suggested to management that the NIO's memo be sent back with a snide endorsement after the United States shot down an Iranian civilian airliner on July 3, 1988, having mischaracterized the aircraft as a military threat.

38. Lord Kelvin, "Electrical Units of Measurement" (1883), cited by John M. Henshaw, *Does Measurement Measure Up? How Numbers Reveal & Conceal the Truth* (Baltimore: Johns Hopkins University Press, 2006), 1.

39. It is encouraging that the DNI is investigating how it assesses foreign powers' will and capacity to fight. See "US Intelligence Agencies Review What They Got Wrong on Russia's Invasion of Ukraine," *PBS Newshour*, June 4, 2022, https://www.pbs.org/newshour/nation/u-s -intelligence-agencies-review-what-they-got-wrong-on-russias-invasion-of-ukraine. The issue was raised on May 10, 2022, in congressional hearings; C-Span, "Director of National Intelligence Avril Haines Testimony on Global Threats and National Security," May 10, 2022, https:// www.c-span.org/video/?519983-1/us-believes-russia-preparing-prolonged-conflict-ukraine (at 1:32:36). There is a long history of the CIA's involvement in the conduct of net assessments. See, e.g., "Secretary of Defense and Director of Central Intelligence, Joint Net Assessment, Executive Version, US and Soviet Strategic Forces, 14 November 1983," declassified from TOP SECRET, https://nsarchive2.gwu.edu/NSAEBB/NSAEBB428/docs/1.US%20and%20Soviet %20Strategic%20Forces%20Joint%20Net%20Assessment.pdf; and "South Vietnam: A Net Military Assessment (cover memo)," April 2, 1974, declassified from SECRET, https://www.cia .gov/readingroom/docs/CIA-RDP79R01099A001100050004-7.pdf.

40. Jeffrey Friedman, *War and Chance: Assessing Uncertainty in International Politics* (New York: Oxford University Press, 2019), 1. Friedman has a bit of a word jumble in the printed text.

41. Micah Zenko, "100% Right 0% of the Time," *Foreign Policy*, October 16, 2012. The CIA and DoD's records predicting combat outcomes from "expert judgment" or common wisdom is not one in which either can take much pride. E.g., the CIA has advertised its incisive call on Israeli prospects before the 1967 war. It not only missed the commencement of the Yom Kippur War six years later but top US government officials had an overly sanguine view of Israeli prospects when the war started, expecting Israel to defeat Egyptian and Syrian forces quickly. A recent national intelligence officer for conventional military issues detailed in his book, *Bombs without Boots*, case after case of missed judgments on the likely character of military conflicts in the last couple of decades; Emile A. Nakleh, "The June 1967 and October 1973 Arab Israeli Wars," in Central Intelligence Agency, Directorate of Intelligence, *Directorate of Intelligence: Fifty Years of Informing Policy, Central Intelligence Agency* (Langley, VA: CIA Center for the Study of Intelligence, 2002). See also NIE 30-73, *Possible Egyptian-Israeli Hostilities: Determinants and Implications*, May 17, 1973, declassified from SECRET, https:// www.cia.gov/readingroom/docs/1973-05-17.pdf; Middle East Status Report—1:00 p.m., October 8, declassified from TOP SECRET, https://www.cia.gov/readingroom/docs/1973-10-08A .pdf; and Anthony M. Schinella, *Bombs without Boots: The Limits of Airpower* (Washington, DC: Brookings Institution Press, 2019).

42. See, e.g., CIA, "Soviet Perceptions of US Naval Strategy," SOV 86-1009D, July 1986, declassified from SECRET, https://www.cia.gov/readingroom/docs/DOC_0000500708.pdf.

43. These documents had borne our opponent's classifications of SECRET and TOP SECRET and now had our highly restrictive classifications. Dozens if not hundreds of these

documents have been declassified and can be accessed through the CIA Freedom of Information Act (FOIA) website. An example is CIA/DO Report FIRDB-312/01545-78, declassified from TOP SECRET, https://www.cia.gov/readingroom/docs/1978-07-28.pdf, formerly Soviet TOP SECRET lecture materials from the Soviet General Staff Academy.

44. Memo from K. Wayne Smith to Dr. Kissinger, June 8, 1971, declassified from TOP SECRET, https://www.cia.gov/readingroom/docs/1971-06-08.pdf.

45. Michael E. Porter, "What Is Strategy?" *Harvard Business Review*, November–December 1996, 61–78, https://orion2020.org/archivo/pensamiento_estrategico/01_1_whatsstrategy.pdf; Porter displays activity system diagrams for Vanguard, Ikea, and Southwest Airlines.

46. Allan R. Millett and Williamson Murray, eds., *Military Effectiveness*, new ed. (Boston: Allen & Unwin, 2010).

4

ECONOMIC ANALYSIS: "INVISIBLE HANDS" AT WORK

Cynthia S. Barkanic

Recently, I was approached by a colleague at the CIA's Center for the Study of Intelligence, who asked, "I'm wondering whether you have a good definition of economic intelligence. Is there any kind of standard definition?" I initially felt embarrassed because nothing immediately came to mind, despite my long career as a CIA economic analyst. I became mildly defensive and asked, "Well, do you know of standard, established definitions of political or military intelligence?" I was relieved when he responded in the negative.

Searching various public sources, I identified three definitions that I offered my colleague (see box 4.1). The first one probably comes closest to describing key job duties during my thirty-seven-plus-year career as an economic analyst at the CIA, but none of them is fully satisfying.

For simplicity's sake, this was my colleague's placeholder language that captures the core mission: "Broadly speaking, economic intelligence involves the collection, analysis, and dissemination of economic information on foreign countries or entities from public and non-public sources. This can extend from basic economic data to specific technologies or industrial processes."

Nevertheless, that conversation stimulated the general question of "what is economic analysis" ever since. So, when the opportunity came up to write the economic chapter for this volume, I jumped at the chance. Not only could the project be a capstone on my long career as an economic analyst at the CIA but it would help me answer these difficult questions in a more rigorous way. Thanks to wise mentors, managers, and peers, over the course of my career, the key and sometimes quirky tenets of economic analytic tradecraft became second nature to me and my professional colleagues.

As for the title of this chapter, the "invisible hand" of course is a concept developed by the eighteenth-century economist Adam Smith to describe the *unseen forces*

BOX 4.1: DEFINITIONS OF ECONOMIC ANALYSIS

- "Economic intelligence can be loosely defined as information gathered about materials and resources that are developed, produced, or managed outside the United States, and the interpretation and presentation of raw information or unpublished data to reports or analyses that inform policymakers and consumers. . . . The CIA, assisted by other government agencies, provides economic intelligence for US policy, with experts monitoring international transactions (including sanctions enforcement and illicit finance); international economic and environmental problems, including trade and finance; defense markets and logistics; geographic resources, including demographics and commodities; civil technology, including aerospace, advanced manufacturing, and emerging technologies; and energy resources."[1]
- "[Economic intelligence] is information concerning the production, distribution, and consumption of goods and services, as well as labor, finance, taxation, and other aspects of a nation's economy or of the international economic system. Economic intelligence allows a nation to estimate the magnitude of possible military threats and is also valuable in estimating the intentions of a potential enemy. In wartime, economic intelligence is a prime indicator of an enemy's ability to sustain a war. This is particularly important when analyzing small nations, such as Israel, where a conflict requires total mobilization and cannot be sustained for long without creating severe economic problems."[2]
- "Economic intelligence (n.): All the actions aimed at stimulating, disseminating, and exploiting the results of research, technological development and demonstration for the benefit and information of companies and other economic agents."[3]

---

that move the free market economy.[4] But at the CIA, the concept of "invisible hands" could also describe the role of largely unseen economic analysts who work behind the scenes, generate analysis, and respond to administration requests—"taskings," as they are known on the inside—on the economic, financial, and political-societal implications of worldwide developments of the moment.

Economic intelligence has long held a place in US history,[5] and it has long been part of the CIA's mission.[6] This chapter digs more deeply into the current contours of the CIA's economic analysis, including the breadth of the roles of economic analysts at the Directorate of Analysis (DA), the rigors and tenets of economic analytic tradecraft, and examples of support for busy and demanding policymakers. In the process, it also outlines some of the challenges that the CIA's economic analysts face in the course of performing their duties.

THE ART OF ECONOMIC ANALYTIC TRADECRAFT

Simply put, economic analysts at the CIA assess foreign economic, trade, and financial interests that affect US security interests and provide accurate and timely coverage of evolving economic stories. Economic analysis typically is based on well-established economic theory, generally accepted methodologies, and an understanding of global economic linkages. Economists working in Mission Centers focus on a range of macroeconomic and microeconomic issues facing a country or region. Country-specific economic analysts must have a comprehensive understanding of how a national economy works, its strengths, and especially its vulnerabilities. They highlight how economic and societal issues can affect development outcomes, pose risks to stability, and may have other spillover effects. They follow areas such as economic decision-making and internal policy debates. They analyze not only what is unique about the economies they follow but also identify themes that may cut across or apply more broadly to other economies.

Economic analysts working transnational issues take a broader, global approach to macroeconomic and microeconomic issues and dive deeply into the technical details of functional issues such as debt, energy security, environment and climate change, finance, trade and sanctions, and transportation. A good example is the long-standing CIA work on the petroleum market, for which they make long-range projections of output, sometimes matching estimates of market analysts and at other times diverging. These assessments can also cover multilateral commercial alliances. Other economic analysts may assess transnational illicit financial activities, including terrorist and criminal networks, money laundering, and foreign corruption.[7] More recently, financial technology, cryptocurrency, and supply chain analysis have become important areas for inquiry.

Economic analysts have a mix of backgrounds. While working at my "day job" as a CIA senior economic analyst, I also served as an Agency hiring adviser for more than the last two decades of my career, interviewing dozens of applicants and looking for specialized backgrounds. The minimum qualification was a bachelor's or master's degree in economics; however, depending on the requirement, the Agency would consider applicants with degrees and/or experience in fields such as banking, business administration, finance, and international management. Naturally, we were looking for candidates with a strong interest in international affairs; awareness of US national security interests; foreign language capability; strong verbal presentation skills; a demonstrated ability to write clear, concise text; and interest in a career that requires regular writing assignments.

CIA economic analysts are number lovers who use conceptual frameworks and models to organize complicated material. These analysts sometimes bristle when they must simplify the story for noneconomist readers or omit technical nuance to reach a broader audience. Perhaps more than any other intelligence discipline, economic analysts use charts, graphics, and other visual techniques to convey statistical data and trends. CIA economic analysts working on macroeconomic issues need knowledge about—and comfort with—such basic statistical concepts as price and exchange rate computations, linking indexes and choosing the proper baseline, and growth calculations and expressions. They need to understand the nuances about certain economic concepts. For example, unemployment in an advanced economy is not the same as unemployment in a developing economy; there may be a higher percentage of people who are vulnerable, or the labor market may be too rigid to respond to changing demands.

By nature, economic analysts' work is often multidisciplinary, and they must understand the political and sociocultural contexts that may underlie certain economic trends. At the same time, economic analyses can contribute to a more complete understanding of a country's general outlook. The CIA's country and regional economic analysis must go beyond formal economic and political structures to reveal the underlying interests, incentives, and institutions that enable or frustrate change. Such insights are important in identifying the agendas of key institutions and individuals vis-à-vis governance and economic development and to provide helpful context for US policy deliberations. Economic analysts focus on how power and resources are distributed and contested, as in social contracts, whereby a particular society's members may cooperate in exchange for state benefits and protection. Regional economists often examine the drivers of unemployment, migration, income inequality, and associated socioeconomic unrest. They may also study the way that established demographic trends affect development and the prospects for developing societies' ability to emerge from poverty. In so doing, they may investigate how regional development is changing—for example, by skipping steps in moving from agrarian societies to industrial ones. In other instances, economic analysts will research the economic effects of global health crises (e.g., the COVID-19 pandemic), technological innovation, climate change, and other environmental factors.

Like other CIA analysts, economic analysts have opportunities to develop deep policy expertise through broadening rotational assignments with other offices in the Agency and across the US government, such as the National Security Council. There are also opportunities for foreign and domestic travel, language training, Agency-wide service, mentoring, and analytic tradecraft and management training.[8] In my case, these included several short tours overseas and in-house Arabic training and maintenance courses. Both were wonderful opportunities to learn, boost my expertise, and make a difference in service to the Agency's mission. A particularly memorable assignment was traveling to a key Middle Eastern country in the late 1980s, when I visited several large public sector industries, such as steel, textile, and cookware factories. Escorted by my good friend Ahmed—who worked as a sherpa for American visitors—I interviewed senior company managers about long-languishing privatization and labor reforms. I wrote up my findings and briefed the US ambassador on the situation and, at his request, also briefed a morning gathering of his key staff members. This was an invaluable, eye-opening opportunity for an economic analyst with only five years under her belt.

Like most analysts, I have taken—and later in my career taught—economic courses at the Sherman Kent School for Intelligence Analysis, the CIA's training institute for intelligence analysts. The school does a tremendous job arming students with best practices for working as analysts in the DA, including in the areas of research, production, and collaboration. The school also rounds out the skill sets of economic analysts, as in the areas of financial markets and banking (an area where I had little expertise when I entered duty at the Agency). It should be added that the virtue of having senior analysts train and tutor junior analysts in the economic discipline is that the instructors have done everything in their field that the newer analysts must master. In this sense, the training is not focused as much on economic theory as it is on how to translate economic analysis into an actionable intelligence assessment. To help inculcate best practices among the Agency's cadre of economic analysts, I helped to establish the CIA's Economic Analysis Steering Group, and I served as one of its two cochairs. This group's purpose was to be a focal point for discussing the development of the discipline and in enhancing collaboration, data sharing, and continuing education across the Agency's Mission Centers.

ECONOMIC COLLECTION: A MIX OF FEAST AND FAMINE

Like analysts in other intelligence disciplines, economic analysts depend on three main sources of economic intelligence: open sources, diplomatic reporting from US embassies and consulates, and clandestine information. Often, economic analysts are focused on information compiled by State Department's economic officers, Treasury Department attachés, and officers of the Foreign Commercial Service; however, the larger stream of reporting is important in painting a fuller picture of a country's economic landscape.[9]

Economic analysts must identify key data sources that preferably are timely, complete, and reliable. Indeed, the current plethora of websites, trade publications, and newsletters is a mixed blessing. In many cases, all but the most recent data can be obtained from open source websites of governments, international organizations such as the International Monetary Fund, and private sector economic analysis companies. Nevertheless, comprehensive economic data collection and compilation can be challenging, even in developed economies—and even more so in less developed countries that often have poor data collection and immature statistical agencies that can be subject to government manipulation for political purposes. In some cases, data quality is determined by how often and when surveys are taken, the questions asked, and the consistency of the questions across survey periods. Moreover, there are general indicators of survey quality to consider, such as sample size, languages used, and survey method. Analysts also must take into consideration seasonal adjustments, such as those for a country's agriculture, retail, and/or construction sectors. In making regional or global comparisons, it is a best practice to use a comparable data set, such as from the IMF or the Economist Intelligence Unit.[10]

For most CIA analytic disciplines, it is standard practice—and basic analytic tradecraft—to task collectors to fill intelligence gaps. But this is often difficult for economic analysts because of prevalent views among some policymakers and collectors that the risk is not worth the reward. Indeed, in my experience, few economic issues rank high in the National Intelligence Priorities Framework—the classified intelligence document produced by the top planners of the US intelligence community, and approved by senior policymakers, that summarizes intelligence gathering priorities and guides collectors. By not gaining high-priority rankings, economic issues do not tend to get enough support for tasking human sources or garnering expensive technical collection, and analysts have to rely primarily on diplomatic and open source reporting. An exception may be economic sanctions that monitor key adversaries like Iran and North Korea, about which senior national security policymakers—not solely those responsible for US economic policies—care deeply. In those cases, classified intelligence reporting can offer unique insights on countries of high-priority interest to the United States.[11]

Economic analysts, like those in other disciplines, must know where there are collection gaps and cultivate good contacts with collectors. It was especially important for me to build these relationships during periods of calm because collectors may not be able to quickly generate new intelligence reporting during times of crisis or active conflict. Economic analysts working on war zone countries may be required to make carefully caveated judgments on the basis of scant information while simultaneously using technical capabilities and intragovernmental relationships to build up the collection necessary to make more confident assessments. Also, many collectors were willing to work on economic topics that by their very nature were more opaque and highly secretive. Those topics include decision-making within foreign governments and institutions, off-budget accounting techniques, underground or black market economic activity, corrupt business practices, and sanctions evasion.

DA economic analysts do work with colleagues in the Directorate of Operations, especially the National Resources Division (NRD), whose mission is to reach out to American academics, business leaders, and banking officials. The NRD often arranges meetings between economic analysts—as well as analysts in other disciplines—to exchange views with knowledgeable Americans who are traveling overseas or have excellent foreign contacts. In such meetings, for example, I have had useful discussions regarding a large foreign economy's liberalization efforts as well as opportunities to debrief NRD contacts on developments in some financial sector developments in the Middle East and East Asia. In addition, some of my most invigorating debates have been with foreign liaison partners, who had very different—and often darker—assessments of common adversaries' economic prospects, plans, and intentions. CIA analysts clearly benefited from such sessions in becoming more aware of the lens through which our foreign partners were looking at the problem sets as well as the driving factors they were prioritizing in their analysis.

Ironically, a key knowledge gap for economic analysts is US financial policy. The Treasury Department and the Federal Reserve, for example, often keep a tight lid on internal deliberations for fear of leaks that could rattle stock markets. While understandable, this nonetheless means that analysts will not have full knowledge of key factors influencing certain economic trends. In some cases, CIA economic analysts can exploit external expertise and engage in outreach and information exchanges as part of rounding out their knowledge, boosting innovation and creativity in their work, and seeking out new and challenging perspectives. While the bureaucratic red tape related to external outreach has become more cumbersome, it still is a best practice, for example, to consult private sector experts on complex issues.

MAKING SENSE OF ECONOMIC DATA
TO ENRICH THE FINISHED PRODUCT

In building out their country economic accounts, economic analysts need to identify key sources of data and incorporate them into their analysis. On the economic vulnerability and warning fronts, they need familiarity with fundamental indicators including foreign exchange reserves, trade flows and balance of payments, monetary aggregates, interest rates, inflation, and government and corporate debt. They also need to be familiar with developments in their country's banking sector, equity market, commercial and investment climate, and regulatory framework. While traditional economic indicators (such as growth in gross domestic product (GDP), foreign exchange reserves, imports, unemployment, and inflation) are key measures of economic activity, less traditional indicators (such as food and fuel availability, observable economic activity, black market exchange rates, and public sentiment about conditions on the ground) can be important alternate or supplemental indicators of economic activity.

The strongest economic intelligence pieces with the most impact are data rich and use numbers to drive the analysis. Nevertheless, numbers almost always require context. Here are some typical analytical techniques that economic analysts use to add value to numbers:

- Static, aggregate indicators—level of debt, government revenue, budget deficits—commonly can be compared with a nation's GDP.

- A country's foreign reserves usually are compared with its level of monthly imports or short-term debt service obligations.
- Discussions involving commodity price changes can benefit from marginal analysis of price change (the effect on an indicator of a $1 change in the unit price of a commodity).
- Economic data referring to a subset of a population should be described as a percentage of other larger groups or the population as a whole.
- Identification when fiscal years begin or end in a target country or region.[12]

In general, economic analysis of large data sets or numbers works best when the data are compared with a recent level of the same indicator, placed in context of a trend, or compared with a historically significant level. Similarly, statistical trends may be compared with a projection or expected level or with similar indicators for the United States or third countries. For noneconomist policymakers, such comparisons can help them digest the policy significance of those data or trends.

Correct interpretation and presentation of quantitative economic data are essential for continuing the CIA's credibility with its economic policy customers. At the CIA, economic analysts engage in robust substantive debates on these topics, including during monthly Economic Analysis Steering Group meetings and Economic Vulnerability Forum meetings. Having served for some years on the steering group, I know that we have conducted important and sometimes long-running discussions about

- the proper way to calculate a real interest rate or changes in real GDP or appreciation/depreciation of a foreign exchange rate against the US dollar;
- when to use GDP at purchasing-price-parity exchange rates versus GDP at market exchange rates;
- the shorter-term versus longer-term effects of currency devaluation on an economy;
- the best way to track inflows of foreign exchange reserves not related to actual exports or investments to warn of a "hot money overhang," which could spur speculators to exit a market and cause an uncontrolled collapse in the exchange rate;
- an appropriate description of how fiscal, balance-of-payments, banking, sovereign debt, and/or currency crises can arise, identifying the warning signs, and postulating how they might play out, including policy (mis)steps and contagion effects;
- the pros and cons of using official country statistics versus tapping IMF or Economist Intelligence Unit databases;

- the merits of presenting economic data in a table, line chart, pie chart, or stacked bar chart; and
- use of assumption checks and alternative analyses to heighten self-awareness, guard against implicit mental mind-sets, and to see the bigger context in which data sets exist.

Informed collection and analysis of economic data can mean the difference between a piece being seen as a thoughtful and convincing assessment or as one relying merely on conventional wisdom or an analyst's opinion. On one hand, the data must drive the analysis. On the other hand, overreliance on data alone risks losing even a willing audience. As a rule, analysts must first look objectively at the data and then work to ensure they are aware of other analyses of the same issue or related issues, particularly those that draw different conclusions. This helps to ensure that their assessments do not ignore or dismiss alternative explanations. Also, economic analysts must avoid the temptation to overload an assessment's prose with data and use graphics instead. A single, compelling statistic will stick with readers, whereas several numbers in each sentence may mean that each number becomes less memorable. Analysts often collaborate with the CIA's graphic designers and other colleagues with graphic design skills to think creatively about data visualization and the best way to illustrate regional economic interactions. This is a useful way to appeal to policymakers who are less inclined to read complex economic assessments.

LESSONS LEARNED FROM CUSTOMER ENGAGEMENT

The CIA's economic analysts typically serve very intelligent policymakers. Thus, it is best when they fill in contextual blind spots or distill the torrent of daily information that few policymakers have the time to read. Even the most gifted policy customer can gain valuable insight from a piece that includes an exploration of the institutional or other factors that shape an economic issue. As a frequent contributor to the President's Daily Brief and specialized economic publications, as well as a briefer to dozens of high-level US policymakers, I have observed a range of customers and found them to be serious readers of intelligence. While serving as a briefer for a senior Treasury Department official, I also was able to see the breadth of the Agency's analytic production on global economic issues. Our analysis also improved over time because of tough feedback that compelled us to raise the bar, and we responded with more rigorous analytic products.

Although pushback was infrequent, those policymakers usually asked smart and thoughtful follow-up questions. Our briefings often went over the allotted time. For example, US policymakers frequently sought greater understanding of a foreign government's political obstacles to meeting Washington's economic objectives abroad. Those briefings would regularly go beyond the economic factors and dive into the socioeconomic conditions, regulatory problems, or deficits in the rule of law that affected the commercial landscape in countries of national interest. Success for analysts is often defined by learning that finished analyses or briefings led policymakers to think about their problems in new ways.

Of course, consumers of economic intelligence are expecting relevance, rigor, and insight. They read the financial press and economic journals and are up to date on most global economic developments, so what they need from the CIA's economic analysis is value-added answers to complex questions, or more narrow reportorial ones, where we have unique information. Economic assessments with a policy impact have spanned country-specific, regional, and global analytic themes. Most economic intelligence articles and longer studies of greatest interest to customers in many agencies share several characteristics. First, they often highlight key foreign economic decision-makers, internal debates over economic policy direction, and key interest group positions on economic issues, particularly those that are at odds with US positions. Second, as mentioned above, the pieces often are multidisciplinary. Some explore how economic forces shape political trends, or vice versa. Others describe the diplomacy of commercial relationships or how leadership dynamics affect economic decision-making. To say that an economy is heading toward a recession may be of marginal value; a more useful warning would be to say that the recession could limit the country's ability to support US policies in the region like counterterrorism.

Third, the prose should be comprehensible to noneconomist readers, without "dumbing down" the analysis. Statistics and data support the storytelling, but they are not the story. To repeat a point made above, such assessments can make an effective use of graphics that organize and summarize economic trends. Line graphs that show changes over time require little text and save the reader from having to do the math that is sometimes required in analyzing multicolored bar charts. While text-heavy charts should be used cautiously, some busy policymakers find charts and matrices the most efficient way to absorb and retain information, and they sometimes ask to keep the graphics as handy cheat sheets. Finally, economic analysis has to focus heavily on implications for the United States. For example, a piece on third-party trade blocs pursuing trade agreements needs to explore what those agreements mean for US competitiveness.

A feature unique to the CIA's analysis is the use of what is called "opportunity analysis." This art form involves finding and assessing potential policy options or opportunities that might exploit US strengths and a competitor's vulnerabilities.[13] This form of analysis in the economic discipline can be enhanced by discussing economic policies that have had success elsewhere in the world while being careful not to propose cookie-cutter solutions to US economic problems. At a minimum, it requires CIA analysts to be attuned to what is already being done on the US economic policy front and to what the limits are to Washington's economic instruments and take these into account. In addition, such opportunity analysis can skirt the criticism of policy bias by presenting the CIA's speculative analysis in the form of multiple scenarios that highlight potential trade-offs and use alternative assumptions or "what if" types of structured analytic techniques. Forming partnerships with data scientists, demographers, and analytic methodologists can further maximize the creativity and speculative impact of opportunity analysis without appearing to have a preferred outcome.

A basic reason to not get too far over the line between policy and intelligence analysis is that policymakers change, as do US economic policies. Every few years—four or eight years, at the most—there is a new set of policymakers, with different priorities, policy preferences, and knowledge levels. As a new administration takes shape and officials take on their portfolios, CIA managers and economic analysts get a better feel for what the new team's policies and intelligence needs will be. First, the CIA must seek clues about how key consumers, or "principals," best absorb information or how they prefer analysis be presented. During this transition period, we learn which customer wants short economic assessments, while others may want detailed studies or background information supporting the CIA's analysis. Adjusting the production process to suit the needs of a new administration takes time, and sometimes there can be disconnects between what a customer wants to receive or already knows about foreign economic politics.

WARNING: AN ADDITIONAL CHALLENGE FOR ECONOMIC ANALYSIS

This chapter has covered some of the collection challenges that economic analysts face. It has touched on how it can be tremendously challenging to go beyond the headlines and find ways to tell smart and connected US policymakers something they do not already know or believe. This is especially true as open source economic and financial information and analyses proliferate and become widely available. The consequences of globalization include the interdependence of markets as well as the speed with which they react to changes anywhere in the world. The inherent nature of global financial markets—which are generally beyond the capability of top decision-makers to predict, let alone direct—raises doubts about the CIA's ability to provide "warning" of financial crises in ways on which US policymakers can reasonably act.

Certainly, the CIA's track record is mixed on this score. Warning remains one of the toughest duties analysts across all disciplines face. First, we must recognize that a major discontinuity may be about to occur, which may be difficult for analysts

---

**BOX 4.2: QUESTIONS AS INDICATORS
OF FUTURE FINANCIAL VULNERABILITY**

This illustrative list of questions centers on financial vulnerability, as was experienced during the 1998 Asian financial crisis, and thus provides a set of indicators that analysts can use to detect financial vulnerability and prepare
to warn:

- *Political leadership and fiscal discipline*: Does the country's leadership acknowledge the extent of economic problems, and is it demonstrating a willingness to impose economic hardship? Has the government made commitments, such as to the IMF or the public, to restrain its spending or increase taxes,
and is it fulfilling these commitments?
- *Monetary policy*: What steps is the government taking to reduce pressure on the currency and/or the
banks? Is it taking risky steps, such as making forward purchases of the currency that commit foreign
exchange reserves? Is it imposing or lifting previously imposed capital controls?
- *Currency stability*: Are exporters exchanging hard currency, reducing pressure on the domestic currency?
- *Balance of payments*: Are there impending pressures, such as a bulge in monthly foreign debt payments?
- *Contagion*: Is the country being affected or likely to be affected by weaknesses in its major trading or
financial partners?
- *Financial sector restructuring*: Is the government closing weak banks, privatizing state-owned banks,
reducing its directed lending, allowing buyouts of foreign banks, putting in place and funding a mechanism to buy bad debt from banks, and strengthening the regulatory regimes of banks and nonbank
financial institutions? Has the trend in the ratio of nonperforming loans to outstanding loans leveled
off or declined?
- *Corporate balance sheets*: How are manufacturers faring with the impact of a weaker currency that could
spur demand for exports, but that has already increased foreign debt and made imported intermediate
goods more costly?

---

accustomed to seeing economic trends continuing and governments muddling
through periodic rough patches. Second, if economic analysts do perceive a possible
surprise, they must then marshal sufficient evidence to convince economic decision-
makers of a major problem that demands action. In some cases, the CIA can fail on
both counts. Our analysts were no more prescient than well-connected financial analysts around the world in warning successfully of the Mexican peso crisis in 1994 or
the East Asian financial crisis in 1998. From these cases and others, economic intelligence analysts have learned that they need a set of indicators to aid them in antici-
pating future financial crises (see box 4.2).

Given the complexities and interdependencies of the global financial and commercial markets, analysts also needed to be asking themselves broader, multidisciplinary
questions to guard against too much reliance on assumptions that the financial future
of a country is likely to remain stable:

- What steps, if any, is the foreign government taking to shore up the country's
financial and economic situation? Are these solutions likely to have an impact
in the near term?

- What political problems, such as looming elections, does the leadership face in dealing with economic problems more effectively?
- What could happen in the next two to three months that could change the country's financial/economic position, including the leadership's ability to cope with problems?

When projecting far into the future, the odds of forecasting the state of the global economy are even more hazardous. One can applaud the National Intelligence Council's Global Trends 2020 and 2025 assessments—published decades ago—for highlighting the possibility of a global pandemic and the possibility of it generating considerable interstate frictions. Yet, even as prescient as those speculative assessments were, they did not venture to assess what a pandemic's financial and economic consequences would be, which we now know have been profound.

LOOKING BACK—AND AHEAD

This chapter has tried to capture what economic intelligence analysts do and how they approach their duties in working with collectors as well as policymakers. The CIA's economic intelligence mission has been unique—unlike the Treasury and Commerce departments, it must go well beyond the economic data and trends and forecast their national security implications. Since its founding, of course, the Agency's execution of this mission has continued to evolve. Beginning in the CIA's early years, and throughout the 1970s and 1980s, economic analysts primarily focused on the state of and changes in the Soviet economy and their implications for its defense capabilities and internal stability. Even then, outside consultants worried that this concentration meant too little attention was given to the state of the "Free World's" economies that were competing with the command economies of the Eastern Bloc.[14] By then, the United States had experienced a more volatile world economy, with the abandonment of the Bretton Woods system, the shocks of Arab oil boycotts, and subsequent gas price hikes that brought on spiraling inflation in the United States. So, as Kenneth Dam, former executive director of the White House Council of Economic Policy (and later a senior official in the departments of State and Treasury) put it in 1975: "Economic intelligence has grown in importance over the last five years. This growth is not a fad. It derives from the change in the nature of policy issues of central concern to the President and his principal advisers."[15]

During my career, the unique economic intelligence mission expanded to encompass—as this chapter describes—financial and economic developments in developed and developing countries, key industrial sectors around the world (e.g., oil or strategic metals), food and water resources, and now cryptocurrencies and climate change. The rise of China as a peer economic as well as political and military competitor also significantly raises the stakes for the United States and places more burdens on the CIA's work across the disciplines, including economics. Our customer base during the Cold War was primarily centered in the White House and a few economic and national security agencies. Yet the very definition of national security has broadened, so our customers now include those far beyond that traditional customer base.

There is no indication that policymakers will face a calmer or more benign economic vista in the future. Ransomware and other cyber-based economic espionage and crimes are on the rise, as are the socioeconomic and supply-chain dislocations caused by global diseases. On the positive side, however, the promise of new data mining and artificial intelligence methodologies to filter and exploit the exploding universe of open source data and social media can aid the CIA's "hidden hands" of economic intelligence analysis into the future.

NOTES

1. Definition by Martin J. Manning, from encyclopedia.com. Manning, as of 2018, was a research librarian in the US Department of State. His published works include Greenwood's *Historical Dictionary of American Propaganda*, www.bloomsbury.com/us/historical-dictionary -of-american-propaganda-9780313058639/.

2. Online definition, drawn from https://www.britannica.com/search?query=economic +intelligence.

3. Online definition, drawn from https://dictionary.sensagent.com/economic%20 intelligence/en-en/.

4. The idea of the "invisible hand," a cornerstone concept of a free market economic system, was first introduced by Adam Smith in *The Theory of Moral Sentiments*, written in 1759. It is worth noting that a number of developing countries have referred in a far different way to the "hidden hand" as shorthand for US covert interference in their domestic affairs. That is not the intended meaning of the term "invisible hand" in this chapter.

5. Martin J. Manning describes the importance of economic intelligence surfacing in 1776, when the Committee of Secret Correspondence of the Continental Congress—considered the first US intelligence agency—sent a gentleman by the name of William Carmichael to Europe to survey several economic matters crucial to the emerging government, such as foreign competition in European markets from tobacco growth in the Ukrainian provinces of the Russian Empire, according to Manning's essay "Economic Intelligence," at http://encyclopedia .com. Furthermore, he describes economic intelligence during the World War I, World War II, and post–World War II eras.

6. For information on the early years of economic analysis at the CIA, see Maurice Ernst, "Economic Intelligence in CIA," in *Inside CIA's Private World: Declassified Articles from the Agency's Internal Journal, 1955-1992*, ed. H. Bradford Westerfield (New Haven, CT: Yale University Press, 1995), 305–30, http://www.jstor.org/stable/j.ctt5vm5td.27.

7. This language is taken largely from the career opportunities section of the CIA's website, http://cia.gov/careers/jobs/economic-analyst/.

8. This language also is taken largely from the career opportunities section of the CIA's website.

9. Within an embassy, there are separate sections covering a wide range of economic topics. Typically, State Department Foreign Service Officers serve in the Economic Section, and they report on their interactions with counterparts in the Foreign Ministry who cover foreign trade matters. The Treasury Department assigns an attaché to key embassies where foreign monetary and financial issues are important. Likewise, the Commerce Department will assign commercial attachés to missions where there is significant US trade, requiring that those attachés represent and facilitate American commercial interests.

10. The Economist Intelligence Unit is the research and analysis division of the Economist Group, providing forecasting and advisory services through research and analysis, such as monthly country reports, five-year country economic forecasts, country risk service reports, and industry reports. For more information, see www.eiu.com.

11. For readers interested in viewing an actual economic intelligence assessment on sanctions monitoring, see the declassified CIA Balkan Task Force Intelligence Reports starting in 1995, https://www.cia.gov/readingroom/docs/1995-09-01A.pdf; and https://www.cia.gov/readingroom/docs/1995-07-21C.pdf.

12. The CIA's "World Factbook" has an entry on each country giving this information; see https://www.cia.gov/the-world-factbook/.

13. Opportunity analysis is not conducted routinely by other intelligence agencies because some believe it crosses the line between intelligence and policy. In truth, it needs to be conducted carefully, without projecting an agency policy preference. At a minimum, the analysis must detail the potential advantages of various options but also their potential costs and risks.

14. See *PFIAB Report on Economic Intelligence to National Security Advisor Henry Kissinger*, https://www.cia.gov/readingroom/docs/CIA-RDP80B01439R000500100018-9.pdf. The report "expresses concern about the inadequacy of economic intelligence and analysis in supporting US economic interests."

15. Kenneth Dam wrote the article titled "Economic Intelligence and Analysis" for the Commission on the Organization of the Government in the Conduct of Foreign Policy in 1975. He sent the draft to the CIA director; see https://www.cia.gov/readingroom/docs/CIA-RDP80B01495R000900070017-1.pdf.

5

SCIENCE, TECHNOLOGY, AND WEAPONS ANALYSIS: LEVERAGING SCIENCE FOR NATIONAL SECURITY

Jane P. Fletcher

When I joined the CIA in the mid-1980s, there was little public information available about the Agency, so I was not quite sure what to expect. A former coworker and close friend at the VA Medical Center had told me that the intelligence community was hiring, and, several months later, the CIA brought me on board as an imagery analyst. During our first meeting, my division manager asked me to describe my previous responsibilities as a microbiologist and then assigned me to the aircraft production account. At the time, I was doubtful, as I barely knew the difference between a fighter or a bomber, much less how to assess foreign aircraft production or air-launched missiles. The CIA expected this and provided extensive on-the-job as well as formal training opportunities that helped science, technology, and weapons (ST&W) analysts leverage their scientific foundational knowledge to master foreign weapons and the related issues to which intelligence consumers need answers. My prior experience as a microbiologist and skills learned as an imagery analyst then led to serving on the then–Arms Control Intelligence Staff, representing the intelligence community at regular interagency meetings and working on multilateral treaties. These experiences and duties also helped me form a more holistic understanding of intelligence collection capabilities, various weapons issues, and customers' needs, which served me well when I was later assigned to the all-source chemical and biological warfare branch.

THE BROAD WORLD OF ST&W ANALYSIS

In its vacancy announcements, the CIA describes science, technology, and weapons analysis as using "scientific and technical expertise to analyze foreign weapons development, weapons proliferation, cyber warfare, and emerging technologies."[1] A mission briefing from over a decade ago by the then–Weapons Intelligence Nonproliferation and Arms Control Center still sums up the goal well: "to prevent surprise and protect the United States and its interests from all foreign weapons threats."[2] Analysts in this field have diverse backgrounds—biological sciences, biotechnology, chemistry, engineering, computer science, mathematics, microbiology, and physics as well as remote sensing or geographic information system—and many also have foreign language expertise. Regardless of their expertise, however, ST&W analysts also must be able to communicate highly technical information and insights into concise, easy-to-understand written and oral products.

This wide range of expertise is necessary because of the increasing numbers of technologies and foreign weapons that ST&W analysts assess, which only have expanded since the late 1980s and early 1990s, when the intelligence community was so focused on the Soviet threat. For example, today's missile analysts are responsible for assessing a wide range of systems, including threats posed by "carrier-killer" or antiship missiles, antisatellite weapons, or foreign adversaries' ballistic or cruise missiles—including modifications to deployed systems as well as those under development. Other ST&W analysts are responsible for assessing emerging or evolving technologies—such as how low-observable or stealth technologies can be used to reduce a variety of signatures, including visual, acoustic, infrared, and radar—that could weaken or defeat US defensive capabilities. Likewise, they may assess quantum computing capabilities that could be used offensively or focus on advanced conventional weapons—including sophisticated precision-guided munitions, heavy military equipment such as aircraft or tanks, and human-portable air defense systems, designed for conventional warfare—that could pose a threat to the United States or its allies.[3] Finally, ST&W analysts also assess foreign weapons of mass destruction (WMD) programs, including adversaries' nuclear, chemical, and biological weapons and their delivery systems. Whatever their focus area, ST&W analysts also assess whether foreign countries are transferring key technologies, weapons components, or actual weapons to other countries as well as identify potential leverage points that could be used to discourage or halt such proliferation.

Because of the breadth and depth of ST&W intelligence analysis, however, it is impossible to adequately describe in detail every possible ST&W focus area in a single chapter. Therefore, to illustrate some of its approaches and challenges, this chapter focuses on WMD issues. We examine ST&W analysis aimed at nuclear, biological, and chemical weapons along with their delivery systems, related technologies, and expertise, with the goal of protecting against weapons that can cause mass destruction or mass disruption. Likewise, this chapter focuses on efforts by foreign *state* programs rather than *nonstate* actors or terrorists.

ST&W CONSUMERS: AS DIVERSE AS THE DISCIPLINE

Consumers of ST&W intelligence are as varied as their information needs, and to bet-ter support policymakers, the military, law enforcement, and others, analysts need to understand their customers' missions, priorities, and responsibilities. For example, many policymakers, often in the State Department or National Security Council, are not interested in the detailed science underpinning ST&W analysis—they only need the bottom-line assessment of the threat, the implications of a particular development for the security of a region, or a judgment on how it aligns (or does not) with any treaty obligations. Other decision-makers, like elements of the Department of Defense (DoD) or Department of Energy, who are responsible for eliminating vulnerabilities by devel-oping countermeasures, will need specific scientific and technical data to understand the physics, chemistry, biology, materials science, or other engineering details under-pinning the assessments. Similarly, DoD military planners need technical information to understand what changes, if any, to military doctrine are required.

As with other disciplines, consumers receive or tap into these ST&W analytic insights through briefings, in shorter and longer intelligence assessments, such as National Intelligence Estimates. Additionally, ST&W analysts support various inter-agency policy groups and delegations as well as serve on task forces, and these forums and exchanges facilitate and catalyze the sharing of insights between con-sumers and analysts. For example, I had the opportunity to twice brief a very senior policymaker on our concerns about a foreign threat that could impede, if not totally deny, the United States' ability to conduct military operations overseas. Drawing on his past experiences with the petroleum industry, he was able to suggest a remedia-tion approach that the intelligence community had not considered.

Given the nature of ST&W analysis, the discipline gets a wide range of questions from its principal consumers. The specific focus varies, depending on the customers' responsibilities and whether they are focused on chemical, biological, nuclear, or deliv-ery systems. Probing these questions, however, reveals that they generally are aimed at *action*—exploring what the United States needs to do, what political or military levers may be available to stall or halt foreign progress, and what the window to act is:

- How big of a threat could it be?
- Where is it being researched? Who is doing the research?
- Where is it being tested? Can the intelligence community monitor tests?
- How hard is it to produce?
- Are the materials and equipment needed for production available? If not, are they seeking or obtaining them elsewhere?
- When will they be able to produce/deploy it?

- Where is it produced?
- How much will they be able to produce?
- How lethal/toxic is it?
- How long does it persist?
- How would it be delivered?
- What are its range and accuracy?
- How would we protect against an attack?
- Can the United States detect and attribute an attack?
- Is it captured by current treaties?

DRIVING AND LEVERAGING COLLECTION

Like analysts in other disciplines, ST&W analysts generally use the same types of information, such as open source intelligence (OSINT), human intelligence (HUMINT), signals intelligence (SIGINT), and geospatial intelligence (GEOINT). Similarly, ST&W analysts generate requirements, inform targeting efforts, and build personal relationships to drive collection. For example, the chemical warfare (CW) community—including analysts and collectors—would periodically hold "sunset reviews" to reexamine technical collection targets and priorities and discuss any needed changes. These face-to-face meetings provided a great opportunity to consider different opinions, learn more about the status of collection accesses as well as any current or anticipated challenges, and reach a consensus on priorities. Importantly, they also optimized limited collection resources as well as fostered the intelligence community's trust and dialogue.

As mentioned in chapter 4, on economic analysis, the National Intelligence Priorities Framework is used to codify the intelligence community's priorities; however, unlike the low-priority challenges that economic analysts often face, many ST&W issues are among the highest. Having a high priority, however, does not always guarantee sufficient attention or successful collection. For this reason, to help our overseas HUMINT collectors better understand ST&W collection needs, other analysts and I traveled to key foreign capitals to explain our priority intelligence gaps and what information was needed to close them. As a result of these investments and other initiatives, one chief of station—the senior intelligence community officer stationed in a foreign country—became excited when he realized he could help and eventually facilitated our access to a proving ground, which increased our confidence in prior reporting and our assessments as well as revealed insights into new weapons systems. Today, with the creation of Mission Centers, ST&W analysts in the Directorate of Analysis work closely with officers from the Directorate of Operations.

Like other disciplines, ST&W analysts may assist in debriefing sources when their technical expertise is needed, especially when access to a source is extremely limited and time is of the essence to obtain critical information. Having participated in dozens of debriefings, I observed how this firsthand access was invaluable in assessing the credibility of sources. Analysts can directly observe a source's demeanor, understand the source's motivation for reporting, clarify the provided information (especially important when it is filtered through translations), and assess his or her expertise. These debriefings can deepen (or in some cases, decrease) confidence in an asset's reporting. When these opportunities arise, it is always a best practice to create and coordinate, when possible, the list of requirements in advance to optimize these face-to-face encounters, which may be fleeting.

PARTNERSHIPS MATTER

As with other disciplines, partnerships are critical to ST&W analysts' success, including regularly exchanging information with other government agencies or departments, including the United States and its foreign partners, and consulting with nongovernment experts as needed. As ST&W analysts know, just because something looks feasible on paper, in a computer simulation, or at a laboratory-scale, it does not mean that it can be successfully used militarily. For example, to assess the threat of chemical weapons, analysts need to understand the properties of the agents (e.g., are they stable in air; do they have high vapor pressures, which make them more of an inhalation threat; or low vapor pressures, which make them more of a terrain-denial, contact, or percutaneous hazard), but they also must know the limitations of physical weapons systems, established doctrines, and how meteorological conditions may affect weapons employment outcomes to assess the overall threats. Collectively, these insights then drive collection, inform debriefings, highlight remaining gaps, and lead to assessments that have higher confidence levels.

Sometimes, the intelligence available dictates these partnerships. For example, in the fall of 1992, a series of open source articles detailed top-secret work conducted by the Soviet Union on CW agents, including binary weapons (consisting of two components that are not lethal until they are mixed to form a CW agent before use), despite Moscow's assurances that it had ceased work on its CW program.[4] These articles warned that international negotiations on what would become the Chemical Weapons Convention did not capture these secret weapons, some of which the Russian scientists described as being "10 times more lethal than VX"—an extremely toxic nerve agent.[5] The articles also outlined facilities and locations involved in the research and testing of these agents, called Novichok or "newcomer" as well as the designators for specific agents.[6]

When this reporting became available, the intelligence community began working to better understand these threats. Although initially there was some resistance about

---

BOX 5.1: ATTRIBUTING CHEMICAL WARFARE ATTACKS

In the spring of 2018, a former Russian military intelligence officer and double agent, Sergei Skripal; his daughter, Yulia; and a British detective sergeant were hospitalized after being exposed to a potent nerve agent, which the Soviets reportedly had developed and Moscow had steadfastly refused to acknowledge.[7] Almost four months later, Charles Rowley and his girlfriend, Dawn Sturgess, discovered the discarded perfume bottle used to hold the agent and also were exposed and hospitalized, and Sturgess died days later.[8] After examining over 11,000 hours of CCTV recordings, British officials identified two Russian GRU agents, Dr. Alexander Mishkin and Col. Anatoliy Chepiga—both recipients of the Hero of Russia award—as the attempted assassins.[9]

Because of yearslong investments and efforts by the United States and its partners, British scientists were able to confirm within 24 hours that a Novichok agent had been used, and this insight undoubtedly helped inform approaches on how to best treat the victims and decontaminate the affected areas. Additionally, the Organisation for the Prohibition of Chemical Weapons confirmed that a type of Novichok agent was used in the assassination attempt,[10] and a November 2020 *Arms Control Today* article reported that A-234 was the Novichok agent used to poison Sergei and Yulia Skripal.[11] Likewise, these partnerships also facilitated the rapid attribution during the 2020 attack, which used a different type of Novichok agent, on the Russian dissident Alexei Navalny.[12]

---

whether this was the community's job, or whether the Defense Department should have the sole responsibility in validating these types of threats, ultimately, the CIA's leadership agreed that it was impossible to reliably analyze intelligence reporting, guide future collection efforts, and confidently characterize the threats posed unless we explored them further. Partnerships with various collectors, chemists, toxicologists, medical personnel, and components of DoD as well as foreign counterparts and scientists accelerated our progress in validating and understanding this threat, developing monitoring capabilities, and informing those charged with assessing existing countermeasures. In the latter case, this collaboration informed efficacy studies of treatments and decontaminants as well as military doctrinal updates. These investments took years and required extensive funding; however, the resulting insights strengthened our defensive posture and would not have been possible without these critical alliances. Over the years, these investments advanced the ability to confidently attribute while also informing responses so that the effects of these attacks were minimized (see box 5.1).

EXPLOITING DIFFERENT DATA SETS AND INTELLIGENCE SOURCES

Unlike other analytic disciplines, though, ST&W analysts often leverage different collection streams and data sets to inform their judgments. For example, MASINT—Measure and Signature Intelligence—is defined by the Federation of American Scientists' Intelligence Resource Program as "scientific and technical intelligence information obtained by quantitative and qualitative analysis of data (metric, angle, spatial, wavelength, time dependence, modulation, plasma, and hydromagnetic) derived from specific technical sensors for the purpose of identifying any distinctive features associated with the source, emitter, or sender and to facilitate subsequent identification, characterization, and/or measurement of the same."[13] Materials MASINT is often used to analyze collected gas, liquid, or solid samples, but MASINT also may include acoustic, laser, radar, radiation, spectroscopic, or other technical data, used to inform analysts on foreign activities as well as the likelihood that they are occurring. Analysts must be cautious when leveraging MASINT data, as it may provide indications that certain activities happened, but it may not provide reliable insights as to *where* or *when* an activity occurred.

Likewise, analysts who assess delivery systems often rely on insights from FISINT—Foreign Instrumentation Signals Intelligence, a subcategory of SIGINT—data that include intercepted electromagnetic emissions, such as "telemetry, beaconry . . . tracking/fusing/arming/firing command systems, and video data links," associated with testing or deployments of foreign systems.[14] FISINT is usually used to inform judgments on foreign systems that are under development, allowing analysts to glean new insights with much higher confidence on a weapon's performance, capabilities, and potential vulnerabilities. For example, telemetry may provide information such as a system's altitude, speed, temperature, and vibration levels while in flight and may provide insights into system failures.[15] Assessing telemetry requires highly specialized training and skills—deciphering what some refer to as "squiggly lines"—but it is an indispensable tool when it is available.

However, obtaining and/or processing these data may present challenges. Access is not always conducive to collecting the data needed, or some countries may encrypt their data. Likewise, the volume of the technical/electronic data may present other challenges when trying to collect, capture, or transmit them; however, when available, these data sources often provide incontrovertible evidence of a country's activities. For example, when Iraq was accused of firing missiles beyond the proscribed range limits the United Nations had allowed, the intelligence community had solid evidence to back up these claims.

Moreover, ST&W analysts may use Foreign Materiel Exploitation to enhance their understanding of a system's design, capabilities, or potential weaknesses, and these insights usually result in assessments with much higher confidence levels. For example, some countries provided the US access to Soviet-produced systems in their inventories.[16] A US government document from March 2021 also lists some foreign equipment holdings, including combat aircraft, air-to-air missiles, surface-to-air missile systems, antiaircraft gun systems, and radars.[17] Foreign Materiel Exploitation can facilitate testing, including against US equipment, to further understand the threat it may pose during a conflict and to develop US countermeasures.

CHALLENGES SLOW DOWN, BUT DO NOT PREVENT, SUCCESS

With few exceptions, nations working on WMD programs generally attempt to conceal their efforts using denial and deception or enhanced security measures, although their motivations may differ. Some have ratified treaties, vowing not to develop WMD, as Iraq did. Others strive to "reach the WMD finish line" before another country can stall or completely halt their progress—an accusation that has been made against Iran. Yet others may look for treaty "loopholes" to exploit while pursuing their programs, as Russia's continued use of Novichok agents demonstrates. Moreover, especially in the case of chemical and biological agents, the raw materials, equipment, and infrastructure are dual-use—meaning they have legitimate commercial applications as well as military ones. This inherent plausible deniability makes it even more important to understand a country's plans and intentions via robust collection and rigorous analytic efforts.

In contrast to some other analytic disciplines, for which a wealth of information may be openly available, foreign denial and deception (D&D) efforts mean that when ST&W information is available, it must be protected. As a result, intelligence information about foreign ST&W programs often is highly compartmented to protect sensitive sources, guard vulnerable or fragile accesses that may have taken years to establish, or prevent dissemination of information that may enable adversaries to attack the United States or its interests. Compartmentation complicates the ability to seek outside expertise or form partnerships with others while occasionally creating apparent disconnects in confidence levels associated with intelligence judgments when analysts cannot fully elaborate on the highly sensitive information that may be underpinning some assessments. These challenges may be mitigated by highly restricting dissemination of certain products or by releasing key information that has been sanitized to protect any sensitive sources and methods.

More than most of the other analytic disciplines described in this book, ST&W analysis requires extensive funding, especially when trying to understand nontraditional threats or develop new technical collection or analytic approaches. Modeling and processing capabilities, licensing fees, data storage, and contracts to leverage diverse, cutting-edge laboratories (including the US national laboratories) require substantial, sustained investments. These costs are essential for confidently analyzing foreign weapons as well as the large, dynamic, novel, or incomplete data sets inherent in or acquired to monitor ST&W issues.

Finally, in cases of WMD use, attributing the source of the material and/or the perpetrator of an attack remains a difficult challenge that requires information that may not always be available. In other words, when WMD are used, it is often easier to determine the "what" than identify the "who." The Syria case described below highlights how the attribution process unfolded in determining who used chemical weapons.

NOVEL ASPECTS OF ST&W TRADECRAFT

ST&W analysts especially need to be aware that sometimes countries pursue novel, less known, or previously abandoned approaches. This may be because these countries lack the technical expertise, raw materials, equipment, infrastructure, or finances needed to pursue the more traditional approaches or because they are attempting to circumvent agreements or treaties that they have signed or ratified. In these cases, ST&W analysts need to guard against mirror imaging and keep an open mind about the significance of information that seems different than US experiences or may be previously unknown or not pursued (see box 5.2). Additionally, ST&W analysts need to be aware that some countries may use an "on-demand" approach, whereby the production of proscribed materials is embedded within legitimate facilities and only produced sporadically, as needed. Such a mobilization approach complicates intelligence monitoring and can help shield foreign detection of their activities while protecting their investments in production by reducing the risk that their facilities will be damaged or destroyed.

BOX 5.2: MIRROR IMAGING IN A WMD WORLD

In its pre-1991 nuclear program, Iraqi scientists primarily used the electromagnetic isotope separation (EMIS) process—which uses large magnets to separate ions of different isotopes of the same element[18]—to enrich uranium (or convert natural uranium into fissile material) because Iraq could acquire the magnets, the technology was relatively simple, and information was accessible in the open literature.[19] Although the United States successfully used EMIS at its first large-scale uranium enrichment facility in Oak Ridge, Tennessee, it abandoned the process after World War II because of its high electrical power demands.[20]

A "mirror-imaging mind-set"—that Iraq would not use EMIS in its nuclear program for the same reasons that the United States had abandoned it—underpinned some of the intelligence community's earlier judgments on Iraq's nuclear program. In describing United Nations' findings during its inspections throughout the 1990s, a 2005 Council of Foreign Relations article noted, "UN inspectors . . . were stunned by the volume of information and material they found and surprised that Iraq's weapons programs were much more advanced than they had expected."[21] In 2005, the WMD Commission echoed this finding, noting that "the Intelligence Community's pre-war assessments had underestimated Iraq's nuclear program and . . . intelligence analysts were determined not to fall victim again to the same mistake."[22]

This EMIS case underscores how analytic tradecraft must rigorously consider potential alternative approaches adversaries may pursue. Doing so also can provide early targeting leads that may otherwise be initially untapped. For example, broadly considering what drivers may factor into a country's calculus in selecting which technical routes to pursue may uncover early indicators of procurement information; highlight potential research, production, or testing sites that should be targeted for collection; and offer other possible opportunities to deter or rollback programs.

A second aspect of ST&W analysis that poses challenges is that key information is often limited or unavailable, which creates a vacuum, whereby analysts lack the feedback needed to adjust or recalibrate their assumptions and judgments. Contrast this with weather forecasters, who receive daily and even hourly feedback on their predictions—can look out the window and see if it rained or snowed, for example—and that helps them understand which factors exacerbated forecast errors. This feedback helps them adjust and improve the reliability of future projections. Likewise, leadership analysts often receive clear feedback on which parties or leader won an election or how a leader acted when faced with a particular crisis. Ditto, as we have seen with the recent Russia-Ukraine crisis, military analysts usually receive feedback on whether their judgments that a country would attack another as well as what factors altered the calculus to go to war were correct. However, a country intent on evading the intelligence community's monitoring of its WMD program can exploit publicly available findings of the postmortems on community failures to better conceal its efforts. This then makes it even more difficult to detect and identify indications of or changes to foreign WMD-related efforts. This gap can exacerbate analytic biases, whereby analysts continue to build their assessments on flawed assumptions, information, or assessments, migrating further from actual conditions.

Especially because ST&W analysis often takes several years to develop a clear picture of a WMD threat, rigorous tradecraft practices become even more essential in providing additional analytic guard rails, especially when feedback is not available. It is even more critical that ST&W analysts clearly lay out the assumptions and information upon which judgments are based as well as any key knowledge gaps that could most affect these assessments. As mentioned above, ST&W analysts especially need to check against the tendency to mirror image when considering what path or options a country might pursue on its WMD journey and stringently avoid focusing only on information that reinforces confirmation bias—a cognitive bias where we only seek or consider information that is consistent with or confirms our own theories or preexisting views.[23] Additionally, all analysts need to guard against anchoring bias, whereby the first information received is believed to be more reliable than any subsequent information received that may contradict the first,[24] as well as availability bias, or a "distortion that arises from the use of information which is most readily available, rather than that which is necessarily most representative."[25] As discussed above, the latter is especially relevant in the case of ST&W analysis, as adversaries tend to carefully guard information about their most sensitive ST&W programs, making it especially difficult to obtain.

Finally, more than most analytic disciplines except for terrorism analysis, ST&W intelligence analysis often is a one-step-forward, two-steps-back journey that one undertakes—sometimes multiple times and over many years—before getting a clearer picture of the threats, as demonstrated with the Al Kibar, Syria, and Novichok cases. Some information received will highlight places, people, motivations, drivers, or activities that previously were not being considered or with which the analyst is unfamiliar, or it may contradict other information. This new information then triggers the intelligence community to delve further or reassess whether their previous judgments are consistent with new reporting.

THE MANY ROLES OF ST&W ANALYSIS

Depending on their accounts, ST&W analysts may provide warning, investigate alleged-use incidents, support arms control, assess threats from crises, detect new programs, or follow milestones and changes in established weapons threats. Regardless of the role, the underlying goal remains to identify any US vulnerabilities or risks to US interests and ease or eliminate them. This may include informing the development of potential countermeasures, highlighting needed doctrinal changes, or identifying opportunities—via diplomatic or other approaches—that could be used to mitigate these, and sometimes these roles may intersect. Several ST&W case studies illustrate these various missions while underscoring how they unfolded and highlighting the various resources and partnerships involved.

Assessing Alleged-Use Events—Syria CW

The intelligence community had monitored and assessed Syria's CW program for decades, but as Syria's civil war continued to escalate in 2011 and 2012 after President Assad's brutal response, the community became increasingly concerned about the security of Syrian CW stockpile and correspondingly intensified its efforts.[26] When the community obtained reports by 2012 that Syria planned to use chemical weapons against its population to quell opposition fighters' resistance, it immediately alerted senior leaders. In August, President Obama warned Assad that any use of chemical weapons would be a redline for the United States.[27] Although this warning seemed temporarily to stall these preparations, by mid-March 2013, increasing indications suggested that chemical weapons had been used. On March 20, the Syrian government alleged that opposition forces had used chemical weapons that killed dozens and asked the UN to investigate.[28] Months later, multiple attacks were reported on August 21, resulting in an estimated death toll of over 1,000 people, including more than 400 children.[29]

By August 2013, based on multiple sources of information, the intelligence community assessed with high confidence that "the Assad regime had used chemical weapons—including the nerve agent sarin—against the opposition on multiple occasions."[30] The more than one hundred videos reviewed showed bodies with no visible injuries that exhibited signs "consistent with, but not unique to, nerve agent exposure."[31] However, hospitals in Damascus treated thousands of patients with symptoms consistent with nerve agent poisoning, and the reported "contamination of medical and first aid workers" as well as the rapid influx of patients and observations from media-aired images of the victims were all consistent with nerve agent exposure.[32] The identification of the specific nerve agent used in the attacks, however, was based on laboratory analyses of samples taken from victims.[33] And although these data verified *what* was used, they did not provide insights into *who* used it.

The final attribution judgment of whether the Syria regime or opposition was responsible drew on several sources of information—including human, signals, open source, and geospatial intelligence. First, "Multiple streams of intelligence . . . indicated that the regime had executed a conventional rocket and artillery attack against the Damascus suburbs in the early hours of August 21."[34] In contrast, there was no credible evidence that the Syrian opposition had the ability to strike multiple locations simultaneously. Second, "Syrian chemical weapons personnel were operating in the Damascus suburb . . . from August 18 until early in the morning on . . . August 21 near an area that the regime uses to mix chemical weapons, including sarin. On August 21, a Syrian regime element prepared for a chemical weapons attack, . . . including through the utilization of gas masks."[35] Conversely, there were no indications before the attack that opposition forces were preparing to use chemical weapons. Third, the intelligence community assessed that the opposition lacked the "capability to fabricate all of the videos, physical symptoms . . . and other information associated with this chemical attack."[36] Finally, the United States "intercepted communications involving a senior (Syrian) official intimately familiar with the offensive" who was worried that UN inspectors would uncover evidence that the regime had used chemical weapons in the August attack.[37]

On August 26, Syrian president Assad denied his regime used chemical weapons, asserting such claims were "politically motivated."[38] However, an independent UN team, which gained firsthand access to victims, medical personnel, first responders, and sites, validated the intelligence community's assessment that sarin nerve agent had been delivered using surface-to-surface rockets to multiple targets in Damascus, while the UN secretary general confirmed, "The results are overwhelming and indisputable."[39] Days later, France also released its declassified intelligence assessment, which concluded that in contravention to the 1925 Geneva Protocol, "the Assad regime used sarin gas in the August 21 attack, and in two earlier attacks in April."[40]

The Syria case is a great illustration of how the different roles of ST&W analysis can intersect. Throughout this case, the intelligence community repeatedly provided strategic and tactical warnings and updates via briefings, phone calls, and written products to senior administration officials and congressional leadership as it investigated the alleged use of chemical weapons and determined who conducted the attacks.[41] Additionally, however, this event later developed an arms control component, and ST&W analysts monitored the status and elimination of Syria's CW agents, stockpile, and infrastructure by mid-2014.[42]

Supporting Arms Control

For more than five decades, ST&W analysts have contributed to advancing various arms control initiatives, including bilateral agreements, multilateral treaties, and confidence-building measures (see table 5.1). These contributions change, depending on the provisions of each agreement and as they evolve over time. For example, some are in the negotiation stages; others have expired, while others never entered into force; and yet others lack verification provisions, such as the Biological Weapons Convention.

ST&W support to arms control begins in the negotiation stages as they work closely with analysts in other disciplines to provide backstopping support by relaying the intelligence community's insights about assessed foreign military and technical capabilities, drivers/motivations, goals, and likely improvements to offensive programs. In addition, analysts can assist in drafting needed language or highlighting potential issues that could create future loopholes, which could be exploited by adversaries. Backstopping may be conducted remotely or in person, serving as part of an interagency group or delegation. My experience in multilateral and bilateral discussions reinforced that it was invaluable to understanding foreign priorities and concerns while helping to underscore potential new opportunities. As with other disciplines, ST&W analysts also have an obligation to ensure that the intelligence community's counterparts are kept abreast of key developments to optimize potential synergies by drawing on their varied expertise as well as ensure that partners are not caught off guard.

In the United States, after an agreement is negotiated, the president submits the treaty for advice and consent to the Senate, where ratification requires its approval by a two-thirds vote. Generally, relevant committees will first consider and report its views to the larger Senate. During this period, ST&W analysts—in addition to other departments, such as the departments of Defense, State, and Energy—usually provide written answers to Senate questions as well as brief the Senate Foreign Relations Committee. Depending on the agreement, the intelligence community also may be asked to brief the Senate Appropriations Committee, Senate Armed Services Committee, and/or the US Senate Select Committee on Intelligence. Regardless of the committee, members and staff generally want to know how confident the intelligence community is in its ability to monitor the treaty as well as what insights the treaty may provide, how the treaty may improve the security of the United States, and/or the national security ramifications of *not* ratifying the treaty. In some cases, these sessions also offer an opportunity for the community to request additional

TABLE 5.1. Illustrative WMD Arms Control Agreements and Treaties

Treaty/Agreement	Opened for Signature	Entered into Force	Parties	Status– in Force?	Comments
Biological Weapons Convention (BWC)	4/10/1972	3/26/1975	183 States Parties; 4 signatories	Yes	Contains no verification provisions
Chemical Weapons Convention	1/13/1993	4/29/1997	193 States Parties; 1 signatory	Yes	Implemented by Organisation for the Prohibition of Chemical Weapons
Intermediate-Range Nuclear Forces Treaty	12/8/1987	6/1/1988	US & Soviet Union	No	US withdrew in 2019, citing Russian noncompliance
Joint Comprehensive Plan of Action (JCPOA)	7/14/2015	10/18/2015	Iran + P5 (China, France, Germany UK & US)	No	US withdrew in May 2018; currently renegotiating
Missile Technology Control Regime (MTCR)	4/16/1987	1987	35 Partners	Yes	Has no formal mechanism to monitor compliance
Nuclear Nonproliferation Treaty (NPT)	1/7/1968	3/5/1970	191 States	Yes	India, Israel, and Pakistan never joined; North Korea withdrew in 2003; International Atomic Energy Agency verifies compliance
Strategic Arms Reduction Treaty I (START I)	07/31/1991	12/5/1994	Initially US & Soviet Union / Russia; Belarus, Kazakhstan, and Ukraine added in 1994	No	Expired on December 5, 2009

Source: Arms Control Association, "Treaties and Agreements," www.armscontrol.org/treaties#:~:text=This%20is%20a%20multilateral %20treaty,and%20use%20of%20chemical%20weapons.&text=This%20is%20a%20legally%20binding%20global%20ban%20on %20all%20nuclear%20explosive%20testing.

resources, if a new treaty will require the community to develop new capabilities and programs.

Not surprisingly, views on the monitorability of an arms control agreement can be controversial. While serving on the then–Arms Control Intelligence Staff, I observed how contentious the intelligence community's judgments could be when another US government department accused the community of trying to sabotage a particular agreement after it assessed that it had low confidence in its ability to monitor its provisions. The community was accused of being too pessimistic and unreasonable and was asked repeatedly to revise its judgments. Although the assessments did not ultimately change, some of these relationships were forever strained. My lesson was that upholding the truth as analysts see it often tests the courage of those trying to present it, especially when faced with others' convictions that an arms control agreement's benefits should supersede "less important" monitoring facts.

Finally, the arms control mission of ST&W analysis may also include developing collection strategies, informing the development of various collection capabilities, and monitoring adversaries' compliance with arms control agreements, which inform policymakers' verification judgments. The latter also can be contentious, and it is critical that the intelligence community explicitly explain the basis for its judgments and not bend to political pressure.

Regardless, arms control is not a guarantee that a country, which has acceded or is a party to an arms agreement or treaty, will abide by its provisions or remain committed to its goals. As such, ST&W analysts must remain vigilant and inform decisionmakers when changes or apparent violations occur. For example, North Korea in early 2003 announced it would no longer be bound by the Nuclear Non-Proliferation Treaty. In the Syria case highlighted above, the UN reported in October 2017 that "the Assad regime was guilty of using sarin nerve agent in the April 4 attack in Khan Sheikhoun."[43] Furthermore, after collecting and analyzing samples, the Organisation for the Prohibition of Chemical Weapons (OPCW) determined in 2018 that Syria had used chlorine multiple times as a weapon as well as sarin, which it reported "very likely used a chemical weapon . . . on March 24, 2017."[44]

Even when updates are made to agreements to close loopholes, some states still find ways to circumvent them. Triggered by the 2018 Skripal assassination attempt, the Chemical Weapons Convention's Schedules of Chemicals—which drive the convention's verification provisions—were amended for the first time since the Chemical Weapons Convention entered into force to include some of the Novichok agents.[45] State parties agreed to this change in November 2019, and the amendment officially became effective on June 7, 2020.[46] However, shortly after the amendments to the schedules were finalized, laboratories in France, Germany, and Sweden as well as the OPCW confirmed that a new variant—A-262, which was not captured by the schedules that had been updated only two months earlier—was used in the August 2020 assassination attempt of a Russian opposition leader, Alexei Navalny.[47] A Bellingcat investigation report, in December 2020,[48] provided confirmation that a Russian Federal Security Service agent admitted over a 49-minute recorded phone call that a team had poisoned Navalny's underwear with the chemical warfare agent.[49] CNN reported that the FSB dismissed the Bellingcat video as "a 'fake,' facilitated by foreign intelligence"; and as with Syria, Moscow has denied that it has ever used chemical weapons.[50]

Assessing Threats from Crises

During various crises, ST&W analysts often serve as reliable sources of expertise on which senior leaders and policymakers may draw. For example, during the 1986 Chernobyl disaster in Ukraine, the 2001 Anthrax letters attacks in the United States, and the 2011 Fukushima reactor tragedy in Japan, analysts were asked to provide briefings, answer questions, and provide daily (or more frequent) updates as events unfolded. During these times, analysts worked closely with the rest of the intelligence community, drawing on imagery, human, and signals intelligence as well as open source and technical data and providing clarity to the jumble of news and other reporting that can result in misinformation or cause panic, which allowed senior leaders to make informed decisions. Likewise, I am certain that ST&W analysts today are following the threats posed by the Russians bombing or occupying nuclear plants in Ukraine as well as monitoring for any indications that the Russians are preparing to use chemical weapons against Ukrainians.

Detecting and Characterizing New Threats: Syria's Nuclear Reactor at Al Kibar

The Al Kibar story exemplifies how ST&W analysis frequently unfolds, often over many years, as well as the critical role of collection and partnerships in ultimately allowing analysts to warn the nation's most senior decision-makers. It also highlights how analysts overcome the extensive denial and deception activities a state intent on concealing its illicit activities may undertake. Although some of the detailed sources and methods remain classified, much of this story has been made publicly available and is recounted here.[51]

In 2001, intelligence became available that senior Syrian officials were collaborating with North Korean nuclear entities.[52] Prompted by this information, analysts searched for other indications of when this cooperation may have begun and discovered "a pattern of . . . technology transfers, cargo shipments, and meetings between high-level officials, dating back to 1997"—four years earlier.[53] Because of the individuals involved, the analysts assessed that these efforts were nuclear-related and for work within Syria. At the time, no other information was available, so analysts provided strategic warning while continuing to seek more information.

In 2005, additional information became available on a Syrian–North Korean project in the Dayr Az-Zawr region, northeast of Damascus.[54] The intelligence community was then able to focus its imagery searches, which led to the discovery of an enigma facility—"a large, nondescript building in a remote area of Syria near the Euphrates River, the closest town's name was al Kibar."[55] Unlike most areas involved in WMD-related activities, there was no obvious heightened security measures—gates, fences, or guards—although its remoteness and siting in a ravine provided natural screening. Moreover, the exterior of the building seemed "designed to look like one of the Byzantine fortresses that dot the Syrian countryside."[56] Nonetheless, analysts also observed that its closeness to the Euphrates River could be an important source of water for future illicit activities.

This sequence of events is not uncommon in WMD analysis. A tip will suddenly highlight a particular area that perhaps has never or rarely been targeted for collection. Because historical imagery may not be available, other types of information may be needed to provide new insights into its purpose. That breakthrough came two years later, in 2007, when a Middle Eastern liaison service provided handheld photographs.[57] The photos showed the interior and exterior of a building that reportedly was in the same region as the enigma facility, and National Geospatial Intelligence Agency analysts were able to confirm that "all of the windows, doors, (and) ventilation holes in the wall matched up perfectly" with the previously identified enigma building.[58] These photos also confirmed that the building contained "a gas-cooled graphite-moderated reactor and included vertical tubes at the top of the reactor for control rods and refueling ports, a concrete reactor vessel and its steel liner, and a water supply to move heat."[59] Moreover, they revealed that the fuel configurations were extremely similar to North Korea's plutonium reactor at Yongbyon, and in fact, during the last thirty-five years, only North Korea was known to have built this type of reactor.[60] It also became clear from the photos that the exterior of the building had been deliberately modified to conceal these similarities. With the Iraq WMD lessons still fresh, analysts considered alternative explanations for the site but were able to rule out that it was intended to generate electricity, serve as a water treatment plant, or be used for research.[61]

Based on these new insights, the intelligence community assessed, "Syria was building a gas-cooled, graphite-moderated reactor. The reactor would be capable of producing plutonium for nuclear weapons, was not configured to produce electricity and was ill-suited for research . . . that North Korea assisted Syria's covert nuclear activity with cooperation going back 10 years . . . (and) that this reactor was part of a Syrian nuclear weapons program," while continuing to monitor the site.[62] Subsequent imagery analysis revealed that the Syrians connected pipes from the river to an underground storage tank beside the building housing the reactor, while a different pipeline was constructed to return water to the river.[63] The analysts noted that these additions would have been necessary to pump water through the heat exchangers to cool the reactor and then return the heated water to the river. By early August, as the pumphouse and pipelines neared completion, the analysts judged that reactor start-up operations were imminent.[64]

On September 6, 2007, the Israelis destroyed the Al Kibar building before nuclear fuel had been loaded into the core, and almost immediately Syria began removing equipment and debris, working at night or under tarps to stymie foreign monitoring, while North Korean nuclear personnel visited Syria shortly after the strike.[65] In October, the Syrians used an explosion in an attempt to destroy the building and obscure its purpose, which instead revealed key internal aspects of the building, including remnants of the "concrete reactor vessel, the shielded heat exchanger rooms, and the spent fuel pool."[66] Syria finally permitted International Atomic Energy Agency (IAEA) inspectors to visit the site—eight months after it was bombed, in June 2008—but only after it moved topsoil from an adjacent hill to cover the reactor and constructed a new building over the former reactor location.[67] Although these denial attempts were unexpected, the IAEA still found evidence of nuclear material—uranium particles— and concluded the structure could have been for a nuclear reactor, at which point Syria ceased its cooperation.[68] Damascus's repeated refusals to resolve international concerns led to the IAEA Board of Governors finding in June 2011 that Syria was in noncompliance with its Non-Proliferation Treaty Safeguards Agreement.[69] As with some of the highlighted case studies in this chapter, Syria has yet to acknowledge that the Al Kibar facility was intended for illicit purposes.

LEARNING LESSONS

Most readers are generally familiar with the controversy surrounding the intelligence community's flawed analysis on Iraq's WMD programs. What few will appreciate, however, is how seriously the CIA studied what went wrong and how to improve its organizational practices and tradecraft. By the summer of 2003, before the outcome of the Iraq WMD story was even known, the CIA began conducting an exhaustive deep dive to understand and reconstruct our analysis, the information underpinning it, and the institutional practices or lack of guard rails that contributed to errors. Former CIA deputy director John McLaughlin elaborated: "Within a couple of months after the end of hostilities, we have already initiated an extensive 'Lessons Learned,' when weapons of mass destruction were not appearing. We put some of our very best people on that case to figure out, scrub everything we said, every resource, every sentence. We covered walls with charts documenting what we had said day-by-day and report-by-report."[70]

A team of approximately ten senior analysts, collectors, and other specialists were reassigned to focus solely on this effort, and to minimize any risk of anchoring or other cognitive biases, only analysts who had never worked on Iraq-WMD issues were selected. Although it was originally believed that the effort would take only a few weeks, it soon became clear that this mission would take months. The pressure and intensity were immense, compounded by the huge volume of information, endless urgent taskings, insanely long hours, sense of responsibility that we felt to "get it right," in addition to the strain it placed on the relationships with our colleagues, who understandably felt as if we were second-guessing their expertise or work.

This experience, however, caused all of us to think about intelligence in ways we had not before. We had been trained to consider foreign denial and deception, assess capabilities, and identify collection gaps. Our study, though, underscored that the intelligence community had not sufficiently focused on probing and making explicit our analytic assumptions, better understanding the sources underlying the reporting, and understanding that positive reporting was inherently prioritized over negative information, while considering alternative explanations for foreign behavior. The group's insights into these analytic tradecraft shortfalls as well as into embedded, institutional practices that exacerbated some of the failings made a difference not just to ST&W analysis but also to analysts, collectors, and managers throughout the community. The group tirelessly worked with others to address some of the institutional hurdles, and to ensure these lessons were not lost, we delivered scores of briefings to the community's leaders, collectors, and analysts as well as policymakers, staffs, and even the presidential Commission on the Intelligence Capabilities Regarding Weapons of Mass Destruction—which, in its footnotes, cited the Review Group's insights on Iraq that helped shape the commission's understanding of the issues.[71] Ultimately, the group's insights and efforts resulted in various information technology, tradecraft, and organizational changes, which improved the transparency into sources and past products, sharpened analytic approaches, and improved the communication of knowledge gaps, judgments, and associated confidence levels.

When the group disbanded, I was fortunate enough to be assigned to the Sherman Kent School for Intelligence Analysis, where I was tasked with ensuring that the Iraq lessons would not be lost within the directorate. And with the help of many, many others, we worked tirelessly to do just that, creating a series of tradecraft journals that codified best practices and shared lessons learned, integrating these findings into courses, and even creating a simulation so that future analysts could experience some of the same dilemmas and learn the lessons firsthand.

Reflecting on the Agency's commitment to being a learning organization, John McLaughlin stated, "In my judgment, we came to the conclusions about what had gone wrong well in advance of any of the commissions that have looked at us. I can tell you from having looked at some of the subsequent products that the American public needs to understand that the [intelligence community] has absorbed lessons from this and now approaches its work on National [Intelligence] Estimates in a way that gives great attention to things like uncertainties and alternative views and makes them very prominent in the document."[72]

THE VALUE OF ST&W ANALYSIS AND LOOKING AHEAD

As highlighted above, ST&W analysis requires a larger financial investment than most of the other analytic disciplines described in this book. In a time of contracting resources, some may ask: Is ST&W analysis worth the investment? Does it really matter? Given the stakes involved, there is no question that it must remain central to the CIA's mission. ST&W analysis has helped minimize loss of life, improve military readiness, reduce potential economic costs, and protect global norms. If a central goal of US national security is to prevent and protect against weapons capable of causing mass destruction or mass disruption, then this discipline undoubtedly is indispensable. For example, the 2018 targeted UK CW attack alone was estimated to cost at least $15 million.[73] Imagine an adversary attacking and destroying crops or livestock and the impact it could have on global food supplies. Treaties that help establish global norms are important in a world with diverse views and goals, and ST&W analysis helps monitor others' activities that may be inconsistent with or threaten those norms.

As with the other intelligence disciplines described, to be successful, ST&W analysis "takes a village," working with technical and human collectors, analytic counterparts, other non-intelligence community scientists, consumers, and the military, to name just a few. The layering of these sources of information, expertise, and perspectives facilitates the insights and strengthens the confidence levels needed to provide warning to protect the United States and its allies. There is no doubt that ST&W analysis is not—and never will be—perfect. Scant information; adversaries determined to conceal their efforts, plans, and intentions; and the lack of access or information can hinder fact finding and result in incorrect judgments. Especially when ST&W analysts are trying to understand new or novel weapons, with which the United States has had little or no experience, there is a learning curve, and, sometimes, it involves luck that *the* critical piece of information needed to fill a gap or point you in a different direction will become available. However, when outcomes turn out differently than assessed, as in the case of Iraq WMD, ST&W analysts are the first to try to understand what went wrong and make the needed changes.

NOTES

1. Central Intelligence Agency, "Browse CIA Jobs—Science, Technology and Weapons Analyst," https://www.cia.gov/careers/jobs/science-technology-and-weapons-analyst/.

2. "WINPAC Mission Briefing," revised June 27, 2001, https://www.cia.gov/readingroom/docs/DOC_0005462544.pdf.

3. US Department of State Archive, Bureau of International Security and Nonproliferation, Advanced Conventional Weapons, https://2001-2009.state.gov/t/isn/acw/index.htm#:~:text=An%20important%20component%20of%20the,munitions%20designed%20for%20conventional%20warfare.

4. Will Englund, "Ex-Soviet Scientist Says Gorbachev's Regime Created New Nerve Gas in '91," *Baltimore Sun*, September 16, 1992.

5. Englund.

6. Will Englund, "Russia Still Doing Secret Work on Chemical Arms: Research Goes on as Government Seeks UN Ban," *Baltimore Sun,* October 18, 1992.

7. Jonathan Mayo, "The Novichok Files," *Daily Mail,* March 2, 2019.

8. "Novichok Poisons Two New Victims: Couple Critically Ill in Salisbury Following Contact with Same Nerve Agent Used on Spy Pair Showed Similar Symptoms to Skripals," *Daily Telegraph,* July 5, 2018.

9. Jemma Buckley, "Novichok Assassin 'Pictured Shaking Hands with Putin,'" *Daily Mail,* October 10, 2018.

10. Alicia Sanders-Zakre, "OPCW Confirms Novichok Use," *Arms Control Today* 48, no. 4 (May 2018): 35.

11. Julia Masterson, "Novichok Used in Russia, OPCW Finds," *Arms Control Today* 50, no. 9 (November 2020): 25–26.

12. Masterson.

13. "Measurement and Signature Intelligence (MASINT)," FAS Intelligence Resource Program, last updated May 8, 2000, https://irp.fas.org/program/masint.htm#:~:text=Measurement %20and%20Signature%20Intelligence%20(MASINT)%20is%20scientific%20and%20technical %20intelligence,sensors%20for%20the%20purpose%20of.

14. "Foreign Instrumentation Signals Intelligence (FISINT)," FS-1037C, last updated August 23, 2000, https://www.its.bldrdoc.gov/fs-1037/dir-016/_2290.htm.

15. Raytheon Missile Systems, "Application to Renew WF2XLI, File No. 0036-EX-CR-2017: Explanation of Experiments and Need for Experimental License for Use of Several Frequency Bands for Lab and Factory Missile Communications Testing," 2–3, https://apps.fcc.gov/els /GetAtt.html?id=187204&x=.

16. FME acquisition efforts are described in declassified documents in the National Security Archive, "Scavenging for Intelligence: The US Government's Secret Search for Foreign Objects during the Cold War," https://nsarchive.gwu.edu/briefing-book/intelligence/2018-01 -31/scavenging-intelligence-us-governments-secret-search-foreign-objects-during-cold-war.

17. "Nellis AFB Heavy Military Equipment Move," https://sam.gov/opp/3e51df19a07740 638ef639d3eff33c37/view.

18. GlobalSecurity.org, "Weapons of Mass Destruction (WMD): Electromagnetic Isotope Separation Uranium Enrichment," July 24, 2011, https://www.globalsecurity.org/wmd/intro /u-electromagnetic.htm#:~:text=The%20first%20large%2Dscale%20uranium,and%20their %20ability%20to%20procure.

19. GlobalSecurity.org, "Iraq Survey Group Final Report: Electromagnetic Isotope Separation Uranium Enrichment," https://www.globalsecurity.org/wmd/library/report/2004/isg -final-report/isg-final-report_vol2_nuclear-12.htm.

20. GlobalSecurity.org, "Weapons of Mass Destruction"; Energy.gov, "Oak Ridge Environmental Management: 30 Years in 30 Minutes," https://www.energy.gov/orem/about-us/history.

21. Council on Foreign Relations, "Iraq: Weapons Inspections: 1991–1998," February 3, 2005, https://www.cfr.org/backgrounder/iraq-weapons-inspections-1991-1998.

22. Commission on the Intelligence Capabilities of the United States Regarding Weapons of Mass Destruction, *Report to the President of the United States March 31, 2005, Official Government Edition* (Washington, DC: US Government Printing Office, 2005), 9–10.

23. Center for Evidence-Based Medicine, University of Oxford, "Catalogue of Bias: Confirmation Bias," https://catalogofbias.org/biases/confirmation-bias/.

24. "Why We Tend to Rely Heavily upon the First Piece of Information We Receive; Anchoring Bias, Explained," Decision Lab, https://thedecisionlab.com/biases/anchoring-bias.

25. Center for Evidence-Based Medicine, University of Oxford, "Catalogue of Bias: Availability Bias," https://catalogofbias.org/biases/availability-bias/.

26. Brian Lessenberry, "Intelligence Integration and the Syrian CW Threat," Center for Strategic and International Studies, February 18, 2015, 2–4, https://www.csis.org/analysis/intelligence-integration-and-syrian-cw-threat.

27. Arms Control Association, "Timeline of Syrian Chemical Weapons Activity, 2012–2022," last updated May 2021, https://www.armscontrol.org/factsheets/Timeline-of-Syrian-Chemical-Weapons-Activity.

28. Arms Control Association.

29. Lessenberry, "Intelligence Integration," 6–7.

30. Lessenberry, 5.

31. White House, Office of the Press Secretary, "Government Assessment of the Syrian Government's Use of Chemical Weapons on August 21, 2013," August 30, 2013, 3–4, https://obamawhitehouse.archives.gov/the-press-office/2013/08/30/government-assessment-syrian-government-s-use-chemical-weapons-august-21.

32. White House.

33. Lessenberry, "Intelligence Integration," 5.

34. Lessenberry, 7.

35. White House, "Government Assessment."

36. White House, 4.

37. White House.

38. Arms Control Association, "Timeline."

39. Lessenberry, "Intelligence Integration," 8.

40. Arms Control Association, "Timeline."

41. Lessenberry, "Intelligence Integration," 5–6.

42. Lessenberry.

43. Arms Control Association, "Timeline."

44. Arms Control Association.

45. Daryl G. Kimball, "CWC States Update List of Banned Chemicals," *Arms Control Today*, December 2019, 10, 32, 49.

46. Masterson, "Novichok."

47. Masterson.

48. For more information on Bellingcat, see https://www.bellingcat.com/about/, which describes itself as "an independent international collective of researchers, investigators and citizen journalists using open source and social media investigation to probe a variety of subjects—from . . . crimes against humanity, to tracking the use of chemical weapons and conflicts worldwide. With staff and contributors in more than 20 countries around the world, we operate in a unique field where advanced technology, forensic research, journalism, investigations, transparency and accountability come together."

49. Bellingcat, "'If It Hadn't Been for the Prompt Work of the Medics': FSB Officer Inadvertently Confesses Murder Plot to Navalny," December 21, 2020, https://www.bellingcat.com/news/uk-and-europe/2020/12/21/if-it-hadnt-been-for-the-prompt-work-of-the-medics-fsb-officer-inadvertently-confesses-murder-plot-to-navalny/.

50. Tim Lister, Clarissa Ward, and Sebastian Shulka, "Russian Opposition Leader Alexey Navalny Dupes Spy into Revealing How He Was Poisoned," *CNN Wire Service*, December 21, 2020, https://www.cnn.com/2020/12/21/Europe/Russia-Navalny-poisoning-underpants-ward /index.html.

51. Michael Morell and Maja Lehnus, CBS News, "Thwarting Syria's Nuclear Program— Intelligence Matters, Declassified," May 26, 2021, https://www.cbsnews.com/news/thwarting -syrias-nuclear-program-intelligence-matters-declassified-podcast/.

52. Morell and Lehnus.

53. Nuclear Threat Initiative, "Al Kibar Plutonium Reactor, Syria," December 6, 2013; James Martin Center for Nonproliferation Studies at Monterey Institute of International Studies, https://www.youtube.com/watch?v=kz6xVVMa2nM.

54. Morell and Lehnus, "Thwarting Syria's Nuclear Program."

55. Morell and Lehnus.

56. Nuclear Threat Initiative, "Al Kibar Plutonium Reactor."

57. Michael V. Hayden, *Playing to the Edge: American Intelligence in the Age of Terror* (New York: Penguin Press, 2016).

58. Morell and Lehnus, "Thwarting Syria's Nuclear Program."

59. Morell and Lehnus.

60. Morell and Lehnus.

61. Morell and Lehnus.

62. Morell and Lehnus.

63. Morell and Lehnus.

64. Morell and Lehnus.

65. Morell and Lehnus.

66. Morell and Lehnus.

67. Nuclear Threat Initiative, "Al Kibar Plutonium Reactor."

68. Nuclear Threat Initiative.

69. Nuclear Threat Initiative. This reference also notes that in February 2009, the IAEA issued "a follow-up report on Al-Kibar ... revealing that additional examination of environmental samples had yielded further traces of uranium ... (and) characteristics of the uranium particles found at the site made it unlikely the uranium came from Israeli munitions, as Syria had previously suggested."

70. PBS, *Frontline*, "The October '02 National Intelligence Estimate."

71. Commission on the Intelligence Capabilities of the United States Regarding Weapons of Mass Destruction, *Report to the President of the United States March 31, 2005, Official Government Edition* (Washington, DC: US Government Printing Office, 2005), 215, 216, 225, 226, 228, 231, 234, 241.

72. PBS, *Frontline*, "October '02 National Intelligence Estimate."

73. "Novichok £11m Bill" [Lancs Region], *Daily Star*, November 30, 2018.

6

LEADERSHIP ANALYSIS: THE WORLDWIDE WHO'S WHO

Jeffrey Waggett

WHAT IS LEADERSHIP ANALYSIS?

Nothing has permeated the American cultural zeitgeist quite like the concept of leadership. An Internet search for the term "leadership" returns over 60,000 results in the book section on Amazon.[1] Neither Spotify nor Apple Podcasts states an exact number, but the same search results in pages upon pages of podcasts.[2] The popular TED website boasts 419 talks, 245 blog posts, and 326 events about "leadership."[3] One can read why leaders should eat last, why leaders should make their bed, and why leaders should be paranoid. Books enumerate leadership's five levels, seven successful habits, and twenty-one irrefutable laws. More seriously, one can read about leadership in a specific context—in business, nonprofits, or government; as a first-time, middle, or senior manager; or for women, minorities, or members of the LGBTQ+ community. Or maybe the most discerning students of leadership would only trust information gleaned directly from leaders themselves—perhaps a former US president, professional sports coach, or *Fortune* 500 CEO.

But at least everyone works from the same page and agrees on the definition of leadership, right? No. Amid the mountain of leadership literature, the ways that writers define "leadership" no doubt numbers in the thousands. Here is just one example. In the mid-1990s at the University of Richmond, my first-year leadership studies curriculum revolved around John Gardner's definition of leadership. An educator, Gardner served under six presidents, founded the advocacy group Common Cause, and, appropriately for this book, served in the Office of Strategic Services (the predecessor of the CIA) during World War II. In his book *On Leadership*, Gardner defined the concept as "the process of persuasion or example by which an individual (or leadership team) induces a group to pursue objectives held by the leader or shared by the leader and his or her followers."[4]

In Gardner's view, leadership falls under the larger topic of "accomplishment of group purpose," asserting that "shared values are the bedrock on which leaders build the edifice of group achievement."[5] Gardner was far from the first to equate virtuous principles with proper leadership, but this value-based foundation of leadership has only become more entrenched in today's mass market leadership literature. Evaluating a "good" versus a "bad" leader is now often based on personal appeal and how followers are treated. Is the leader relatable? Authentic? Does the leader have a positive attitude and uplifting vision? Are followers included in the decision-making process? Is the leader–follower relationship beneficial to both sides? Does the leader inspire or motivate followers to be their best selves or accomplish their highest personal potential? None of these questions are particularly relevant to an intelligence analyst—and popular contemporary sources on leadership offer little help to understand why.

REFRAMING THE DISCIPLINE AS LEADER ANALYSIS

How, then, does a practitioner explain to those unfamiliar with intelligence analytic disciplines what leadership analysts do? Although the CIA calls it leadership analysis, in the remainder of this chapter, I refer to it as *leader analysis*. This is not a simple matter of semantics. The term "leader analysis" helps the reader differentiate between serious intelligence analysis and airport bookstore, pop culture pseudoscience. For intelligence insiders, the change honors decades of effort to elevate the discipline above simplistic perceptions that our analysts have been mere biographers no better than *People* magazine writers who lack analytic rigor.

Rebranding the discipline as leader analysis would also underscore that my colleagues are less interested in the relativistic, value-laden aspects of contemporary leadership discussions. In fact, overemphasizing its moral aspects would make intelligence assessments of foreign leaders laughably straightforward; Russia's Vladimir Putin—bad leader. China's Xi Jinping—bad leader. Ukraine's Volodymyr Zelensky—great leader! US policymakers would not find this particularly helpful.

Analysts instead need to evaluate their targets in the contexts of the society, culture, and political system where they operate.[6] This helps to ensure that the individual and cultural values of the subject remain the key analytic drivers. Minimizing the influence of their own United States–based values enables analysts to maintain the intellectual detachment required to consider and assess the full range of potential options that a foreign leader may consider. This approach also helps analysts communicate their assessments with as much objectivity as possible and thus enables US policymakers to decide whether and how the US government ultimately engages with foreign officials.

The primary focus of a leader analyst is on *individuals who matter*, which, in the context of intelligence, can be clearly defined as those who promote, hinder, or harm progress on issues of concern to US civilian and military officials. Individuals who matter include those beyond a country's titular head, the political and economic elite, and senior military officers. Analysts may follow figures outside the government, such as rebel groups in exile.[7] They may also work to anticipate upcoming leaders or significant actors beyond the traditional political or military elite. For example, a weapons proliferation analyst and I collaborated in the early 2000s to cowrite the first leadership profile on the then-up-and-coming but soon-to-be-infamous Pakistani nuclear scientist A. Q. Khan, who became a major nuclear proliferator. (At the time, Khan was known only by his actions and reputation; we did not have a photo of him or even know what his voice sounded like.) Other such assessments have been made on Indian nuclear scientists and advisers.[8] Who might matter in the future? Will multibillionaire foreign businesspeople amass more power than sovereign states? Who among them will influence other foreign leaders or have an impact on global politics in new ways?

WHO ARE LEADER ANALYSTS?

Leader analysts are the extroverts of the CIA analytic corps—which is admittedly like being crowned the largest chihuahua in the litter. Within the CIA's introverted Directorate of Analysis (DA), leader analysts have a special esprit de corps based on a unique and proud history. Other CIA offices were organized on the basis of regions of the world or specific technical areas throughout the 1980s and 1990s, but leader analysts worked together in a separate discipline-specific office. This Office of Leadership Analysis (LDA) was created to elevate biographic collection from a central reference function to an analytic discipline equal to political, economic, and military analysis. LDA sought to build and legitimize its rigorous analytical foundation, building on the emerging discipline of political psychology and challenging analysts to develop a range of analytic techniques. LDA fostered a sense of community within this discipline, which survived the dissolution of LDA in the late 1990s and integration of leader analysts into the Agency's regional offices. At that time, leader analysts were often regarded within the DA as mere "biographers"—even as the increasingly sophisticated leadership profile became the most requested and uniformly praised CIA analytic product. The analysts in this discipline bonded over their unique role as intelligence collectors—see the discussion below—and would informally share best practices on how to interview US officials for leader intelligence. Unsurprisingly, leader analysts subsequently formed the DA's first discipline-specific analytic steering group.

I was the first CIA leader analyst hired with an academic degree in leadership studies when I began duty as a graduate fellow in 1997. At that time, my alma mater had just stood up the first undergraduate leadership studies program, when the Jepson School of Leadership Studies opened at the University of Richmond in 1994. Other programs followed, but most leader analysts have academic backgrounds outside leadership studies and represent a wide variety of experiences. An effective CIA leader analysis team combines functional generalists with subject matter experts and includes a diverse cross-section of backgrounds—making the leader analysis discipline open to everyone.

HOW THE DISCIPLINE FUNCTIONS

What do analysts assess once they identify foreign individuals who matter? Simply stated, all policymaker requirements regarding foreign leaders ultimately boil down to two questions centering on one essential criterion: efficacy. First, how effective is this individual at promoting, hindering, or harming US goals and interests? Second, what information will help policymakers find the most effective and practical approach to support or undermine this individual? Providing input on these two questions for US policymakers requires analysts to evaluate a wide range of issues associated with a foreign leader: motivations, political associations, personal strengths and weaknesses, subject matter expertise, biographic details, and even their physical and mental health (see box 6.1).

Once analysts identify the most influential foreign individuals vis-à-vis the United States, they assess their intentions, plans, and ability to make an impact on US national security. Analysts can then, finally, evaluate options available to policymakers that may potentially shape these foreign leaders' behaviors to benefit US policy or at least constrain their attempts to undermine US goals.

Leader analysts study how key foreign leaders maneuver and exert influence within their political system to achieve their desired goals—in other words, how they demonstrate leadership within their own cultural norms. Analysts must be careful to convey this process to US policymakers in an objective and accurate way. Assessments of leaders are no place for overly emotive, dramatic, or evocative language. In general, analysts prefer to use specific terms that have well-established academic rigor and are clearly supported by available reporting. A single adjective can have a profound influence. For example, the journalist Melissa Chan makes a compelling case that the most accurate way to describe present-day China is "fascist." She cites specific leadership methods employed by Chinese president Xi Jinping and actions of the Chinese government that are consistent with the definition of the word. Her editors complained in 2009 that describing China as "authoritarian" was too much

BOX 6.1: INSIDE THE BODIES AND MINDS OF FOREIGN LEADERS

Foreign leaders' physical and mental health can affect their behavior and decision-making. The prospect of death can impel a hasty act to secure a legacy, while chronic conditions like hypertension, diabetes, depression, or cancer can deplete their stamina, fog their memories, or create other barriers to clear thinking. Thus, intelligence analysts need to consider potential ailments found in the body and mind when assessing a leader's decisions. For example, monitoring the ailing Soviet octogenarian leadership of the 1980s was a tipoff to the succession process that brought the spry Mikhail Gorbachev to power. Similarly, the image of the ailing and alcoholic Boris Yeltsin being steadied by President Bill Clinton during a presidential meeting in the 1990s reflected Russia's depleted status after the end of the Cold War.[9]

Although not formally part of the leader analysis discipline, almost from the CIA's beginning there have been specialists who examine how mental and medical conditions can affect leaders' decisions. Over the years, these analysts have toiled within a variety of centers, including the Medical and Psychological Analysis Center and, later, the Center for Analysis of Personality and Political Behavior. In practice, this VIP medical group is made up of seasoned physicians, psychiatrists, psychologists, and sometimes sociologists. They must have superior analytic skills and be able to make what some have called "remote diagnosis" based on very indirect and incomplete medical or psychological information.[10] Like leader analysts, they depend primarily on observing a "patient" from afar, reviewing videos of leaders' speeches and interactions with other world leaders, and combing through what limited human and technical intelligence reports reveal about the state of a leader's physical or mental condition.[11]

Examining the state of a world leader's health has never been easy and usually is controversial. A few cases illustrate this. In the 1979 Iranian Revolution, policymakers were puzzled by the shah's inability to take vigorous measures to quell the unrest; few knew that he was suffering from late-stage leukemia and was receiving treatment from French cancer specialists.[12] Almost contemporaneously, the Carter administration was reading leader profiles of Anwar Sadat and Menachem Begin, who suffered from bouts of depression, prepared in part by the head of the Center for Analysis of Personality and Political Behavior, Dr. Jerrold Post. During the Clinton administration, senior intelligence officials also were briefing congressional committees on former Haitian president Aristide's mental illness and treatment in a Canadian mental institution before taking office. A final example of such analysis is Dr. Post's congressional testimony regarding Saddam Hussein's personality, in which he challenged the notion of Saddam being a "madman."[12] Instead, he characterized him as "dangerous in the extreme" but "a judicious, effective political calculator who is by no means irrational, using different premises of rationality."[14]

US policymakers have both applauded these medical insights and also shuddered when they became public. The Carter White House was effusive in its praise of the leadership profiles before the Camp David meetings, leading to Dr. Post being awarded the CIA Medal of Meritorious Service. Conversely, Clinton administration officials dismissed the revelations of Aristide's mental health issues and were furious about senior intelligence officials' congressional testimony.[15]

editorializing; she countered by noting how many articles written before the 2008 Summer Olympic Games in Beijing that failed to mention Chinese authoritarianism influenced readers in a much subtler way.[16] Like Chan, analysts argue over the proper way to describe foreign leaders and their methods and certainly do not default to how foreign leaders might describe themselves or their country. (For instance, the Democratic People's Republic of Korea—North Korea—is certainly neither a democracy nor a republic.) CIA assessments also assiduously avoid trendy leadership jargon or moralistic buzzwords, although the judicious use of value-laden adjectives (e.g., brutal, repressive, collaborative, inclusive) is often the most efficient and effective way to brief US intelligence consumers. They, after all, understand human motivation and actions through the lens of US ideals and standards. Beyond effective communication, however, value judgments lie outside the realm of this discipline as well as others at the CIA.

Leader analysis can take different forms, depending on the policymaker's policy focus and the amount of information desired by US officials. Two-page leadership profiles focus exclusively on an individual foreign leader and his or her individual circumstances and point of view. The similarly brief leadership note may complement a profile with a deep dive into a related topic—perhaps a more detailed look at the leader's changing position on a critical issue or the evolving power dynamics within his or her political party. Analysts may provide longer assessments to introduce a US policymaker to a new player on the scene, examine issues like succession that touch on multiple leaders, or offer specialized insights such as medical analysis or psychological profiles.

Leadership Profiles

The most requested CIA analytic product—year after year—is the two-page leadership profile. Analysts tailor leadership profiles (LPs) to prepare US policymakers and officials for meetings with their foreign counterparts. These meetings range from reoccurring, lower-level diplomatic or military exchanges to extraordinary presidential summits. For example, President Jimmy Carter was provided three LPs before his 1978 Camp David summit: one each on Egyptian president Anwar Sadat and Israeli prime minister Menachem Begin, and he was also given a third LP comparing their personalities and negotiating styles (see box 6.2). After his diplomatic success, Carter thanked the CIA and singled out the LPs for special praise: "After spending 13 days with the two principals," he said, "I wouldn't change a word."[17]

The structure of LPs has remained stable for decades while still proving to be remarkably flexible. Over time, the discipline has expanded profiles to cover subjects with whom US officials cannot (or do not want to) meet, such as terrorist leaders. Creating an inaugural LP on a new *individual who matters* helps to coalesce current leader analysis, identify intelligence gaps, draft intelligence requirements, and ensure that the individual remains a focus of US intelligence for as long as the subject remains of interest or a threat.

LPs follow a formula and are ensured to be timely, useful, and relevant, whether the requester is meeting with the profile subject for the first or fiftieth time. First comes practical personal information, then more details on the individual's motivations, followed by personal background and personality traits. For example, an LP tells US policymakers how to pronounce the leader's name, what positions and titles she currently holds and previously held, and, if a photograph is available, what she looks like. The opening paragraphs could discuss issues ranging from the foreign leader's goals

---

BOX 6.2: DECLASSIFIED LEADERSHIP PROFILE OF
EGYPT'S PRESIDENT, ANWAR SADAT, AUGUST 23, 1978

Anwar al-SADAT   EGYPT
(Phonetic: saDAHT)
President (since September 1970)
Addressed as: Mr. President

When Anwar al-Sadat, a former revolutionary and ardent nationalist who rose from peasant origins, assumed the Presidency after the death of Jamal 'Abd al-Nasir, it was widely assumed that he had neither the strength nor the political astuteness to be successful. He has, however, long since shaken his image ██████████████ and proved to be a moderate leader and a pragmatic politician and diplomat. He has become known for his realism, political acumen, and capacity for surprising, courageous and dramatic decisions. ████████

██

██ He has continued to seek a peace settlement with remarkable self-confidence and optimism in the face of both risk and failure.

Leadership Style
Sadat's dominance of the decision-making process—especially in foreign policy—has become increasingly evident in the peace talks with Israel: senior foreign affairs advisers are not always certain what the President has in mind, and they must refer major decisions to Sadat personally.

██

Sadat ██ believes that Egyptians are superior to other Arabs. He takes pride in his peasant origins and in his reputation for being sensitive to his people's needs. He wants to go down in history as the man who improved the economic and social well-being of the ordinary Egyptian. Sadat has, however, far less understanding of or interest in economic matters than he has in foreign affairs or politics, and he devotes little time to this major problem area. A consummate politician, he looks at most issues in political terms, and if he is confronted with policy problems in which political factors and economic considerations are in conflict, his decision is likely to be informed by the former.

██

Personal Data
In accordance with his upbringing, Sadat remain a deeply religious man. He speaks good English but he does not always pick up nuances or follow complex reasoning. Soft spoken and serious, the 59-year-old President is warm in manner. His wife, Jihan, is an elegant, graceful woman. The couple has four children.

23 August 1978

Source: Leadership Profile of Anwar al-Sadat, August 23, 1978, declassified, https://www.cia.gov/readingroom/docs/1978-08-23b.pdf. There are several redacted sections, indicated by blacked-out text.

---

or motivations for an upcoming meeting to whether this individual has the authority, connections, or expertise necessary to advance or hinder issues on the meeting agenda. Perhaps the foreign official is more pro-US relative to their political or ministerial rivals, so that a positive outcome with his or her US counterpart would boost their career prospects. Or maybe the profile subject was the primary decision-maker on an issue when she last met with US officials, but her influence has waned significantly since a protégé became embroiled in a scandal.

The next paragraph or two would probably address the broader domestic political context in which the subject is operating. For example, will the recent downward trend in public opinion polls dampen the risk tolerance of a previously audacious leader—or make her double down on a political gamble? After this point, the profile would present additional leader analysis based on past career experiences and other background material.

Achieving timeliness with a leadership profile is generally easy by providing the most up-to-date intelligence reporting just before the meeting with the foreign leader. Usefulness is also generally straightforward. Profiles, like intelligence products provided by analysts in other disciplines, typically determine what is useful based on topics and issues on the meeting agenda or those prioritized by the US official. For example, if the CIA is providing a senior Pentagon official with assessments of a counterpart military's capabilities and resources, that official might wish to know the visiting defense ministry official's attitudes toward military-to-military relations with Washington, her commitment to raising her country's defense spending, and her position on potential arms sales.

Relevance can be harder. US policymakers look to leader analysts for insights that will enable them to create a personal bond with their counterparts. Any personal detail might be relevant, but only if the analyst knows enough about the foreign leader *and* their US counterpart. For a US official who is an expert skier, knowing that her counterpart grew up near a world-famous ski slope could be useful, but not so much for other US officials. Shifting contexts and leaders who cover broad or multiple portfolios is also challenging. The fact that a foreign official graduated from a university known for its conservative economic philosophy may be relevant for a US commerce official before trade talks but is less so when that foreign official later attends a multilateral meeting on a noneconomic topic.

Leadership profiles are most effective when analysts can tailor their content with timely analysis and context for a specific consumer and purpose. But the sheer volume of interactions between US officials and their foreign interlocutors makes it impossible for leader analysts to shape and customize every LP to meet every need. The set structure of LPs allows analysts to retain unchanging biographic data at an LP's end. Then, my colleagues and I kept multiple introductory paragraphs on hand, which were updated and slotted into the LPs used for different US policymakers. Depending on the context, we might highlight how a senior foreign political leader was facing internal difficulties in one area—say, their economic agenda—but remains steadfast and influential in her government's foreign policy. A stock general leadership profile that addressed a balance of issues was used for last-minute requests. Analysts also maintain leadership notes that detail critical issues currently affecting a profiled leader.

Notes are essentially expanded—but still brief—sections of an LP that either deserve a more nuanced look at a relevant topic or require a discussion of multiple leaders.

Succession Analysis

Unique among the analytic disciplines and in defiance of the inherent ambiguity of intelligence in general, leader analysts can definitively state with 100 percent accuracy that a foreign individual who matters will not matter forever. Leaders leave office through retirement, well-established processes like elections, extrajudicial military coups, or—ultimately and inevitably—death. In whatever manner a succession occurs, US policymakers need to know whether new leaders mean more of the same or are indicative of a potential seismic shift for a country or entity. Leadership succession issues represent the bread and butter of long-form leader assessments.

Most often, succession analysis is presented through a variety of products that build off each other and present different facets of the story in different ways. A foundational intelligence assessment might introduce a potential new successor, detailing her views toward the United States, how her strengths and weakness might affect her advancement, and clearly outlining what we do and do not know about her. A stand-alone graphic may follow up with a detailed overview of her allies and adversaries, their placement within the government, and their relationships with the current regime. Over time, additional intelligence assessments would address how significant events—such as a terrorist attack or the arrest of a corrupt protégé—might affect her advancement or views toward the United States. Finally, succession analysis culminates with an assessment of how her success or failure will help, hinder, or harm US interests.

The ascension of Mikhail Gorbachev—the eighth and last leader of the Soviet Union—represents one of the best (declassified) examples of CIA succession analysis.[18] CIA leader analysts correctly tracked how the personal motivations of two powerful rivals played a pivotal role in selecting Soviet leaders in the mid-1980s. Soviet defense minister Ustinov and Soviet foreign minister Gromyko—eager to maintain their strong influence in defense and foreign policy—joined forces in early 1984 to back the politically weak, seventy-two-year-old Konstantin Chernenko. Eighteen months later, Chernenko became the third elderly Soviet leader to die in office over a three-year period, and the Soviets were all but forced to turn to the next generation of leaders. CIA leader analysts had previously identified fifty-four-year-old Gorbachev as the most probable selection, despite perceptions among Soviet powerbrokers that his policy views could be "too pro-American." After succeeding Chernenko in 1985, Gorbachev instituted a dramatic series of domestic political reforms and foreign policy initiatives that ultimately helped end not only the Cold War but also the Soviet Union itself. Gromyko, who died in 1989, lived long enough to see how the series of rapid Soviet leadership successions—in which he played a key role—led to profound, yet unintended, systematic changes. He was staunchly anti-American and certainly would not have appreciated the irony.

The declassified CIA succession assessment that correctly pointed to Gorbachev's rise offers a glimpse into a few of the analytic methods used by leader analysts. For example, content analysis evaluates a leader's published statements—with a focus on themes and action verbs—to identify leadership traits, motivations, and even cognitive styles. Analysts twice cited Gorbachev's rhetoric as support for his more pro-American views, with one of these examples directly contrasting Gorbachev with his main rival. Timeline analysis helps compare individual experiences with others, contextualize key life and world events, and identify common traits of previous successful leaders—like taking on prominent and important roles. Analysts referenced a report that said Gorbachev was perceived to be "in charge" in Moscow when Chernenko was on vacation, suggesting that a Politburo decision had accorded him the honor. Finally, analysts evaluated Soviet group dynamics and elite preferences to identify mentor links and common values. The assessment contains multiple references to Gorbachev's positive relationship and policy commonalities with Ustinov, who supported Gorbachev even when his approaches may have been outside the political norm.

Long-Form Analysis

Unlike leadership profiles, long-form assessments do not use a standard template or a consistently structured format. In addition to succession issues, long-form leader analysis offers more detailed evaluations of foreign leaders or covers specific leadership topics of interest. For example, in 2002, I drafted the first in-depth assessment of Vice President Hu Jintao—China's putative next-generation successor—before his first visit to the United States to meet with Vice President Dick Cheney. A two-page LP would have simply not been sufficient for such a momentous occasion. More recently, CIA leader analysts almost certainly provided the president with long-form assessments of Putin's mind-set, decision-making process, key influencers, and other critical topics in the run-up to Russia's invasion of Ukraine. Leader analysts also frequently contribute to the long-form products of other analytic disciplines—usually in the form of boxed text outside the main narrative—to provide a brief look into how leadership dynamics may affect a political, economic, or military decision. More broadly, leader analysts provide insights to inform community-wide strategic assessments like National Intelligence Estimates.

POLICY SUPPORT: FROM TACTICAL TO STRATEGIC

Leader analysts serve a broad and diverse range of US policymakers, from the president to the vice president, Cabinet secretaries, Joint Chiefs of Staff, National Security

Council officials, and more. Any US policymaker who meets with or needs to know more about a foreign official or about the impact of leadership struggles is a potential consumer of this discipline's analysis. As is discussed below, they are also potential intelligence sources. Analysts frequently provide intelligence briefings for the most tactical situation of all: one-to-one meetings between two individuals. In my own career, I have prepared numerous US policymakers on individuals within my portfolio of Chinese foreign policy leaders. Still, I was nervous preceding a 2001 briefing of the secretary of energy on a senior Chinese diplomat. Up until then, I had usually provided US officials with a written analysis or, less frequently, with in-person briefings well in advance of meeting their Chinese counterparts. This briefing, however, had been delayed several times and was taking place at the last minute—literally. The secretary was meeting the diplomat right after my briefing, to the point that I was instructed to depart his office by a secondary exit to avoid coming face-to-face with the visiting diplomat when he entered the secretary's office.

My colleagues and I always knew that what we told US officials could shape how a key US policy objective might be handled in an upcoming meeting. Every analyst accepts the pressure of representing the CIA, knowing any misstep or forgotten talking point might have immediate consequences. But now I knew that the leader assessment on which I was about to brief the secretary would be fresh in his mind and—within minutes after my departure—probably affect his first interaction with this Chinese official. The importance of our discipline never seemed more real than at that moment; but thankfully, my brief proved on the mark.

At other times, analysts must find novel ways to prepare for face-to-face meetings. In the case of busy US policymakers, they often absorb information about other people more efficiently and viscerally through visual media. Before President George W. Bush's first meeting with Chinese president Jiang Zemin in October 2001, we produced a series of video leadership profiles that Bush and his advisers watched on Air Force One en route to Shanghai. In one video, we included a clip of Jiang—who loved being on the world stage—lumbering halfway across a stage to embrace UN secretary general Kofi Annan in a slow-motion, awkward hug. This scene—which could have never been as effectively conveyed in a written product—reportedly alarmed White House personnel, who directed US officials in charge of protocol to ensure that the president would not be subjected to such a public display of warmth from a communist leader. Videos have proven to be effective tools, including those produced earlier for President Reagan, who as a former actor particularly enjoyed watching CIA-prepared video profiles of his foreign counterparts.

In addition to such tactical support, the discipline is engaged in supporting strategic decisions, often in conjunction with assessments from the CIA's other disciplines. In these cases, leader analysts must address issues that affect the highest US national security priorities, where conveying the mind-set of foreign leaders can complement assessments of an adversary's political objectives or military capabilities. Assessing leaders' motivations, redlines, and tolerance for costs and risks is more helpful than attempting to forecast a leader's or leadership's specific response to a hypothetical situation.

For example, in the early 2000s, I found myself on an aircraft carrier stationed at a strategically important US naval installation in East Asia. Senior US Navy planners were (and still are) laser-focused on the US Seventh Fleet's probable role in a US response to a potential conflict between China and Taiwan. For nearly an hour, my three CIA military analyst colleagues answered questions from a panel of high-level US Navy officers—expertly diving deep into esoteric detail on Chinese military doctrine, capabilities, and tactics relevant to a potential cross-Strait invasion of Taiwan. As the briefing was about to end, a US Navy captain, who had been quiet up until then, suddenly pointed at me:

> Captain: "I have a question for the leadership guy. I'm in charge of fleet strategic planning. My question is: what percentage of Chinese invaders would we have to eliminate to convince Chinese leaders not to send a second wave?"
>
> Me: "I'm sorry, sir. I am not sure I can answer that for you."
>
> Captain: "Why? Does the CIA not know? Is the intelligence not specific enough?"
>
> Me: "No, sir. I mean a percentage would be misleading in the overall context of your question. Saying the answer is 100% would imply the US military could eliminate every invader in the first wave and Beijing would then call off a second wave. But that is not true because, regardless, there definitely will be a second wave."
>
> Captain: "And a third?"
>
> Me: "Yes. And followed by whatever number of waves might require equipping Chinese soldiers with water wings to swim across the Strait."
>
> Me: "Sir, the only way to stop a second wave is to prevent the first one from happening. No Chinese leader—and possibly also the entire party—could survive making the political call to stop an invasion of Taiwan once it started."
>
> Captain: "And any China/Taiwan conflict would require planning for an inevitable expansion outside the Taiwan Strait theater."

In this case, the military analysts had fully briefed on their assessment of what a cross-Strait invasion might look like, while the leader analyst focused on the motivations and political calculus that might drive China's political leaders to order such an attack. Hence, the implication of our briefings was that preventing a wider war with Beijing would not—could not—be achieved through military means alone.

CIA analysts also tackle strategic issues associated with potential leadership changes. US policymakers are keenly interested in how they can foster or promote up-and-coming foreign leaders who are favorably inclined toward the United States, especially when a current crop of leaders is perceived as roadblocks to US interests. The effects of new leadership can occur over time as a new generation comes to power or when a leader is dramatically replaced or suddenly dies. Analysts attempt to identify potential new leaders early in their careers or as soon as possible when opposition forces emerge. Importantly, actions by US officials might influence the prospects of a rising leader. Requesting a meeting with or even merely acknowledging a new political star in some adversarial countries, or even some allied with the United States, may damage that leader's prospects. Or, counterintuitively, a well-timed engagement on a specific issue with such an individual can provide a boost to that person's standing. In other cases, such as with terrorist groups, analysts may warn US officials that a leadership change would be, relatively speaking, detrimental because prospective successors would be even more radical and dangerous—especially if US counterterrorism operations were believed responsible for the death of that leader.

Leader analysts can be challenged by the question of when to provide US policymakers with their assessments of potential leadership changes. Such successions often play out over many years. For example, during George W. Bush's presidency, while I was serving as an assistant to Michael Morell, the president's briefer, I would often be asked how a President's Daily Brief item could be improved. One day, a PDB article analyzing China's ongoing generational leadership succession came from my own office. Morell asked me "What's wrong with this?" Not seeing a problem, I blurted out: "Nothing, but why now?" I had passed the test when he nodded, yet I could not help thinking—but if not now, when? In this case, President Bush—whose father had represented the United States in Beijing before he led the CIA—had a personal interest in China, which perhaps merited addressing the Chinese leadership succession in the PDB more often than we may have otherwise.

ANALYSTS AS COLLECTORS

Just as this discipline is unique in the kinds of analysis it performs, it also plays a more direct role in the collection of information on foreign leaders. While Directorate of Operations (DO) case officers can involve analysts from any discipline in the debriefing of clandestine assets (as mentioned in other chapters), only leader analysts operate as their own "targeters" and collectors.

Every leader analyst's portfolio consists of a certain type of leader (e.g., Russian military commanders or Pakistani foreign policy officials). Analysts work with the DO's collection management officers (CMOs) to identify information gaps associated with those targets. In addition, analysts also keep track of people who have direct overt experience and contact with these key leaders as potential sources. Together with CMOs, they determine whether these individuals could best fill information gaps and, if so, how they can be approached. This is essentially the same targeting process used to guide clandestine intelligence collection in the DO.

Once identified, the analyst will seek opportunities to engage these individuals for interviews. The most obvious sought-out "sources" are US policymakers who meet with foreign leaders on a regular basis in an official capacity. In these instances, US consumers of leader analysis are also intelligence sources—an aspect unique to this analytic discipline. US officials might meet with their foreign counterparts during official travel overseas, during their postings at US diplomatic and military postings, at public events, or even in social settings on occasion. Analysts on occasion travel overseas to collect intelligence directly from these US officials. If appropriate, DO officers will support analyst meetings with foreign intelligence partners; for example, a friendly foreign intelligence service might have more interactions with a third country's foreign diplomatic or military services than would be the case for the US intelligence service. After an interview, analysts capture what they have learned in official analytic collection memos, which are then coordinated for use in future finished intelligence products. (Analysts ensure that a US policymaker is aware when a leader assessment contains information gleaned from that very same policymaker to avoid dangerous cases of "circular reporting.")

In countries with a free (or at least relatively open) civil society, analysts may also seek out other identified individuals such as US and foreign academic experts and businesspeople who have met with key leadership targets. Conversely, a leader analyst who covers an authoritarian country would have fewer opportunities for interviewing such sources, even if it were safe to do so. Analysts would then focus their collection efforts on identifying third-country officials and subject matter experts who may meet with leaders of the target country. These analysts would more often visit these third-party countries or those with interests that align with the United States.

Back in Washington, leader analysts must be familiar with and track the activities of many different US government agencies—not just the national security apparatus. Often, up-and-coming foreign leaders are not stovepiped in their own political systems to positions tied to their potential future areas of influence. For example, an analyst who covers South African economic leaders may often interview US officials at the departments of Commerce and the Treasury about those individuals. But if the political protégé of an African finance minister was serving at its Ministry of Forests,

Fisheries, and the Environment, that leader analyst might want to debrief US officials at the Environmental Protection Agency who had met with this rising political figure.

Leader analysts conduct interviews with these various potential sources to collect subjective observations and background information. They will ask questions about the foreign official's personality, subject matter expertise, willingness to engage outside their official talking points, level of deference to their colleagues, policy consistency with previous meetings, and similar topics. Analysts will also collect previously unknown facts about the foreign leader, such as educational background, previous professional experience, biographic details, or even personal interests and hobbies.

While the discipline has such a unique role in collecting information on foreign leaders, it must also guard against several pitfalls. First, leader analysts must be aware of their own personal biases by virtue of being the collector of information they must then analyze. In his seminal work *Psychology of Intelligence Analysis*, the veteran CIA officer Richards Heuer discusses the cognitive bias inherent in information that is "vivid, concrete, and personal."[19] Unlike data gleaned from written intelligence reports produced by others, leader analysts are personally engaged in the initial collection of information via an interview. The analytic danger that Heuer identifies is clear: "Information that people perceive directly, that they hear with their own ears or see with their own eyes, is likely to have greater impact than information received secondhand that may have greater evidential value."[20] Analysts as collectors must mitigate against this "vividness bias" through a deliberate coordination process with other analysts of their postinterview reports as well as any finished intelligence based on these interviews. Analysts cannot allow themselves to become enamored with their own collection efforts to the detriment of the wholistic picture presented by all-source reporting.

Second, analysts must also understand how US policymaker bias affects their ability to effectively brief and debrief US officials. Generally, most high-level US policymakers are "people persons." The CIA trailblazer Helene Boatner—the inaugural director of the previously mentioned Office of Leadership Analysis—observed that US policymakers have a particular view of how the world "should operate" and regard the present world as "shapeable."[21] These officials, therefore, view meetings with foreign leaders as prime opportunities to move the world toward how things should be. This confidence and vision can skew their assessments of foreign counterparts' personal agendas and influence within their governments.

After meeting with a foreign leader, however, the "vividness" bias can begin to affect US officials' own reporting on such exchanges. They may even stop reading leadership profiles of leaders they meet with frequently or think they know well. Analysts must account for this bias, especially if our assessment of a foreign official changes. But analysts can do only so much when the vividness bias leads a US official to develop erroneous initial impressions of a foreign contact. CIA leader analysis—even when meticulously thought out and based on a range of multiple sources—cannot inform a US policymaker when he believes he has taken the measure of his counterpart's soul. President Bush famously declared exactly that in 2001 after his first meeting with Vladimir Putin, whom Bush evaluated as "very straightforward and trustworthy," an assessment that was not shared by many other observers.[22]

USING OTHER INTELLIGENCE SOURCES

Leader analysts primarily rely on four types of intelligence reporting—diplomatic cables, open source, clandestine HUMINT, and SIGINT—each of which has strengths and weaknesses specific to leader analysis.[23] Overall, this discipline relies primarily on copious amounts of open source and diplomatic reporting, using some clandestinely acquired sources more for the unique insights that foreign leaders would prefer not to acknowledge or have made public. Outside sourcing issues, this discipline requires massive data storage and robust search capabilities to enable analysts to follow a foreign individual over their decades-long careers.

Diplomatic Reporting

State Department reporting offers analysts a treasure trove of information on foreign leaders. Official diplomatic cables from overseas posts summarize meetings between US officials and their foreign counterparts. Analysts can review such reports—which in some cases span years—to assess how a foreign leader's actions and attitudes toward the United States might have shifted. Analysts use a variety of reporting sources, including HUMINT, to determine if a foreign leader is a subject matter expert or generalist; in other cases, analysts can assess how well a foreign official represents government policies. For example, analysts sometimes find that a foreign diplomat's nonpublic views diverge from their public comments.

Like all reporting streams, analysts must be alert to biases introduced by the sources as well as the collectors themselves. Diplomatic reporting from the perspective of American officials can introduce subjectivity problems. Was the foreign leader described as difficult or unknowledgeable because he refused to agree with a US demand? Did US officials report unsubstantiated progress from a meeting because they met with a longtime, affable foreign interlocutor? Political appointees in ambassadorial positions also may carry strong personal agendas that can taint their own reporting. Professional diplomats are incredibly capable and well trained in drafting reporting cables, but they too wish to promote US foreign policies, and their unconscious bias could be to see a glass half full rather than half empty. Analysts must account for this potential confirmation bias and recognize that the

State Department's reporting is generally slower to reflect changing foreign leader circumstances.

Open Source Overload

Leader analysts have a love/hate relationship with open source intelligence. For analysts who cover democratic leaders (or at least those who operate under the eye of a relatively free press), open source intelligence provides access to official and unofficial biographies, interviews with leaders, social media posts, public polling data, investigative journalism, opinions from diverse pundits, fact checkers, and on and on. For other analysts who cover authoritarian leaders in closed political systems, the diversity of open sources may be markedly less, but—perhaps surprisingly to outsiders—the sheer volume remains a challenge.

Collection, therefore, is not the problem. Most leader analysts are awash in a constant stream of open source information. The issue becomes how to store such a vast amount of data and then sorting through it all with a high degree of efficiency. But why store everything? In other analytic disciplines, storage and selection of the most relevant information might be more straightforward when focused on a country's current military, economic, or political developments. Leader analysts, however, may not know which foreign individuals will ultimately be relevant or what piece of information may be useful in the future. There is no singular path to becoming a world leader or influential official, which means that analysts must track many individuals who potentially may or may not matter. And when an individual does rise above the pack to lead, maybe his link to a certain school or relationships with other colleagues led to her rise. Or perhaps a random detail like a hobby has been insignificant for years—until a common love of fly-fishing or baseball or historical novels breaks the ice between a new US ambassador and her foreign counterpart.

Open sources in more closed societies are no less important. Beyond biographic details, analysts pore over long, pedantic official speeches, state-controlled press releases and photographs, and every known propaganda outlet to search for elusive clues, hints, and implications. Did a leader slightly change the wording of standard political dogma during the annual address to the nation on purpose? Why was a military general appearing less frequently in photographs published in the official party magazine? When the new Politburo Standing Committee was introduced, what factors—and more important, who—determined the order the members appeared in line as they walked on stage? Knowing the answers to if, why, and how requires tracking long-standing leadership trends, seeing when these patterns change, and shifting through reams of data to understand the context.

This is possible only when enormous amounts of data are saved and can be searched effectively. Office of Strategic Services researchers during World War II

knew this when they recorded and organized biographic information on Axis leader-
ships in vast, paper-based indexes. Ever since, leader analysts have been a driving
force in information management, keeping the CIA analytic corps at the cutting edge
of advanced, automated data processing and information systems.

Clandestine HUMINT

Clandestine HUMINT reports provide leader analysts a peek behind the decision-
making curtain. Such sources—usually from CIA case officers or the Defense Intelligence Agency's defense attachés—may indicate a civilian or military official's
statements differ from how the individual privately views an issue or plans to address
it. This HUMINT also provides insights into the internal, behind-the-scenes battles
among foreign officials, even as their government might seem in lockstep publicly. It
does not take much imagination to appreciate the value in knowing what your adversary says in private about their peers, colleagues, and you.

Analysts must be extremely careful to avoid overweighing the significance of
information provided via clandestine HUMINT sources. Leader analysts are particularly challenged in three ways. First, this reporting is not inherently "better" simply
because the information was acquired via clandestine collection. Often, how the information was obtained—not its substance—causes a report to be highly classified. Is
it useful to know information in the open press is supported by secret sources with
inside access? Of course. Yet a single clandestine source close to a foreign leader is
rarely the silver bullet for supporting a particular intelligence judgment.

Second, clandestine reporting is no less subject to unconscious cognitive bias than
reports from US diplomats, journalists, or academics. CIA clandestine reports include
source reliability descriptors, and the DO seeks to ensure that analysts understand
the context from which the source is reporting. Diligent analysts in all disciplines
consider the inherent prejudices of each HUMINT source, knowing that praise from
a source within the foreign leader's circle means much less than criticism from that
same source. As the name suggests, all HUMINT sources are humans who can be
biased by personal animosities, ambition, or other self-serving motivations.

Finally, this discipline must keep firmly in mind that HUMINT sources report a
snapshot in time and accept that analysis focused on an individual is perhaps more
fleeting than other disciplines. Even the most reliable and plugged-in clandestine
asset may report information that was 100 percent accurate when passed to a case
officer but was incorrect by the time the analyst reads it. This is especially true during
leadership transitions or before a leader makes a major decision. Jockeying among
up-and-coming leaders can be intense. In closed, authoritarian systems, an analyst
may read a CIA HUMINT report that says the protégé of the current leader is set to
take over; yet the next week, the same clandestine source may report that the protégé's

chief rival will become the next party leader. It is easy to see that both reports can be true when they are provided by the same source. Circumstances and perspectives can change. At other times, two trusted clandestine sources might report the exact opposite information. In the give and take of a leadership succession struggle, both can still be accurate reporting.

The leader analyst must keep HUMINT reporting in the context of other contextual factors and events when trying to anticipate how a foreign leader will act. For example, US intelligence was widely credited with predicting that Russia would invade Ukraine.[24] Let us assume that this assessment was, at least in part, based on reporting from a trusted HUMINT source. How would we evaluate this source if Putin had not invaded? What if a leader analyst told President Biden that Putin, without a doubt, had decided to invade Ukraine, and the United States and its NATO allies then took unprecedented actions (beyond even those that were taken)—immediate, historic levels of economic sanctions; massive NATO troop redeployments; raised strategic nuclear threat levels. And Putin . . . blinked? Should we not trust that clandestine asset again? This hypothetical is simplistic and observable—of course, the HUMINT report was overtaken by events. Most often, however, leader analysts do not have the luxury of a clear cause and effect that would make the evaluation of an "incorrect" HUMINT report this easy and obvious.

SIGINT

By volume, leader analysts use signals intelligence less than the other intelligence sources discussed above. SIGINT rarely provides an immediate and definitive answer to long-term leader analysis questions. Like HUMINT, leader analysts must take information collected via SIGINT with the same grains of salt—humans are biased, subjective, and inaccurate. Furthermore, unlike HUMINT, the leader analyst may not know important information regarding the biases or viewpoints of who is speaking or whether the information being conveyed in the SIGINT was directly observed or obtained second- or thirdhand.

Intercepted communications can, of course, provide insights into how foreign leaders think and what positions foreign officials may take in upcoming meetings with US officials.[25] Over the years, foreign leaders and officials have become far more aware of the possibility of SIGINT collection because of the successful targeting of terrorists since 9/11, advances in computer security technology, increased public sensitivity to privacy issues, and occasional high-profile leaks of US intelligence capabilities. On a rare occasion, a SIGINT report may still provide unique and valuable intelligence that confirms other information or reveals new details. Analysts cannot, however, control or rely on SIGINT as a consistent source of reliable intelligence. In all-source leader analysis, SIGINT represents the serendipitous icing on the cake.

CONCLUSION

Leader analysis as an intelligence discipline has a long, proud history dating back to World War II and the Office of Strategic Services. Yet two key, mutually reinforcing challenges threaten to undermine the distinct and valuable contributions that CIA leader analysts provide to US policymakers.

The first challenge is external. In academia, the field of leadership studies has matured, backed by rigorous research and studied by scholars around the world. But, as the opening of this chapter showed, leadership has become a pop culture buzzword. Everyone views themselves as a leadership expert, and every hot take is deemed equally insightful. At any given moment, hundreds of websites, television shows, and opinion platforms offer fast-and-furious "leader analysis" that too often dramatizes the superficial and trivializes the serious. This sheer volume—loudness and quantity—lowers the quality of discourse and floods reporting channels with data. What was a wave of open source information has become a tsunami. It is easier and more likely than ever for a CIA leader analyst to miss critical information and lose the trust of policymakers, which then only further undermines the value of true expertise.

The second challenge is internal. My career as a CIA leader analyst began in 1997, not long after the disbanding of the Office of Leadership Analysis. At first, my office had two separate teams, one for leader analysis and one for political analysis. Within a few years, the teams were merged into the "leadership politics" team, although each team member remained a leadership or political analyst. Over time, even this distinction has eroded, as analysts have become "dual hatted" and leader analysts have increasingly become "political analysts who write leadership profiles." All disciplines train their practitioners—to some extent—to write and contribute to multidisciplinary analytic assessments. This expectation, however, cannot be confused with having analysts from one discipline write another discipline's products. Preventing this, ironically, requires leadership. Long the smallest analytic cadre, the number of leader analysts is likely to degrade further as the percentage of leader analysts in management continues to fall. This probable development is especially striking as our modern world produces more and more leaders—some of whom exert influence in nontraditional contexts unimaginable even a few years ago. Year after year, US policymakers place a high value on leader analysis. The CIA's Directorate of Analysis should too.

Leader analysts understand that policies do not just happen. Military capabilities are not (yet) autonomous. Economies do not rise and fall on their own, and terrorist attacks are not spontaneous. All are driven by *individuals who matter*. Former US secretary of state and national security adviser Henry Kissinger once remarked, "As a professor, I tended to think of history as run by impersonal forces. But when you see it in practice, you see the difference personalities make."[26]

From observing Hitler to Bin Laden to Putin, leader analysts see this difference with crystal clarity.

NOTES

1. Amazon.com, https://www.amazon.com/s?k=leadership+books&rh=n%3A283155&dc &crid=2KKDGX0X60SSP&qid=1645465725&rnid=2941120011&sprefix=leadership+books %2Caps%2C133&ref=sr_nr_n_1).

2. Spotify.com, https://open.spotify.com/search/leadership/podcasts; Apple Podcast application.

3. TED.com, https://www.ted.com/search?q=leadership.

4. John W. Gardner, *On Leadership* (Washington, DC: Free Press, 1990), 1.

5. Gardner, xii–xiii.

6. Because this chapter deals with the specific analytic discipline focused on leaders, it uses the term "analyst" to designate "leader analyst," unless otherwise noted.

7. An interesting declassified example is by the CIA Directorate of Intelligence, *India: Transition Time in the Nuclear Leadership*, Intelligence Assessment, NESA 84-10049, February 1984, declassified from SECRET, https://www.cia.gov/readingroom/docs/CIA-RDP84 S00927R000300050005-2.pdf.

8. "India's Key Nuclear Advisers," *Near East and South Asia Review*, NESA NESAR 85-024, November 8, 1985, declassified from SECRET, https://www.cia.gov/readingroom/docs /CIA-RDP87T00289R000100260001-0.pdf.

9. Examples of assessments provided to decision-makers are National Intelligence Daily, *Bulgaria: Zhikov's Health*, November 26, 1982, declassified from TOP SECRET, https://www .cia.gov/readingroom/docs/CIA-RDP84T00301R000600010099-3.pdf; and President's Daily Brief, "Communist China" (discusses Mao's health), October 9, 1971, declassified from TOP SECRET, https://www.cia.gov/readingroom/docs/DOC_0005992910.pdf.

10. Myles Maxfield, Robert Proper, and Sharol Case, "Remote Medical Diagnosis," *Studies in Intelligence* 23, no. 1 (Spring 1979), https://fas.org/cia/product/remote.pdf. Another insightful declassified product is by Myles Maxfield and Edward G. Greger, "VIP Health Watch," *Studies in Intelligence* 7, no. 2 (Spring 1968): 53–63, declassified from SECRET, https://www.cia.gov/readingroom/docs/VIP%20HEALTH%20WATCH%5B14747229%5D.pdf.

11. Jonathan D. Clemente, "In Sickness and in Health," *Bulletin of the Atomic Scientists* 63, no. 2 (March–April 2007): 38–44, https://journals.sagepub.com/doi/pdf/10.2968/063002010.

12. Clemente, 40.

13. Jerrold Post, "Saddam Hussein of Iraq: A Political Psychological Profile," *Political Psychology* 12, no. 2 (1991): 79–89, https://www.jstor.org/stable/3791465.

14. Jane Mayer, "Saddam on the Couch," *New Yorker*, October 20, 2002, https://www.new yorker.com/magazine/2002/10/28/saddam-on-the-couch.

15. George Gedda, "Clinton Backs Aristide as Haitian Rebuts Critics' Mental Health Claims," AP News, October 23, 1993, https://apnews.com/article/b441d6d6cd8e1bb36042e 02c911d7b7d.

16. Melissa Chan, "Opinion: China Isn't Just 'Authoritarian' Any More; It's Scarier," *Washington Post*, January 31, 2022.

17. "President Carter and the Role of Intelligence in the Camp David Accords," 2014, 15, http://www.foia.cia.gov/cartercampdavidaccords. Declassified Leadership Profiles can be viewed at https://www.cia.gov/readingroom/docs/1977-07-07.pdf, for Begin; https://www.cia.gov/readingroom/docs/1978-08-23a.pdf, for Dayan; and https://www.cia.gov/readingroom/docs/1978-08-17.pdf, for Kamil. An interesting National Intelligence Daily article on Dayan is at https://www.cia.gov/readingroom/docs/1977-09-17.pdf.

18. Memorandum prepared for meeting with Secretary [of State] Shultz, *Generational Policy Perspectives within the Soviet Leadership*, September 7, 1984, declassified from SECRET, https://www.cia.gov/readingroom/docs/CIA-RDP86B00420R000501010010-4.pdf.

19. Richards J. Heuer Jr., *Psychology of Intelligence Analysis* (Langley, VA: CIA, Center for the Study of Intelligence, 1999), 116.

20. Heuer.

21. Helene Boatner, "The Evaluation of Intelligence," *Studies in Intelligence* 28, no. 2 (1984): 66.

22. C-Span, "User Clip: Bush Saw Putin's Soul," June 17, 2001, https://www.c-span.org/video/?c4718091/user-clip-bush-putins-soul.

23. A dated but remarkable declassified study of intelligence sources and analysis involved in Chinese leadership assessment is by DCI Intelligence Community Staff, *Appraisal of Intelligence Sources and Analysis in the Fall of Teng Hsiao-p'ing and in the Rise of Hua Kuo-feng*, DCI/IC 78-2318, January 31, 1978, declassified from SECRET, https://www.cia.gov/readingroom/docs/CIA-RDP82M00311R000100170001-3.pdf.

24. Zachary B. Wolf, "How US Intelligence Got It Right on Ukraine," CNN, February 26, 2022, https://www.cnn.com/2022/02/26/politics/us-intelligence-ukraine-russia/index.html.

25. An example of valuable SIGINT from decades ago is GAMMA GUPY, the interception of communications of limousines of senior Soviet officials until 1971; see Office of the Director of National Intelligence and Office of the National Counterintelligence Executive, *Unauthorized Disclosures of Classified Information*, September 2011, https://nsarchive2.gwu.edu/NSAEBB/NSAEBB506/docs/ciasignals_42.pdf.

26. Here, Kissinger was in a background talk with reporters in January 1975, as quoted by Walter Isaacson, *Kissinger* (New York: Simon & Schuster, 1992), 13.

7

COUNTERINTELLIGENCE ANALYSIS: CATCHING SPIES AND COUNTERING FOES

James B. Bruce and Blake W. Mobley

WHAT IS COUNTERINTELLIGENCE ANALYSIS?

If spying is the world's second-oldest profession, the practice of counterintelligence (CI) is the third—and it hardly lagged the second.[1] Spying naturally gave rise to spy catching. And some form of "analysis" has always been part of that spy-counterspy interaction. CI analysis *as a discipline* has evolved over time as have other analytic fields, but it arrived late and faced resistance in the CIA.[2] In its early years after World War II, CI analysis was not a distinct area of study—a rigorous way to uncover secret hostile activities—and seemed an unwelcomed stranger in the den of intelligence operations. Only in the last several decades, beginning roughly in the mid-1980s,[3] has analysis come to play an increasingly significant role in CI.

At the CIA, counterintelligence is one of its three major intelligence missions, the others being foreign intelligence and covert action (see box 7.1). An authoritative definition is given in Executive Order (EO) 12333:

> *Counterintelligence* means "information gathered, and activities conducted to identify, deceive, exploit, disrupt, or protect against espionage, other intelligence activities, sabotage, or assassinations conducted for or on behalf of foreign powers, organizations, or persons, or their agents, or international terrorist organizations or activities."

Typically, hostile intelligence actions emanate from adversary countries such as Russia, China, Iran, and North Korea. But often, friendly services or even allies such as Israel and France conduct hostile operations against American targets.[4] Moreover,

BOX 7.1: INTELLIGENCE MISSIONS

- Foreign, or "positive," intelligence (FI) provides information to policy and military leaders to bolster their decision advantage over adversaries.
- Counterintelligence (CI) aims to counter, defeat, or degrade the activities of foreign intelligence services. As part of it, counterespionage (CE) seeks to detect and neutralize American spies working inside the US government.
- Covert action (CA) exercises political, economic, or cultural influence abroad clandestinely–that is, in ways that conceal the identity and means of intelligence services, foreign intelligence entities, and states conducting it.

nonstate actors—including terrorists, drug cartels, and other criminal organizations—can operate surprisingly effective intelligence and CI services.[5]

A working definition can cast CI in specific terms. CI aims to counter the activities of foreign intelligence services that seek to (1) steal our national secrets, (2) penetrate and degrade our intelligence services, and (3) influence our society (people, politics, etc.) through clandestine and covert means. Each of the three poses a vital threat to our country.

First, jointly with good security, CI is needed to protect our own national secrets—including, for example, our military contingency plans, command-and-control of forces, and advanced defense technologies.[6] Foreign espionage that also targets our commercial or proprietary secrets can undercut our competitiveness in the marketplace—costing jobs and hemorrhaging large investments. Senior officials have exposed some of the vast efforts made by foreign services. The director of the FBI, Christopher Wray, referred in 2020 to "the greatest long-term threat to our nation's information and intellectual property, and to our economic vitality—and that's the counterintelligence and economic espionage threat from China."[7] Wray noted, "Even as we speak, the FBI has about 1,000 investigations involving China's attempted theft of US-based technology, in all 56 of our field offices, spanning almost every industry and sector." Foreign intelligence attacks against our defense secrets come to light for the public when legal actions result in multiyear convictions. Compromises against our classified military communications by John Walker and others, for example, can jeopardize our nuclear submarines, air, land, and sea forces; our troops; and our ability to defend our country and allies.

Second, without effective CI, efforts to recruit and run assets or operate clandestine technical collection systems abroad can be compromised and defeated. The treachery of CIA officer Aldrich "Rick" Ames devastated our HUMINT collection efforts in the USSR—compromises that were compounded by the extensive espionage of FBI special agent Robert Hanssen and others.[8] Assets recruited and run for years by the CIA and other parts of the US intelligence community—providing information on Russian military technology valued by US officials at well over $1 billion as well as more general insights into Soviet and Russian perceptions, intentions, plans, and actions—disappeared.[9] As many as ten of these assets were executed, and others received lengthy prison sentences. US technical collection efforts that cost many millions of dollars and also risked lives were defeated by the betrayals of former CIA officer Edward Howard and former National Secuirty Agency (NSA) officer Ronald Pelton.[10] Ineffective CI allowed an al-Qaeda associate to carry out a devastating attack against a CIA base in Khost, Afghanistan, in December 2009, killing seven CIA officers and contractors as well as a Jordanian intelligence officer and a cooperating Afghan.[11]

Third, covert action that is not accompanied by good CI can be revealed and rendered ineffective. Compromises resulted in the capture and deaths, or lengthy prison sentences, of assets recruited or inserted into hostile states intended to support efforts to undermine hostile authoritarian regimes. US intelligence activities in Cuba were seriously compromised by Defense Intelligence Agency (DIA) analyst Ana Montes. As noted in the declassified Department of Defense Inspector General report, "Throughout her career at DIA, Montes had access to [DIA] decision-makers, intelligence collectors, operational plans, sensitive programs and military exercises."[12] She provided a steady stream of our most closely held secrets to the Cuban government.

Finally, Russia's significant covert intervention in the 2016 US presidential election highlighted foreign attempts to influence US publics, and in particular our elections through covert action.[13] There is nothing new in the purpose and goals, but technologies, techniques, and the scale of operations have taken massive leaps. Before the US entry in World Wars I and II, European belligerents used overt and covert approaches—and mixtures of the two—to sway US public opinion. For example, British authorities operated a large influence operation before World War II based largely in New York.[14] German authorities published false documentary evidence in the United States, such as *Polish Acts of Atrocity against the German Minority in Poland* in 1940, to justify the attack that started World War II in Europe.[15]

Thus, in both foreign intelligence and CA, the effectiveness of CI is vital to the success of the whole intelligence enterprise. Given its central importance, the role of analysis is key to whether counterintelligence succeeds or fails. Given the broad scope of hostile foreign intelligence operations against the US government and the American private sector, we focus on the role of CI analysis in support of operations as illustrative of the broader discipline.

WHAT MAKES CI ANALYSIS UNIQUE?

Unlike other disciplines described in this volume, the bulk of counterintelligence assessments are not designed primarily for policymakers. Instead, most CI analyses are tailored to support intelligence operations, such as gathering foreign intelligence (FI), carrying out covert actions (CA), or, to a lesser degree, counterespionage (CE) investigations to catch spies in our own country working for a foreign power. To be clear, some CI analysis benefits intelligence consumers in the White House and other policy consumers. Still, as we explain below, the bread-and-butter job of CI analysts is working together with operations officers.

Operations

In broad terms, operational analysis provides decision-makers within the Directorate of Operations (DO) with judgments and insights about foreign intelligence entities (FIEs), such as the Russian Intelligence Services (the SVR operates abroad, the FSB domestically—both formerly in the KGB) or the Chinese Ministry of State Security. Those in charge of operations generally care deeply about this line of analysis. Baseline assessments of FIEs—dissecting them, top to bottom—may include their history and personnel, the FIE's technical and human intelligence capabilities, surveillance methods, and patterns of targeting and recruiting US citizens, among other things. CI analysts can also play a critical role in the DO targeting process, identifying FIE officers overseas who may be suitable targets for recruitment. This analysis may include examining their social networks, pattern-of-life issues (e.g., daily habits and routines), job responsibilities, family needs, and their psychological needs, including whether they are favorably disposed or hostile to Americans and the United States.

Counterespionage

A closely related type of CI analysis is referred to as counterespionage for catching and neutralizing spies in our own country. In this instance, the FBI is an especially important intelligence community partner—and the Department of Justice is also a customer should a prosecution be pursued. Cooperation between the CIA and FBI can prove critical to identifying and catching spies both domestically and overseas. Within the Counterintelligence Mission Center (CIMC), the Counterespionage Group enjoys interagency participation and is headed by the FBI. The FBI's domestic responsibilities span its role as a law enforcement agency, as the above quotation by FBI director Wray indicates. Still, the overlapping jurisdictions and some bureaucratic rivalry both abroad and at home has led to friction within the national security enterprise.

Policy

The third type of CI analysis is produced for policymakers. The foremost purpose of this analysis is to provide assessments of the principal intelligence threats facing the

US government and the American private sector. This is very different from the support given to operators. Although less frequent, there are at least three areas where CI analysis can rise to the level of senior policymaker interest.

First, many of our key adversaries and even friendly powers rely on their intelligence and counterintelligence services to shape and implement their foreign and domestic policies—these include Russia, China, North Korea, Iran, Pakistan, Egypt, Saudi Arabia, and Turkey, to name a few. To understand and anticipate shifts in the policies of these countries, policymakers often need to understand the influential roles their intelligence services play. Second, foreign intelligence services are key players in transnational issues such as terrorism, drug trafficking, human trafficking, and proliferation of nuclear and other weapons of mass destruction. The CIA is often working with these liaison services. Thus, CI analysis can inform policymakers when a key intelligence partner in such efforts changes course or curtails cooperation with the United States. Third, CI analysis can warn policymakers when an FIE's actions threaten US national security interests. For example, such an analysis might forecast how rapid advances in technology—such as artificial intelligence, biometrics, and telecommunications—could enhance an FIE's ability to detect and reveal the activities of US intelligence officers or assets as well as American diplomats, businesspeople, and expatriates when they travel and work abroad.[16]

CI ANALYSTS: ROLES AND METHODS

Most practicing CI analysts in the DA work within the CIMC as their "home base," and a small cadre of those analysts are seconded to other parts of the CIA, the intelligence community, and the executive branch. CIMC is home to a large group of analysts, each of whom is assigned to one or several "accounts" corresponding to geographical and functional areas. Many of these analysts are hired directly from academia after they have completed an advanced degree in any number of fields like history, political science, or international relations. Some analysts will transfer from other parts of the DA because of their interest in counterintelligence. Analysts in CIMC undergo the same analytic training as the rest of their colleagues. There are a variety of short CI analysis-specific courses available to analysts in CIMC; however, for the most part, analysts will learn CI specifics "on the job." At the core of CI, analysts encounter a basic truth—as we do our work, there are adversaries on some far shore, in a classified vault or other secret location, analyzing us just as dutifully as we analyze them. It is our brains versus theirs. Outwitting the adversary's CI analysts can be the key to gaining an upper hand. To CI analysts, it can feel like playing a chess game in the dark, with brief glimpses of an often-opaque chessboard.

How Do CI Analysts Work?

CI analysts have a wide variety of daily routines, but many begin their day, as do analysts in other disciplines, by reviewing cable traffic, open source news, classified intelligence reporting, and signals intelligence from the prior day. CI analysts typically monitor one or several FIEs and will be alert to any information that changes their views of widely accepted assessments of FIE activities (what is commonly known in the DA as an "analytic line"), while also paying attention to information that could support a new analytic line or a warning piece useful to policymakers. Analysts often work closely with the DO and its stations to monitor an FIE and will devote extra time reading station cable traffic and HUMINT reporting in their area of responsibility.

Arguably the most difficult step of the process is making sense of the deluge of daily intelligence inputs. For CI analysts, assessing the relevant information can be particularly daunting, for several reasons. First, the target of inquiry is an FIE, which is actively obscuring its activities and engaging in deception for the purpose of misleading its spectators. Second, CI analysts immerse themselves in the minutiae of voluminous intelligence reporting; moreover, they review the personal details of each source of that reporting, which expands the amount of information that needs to be examined. All analysts will have some techniques for managing the enormous volume of reporting. Some use Microsoft Word documents or Excel spreadsheets to organize key pieces of evidence that appear relevant for analysis of their particular account. Organizing data around timelines to appreciate the order of events and to avoid losing sight of key political dates (both past and approaching) is a common technique. Many analysts use concept mapping software, like Analyst's Notebook, to organize and visually analyze data in expansive charts with lines connecting related persons, events, buildings, and devices. Once a preponderance or key piece of data are collected, analysts then begin to apply structured analytic techniques, such as analysis of competing hypotheses, signposts of change analysis, and alternative futures and scenarios analysis—techniques they learned in DA training—to refine their thinking and prepare an assessment for operators or policymakers. Occasionally, analysts will have access to a trained facilitator, who can aid in the brainstorming process.

Working with Collectors

CI analysts are "all-source" analysts, albeit generally with a greater focus on HUMINT as compared with the other INTs. What may distinguish CI analysts is that often they have access to reporting that is not disseminated to other parts of the government but rather remains within the DO. CI analysts will often see the cable traffic that describes an operation or a case officer's interactions with a source or provides a sensitive station assessment of a source. Analysts will not use this information directly in a piece of finished intelligence, but it will shape how they judge the credibility of that source's reporting. In some cases, critical information useful to analysts never makes it past the cutting room floor. For example, one of the authors had access to undisseminated "raw" SIGINT. Working alongside NSA and DO officers, he was able to assemble that information into a longitudinal (multiyear) SIGINT report on an FIE's surveillance capabilities. After it was disseminated to the broader intelligence community as an intelligence report, analysts were able to cite it in a finished intelligence product that advanced a developing analytic line and aided a station's efforts to track and circumvent the FIE's surveillance.

WHOM DO CI ANALYSTS SUPPORT?

As mentioned above, the CI discipline is very different from the traditional DA focus on informing policymakers, in which the bulk of the analysis is provided in various forms to those in the White House or in Cabinet agencies. In fact, the primary focus of the CI discipline is on providing information and insights to operators who must launch operations in denied areas or be alert to hostile intelligence services' attempts to penetrate and disrupt US intelligence operations. The focus on operators is more similar to how the CT analytic discipline has gradually evolved to become integral to successful counterterrorism efforts.

Supporting Operations

The creation of the Counterintelligence Center (CIC) in 1988, and the colocation of CI analysts with operations officers in the DO, greatly enhanced the analytic contribution to evaluating CIA HUMINT. As a new Mission Center, CIC became the CIMC in 2015, further integrating the DA and DO counterintelligence personnel and mission objectives.[17] They are no longer "outsiders" but are rather an integral part of that collector organization. Thus, analysts could build relationships—and build trust—in their new roles as colleagues in the same organization. By providing unprecedented access to operational information rarely shared previously with analysts, this organizational integration afforded new CI analysis opportunities. Drawing on the authors' firsthand experiences, we identify several areas where CI analysis has benefited HUMINT collection efforts.

Asset Validation

It is fair to say that, by most measures, CI analytic work that helps establish an asset's bona fides is an important contribution to the overall mission of the CIA. CI analysts support operational elements at Headquarters and in the field to evaluate human sources on several dimensions:

- Are they authentic? Are they who they say they are? And do they have access to secrets that they claim and we need?
- Are they reliable? Do they respond to their case officers' taskings in a diligent, consistent, and trustworthy manner?
- Are they providing valuable information or only low-grade or even false material? Are they fabricating what they allege is classified or closely held information?
- Are they under "hostile control" by the FIE? Is the intelligence service in their home country controlling or working with the source to manipulate and deceive us?[18]

Human sources are considered vetted and credible when they meet these and other key criteria. Identifying hostile control is especially challenging when evaluating human sources working within or closely with an FIE. The closer human sources are to an FIE, the more likely it is that they might have been trained to identify, avoid, and report contact with American diplomats and citizens. Human sources will also be aware of the greater surveillance scrutiny they will receive from their FIE and its counterespionage cadre as well as the severe penalties they or their families would pay if caught spying.

Asset validation is inherently, but not exclusively, an analytical process. It goes on during all phases of an operation, such as spotting and assessing (e.g., targeting), developing, recruiting, and running a foreign agent. Numerous CIA operations have failed because of an inability to identify a double agent—an agent thought to be bona fide but in reality under the control of a hostile intelligence service. Double agents can discover key elements of CIA operational tradecraft, such as case officer identities, locations of safe houses and dead drops, and clandestine communications techniques. They can provide false and misleading reporting to deceive human intelligence collection that is disseminated to senior policymakers. In a worst case, they occasionally have penetrated CIA stations or bases as happened in Khost, Afghanistan, in 2009. Countries that have enjoyed success in running double agents against the CIA (and other US intelligence services) include Cuba, the Soviet Union, Russia (and its Cold War allies, e.g., East Germany), China, and Iran.

Defectors

Analysts in all the disciplines benefit from direct access to defectors, émigrés, and, on rare occasions, in-place assets. Firsthand debriefings of defecting intelligence and military officers can open a rich mine of information. Defectors from hostile countries—mainly Russians but also Chinese, North Koreans, and others—can provide firsthand evidence concerning perceptions, interests, intentions, plans, personnel, structures, and capabilities of FIEs and military services. Moreover, CI analysts with a deep understanding of the FIE can extract insights about the internal culture of FIEs and their operational environments. In one instance, one of the authors of this chapter conducted extensive debriefings of an undisclosed defector (a particularly sensitive source not routinely available for wider debriefings) on internal stability in a key adversary country. The debriefings resulted in a comprehensive but internal-use-only assessment exploring rare insights of an intelligence defector.

Counterintelligence Inspections

The CIA Directorate of Operations routinely conducts CI inspections of its stations and bases abroad to ensure they are fully aware of and responsive to CI threats they face. As part of a CIC inspection team, one of the authors of this chapter participated in the inspection of a Latin American station. Insights derived from a rigorous analysis of select station files, and interviews of key operations officers assigned there, enhanced the examination and vetting of several problematic cases in various stages of development. They also identified some station vulnerabilities to the host country's service's technical threat to station operations.

Counterespionage Analysis

Spy catching (or "mole hunting") certainly ranks as a priority function in counterintelligence. The United States has been a priority target of more than 200 countries and other FIEs since the beginning of the Cold War, and key adversaries and even "friends" have scored major espionage successes with Americans willing to spy against their country (see box 7.2).[19] Although analysis can fill a critical gap in counterespionage (CE) work, historically it has played an understated role, often barely included. Instead, CI officers traditionally have relied on three methods to identify a spy (or mole) in their midst:

- *Penetrating* an FIE by recruiting one of its officers who can report on—or at least provide useful leads to—spies. FBI officer Robert Hanssen was positively identified through a penetration source who provided a file with revelatory information including a recording of his voice.
- *Defectors* from an FIE may provide information about spies their FIE is running or had run in our country. The most senior KGB officer to defect to the United States, Vitaly Yurchenko, provided information that led to the identification and capture of CIA operations officer Edward Howard, and NSA officer Ronald Pelton, who compromised highly compartmented US communications intercept capabilities. A high-ranking Chinese intelligence defector identified Larry Wu-tai Chin, possibly the longest-serving US spy, with over

three decades reporting to Chinese intelligence and working in the CIA's Foreign Broadcast Information Service. A Cuban defector exposed Castro's stun-
ningly effective double agent operations against the CIA (and the FBI).

- *Tip-offs* from alert coworkers of an individual whom they suspect might be a
spy. For example, Ana Montes, a senior Defense Intelligence Agency analyst
who spied for Cuba, was initially identified as a security risk by a colleague
who twice reported his suspicions of a pattern of small clues and unusual
behavior he had seen in her, though nothing conclusive. Similarly, US Navy
intelligence analyst Jonathan Pollard, who spied for the Israelis, was also first
suspected because of a coworker's tipoff. Not all tipoffs succeed. John Walker
Jr., a US Navy chief warrant officer and communicator, was flagged to the FBI
by his ex-wife, but her tip was disregarded and Walker's spying continued
for years.

While vital in some cases, such techniques were not always sufficient to identify counterespionage threats quickly enough. Along with standard law enforcement investigative techniques, analysis is also needed to detect spies and direct the
evidence-gathering process (investigations) to support an arrest and successful prosecution. While the CIA plays a strong role in counterespionage analysis, other US

BOX 7.2: SELECTED ROGUES' GALLERY
OF AMERICA'S MOST DAMAGING SPIES

Robert Hanssen
FBI special agent and senior counterintelligence officer, arguably the most damaging spy in post–World War II American history. With several inactive periods, Hanssen's espionage for the Soviet Union and Russia spanned twenty-two
years. He compromised the special access, continuity-of-government program; all aspects of the FBI's CI operations,
including its Soviet recruitments; and a tunnel project for SIGINT access under the new Russian embassy in Washington. Other major compromises affected all US intelligence collection disciplines, with only one in three US spies
causing this level of damage. CI investigation flawed by biased analysis that focused on an innocent suspect. He
was arrested in 2001 after a Russian source provided his KGB file and was sentenced to life in prison, where he died.

Aldrich Ames
CIA operations officer motivated by greed who compromised at least a dozen CIA and FBI penetrations of Soviet
intelligence and military organizations, of whom at least ten were executed. Also passed huge amounts of highly
classified analysis that revealed sensitive US collection methods, including from National Intelligence Estimates on
Soviet and Russian arms control, biological weapons, and related topics. Like Hanssen, Walker, Conrad, and Chin,
Ames's compensation exceeded $1 million. His nine years of spying (1985–94) were aided by six years of failed inves-
tigations. When analysis was introduced to "follow the money," that finally pinpointed the most serious betrayal in
CIA history. He was sentenced to life in prison, where he died.

John Walker
US Navy communications specialist ran a spy ring that included his brother and son. An eighteen-year spy (1967–85),
Walker passed cryptographic keys and codes to the KGB enabling access to as much as 80 percent of US Naval

communications, including with submarines, allowing the Soviets to decipher a million encrypted naval messages. This compromise severely weakened US strategic nuclear deterrence and afforded the Soviets a significant military advantage had we gone to war. Caught after a disregarded tip by his ex-wife was validated eight years later by another from his youngest daughter. Sentenced to two life terms and died in prison in 2014.

Clyde Lee Conrad

He ran a fourteen-member spy ring for Hungarian intelligence—that shared their take with the Soviets—at a US Army installation in Germany. During his fourteen years of treachery (1974-88), Conrad's army network passed thousands of top-secret US and NATO documents, such as war plans that included tactical nuclear weapons to defend Europe against a Soviet and Warsaw Pact attack as well as troop numbers, strategy, and location of missile sites and other targets. After years of poor Army CI, matching the Navy's record in the Walker case, financial tracking analysis—and rare use of a US double agent—led to Conrad's arrest. Sentenced to life, he died in a German prison in 1998.

Ana Montes

A senior analyst at DIA, she worked for Cuban intelligence for sixteen years (1984-2001). Like Hungary, Cuba shared this information with the Soviets. She compromised a highly sensitive special access collection program; all US intelligence capabilities against Cuba, including CIA operations; many capabilities in Latin America; and significant amounts of finished intelligence. Unlike most US spies, she was motivated by ideology rather than greed. An unapologetic Castro supporter, she also became an agent of influence inside the US intelligence community by shading her analysis and using her position as a senior analyst to show Cuban views favorably. A coworker's tip about her Cuban sympathies helped lead to her capture. Sentenced to twenty-five years, she was released in early 2023 on good behavior.

Ronald Pelton

He was a former NSA analyst with a near-photographic memory of his access to nearly all NSA collection programs. Insolvent and needing money, he walked into the Soviet embassy in Washington in 1980. Vitaly Yurchenko, the KGB officer who welcomed him there, defected to the United States five years later. Yurchenko's information, along with good analysis, identified Pelton. Among Pelton's most damaging compromises were the undersea cable tap operation of Soviet military communications, then a heavily compartmented special access program, along with NSA decryption capabilities and other highly sensitive information. He was sentenced to three life terms but released in 2015 (he died in 2022).

Jonathan Pollard

US Navy intelligence analyst who spied for Israel (1984-85). His espionage production over such a short period was prodigious, surpassing more than a million pages of classified intelligence, chiefly analysis, much of which offered detailed information on US collection capabilities. A journalist has credibly reported that Israel passed much of that to the Soviets to facilitate Jewish immigration to Israel. Identified, like Montes, after a coworker's reports of security concerns. Sentenced to life imprisonment and paroled in 2016.

Larry Wu-tai Chin

He spied for China for thirty-three years (1952-85), the longest record for known US traitors. Beginning as a translator in Okinawa for the Foreign Broadcast Information Service, Chin immigrated to the United States in 1961, gained citizenship in 1965, and transferred to Foreign Broadcast Information Service headquarters in Virginia in 1970, becoming a top-secret, cleared CIA employee. He was a Chinese penetration when he started as a CIA contract translator until he was arrested in 1985 based on reporting of a Chinese source and good FBI analysis. Assessing the damage of his compromises is difficult, but CI expert Michael Sulick concludes that owing to Chin, there was "undoubtedly little raw intelligence and analysis [on China] in CIA hands that the Chinese had not seen." Convicted in 1986, he committed suicide before sentencing.

Sources: Michael J. Sulick, *American Spies: Espionage against the United States from the Cold War to the Present* (Washington, DC: Georgetown University Press, 2013); James M. Olson, *Gabriel: The Art of Counterintelligence* (Washington, DC: Georgetown University Press, 2019); David Major and Peter C. Oleson, "Espionage in America," in *AFIO's Guide to the Study of Intelligence*, ed. Peter C. Oleson (Falls Church, VA: Association of Former Intelligence Officers, 2016), 434-35; Personnel Security Research Center, *Espionage and Other Compromises to National Security: Case Summaries from 1975 to 2008* (Monterey, CA: PERSEREC, 2009).

intelligence agencies, notably the FBI, also have major roles. Analysis for spy catching uniquely involves interagency cooperation.

Few CE cases better illustrate the importance of analysis than that of CIA traitor Aldrich Ames. Lacking a penetration, defector, or a coworker tipoff, analysis was essential to uncover Ames's nine-year treachery. In 1985, Ames passed a large tranche of documents to a Soviet embassy officer during a sanctioned meeting he held under the guise of an authorized plan to recruit this diplomat. Almost immediately, his actions resulted in the loss of at least twelve CIA assets inside the Soviet Union, of whom ten were executed.[20] He also compromised two very sensitive technical collection programs. After almost nine years of many missteps, interagency rivalries, and insufficient analytical resources, Ames was identified and arrested. Why did it take nine years? The CI staff, and later, the CIC, were slow to organize and to assign needed analytical resources to the mole hunt.[21] Instead, they conducted a slow-motion array of misdirected and time-consuming reviews of all the compromised assets as well as the Agency's operational communications systems (fearing compromise based on a KGB deception) and then re-reviewed earlier CI leads from the 1973–75 period. Separately, the office of security interviewed all officers who had served in Moscow or traveled there between 1985 and 1986. None of these efforts hit paydirt or even got close.

In 1989 an Ames colleague reported that his lifestyle had taken a huge boost that could not be easily explained by an Agency salary. A security officer reexamined Ames's personnel and security files and began a financial analysis to "follow the money." This officer eventually identified large bank deposits that were later correlated with documented meetings Ames held with a Soviet embassy officer. Analysis revealed that between 1985 and 1991, Ames had banked more than $1.3 million in unexplained income. Related correlations of his activities with his foreign travel further tied Ames to his espionage for the KGB.[22]

In hindsight, the Ames investigation suffered from insufficient analysis for many years, partly because operations officers lacked an appreciation for what analysts can bring to the table. Other than the financial analysis, there was little analytical effort for much of the first five years of the Ames investigation. The CIA Inspector General's inquiry into the Ames investigation acknowledges that a "good CI analyst needs a great deal of general and particular knowledge to make the mental connections necessary to conduct a CI investigation." But as defined by the Ames investigation, in practice this meant knowledge of the KGB, knowledge of the compromised 1985–86 cases, and operational experience. But no mention is made of having knowledge of analytic methods or training. The Inspector General's inquiry appropriately found that "a very narrow view of the scope and nature of CI investigations ... presents significant risks both to the Agency and successful prosecutions in the future."[23] As CIMC has added more analysts to its activities, this weakness has somewhat diminished. But the organizational culture of the DO, as former director of central intelligence Robert Gates highlighted years ago, has been institutionally resistant to analysis.[24] This deeply rooted legacy, notwithstanding recent gains in CIMC, remains an obstacle to consistently applying good analytic tradecraft to significant CI risks.

Supporting Policymakers

Interactions with policymakers present their own taxing demands. Most policymakers are not familiar with counterintelligence issues or techniques. They are busy and have limited time and attention to absorb new information that fails to address their immediate concerns. Taken together, these conditions highlight the importance of educating policymakers about counterintelligence and its relevance to them as clearly and concisely as possible. One of us participated in a team at CIC that hit a happy medium. In covering an important FIE for our senior military leaders, CIC's lead analyst on that foreign intelligence service had established a deep rapport with senior consumers by creating a weekly report for them and providing raw intelligence updates on the FIE and its activities. As with the core disciplines, sensitivity to consumers' needs, the pressures they face, timing, the rhythm of policymaking, and knowing what drives their decisions can be critical to delivering counterintelligence products with maximum impact.

So, what kinds of CI issues rise to the level of senior policymakers? Some were noted above, but others deserve our attention. First, FIEs often play a critical role in foreign powers' domestic politics, especially in authoritarian countries. FIEs monitor opposition groups, serve as tools of oppression, and influence policy formation and execution. One cannot begin to discuss Russian, Chinese, Iranian, or North Korean internal politics without a deep consideration of their FIEs' domestic roles.[25] These FIEs often are instruments (and even shapers) of foreign policy. The breadth of activities is vast. Policymakers are provided regularly with assessments of FIEs' activities in arming potential US opponents (e.g., Iran's support for Hezbollah) or carrying out violent actions like assassinations and kidnappings.[26] The successful and failed assassination attempts against former Russian intelligence officers in the United Kingdom (Alexander Litvinenko in 2006; Sergei Skripal in 2018) are examples of high-profile policy matters. Not all FIE actions are malicious, but some can complicate relations with the United States nonetheless. In 2010, for example, CIC was able to explain that an important foreign intelligence partner on many transnational issues had misinterpreted US actions, depicting them to their leaders as internally destabilizing measures. CIC analysts helped US policymakers understand the foreign intelligence service's duplicitous and bizarre behavior.

Second, US policymakers need to be aware of the nature and scale of intelligence and counterintelligence threats to align our resources effectively. The allocation of personnel, funds, technologies, and diplomatic efforts generally need to be paired with carefully crafted laws, regulations, and orders. Thus, senior CIA officials appear frequently before congressional committees to explain threats and needed counter-measures.[27] As an example, policymakers have become more aware of FIE attempts to influence American domestic and foreign opinions through disinformation and propaganda campaigns.[28] Russian and other FIEs' attempts to influence US elections stand out. An example of KGB covert attempts to derail alliance politics and arrange-ments were infiltration of peace movements and campaigns that claimed the United States was behind the HIV/AIDS epidemic (Operation INFEKTION).[29]

Third, policymakers are rarely fully aware of the scope of FIE efforts to acquire sensitive technologies.[30] FIE targeting lists well exceed military applications. Chris Krebs (former Cybersecurity & Infrastructure Security Agency director) stated pub-licly, "The big four—Russia, China, Iran, and North Korea—we have seen to some extent all four of those countries doing some kind of espionage or spying, trying to get intellectual property related to the [COVID] vaccine."[31]

Finally, prominent espionage cases and significant unauthorized disclosures of highly classified information, such as those of Edward Snowden, can have a politi-cal blowback. The revelation of espionage or sensitive leaks can trigger substantial political and diplomatic responses.[32] Especially when allies are caught spying on each other, it is hard to avoid a public response. This was certainly the case when US Navy analyst Jonathan Pollard was caught spying for the Israelis and when US espionage abroad is revealed. Another dimension of this is when an allied service is revealed to have had an officer who compromised joint secrets. During the Cold War, the British suffered through several such embarrassments, including the loss of the US "Berlin tunnel" that tapped into Soviet communications, due to George Blake's treachery,[33] Kim Philby's numerous compromises,[34] and Geoffrey Prime's SIGINT disclosures to the Soviets.[35] Liaison relationships inevitably introduce the risk that shared intelli-gence will be compromised, as happened when the Norwegian diplomat Arne Treholt provided NATO secrets to the Soviets in the 1970s and 1980s, and the Frenchman Pierre-Henri Bunel did the same for the Serbs in 1998. More recently, the reported Russian penetration of Germany's foreign intelligence service may also risk strained diplomatic relationships and jeopardize mutually beneficial intelligence sharing.[36]

CHALLENGES TO CONDUCTING CI ANALYSIS

Just as analysts in the core disciplines face difficult challenges, so too do CI analysts encounter obstacles that conspire to make their jobs harder than need be. Three facts are illustrative: Counterintelligence has no history of finding a natural home in the Agency; the CIA did not even have an organization to conduct it for its first seven years, until the CI staff was founded in 1954, and its chief for the next twenty years was the controversial James Angleton. Nor, as noted, has CI provided a welcoming environment to conduct analysis. And overriding secrecy and operational compartmentation can also inhibit both the conduct of analysis and internal receptivity to its products.

Organizational Resistance and Politics

Before the 1988 creation of the CIA's Counterintelligence Center, which superseded the smaller CI staff, analysis was not recognized as a discrete CI specialty. "Analysis" (aka investigations—see box 7.3) then was conducted mostly by operations officers who were well grounded in operational tradecraft and risks but were unversed in the specialized analytic training and methods used by analysts. As mentioned in this book's introductory chapter, DO operators and DA analysts also have been schooled in different organizational cultures. This operational/analytical cultural divide often had the unintended effects of diminishing the value and impact of analysis for both its operational and even its policy customers. Moreover, the CI staff focused operators on investigations or preparing case studies of past operations such as the Rote Kapelle, the World War II Soviet espionage network in Nazi-occupied Europe.[37] Thus, CI managers felt little need to involve professional analysts in its sensitive operations.

That mind-set began to change with the establishment of the CI Center, which initiated a concerted effort to integrate analysis into the closeted world of counterintelligence. As James Olson, former chief of the CIA's Counterintelligence Center, explained it, the main idea of the new center was to bring together experts from the Agency's various components and disciplines to work CI issues together. In his view, "This was groundbreaking and heretical. A lot of naysayers said it could not be done." Most importantly, he brought in analysts: "We set them up in their own unit, the Analysis Group, and turned them loose on counterintelligence analysis. Wonderful things

---

BOX 7.3: ANALYSIS VERSUS INVESTIGATIONS

Analysis and investigation activities are related but far from synonymous. *Investigations* comprise a straightforward process of gathering facts and evidence relevant to a question, such as using reference documents, directories, conducting traces, interviews, and the like. *Analysis* is the cognitive process—often using rigorous analytic techniques—of making sense of the gathered information to produce judgments, insights, and forecasts. For example, mountains of "facts" and tidbits of potentially relevant information must be disaggregated, sorted, weighed, evaluated, and connected in ways to formulate answers to tough research questions. That is what finally happened when *analysis* of information produced in the Ames investigation began to focus on his unexplained income (discussed above) and led to his correct identification as the spy who betrayed at least a dozen CIA recruitments of Soviet assets lost in 1985-86.

happen when good analysts in sufficient numbers pore over double-agent reports, presence lists, signals intelligence, audio and [telephone tap] transcripts, maps, travel data, and surveillance reports."[38] Olson was right, even as it took some time for analysts to prove they were worthy partners of operations officers, many of whom were openly skeptical of the value of analysis.

Analysts can also run up against organizational politics between Washington Headquarters and overseas operations. Working with DO operators, one of the authors came to better understand their needs, mind-sets, and daily pressures, and improved his analytic support. However, he also witnessed firsthand the CIA's internal, bureaucratic tensions between Headquarters managers and stations overseas. Headquarters represents the broader corporate interests of the Agency, but stations have the narrower task of supporting intelligence operations and recruiting sources overseas with actionable intelligence. Stations often need to develop collaborative relationships with local services to accomplish these goals.

What happens when a liaison service cooperating with a station is also engaged in clandestine intelligence operations targeting the United States? In one case, CI analysts and DO managers at Headquarters wanted to issue a warning for US policymakers about an FIE's obstructive intelligence operations. However, the station worried that a negative US policy response would hinder its joint counterterrorism partnership and potentially reveal the sensitive human sources involved in uncovering the FIE's clandestine operations. Headquarters analysts believed some warning could be provided with a request that policy officials not discuss this concern with diplomats from the host country. The station was skeptical that US officials could restrain themselves. An ill-timed disclosure could be disastrous for counterterrorism efforts and CIA sources. The station naturally would prefer to handle its resolution more quietly or patiently, as this is its backyard. Also, analysts who push a story too aggressively may find that their rapport with the station is damaged, and so they must strike a careful balance. In this case, a short list of policymakers was briefed on the matter and, fortunately, none of them insisted on issuing a démarche to the country's officials.

Secrecy and Compartmentation

Heavily compartmented operations can also diminish the analytical function in CI. The operational environment is characterized by the vital necessity of protecting agent identities from the risk of disclosure, along with particularly sensitive foreign operations and espionage investigations. These routine operational activities impose higher levels of classification and strict need-to-know requirements. These necessary limitations reduce the number of people cleared for operational access drastically, especially constraining the analytical attention given to potentially serious CI problems. For example, some years ago, a Pentagon official insisted that several sensitive, highly compartmented collection operations should be examined because their intelligence reporting looked to some customers like deceptive information intended to mislead US policymakers. Their fear was that the CIA was an unwitting conduit just passing along foreign deceptive reporting to the Pentagon under the guise of its being authentic (or validated) intelligence. If so, this would mean a significant US counterintelligence failure to counter foreign deception.

After protracted negotiations among senior CIA managers, an interagency analysis of several heavily compartmented programs revealed significant problems. In one case, the interagency CI team learned that the program under study had almost certainly been penetrated and that CI concerns were indeed warranted owing to the deceptive materials identified. The conclusion was that a CIA source had been poorly vetted. In another case, sufficient operational materials required for analysis were withheld, and the study was unable to complete the analysis without the needed access. In a third case, senior CIA officials reluctantly decided that, lacking access to the materials needed, scarce analytical resources would be squandered on a fruitless effort. The comprehensive multiprogram study ended at that point.

This experience captures how important it is for analysts to have complete access to information if they are to produce accurate and complete judgments about the validity of sensitive collection operations and the intelligence they provide. Notably, since analysts are often asked by the DO to validate HUMINT information—but may not be told that their judgments may also be used to help validate the source who provided that information—it is vital that analysts fully learn a key lesson of this special study, namely, that *they are unable to assess the validity of collected information from human sources alone without also examining operational information pertaining to the source.* Sadly, incomplete access for CI, as well as other analysts, remains a commonplace practice. Especially in the early years, it was more the rule than the exception. The challenge of getting needed operational information to support thorough analysis to vet assets and the information they provide, despite some grudging improvements, continues to hobble CI analysis. In other disciplines, too, getting access to granular DO source descriptions and other operational details has also been a problem, only gradually improving since the weapons of mass destruction (WMD) commission identified this as one source of the flawed 2002 National Intelligence Estimate (NIE) on Iraq's WMD programs.

CI and Cognitive Bias

As explained in the introductory chapter and cited in previous chapters, intelligence analysis has given much attention to detecting and correcting for cognitive bias and preventing it from distorting intelligence findings. Since analysis is a cognitive process, anything that can distort cognition—that is, interfere with objectivity—can be addressed as cognitive bias. It is every bit as important in CI analysis as in the core analytical disciplines. Confirmation bias, for example, is often present in major intelligence failures, including CI cases. In 2002, one of the many flaws of the Iraq WMD NIE was its use of a biological weapons (BW) source, codenamed CURVE-BALL, who later proved to be a fabricator. With no direct vetting of the source, which came through a trusted liaison service, analysts accepted this information as valid largely because it confirmed what they already believed to be Saddam's active (but in reality shut down) BW programs.[39] They failed to identify and correct for confirmation bias. While the deeply flawed NIE failed on many counts for numerous reasons,[40] its "high confidence" BW judgment based on this source was, in the first instance, a CI analysis failure. Had CURVEBALL been properly vetted—either by German intelligence before the fabricated information was shared, or by the DIA that first received it, or by the CIA before its usage in a high-visibility NIE with consequential policy implications—serious analytic failure would have been averted. Accepting unvetted but plausible information from an unvetted source all too easily "confirmed" what had been true twelve years earlier—but not true in 2002—and thus the existing analytical line. No less than in the core disciplines, mitigating cognitive bias through the use of structured analytic techniques is a key tenet of counterintelligence analysis.

A similar instance of uncorrected confirmation bias in CE analysis with devastating personal consequences is seen in the FBI's fingering the wrong suspect when CIA officer Brian Kelley was wrongly accused of being a major spy. Here, the FBI was convinced the spy was a CIA officer and interpreted and misinterpreted all evidence to support that erroneous belief to the exclusion of all other potential suspects. Yet three years later, the FBI learned from information provided by a Russian source that the real traitor was instead its own Robert Hanssen. Apart from the tragedy visited on an innocent man, Hanssen's damage to US national security continued unabated while the FBI was off the scent, and he ably extended his nearly unparalleled period of undetected espionage to twenty-two years.[41]

Finally, career counterintelligence officers are at risk of developing their own unique biases as well. Long-term CI analysts are not immune to a particular bias toward believing that spies are ubiquitous and perhaps even close at hand. It is an unpleasant mix of confirmation bias and anxious hypervigilance. Recalling how the DO culture and even its Soviet operations were corrupted by the zealous suspicions of James Angleton, who headed the CI staff for twenty years, CI expert James Olson counsels CI practitioners to not "stay too long" in counterintelligence lest the bug of paranoia set in—calling it an occupational hazard of CI work.[42] The savvy CI practitioner knows this well and will use it offensively against adversaries to great effect—sowing paranoia has proven to be an effective means for disrupting foreign intelligence organizations and destabilizing insular terrorist groups, such as the British did with the Provisional Irish Republican Army and the Abu Nidal Organization in the 1980s.[43]

Evaluating Liaison Reporting

Evaluating sources from liaison services also is particularly challenging. As the example of CURVEBALL illustrates, liaison services of even our closest allies are not always sufficiently rigorous to avoid being fooled by fabricators. Moreover, liaison reporting can often be designed as much to influence as to inform the US government. Therefore, CI analysts must carefully examine liaison sources for reliability. Understanding a so-called friendly service's motives for sharing information is part of the challenge. For example, information that Israel shares regarding Iran's nuclear program is designed to influence US policy while also providing insight into Iran's plans and intentions. Often, other governments are trying to influence a US president's attitudes toward issues that matter to them, so their services face the temptation to skew their reporting in a direction favorable to their own government's assessment of a problem. For these reasons, using liaison-based intelligence will almost always come with the caveat that the information may be intended "to influence as well as inform." Sometimes, such liaison practices are reinforced at the highest levels, as when a KGB defector's reporting from the United Kingdom was fully supported by British prime minister Margaret Thatcher's efforts to influence US president Ronald Reagan to moderate US policy toward the Gorbachev regime during an insecure and unstable period in the Soviet Union.[44]

Additional sourcing challenges can arise when receiving intelligence on clandestine violent groups from an allied or semicooperative FIE (see box 7.4). Such groups draw a high level of scrutiny from the FIEs of the countries where they are based, particularly when they threaten to undermine political stability. Where the FIE is aggressively monitoring a clandestine group within its borders, it is more difficult for the CIA to unilaterally collect HUMINT and, perhaps, difficult to judge if that FIE is providing us with reliable intelligence on the group. But whether the FIE is providing us with *all relevant* information about the group cannot easily be known—perhaps the group is considering a plot against American citizens overseas and the FIE would rather not have the CIA learn that information until it has been more strongly confirmed. A prime example of this might be the Pakistan Inter-Services Intelligence reporting on the Taliban's activities in Pakistan. The fewer direct points of human and technical intelligence that the CIA has about a terrorist group target, the less able analysts are in corroborating the liaison reporting. Again, operational details matter to sound CI analysis, and these are even more elusive in liaison reporting than in our own operations.

BOX 7.4: CI CHALLENGES PRESENTED BY NONSTATE ACTORS

While understanding how large foreign intelligence bureaucracies behave is an indispensable lens for CI analysts, understanding how small clandestine groups behave is also critical—and the differences can be remarkable. The rise of violent nonstate actors, such as terrorist groups, have challenged traditional notions of how intelligence services behave and, consequently, how CI analysts must vet and evaluate them. Small group dynamics—such as the impact of familial relations within groups, the impact of informal hierarchies and decision-making, and the higher risk tolerances of those who self-select into terrorist groups—are a few of the new features that can influence intelligence sources. In the shadow of martyrdom, analysts need to reconsider whether an asset supplying deadly information to the US government is grounds enough for confirming the asset's loyalty to us.

In one instance, the CIC received a stream of HUMINT-based intelligence from a key CIA liaison partner that two major terrorist groups were sharing training, materials, and intelligence, which was a worrying trend. Would cooperation between these two major groups result in intelligence and counterintelligence gains for both as they engaged in their own liaison relations, sharing lessons learned and methods? In a curious twist, a second key CIA liaison partner in the same region downplayed concerns about these groups' potential cooperation. CI and CT analysts had to consider the information each group provided and separate what each of two liaison partners might be trying to gain by influencing the CIA with their divergent perspectives. The answer is rarely straightforward with liaison intelligence reporting. While liaison services may be manipulative, they might also be victims of their own cognitive biases or paranoia.

CONCLUSION

The relatively recent infusion of professionalized analysis into counterintelligence has certainly strengthened the CIA's long struggle with improving the quality and reach of CI generally. In this respect, the verdict is in: Over the last thirty or more years, CI analysis at the CIA has become a significant contributor to the performance, effectiveness, and impact of its counterintelligence elements. Its contributions are seen in its myriad types of support to FI and CI operations, to national policymaking, and to the counterespionage mission. Against early resistance and institutional skepticism, and notwithstanding any halting performance on its learning curve adapting to a new field and working in an unfamiliar organizational culture, the accomplishments of CI analysts clearly seem to have paid a healthy return on the investment of bringing them aboard. Based on track record alone, its future role in CIMC would seem assured. If that was an experiment, it must be declared a success.

We believe that CI analysis has improved HUMINT operations and policymaker support, and will continue such enhancements. But the new discipline remains a work in progress. As CI analysis techniques mature and more directly support an improving counterintelligence effort, the number of doubters will continue to dwindle and its advocates will increase. CI analysis is far from having reached its full potential. Depending on the evolution of DO culture and management support, it has much more to offer, specifically in asset validation, counterespionage, and other facets of counterintelligence where its analytical potential has barely been tapped. As the seasoned CI expert James Olson reminds us, "Wonderful things happen when good analysts in sufficient numbers . . . find the clues, make the connections, and focus our efforts in the areas that will be the most productive."[45] If CI were to be deprived of these recently discovered and demonstrably proven force multipliers, it would be seriously disadvantaged. Given the stakes and knowing its history, no rational decision-making process would want to gamble on a much-impaired CIA counterintelligence capability.

NOTES

1. This felicitous phrase has murky origins. Many of us saw it first as the title of the book by Phillip Knightley, *The Second Oldest Profession: Spies and Spying in the Twentieth Century*, originally published in 1986.

2. Before the creation of the CIA in 1947, the FBI had the national-level counterintelligence portfolio that spans law enforcement. Today CI is widely distributed across the IC and DoD, with the FBI having preeminence in domestic CI, the CIA principally engaged abroad, and DoD with defense-related CI functions both at home and abroad.

3. James M. Olson, *To Catch a Spy: The Art of Counterintelligence* (Washington, DC: Georgetown University Press, 2019), 50–53.

4. "A former French foreign minister, Bernard Kouchner, also suggested the European outrage may be less about the spying crossing any moral line and more about the extent of the United States' intelligence dominance. 'Let's be honest, we eavesdrop, too,' he told a French radio station. 'Everyone is listening to everyone else. But we don't have the same means as the United States, which makes us jealous.'" Max Fisher, "Why America Spies on Its Allies (and Probably Should)," *Washington Post*, October 29, 2013, https://www.washingtonpost.com/news/worldviews/wp/2013/10/29/why-america-spies-on-its-allies-and-probably-should/. Former CIA director James Woolsey has stated that the United States has spied on friendly countries, including in the economic realm: https://www.heise.de/tp/features/Former-CIA-Director-Says-US-Economic-Spying-Targets-European-Bribery-3446922.html. See also James Woolsey, "Why We Spy on Our Allies," *Wall Street Journal*, March 17, 2000.

5. Blake W. Mobley and Timothy Ray, "The Cali Cartel and Counterintelligence," *International Journal of Intelligence and Counterintelligence* 32, no. 1 (2019): 30–53.

6. Unlike counterintelligence, with its offensive and defensive aspects, *security* comprises mostly defensive measures such as fences, guard dogs, locks, safes, vaults, and encryption to protect people, installations, documents, and communications.

7. FBI, "Christopher Wray, Responding Effectively to the Chinese Economic Espionage Threat," February 6, 2020, https://www.fbi.gov/news/speeches/responding-effectively-to-the-chinese-economic-espionage-threat.

8. Sandra Grimes and Jeanne Vertefeuille, *Circle of Treason: A CIA Account of Traitor Aldrich Ames and the Men He Betrayed* (Annapolis: Naval Institute Press, 2012). David Wise, *Spy: The Inside Story of How the FBI's Robert Hanssen Betrayed America* (New York: Random House, 2003).

9. David E. Hoffman, *The Billion Dollar Spy: A True Story of Cold War Espionage and Betrayal* (London: Icon Books, 2018); Barry G. Royden, "Tolkachev, a Worthy Successor to Penkovsky," *Studies in Intelligence* 47, no. 3 (2003).

10. Robert Wallace and H. Keith Melton, *Spycraft: The Secret History of the CIA's Spytechs from Communism to al-Qaeda*, with Henry Robert Schlesinger (New York: E. P. Dutton, 2008).

11. Joby Warrick, *The Triple Agent: The Al-Qaeda Mole Who Infiltrated the CIA* (New York: Doubleday, 2011).

12. Office of the Inspector General, Department of Defense, "Report No. 05-INTEL-18: Review of the Actions Taken to Deter, Detect, and Investigate the Espionage Activities of Ana Belen Montes," June 16, 2005, p. 12, declassified from TOP SECRET/CODEWORD/NOFORN. Montes worked for the Cubans between 1985 and her arrest in 2001. See also Scott Carmichael, *True Believer: Inside the Investigation and Capture of Ana Montes, Cuba's Master Spy* (Annapolis: Naval Institute Press, 2007).

13. ODNI, *Assessing Russian Activities and Intentions in Recent US Elections*, Intelligence Community Assessment (ICA), January 6, 2017, https://www.dni.gov/files/documents/ICA_2017_01.pdf; ODNI, *Foreign Threats to the 2020 US Federal Elections*, Intelligence Community Assessment (ICA), March 2021, https://www.dni.gov/files/ODNI/documents/assessments/ICA-declass-16MAR21.pdf. The SSCI investigations Wikipedia page has links to the committee's studies of Russian intervention in the 2016 election (recall this is a Republican-chaired committee), https://en.wikipedia.org/wiki/Senate_Intelligence_Committee_report_on_Russian_interference_in_the_2016_United_States_presidential_election. The studies include "Volume I: Russian Efforts against Election Infrastructure," "Volume II: Russia's Use of Social Media," "Volume III: US Government Response to Russian Activities," "Volume IV: Review of the Intelligence Community Assessment (Additional Declassifications of Volume IV: Review of Intelligence Community Assessment)," and "Volume V: Counterintelligence Threats and Vulnerabilities."

14. Henry Hemming, *Agents of Influence: A British Campaign, a Canadian Spy, and the Secret Plot to Bring America into World War II* (New York: PublicAffairs, 2019); Richard Spence, "Englishmen in New York: The SIS American Station, 1915–21," *Intelligence and National Security* 19, no. 3 (September 2004): 511–37.

15. Published by the German Library of Information in New York City.

16. CI analysts, sometimes in conjunction with the DO desk or a CI Referent, will provide defensive CI briefings for officers traveling overseas to provide insight into the surveillance capabilities and tripwires for various FIEs active in areas of travel.

17. "Counterintelligence at CIA: A Brief History," Central Intelligence Agency, News and Information, March 23, 2018, https://web.archive.org/web/20180328184734/https://www.cia.gov/news-information/featured-story-archive/2018-featured-story-archive/counterintelligence-at-cia-a-brief-history.html.

18. "Terms and Definitions of Interest for DoD Counterintelligence Professionals, Office of Counterintelligence (DXC), Defense CI & HUMINT Center, Defense Intelligence Agency, 2 May 2011," https://www.dni.gov/files/NCSC/documents/ci/CI_Glossary.pdf.

19. Since 1947, US spies passed, or tried to pass, classified information to (at least) 26 foreign countries and to al-Qaeda. Russia (including the Soviet Union) has enjoyed the greatest success, with roughly 86 penetrations of US national security organizations from 1947 to 2007. During this period, the former Warsaw Pact countries of East Germany, Hungary, Czechoslovakia, and Poland ran 29 US spies; China ran 13; and Cuba ran 9. The loss of US classified information due to these combined 137 penetrations was wide-ranging and exceptionally damaging. As many as 10 allied or friendly countries—such as Israel, the Philippines,

and Taiwan—can also claim espionage successes against the United States. Defense Personnel Security Research Center (PERSEREC), 2009; Katherine L. Herbig, *Changes in Espionage by Americans: 1947–2007*, Technical Report 08-05 (Monterey, CA: PERSEREC, 2008); and David Major and Peter C. Oleson, "Espionage in America," in *AFIO's Guide to the Study of Intelligence*, ed. Peter C. Oleson (Falls Church, VA: Association of Former Intelligence Officers, 2016). James B. Bruce, Sina Beaghley, and W. George Jameson, *Secrecy in US National Security: Why a Paradigm Shift Is Needed*, PE-305-OSD (Santa Monica, CA: RAND Corporation, 2018), 16, notes 49–50.

20. These are generally accepted tallies with a small margin of uncertainty. Three US spies (the CIA's Edward Howard and Aldrich Ames, and the FBI's Robert Hanssen) accounted for multiple lost US penetrations, and some had been compromised by more than one of them. An authoritative study notes that the KGB could have had as many as twenty investigations going on during that period. Sandy Grimes and Jeanne Vertefeuille, *Circle of Treason: A CIA Account of Traitor Aldrich Ames and the Men He Betrayed* (Annapolis: Naval Institute Press, 2007), 85.

21. Grimes and Vertefeuille, chap. 10.

22. Grimes and Vertefeuille, 142–43.

23. Unclassified Abstract of the CIA Inspector General's Report on the Aldrich H. Ames Case, "The Aldrich H. Ames Case: An Assessment of CIA's Role in Identifying Ames as an Intelligence Penetration of the Agency," October 21, 1994, paras. 67–68, http://www.tscm.com/Hitzreport.html.

24. Robert M. Gates, *From the Shadows: The Ultimate Insider's Story of Five Presidents and How They Won the Cold War* (New York: Simon & Schuster, 1996), 206–7.

25. See Directorate of Intelligence, "China: Reorganization of Security Organs," August 1, 1983, declassified from SECRET, https://www.cia.gov/readingroom/docs/CIA-RDP85T00287R000401310001-4.pdf; Directorate of Intelligence, *USSR Monthly Review*, SOV UR 83-005X, April 1983, declassified from SECRET. All lead articles in the issue are devoted to "The KGB as an Instrument of Soviet Policy," https://www.cia.gov/readingroom/docs/CIA-RDP84T01083R000100050002-2.pdf.

26. See this unclassified speech: CIA, "Soviet Active Measures and Disinformation," May 16, 1986, https://www.cia.gov/readingroom/docs/CIA-RDP89G00720R000500060008-2.pdf; "Interagency Intelligence Assessment: Iran's Use of Terrorism," NI IIA 87-10012C, September 1987, declassified from TOP SECRET, https://www.cia.gov/readingroom/docs/CIA-RDP91T00498R000800100002-2.pdf; Current Intelligence Memorandum, "Possible KGB Involvement in Murder of Polish Priest," SOVA M-10013CX, declassified, https://www.cia.gov/readingroom/docs/CIA-RDP87M00539R001602330007-7.pdf. An older (1964) study of KGB assassination and kidnappings examines now-historical cases, from *Studies in Intelligence*, https://www.cia.gov/readingroom/docs/CIA-RDP78T03194A000400010014-6.pdf.

27. CIA, "HPSCI Briefing," September 20, 1983, https://www.cia.gov/readingroom/docs/CIA-RDP85B00263R000200170002-2.pdf; CIA, "Hostile Intelligence Threat, 22 July 1986," https://www.cia.gov/readingroom/docs/CIA-RDP88G01116R000400410013-9.pdf.

28. See CIA, "Soviet and Cuban Clandestine Activities against U.S. Policies," July 30, 1984, https://www.cia.gov/readingroom/docs/CIA-RDP86M00886R001000040005-5.pdf.

29. CIA, "Soviet Involvement in the West European Peace Movement," undated, https://www.cia.gov/readingroom/docs/CIA-RDP85M00364R001001530019-5.pdf; Directorate of Intelligence, Worldwide Active Measures and Propaganda Alert, February 1987, declassified

from SECRET, https://www.cia.gov/readingroom/docs/CIA-RDP88T00986R000100010001
-2.pdf; Thomas Boghardt, "Operation INFEKTION: Soviet Bloc Intelligence and Its AIDS Disinformation Campaign," *Studies in Intelligence* 53, no. 4 (December 2009): 1–24.

30. CIA, "Soviet Acquisition of Militarily Significant Western Technology: An Update," September 1985, https://www.cia.gov/readingroom/docs/CIA-RDP96B01172R000700060001-8
.pdf.

31. CNBC, "Former Cybersecurity Chief Says Russia, China, Iran and North Korea Are Trying to Steal Coronavirus Vaccine IP," December 6, 2020. Krebs stated this on CBS's *Face the
Nation*, https://www.cnbc.com/2020/12/06/former-top-cybersecurity-chief-says-russia-china
-iran-and-north-korea-are-trying-to-steal-coronoavir.html.

32. "H. Rept. 114-891: Review of the Unauthorized Disclosures of Former National Security
Agency Contractor Edward Snowden by the House Permanent Select Committee on Intelligence, 114th Congress," https://www.congress.gov/114/crpt/hrpt891/CRPT-114hrpt891.pdf.

33. Steve Vogel, *Betrayal in Berlin: George Blake, the Berlin Tunnel and the Greatest Con-
spiracy of the Cold War* (New York: HarperCollins, 2019).

34. Ben Macintyre, *A Spy among Friends: Kim Philby and the Great Betrayal* (New York:
Crown, 2014).

35. National Security Agency, "American Cryptology during the Cold War, 1945–1989;
Book IV: Cryptologic Rebirth, 1981–1989," 1999, 422–24, declassified from TOP SECRET,
CODEWORD, 407.

36. Gabriel Rinaldi, "Suspected Russian Spy Arrested at German Foreign Intelligence
Agency," *Politico*, December 22, 2022, https://www.politico.eu/article/suspected-russia-spy
-arrested-germany-foreign-intelligence-agency/.

37. Olson, *To Catch a Spy*, 63–64.

38. Olson, 52–53.

39. The CI failure with Curveball is best told in the authoritative WMD postmortem, Commission on the Intelligence Capabilities of the United States Regarding Weapons of Mass
Destruction, *Report to the President of the United States, March 31, 2005* (Washington, DC: US
Government Printing Office, 2005): 83–111. A senior operations officer provides a firsthand
narrative highlighting the difficulties of vetting this elusive liaison source, and a controversial
rendering of how discrepant interpretations of Curveball's bona fides were variously handled
by DI analysts and senior managers at the Agency's highest levels, in the book by Tyler Drumheller, *On the Brink: An Insider's Account of How the White House Compromised American
Intelligence* (New York: Carroll & Graf, 2006). A journalist's breezy and less nuanced interpretation is that by Bob Drogan, *Curveball: Spies, Lies, and the Con Man Who Caused a War* (New
York: Random House, 2007).

40. Owing to a toxic mix of poor collection and poor analysis, the 2002 NIE was wrong on
four of the five WMD issues examined—chemical weapons, biological weapons, nuclear recon-
stitution, and UAV delivery systems. James B. Bruce, "The Missing Link: The Analyst Collector Relationship," in *Analyzing Intelligence: National Security Practitioners' Perspectives*, 2nd
ed., ed. Roger Z. George and James B. Bruce (Washington, DC: Georgetown University Press,
2014), 167–68.

41. Falsely accused, Kelley was suspended from the CIA and spent the next three years
effectively under house arrest awaiting formal charges before Hanssen was caught, and Kelley was finally cleared after further delay and allowed to return to work. Before the false FBI

accusations, Kelley's sterling CI performance in both his Air Force career and subsequent work at the CIA was further bolstered through his remarkable analysis that identified a KGB illegal whose shoddy tradecraft led to the US capture of Felix Bloch, among the most senior American spies ever caught. See David Wise, *Spy: The Inside Story of How the FBI's Robert Hanssen Betrayed America* (New York: Random House, 2003), chaps. 24 and 25. See also US Department of Justice, Office of the Inspector General, "A Review of the FBI's Performance in Deterring, Detecting, and Investigating the Espionage Activities of Robert Philip Hanssen," August 2003, 17; and Leslie Stahl, "The Wrong Man," *60 Minutes* segment, CBS, February 2, 2003.

42. This is the ninth of Olson's "Ten Commandments of Counterintelligence," in *To Catch a Spy*, 63–66; commandments originally published in *Studies in Intelligence*, no. 11 (Fall–Winter 2001): 81–87.

43. Blake Mobley, *Terrorism and Counterintelligence: How Terrorist Groups Elude Detection* (New York: Columbia University Press, 2012), 244–47; David Ignatius, "Paranoia Could Be the Best Weapon against the Islamic State," *Washington Post*, December 2, 2014, https://www.washingtonpost.com/opinions/david-ignatius-paranoia-could-be-the-best-weapon-against-the-islamic-state/2014/12/02/771de21e-7a5f-11e4-9a27-6fdbc612bff8_story.html. In one instance, the British announced in the UK press an exaggeratedly high figure for the spoils of a PIRA bank robbery, which led to a series of internal PIRA shootings as members were believed to be stealing from the organization. A PIRA spokesperson summed up the damage from this and similar offensive counterintelligence operations: "[The British] almost destroyed us. They create paranoia in our ranks and left us severely damaged." Quoted by Tim Pat Coogan, *The IRA: A History* (Niwot, CO: Roberts Rinehart, 1993), 267.

44. An excellent example is the controversy engendered among senior CIA and NIC analysts over whether Britain was using the reporting of its high-level KGB defector Oleg Gordievsky—who was introduced to President Reagan in the Oval Office—to persuade Reagan to pivot to a less hostile posture toward the Soviet Union during the so-called war scare of 1983, when the KGB apparently believed the United States was preparing a surprise nuclear attack against the USSR under the cover of the NATO exercise Able Archer. See Ben B. Fischer, *A Cold War Conundrum: The 1983 Soviet War Scare*, CIA CSI Monograph 97-100002 (Langley, VA: CIA, 1997), 26–27, 35–37.

45. Olson, *To Catch a Spy*, 53.

8

COUNTERTERRORISM ANALYSIS: PREEMPTING THREATS

Clark Shannon

A counterterrorism analyst has an unenviable task—namely, to solve a crime before it happens. This mission involves several challenging subtasks, including gaining insight into a terrorist's plans, intentions, and operational capabilities before an attack occurs. Once reasonably understood, the counterterrorism (CT) analyst at the CIA next must persuade others to take action to prevent or blunt the attack. Most controversially, the analyst may also be asked to comment on how to prevent the next planned attack, which in some respects is more in the policy realm than intelligence. Rightly or wrongly, the failure to deliver on any one of these duties may be laid at the doorstep of the analyst to explain how his or her efforts fell short. Analyzing threats and issuing warnings is the "purest" form of counterterrorism analysis because an attack or disruption offers some clarity. Other aspects of CT analysis are opaque, even in hindsight, and include support for operations and answering policymakers' questions, such as, Are America's terrorist adversaries losing strength or just lying low while rebuilding? What are their objectives and key vulnerabilities? Are the military and law enforcement actions designed to suppress terrorism in a particular country making the situation better or worse? Despite the manifold challenges in answering these questions, the analyst has few reliable guideposts and metrics for success.

This chapter offers a perspective on the evolving discipline of counterterrorism analysis at the CIA. There is little academic literature and few journalistic accounts exist on CT practices or tradecraft in the intelligence community, and just like the phenomenon of terrorism itself, this category of analysis is hard to define with much precision and is not well understood either inside or outside the community.[1] Moreover, the CIA is just one element in the US government's larger CT enterprise, which includes analysts at other departments and agencies who support targeting by law enforcement and military operators and collection efforts in other parts of the community as well as policy decisions and protective security measures both at home and abroad.

This chapter aims to fill a gap in the intelligence and terrorism studies literature and highlight what CT analysts at the CIA do, their key partners and interactions in the US government's counterterrorism enterprise, and how analysts in the CIA Counterterrorism Mission Center (CTMC) accomplish its threefold declared mission to "preempt, disrupt, and defeat" international terrorism. The focus is on CIA analysis of the transnational jihadist movement led by al-Qaeda and the so-called Islamic State, or ISIS, and their offshoots. However, many of the observations about the analysis would apply to departments and agencies in the intelligence community other than the CIA as well as analysis of other militant groups with a more national or sectarian focus, such as the Palestinian Hamas group or Lebanese Hezbollah.

In surveying the work of the counterterrorism analyst, I offer firsthand impressions of how the CIA and other community analysts have contributed to national security. My argument is that the CIA's biggest contribution since the 9/11 attacks has been in support of the first two CTMC objectives—namely, to preempt attacks through offensive actions and to disrupt terrorist networks. Analysts contribute by assessing the adversary, helping to set targeting priorities, and delivering warnings that trigger others to take both offensive and defensive measures. The absence of large-scale attacks within the United States since 2001 and systematic dismantling of the leadership cadre and external attack apparatus of al-Qaeda and ISIS are major accomplishments where analysis has played a role.

Nonetheless, the analysts' contribution to America's fight to "defeat" terrorism has proved less consequential, as policymakers have struggled to grasp the evolution of the threat and pursue strategies that are flexible and tailored to local conditions. Perhaps future historians reviewing CIA analysis will conclude that intelligence assessments of the transnational jihadist phenomenon focused too much on tactical and operational questions rather than on terrorist strategy and how counterterrorism augments or erodes the accomplishment of other national security goals, and that analysts could have been more precise in laying out a hierarchy of threats to help policymakers avoid the temptation to deal with "everything everywhere." Also, they may conclude that analysts should have taken a more deliberately multidisciplinary approach that weaves political and terrorism analysis into a single narrative to illuminate the complex interplay between terrorists, state actors (including the United States), and the political, economic, and social context where terrorists operate.

THE EMERGENCE OF THE CIA'S ANALYTIC WORK ON TERRORISM

Unlike the analytic disciplines discussed earlier in this volume, counterterrorism analysis at the CIA is relatively new. Before the 9/11 attacks, CT analysis at best was only a "niche" subject for a handful of career analysts.[2] For example, in the 1970s, the

CIA's Directorate of Intelligence (DI)—the Agency's analytic element, now known as the Directorate of Analysis (DA)—began to write profiles on terrorist groups, compile statistics on international terrorism, and assess macro-level trends in terrorist activity.[3] By 1986, Iranian- and Libyan-backed terrorism and Palestinian militant violence had moved to near the top of the national security agenda. Accordingly, the Reagan administration expanded the CT analysis mission across the US government and authorized the creation of the director of central intelligence's Counterterrorist Center (CTC)—since 2015 known as the Counterterrorism Mission Center (CTMC)—to enable a more proactive and muscular response to anti-American terrorism. This included developing an operational apparatus to disrupt attacks, pursue fugitive terrorists, and maintain an effective operational reach against terrorist groups whose activities spanned many countries and regions.

Despite having a home in the CTC, analysis of terrorism remained on the periphery of the DI's core mission and faced bureaucratic hurdles as well (see box 8.1). Unlike other disciplines, the primary customers of terrorism analysis were not the president, senior Cabinet officials, and National Security Council (NSC) directors but rather operational counterparts in CTC. Those officers drawn from the CIA'S Directorate of Operations (DO), the FBI, and the National Security Agency (NSA) looked to CT analysis for background knowledge, situational awareness, and targeting support for collection and law enforcement operations. While policymaker engagement with CTC analysis grew along with concerns about al-Qaeda in the 1990s, analysts working there were generally at a disadvantage in terms of visibility and professional advancement. This persisted despite attracting some of the CIA's most talented

---

BOX 8.1: TURF AND TERRORISM

Creating an analytic discipline on counterterrorism had its share of birthing problems. The CIA leadership's decision to create a new bureaucratic element like the CTC in the 1980s was not popular with the traditional and powerful regional divisions in the Directorate of Operations nor with the analytic directorate's regional offices. In their own way, each directorate viewed the CTC's transnational focus as an encroachment on its turf and also as competition for resources and personnel. Importantly, however, the first CTC director, Duane "Dewey" Clarridge, insisted that the new center include its own analytic team to help guide operations. Evoking the lessons learned from the ill-fated Bay of Pigs operation, when operators excluded analysts from their planning, Clarridge's stewardship was critical to establishing a key role for analysis in the first such multidirectorate center.

The CTC was also the first center to incorporate representatives from multiple agencies. Administratively housed in the Directorate of Operations, the CTC hosted representatives from other departments and agencies—such as the FBI, NSA, and Federal Aviation Administration—as well as a small cadre of CIA analysts on loan from their directorate's "home base." The philosophy of the CTC was to avoid the separate "silos" (or separation) of information and action that historically has existed among the many domestic and foreign policy agencies.

Source: Timothy Naftali, "US Counterterrorism before Bin Laden," *International Journal* 60, no. 1 (Winter 2004-5): 25-34. See also Nicholas Dujmovic, interview on CSPAN, *Washington Journal*, April 17, 2021, https://www.c-span.org/video/?510576-5/washington-journal-nicholas-dujmovic -discusses-60th-anniversary-bay-pigs-invasion&event=510576&playEvent.

officers—including future CIA director John Brennan, who led an analytic team in CTC, and Paul Pillar, a highly regarded political analyst and manager who later wrote the most comprehensive and authoritative book on terrorism's place in US foreign policy.[4] In fact, analysts in the CTC were detached from the DI's traditional offices, without the benefit of a career service, promotion board, peer networks, and the training and development opportunities afforded to other DI analysts.

The bureaucratic tide turned toward the end of the 1990s. While serving at the Department of State and subsequently in the office of the deputy director of intelligence, I observed how functional issues such as terrorism, weapons proliferation, and financial intelligence increasingly were on the minds of policymakers grappling with globalization and transnational threats. The 1998 attacks on the US embassies in Kenya and Tanzania, a series of failed and foiled plots in 1999, and the 2000 attack on the USS *Cole* in Yemen further elevated counterterrorism as a distinct focus of analysis. Then–CIA director George Tenet acknowledged the need for a major realignment of analytic and operational resources in the CIA and across the intelligence community, but action came too late to avert the 9/11 attacks. At that time, the CIA had a tiny number of analysts dedicated full time to al-Qaeda and assigned to the CTC, and it had only a limited focus on assessing foreign terrorist threats to the US homeland. Similarly, the FBI had only a couple of analysts dedicated full time to al-Qaeda.[5] I was among the few dozen analysts who worked in the CTC at the time, after having joined the Analysis Group in August 1999.[6] By comparison, the US Department of State had about twenty analysts dedicated to analyzing threats to US diplomatic personnel and missions, consistent with America's overwhelmingly defensive CT posture at the time.[7]

After 9/11, CIA leadership pivoted the entire organization toward counterterrorism in support of the so-called global war on terrorism. The CTC's Analysis Group expanded to become a full-size office, where it assigned many more analysts to do what just a few had done before September 11. Over the next two decades, hundreds of analysts would rotate through the CTC, many of whose work on high-profile terrorism issues would advance their careers, sometimes reaching positions as President's Daily Brief writers, senior analytic managers, and policymakers. Terrorism analysts now enjoy the same status and career prospects as those in other offices across the directorate. The CTC served as the model for a 2015 Agency-wide reorganization under John Brennan's direction that merged analytic and operational units under new "Mission Centers" dedicated to a specific geographic region or functional issue.

Yet, even after 2001, when counterterrorism moved to the forefront of the Agency's mission, it has struggled to reconcile the analytic standards, methods, product lines, and thresholds for writing and briefing on terrorism issues with the CIA's traditional analytic disciplines. In this sense, there remain many challenges to counterterrorism's status as a distinct analytic discipline.

IS COUNTERTERRORISM AN ANALYTIC DISCIPLINE?

Like terrorism itself, the analysis of terrorism is difficult to categorize with much precision. The terrorist challenge has been depicted as a criminal act, expression of politics, mode of warfare, form of propaganda, and perversion of religion.[8] Each framework offers some insights, so one needs to use multiple lenses to view terrorism. Political, military, economic, social, or psychological approaches each offer distinct insights on the phenomenon, as evidenced by the burgeoning field of "terrorism studies" that today spans multiple academic fields. Even so, terrorism experts both inside and outside the intelligence community have struggled to develop a set of shared concepts, definitions, and general theories.[9] On reflection, counterterrorism analysts and managers have continued to grapple with fundamental conceptual issues, such as what drives terrorism, how to organize analytic efforts against the phenomenon, and how to distinguish between counterterrorism success and failure. As a result, CT analysis is probably best understood as a discipline that reaches across and integrates the various analytic disciplines across the CIA and other departments and agencies.

CIA managers both before and after 9/11 recognized the need to promote counterterrorism analysis as a discipline and equip analysts with the tools to produce analysis that has explanatory power. Between 1999 and 2001, the CTC routinely consulted with leading scholars in the field of terrorism studies and enlisted one to organize the equivalent of a college seminar in house for analysts. After 2001, the CTC developed a robust outreach program to draw on the insights from a wide range of academic experts, security professionals, and journalists, including by hosting the terrorism researcher Bruce Hoffman as a scholar-in-residence from 2004 to 2006.[10] The CIA drew on its outreach to terrorism experts to create a training program at the Sherman Kent School for Intelligence Analysis, which I organized, for both entry-level analysts and for mid-level CT practitioners who aspired to join the analytic directorate's senior ranks.

As a course director and instructor in CT analysis at the Sherman Kent School, I shaped the initial terrorism analysis curriculum around methods and techniques from other disciplines. One of the core approaches we adopted was a model that the former Defense Intelligence Agency weapons analyst John Bodnar developed and labeled as the multidimensional analysis model as a means to extract strategic insight from highly fragmented data.[11] Under this model, analysts record and code all relevant activities as reported in the intelligence on a timeline to detect indicators and potential progression in a terrorist adversary's plans and activities. Timelines illuminate the "what" and "when" questions. In addition, analysts would situate the persons and other entities and their connections in a link chart. By including place names or geographic coordinates, analysts create a spatial "map" that answers the "where" and "how" questions.

Finally, analysts situate the same entities in an organizational chart, either formal or inferred from one individual's assessed influence over another to reveal "who" and "why" the adversary is acting in a certain manner. Taken together, Bodnar's model helps analysts answer the fundamental questions about a clandestine group, drive further collection to address gaps, and glean insight into a group's plans, intentions, and capabilities when solid intelligence on senior leadership is lacking. Furthermore, analysts could draw on this model to develop indications and warning of planned terrorist attacks, much as military analysts use the same approach to anticipate and warn of interstate conflict.[12]

WHO ARE CT ANALYSTS?

The CIA enlists officers with a wide range of backgrounds and experiences to support the counterterrorism mission in the CTMC, consistent with the need for a multi-disciplinary approach to terrorism. Given the primary focus on al-Qaeda and ISIS, a significant number of CT analysts have studied Arabic. Similarly, analysts who cover terrorist finances, weapons, or communications practices, for example, often bring specialized expertise but do not delve much into cultural factors or the details of one group over those of another. Some analysts completed courses on terrorism while in college, but most did not, and there is no single profile for who will succeed as a CT analyst. The late Terry Bishop, who was one of the most productive analysts assigned to the CTC immediately after 9/11, had previously focused on Russian leadership. Bishop thrived in the CTC because he had an abiding curiosity about all types of ruthless and conspiratorial leaders; accordingly, he was able to apply the same energy and creativity to understand al-Qaeda's senior leaders that he had applied to Vladimir Putin and his inner circle.[13]

Although counterterrorism analysts have varied expertise and academic backgrounds, the most talented among them have an intellectual and emotional disposition that allows them to take a clinical, detached view of a subject that by its nature aims to arouse an emotional response. Experienced CT analysts recognize that provoking fear, anxiety, and irrational reactions by governments and the public is at the center of terrorist strategy and that terrorists win by inflicting psychological, not physical, damage.[14] In this context, presidents, politicians, journalists, and the public—especially in modern liberal democracies—may struggle to separate reason from emotion in responding to terrorism. Retrospective accounts and public opinion polls in the aftermath of 9/11 support the notion that mass anxiety and fears of a second wave of attacks shaped President George W. Bush's counterterrorism policy and influenced his decision to invade Iraq in 2003.[15] Similarly, the fear of a resurgent threat from Afghanistan drove every US president since 2001 to maintain

US troops in Afghanistan,[16] despite less evidence each year that al-Qaeda organized external operations from there.[17] Counterterrorism analysts are not immune to emotional biases, which can result in excessive warning, customer fatigue, and intelligence failures.[18] Therefore, a key measure of the analysts' performance is the degree to which they can characterize terrorism challenges in a way that helps decision-makers avoid misplaced complacency in the absence of an immediate terrorist threat or, alternatively, panicked overreaction to terror that can lead to costly and misguided policies.

A UNIQUE MISSION

Counterterrorism analysis is not only distinguished by its inherently multidisciplinary approach. Just as important, its work is designed and expected to prompt action. Unlike analysts in the traditional disciplines whose finished intelligence primarily supports the decision-making *process*, CT intelligence at the CIA aims to achieve a particular *outcome*. The process-versus-outcome distinction matters because analysis in support of the latter is skewed heavily toward action. Moreover, the CTMC is a hybrid unit that not only combines the tasks of intelligence collection and analysis but also includes covert action; hence, CT analysts are attuned to the fact that their work could appear to be "grading the homework" of their operational counterparts. Analytic managers under this organizational structure have a special responsibility to review the analysis for any subtle "conflict of interest"—that is, an inclination for CT analysts to favorably assess those courses of action that they or their operational colleagues supported.

To be sure, the counterterrorism analyst's focus on a particular operational or policy outcome is not unique. It has parallels in the fields of counterintelligence, counterproliferation, and counternarcotics analysis. In each of these domains, the CIA opted in the 1980s and 1990s to emulate the CTC organizational model and assign analysts to centers where the analysis is integrated with operations. While counterterrorism analysts aim to stop terrorist attacks, counterintelligence analysts work to stop spies working against the United States, and counternarcotics analysts seek to stop drugs crossing our borders. For each of these functional centers, the analytic focus is transnational and operational, and involves both state and nonstate actors. However, the targets of concern to these other centers—traffickers, spies, and smugglers—engage in illicit activity for personal, professional, or commercial reasons without an overt political agenda. As a result, the intelligence centers that tackle those problems have a reasonably reliable set of metrics—arrests, disruptions, interdictions, and seizures—to assess progress toward a desired operational outcome. CT analysts have a different type of target because terrorists engage in political violence to manipulate governments and public confidence. Therefore, counterterrorism reflects a dynamic interaction between the CT actor, terrorist adversary, and the audience, which confounds easy measures of success.

The CT analyst's focus on small, conspiratorial groups highlights another key difference from the traditional disciplines—that is, the fragmented nature of terrorism intelligence. Gregory Treverton, former chair of the National Intelligence Council, argues that the country analyst has the advantage of a conceptual schema of known leaders and national institutions, and a historical narrative that allows the analyst to glean insight from vague or incomplete reports to continue the "story" about the country.[19] By contrast, Susan Hassler, a former colleague at the CTC, recounted how a terrorism analyst—working without a similar guide—can become disoriented from the deluge of fragmentary and often contradictory intelligence. Hassler contrasts CT to her previous job, where she could weave a compelling analytic story by drawing on history and "predigested" intelligence in the form of well-composed analysis or meeting notes from US diplomats, authoritative reports from major media outlets, and clandestine reports drafted in response to formal intelligence requirements.[20]

WHERE THE CIA FITS IN AMERICA'S COUNTERTERRORISM ENTERPRISE

Just as CT analysts work in a hybrid organization alongside operations officers inside the CIA, they also collaborate with counterparts in other departments and agencies across the US government. Interagency relationships have evolved over time, and vary from one country to the next, but in general the closest partners for CIA counterterrorism analysts have been staff members of the NSA; the FBI; the US military, especially the Joint Special Operations Command (JSOC); and the National Counterterrorism Center (NCTC). The NSA, FBI, and the military bring unique collection and operational capabilities of value to the CIA, while the NCTC is more of a peer institution for the CTMC than a traditional partner.

One of the more revealing indicators of the depth of the CIA's interagency relationships is whether the CIA allows officers from the other department or agency to sit in the CTMC workspaces and have access to the center's vast database of clandestine operational cables and records. The CTMC and the FBI's international terrorism section cemented their commitment to work jointly in 1995 by exchanging senior-level officials. The two agencies agreed that one of two deputy chiefs in the CTC would be an FBI official, and one of two deputies at the FBI's comparable center would be from the CIA.[21] Similarly, the CTMC has hosted NSA representatives in the center since long before 9/11 to facilitate intelligence sharing. The FBI and NSA liaison presence is critical because CIA officers do not have authority to access those agencies' sensitive operational information, especially on US persons. The CTMC also struck an information-sharing arrangement with the JSOC.

Although US law bounds each organization's authorities and jurisdiction, the drive to collaborate inevitably becomes a source of confusion, and in some instances competition, between the CIA and the various departments and agencies. Disagreements tend to boil down to the question of which agency has primacy in a geographic area or specific case. A colleague of mine once described the CIA's organizational culture as one of "competitive collegiality." In practice, this meant that individuals would strive to maintain good relations while they competed with each other for status and resources. The same principle might apply to the CIA's interagency relationships.

The CIA's and FBI's missteps before 9/11 are well documented and need not be recounted in this chapter. Suffice it to say that the FBI's focus on protecting information for criminal prosecutions and the CIA's penchant for not sharing operational information outside the Agency produced information gaps that became unacceptable after the 9/11 attacks. Those shortfalls in communication and sharing between law enforcement and intelligence contrast sharply with the extraordinary partnership between the CIA and FBI that exists today. The post-9/11 reforms were transformative for both agencies and brought them into closer alignment. In a 2015 congressionally directed study of the FBI's CT procedures, reviewers judged that the FBI's relations with the CIA domestically and overseas are "arguably the strongest . . . in their collective history."[22] The FBI's collection and dissemination of human intelligence, obtained both from confidential human sources and from FBI agents, has skyrocketed and, in many cases, FBI human intelligence eclipses the CIA's efforts in the online domain.

The CIA's other key interagency partner for counterterrorism operations has been the US military, which, like the Agency, pivoted to the counterterrorism mission with the wars in Afghanistan and Iraq. The CIA also had to adjust its practices for information sharing during this era to enable military operations that relied on sensitive intelligence. According to one account, after the JSOC established its first joint intelligence task force at Bagram Air Base in Afghanistan, CIA officers set up police tape to separate the Agency analysts from military counterparts.[23] Soon, however, the CIA was supporting what JSOC commander General Stanley McChrystal called the "fight for intelligence" through raids mounted in quick succession to obtain raw intelligence from documents and debriefings and, in the military's jargon, get inside the enemy's "decision cycle."[24] CIA analysts gained a mountain of intelligence from JSOC operations, while CIA operators leaned heavily on the military to provide facilities, security, logistics, and operational platforms in hot war zones and areas of active hostilities.

While the CIA's interagency partnerships with law enforcement and the military have an operational focus, the CIA also maintains partnerships in the community to advance intelligence collection and analysis. CTMC analysts engage every day with counterparts at the NSA, generating requirements, providing feedback on reports, and clearing tearlines with NSA-derived information to share with US and foreign partners.[25] For the CT analysts in particular, SIGINT is the lifeblood of counterterrorism, the most consistently reliable and useful source on organizations and networks and their plans. Unfortunately, most CIA analysts still have only a limited understanding of the NSA's capabilities, processes, and its relations with foreign SIGINT partners because of the NSA's strong protective shield around its unique access and methods—not to mention its sensitive US persons data.

Finally, analysts in the CTMC and the National Counterterrorism Center have built a productive relationship, although the twin organizations still compete as often as they collaborate. In 2005, Congress created the NCTC as part of the Office of the Director of National Intelligence, who would oversee the intelligence community, including the CIA. Many observers viewed the NCTC as a punitive measure for the CIA's failure to prevent the 9/11 attacks and an easy way for Congress to demonstrate bipartisan agreement.[26] The intent of the legislation authorizing the NCTC was to develop a central repository for foreign intelligence, a terrorist identity database warehouse, and a platform for domestic FBI operations. However, Congress also envisioned more strategic analysis from the NCTC that would help compensate for what the commission deemed a "lack of imagination" by analysts before 9/11. Inevitably, forming the NCTC sparked an analytic turf war with the CIA because Congress and the Bush administration made no parallel effort to rescind the CIA's CT mission.[27] Over time, the CTMC and NCTC analysts reached a balance, in particular after a 2006 intelligence community directive affirmed the NCTC's statutory role as the lead agency for all-source integration and analysis of terrorism. The NCTC has supplanted the CTMC in providing the high-visibility "scene setter" briefings for interagency meetings and in producing integrated, community-wide terrorism analysis. In part, this made sense because the NCTC's independence from any policymaking or operational department or agency gives the NCTC the imprimatur of analytic objectivity.

How CT Analysts Enable Collection

In addition to working with counterpart analysts and operators, CT analysts work with collectors of all sorts. Fran Moore, a former director of analysis for the CTC and later the deputy director of intelligence, urged CTMC officers to be "360-degree analysts"—that is, officers who take a full-spectrum view of their responsibility to support the policy customer as well as collectors and other operational partners in CIA field stations, foreign government services, law enforcement, and the military.[28] The 360-degree CT analyst is a rough equivalent to the "enabler" analyst that the editors highlight in the introduction to this volume. By virtue of their affiliation with a hybrid center, the counterterrorism analysts at the CIA have an established channel to feed collection requirements and provide feedback on disseminated reports to operations officers in CIA field stations, technical and HUMINT targeters, DO collection management officers, and collectors in other departments and agencies. One of the formal mechanisms where CT analysts play a key role to drive collection is through the NSC-chaired interagency body known as the Counterterrorism Security Group (CSG), which was established after President Bill Clinton signed Presidential Decision Directive 62 (PDD-62) in May 1996. The CSG has a storied history in the pre-9/11 era and continued to function as of the early 2020s. The NSC-chaired body includes senior representatives from several departments and agencies who meet weekly to review specific threats. In preparation for the CSG, the CIA's analytic partners in the NCTC draft talking points on reported threats worldwide, which range from a planned attack against US forces operating in Syria to a group of teenagers in Europe who are brandishing weapons on social media and declaring their loyalty to ISIS. The talking points were generally more than twenty pages long, and the CIA was expected to provide background and context on raw intelligence reporting and specify what follow-up actions the CIA and our foreign partners are taking in response to the threat. The CSG reviews an enormous volume of uncorroborated and unrealistic threat information, but the forum nonetheless is a model for terrorism warning and response because the process is customer-designed by the NSC, analyst-built, and collector fueled. All but the most sensational threats are treated as valid until customer-driven collection proves otherwise or else law enforcement or military operators take action to preempt or disrupt the threat. The CSG process can be likened to a sort of combined-arms training exercise to synchronize and test the terrorist threat warning system and ensure that it functions when a serious threat emerges.[29]

The CSG and other threat review processes rely on an indications-and-warning model to anticipate planned attacks, which helps analysts guide collection. The model rests on one or more hypotheses about how an attack might take shape, so uncertainties and inconsistencies in the reporting that do not align well with the hypotheses in the indications-and-warning model tend to prompt questions from analysts and other CSG members that in turn require additional reporting. When done well, the process can create a virtuous circle where the threat analysis drives an operational response such as an arrest, which in turn yields additional collection in the form of debriefing reports, captured documents, and seized electronic devices. Finally, the analyst might prepare a retrospective analysis for policymakers on the suspects, their activities, and the impact of the disruption.[30]

WHAT CT ANALYSTS DO

The counterterrorism analyst's mission is clear even if the tasks vary. At the CIA, analysts support the three priority objectives laid out in the CTMC charter: to "preempt, disrupt, and defeat" the terrorist adversary. First and foremost is the analyst's requirement to warn of planned or potential plots against US persons or interests, which should trigger law enforcement, the military, or security services to take preemptive action to thwart the attack. In addition, CT analysts support ongoing efforts to disrupt the wider network of terrorist leaders, facilitators, and backers, and evaluate the impact of such efforts. A third key objective—to defeat terrorism—is the most ambitious and is deeply intertwined with other policy goals that intersect with counterterrorism. For the analyst, delivering on this requirement entails leveling policymaker expectations and describing what defeat of terrorism looks like. This chapter examines all three missions in turn.

Preemption: From Analysis to Action

For more than three decades, one of the CIA's top counterterrorism missions has been to support preemptive action against known terrorists to damage their organizations and destroy their safe havens. Often portrayed as a seismic shift in US policy after 9/11, the CTC laid the groundwork for this approach starting in 1986, to support operations with US special forces and develop access to denied areas using unmanned aerial vehicles to surveil high-profile terrorist targets. Over time, support to offensive counterterrorism operations using ground and air assets has moved to the forefront of the CIA's counterterrorism mission.[31]

Analysts play a variety of roles in helping the CIA preempt attacks and attackers, although their key contributions are at the front and back ends of CT operations. Analysts help set priorities for specific operational targets by mapping the structure of terrorist networks and organizations to identify who holds the most influence and the specialized skills relevant to external operations, in particular those persons who have access or extensive contacts in the West. The CTMC maintains a library of "extremist profiles" on terrorist leaders worldwide, which is updated on a regular basis and includes a section designed to guide targeting decisions. Cofer Black, the colorful chief of the CTC when 9/11 occurred, described his operational role to me as the equivalent to a saber-toothed tiger, "with sharp teeth, long claws, and the strength to pounce and devour prey." "But," Cofer added, "this animal has very narrow-set eyes and a tiny brain. I need your brains to point in the right direction."[32] With priorities set, the CT analyst yields primary responsibility to a separate category of intelligence professionals known as "targeters" as well as operations officers. Targeters have highly developed technical skills and carry out the bulk of the investigative work on terrorists who are authorized targets for preemptive strikes. Targeters and analysts work under the same chain of command in the CTMC, with the targeters supporting internal customers, while analysts are mainly engaged with the policymaking community.[33]

CT analysts also help on the back end of operations by providing "after-action" evaluations of the strategic, operational, and tactical impact of preemptive strikes. Although a broader assessment of targeted killings of foreign terrorists by the US government is beyond the scope of this chapter, my own experience in providing information and analysis to help responsible US government officials tackle these complex issues surrounding preemptive strikes underscores the importance of including the political and social contexts to these impact assessments. In hindsight, one must acknowledge the possibility that in some cases doing nothing may have been a better course of action. The case of Abu Ali al-Harithi illustrates how analysts, targeters, and operators may not always appreciate the hidden costs of such preemptive strikes (see box 8.2).

Looking back, the killing of Abu Ali in a missile strike may have rallied local support for al-Qaeda in Yemen and spurred retaliatory attacks against the United States. Oblique public claims of credit for the attack by the secretary and deputy secretary of defense immediately after the strike undoubtedly damaged the legitimacy of the Yemeni government. Within weeks, local jihadists killed American missionaries working in Yemen and later claimed a series of anti-Western attacks in Abu Ali's name to avenge his death. When al-Qaeda rolled out an organizational affiliate in Yemen in February 2006, the new leader, Abu Basir Nasir al-Wahishi, announced that he was taking up Abu Ali's mantle.[34] The case of Abu Ali highlights the unavoidable trade-offs analysts from across US government departments and agencies must consider

---

BOX 8.2: THE NOVEMBER 2002 TARGETED KILLING OF ABU ALI

Qaed Salim Sinan al-Harithi, also known as Abu Ali al-Harithi, was a senior al-Qaeda associate in Yemen and a suspect in the October 2000 attack on the USS *Cole*, which killed seventeen sailors.[35] CIA director George Tenet later identified Abu Ali in congressional testimony as a confirmed senior al-Qaeda leader killed by the United States in a remote area of central Yemen.[36] The CIA had included Abu Ali in a list of suspects soon after the *Cole* bombing. He was an influential tribal figure and longtime associate of Osama Bin Laden who had organized Bin Laden-funded training camps in Yemen. Thus, Abu Ali was a natural candidate to have lent support to the attack.[37]

However, a 2011 scholarly review of al-Qaeda's trajectory during this period based on primary and secondary sources indicates that both jihadists and Yemeni intelligence officials discounted Abu Ali's role in the attack. Close observers saw him more as a respected tribesman rather than formal leader involved in plotting or carrying out terrorist attacks.[38] This information tracked with the CIA and FBI's own investigations that highlighted the central role of Saudi al-Qaeda members Abd al-Rahim al-Nashiri and Walid Bin Attash, operatives deployed from Afghanistan with no organizational base inside Yemen.[39]

when evaluating a targeted killing. For strikes to have a strategic impact, the group either must be vulnerable to a struggle over succession or not have a more capable and dangerous successor waiting in the wings. Similarly, strikes are less likely to cause blowback when focused on targets that lack deep connections to the local landscape through ethnic, tribal, or ideological ties.[40]

Disruption: Working with Others

In addition to preemptive strikes, analysts support nonkinetic operations to disrupt the plans and capabilities of al-Qaeda and ISIS-associated groups and networks. This can take the form of hostile surveillance to sow uncertainty in terrorist networks, police investigations and arrests of suspected operatives, and financial sanctions and travel restrictions to squeeze terrorist resources and mobility. The specific requirements for the CIA's analytic support depend on the nature of the threat; operating environment for US military, intelligence, and law enforcement personnel; capabilities of local partners; and the political and social environment. As with preemptive strikes, the analyst's main contributions are typically at both ends of the operational timeline, first helping set priority targets for disruption and working with partners to support operations and later assessing the effects.

Threat assessments and warning products from the CIA and other agencies have helped shape countless disruption operations worldwide over the past two decades. Of course, disruption is less viable in the countries where political order is weak and terrorist violence is highest—Afghanistan, Burkina Faso, Iraq, Mali, Niger Somalia, Syria, and Yemen. Such places are challenging intelligence collection environments and the local security services have limited will or capability to disrupt threats, which are mainly directed at local and regional targets. In Europe and other Western nations, the prospects for collecting actionable intelligence are higher. There, the CIA has robust intelligence sharing and often has unique insights into what our British counterparts call the "upstream" operatives in hot war zones who direct or enable attacks in the West. For example, from 2014 to 2017, US and Western government CT analysts focused heavily on ISIS's external operations apparatus and media operatives located in Syria and Iraq who often had extensive contacts in the West and could drive terrorist plots. A European terrorism researcher counted 69 terrorist plots in Europe associated with ISIS during this period, of which 32 were completed attacks.[41] The high proportion of disrupted attacks attests not only to the effectiveness of the European services but to the level of US intelligence sharing that enabled the European services to map terrorist networks and thwart attacks.

Another contribution analysts make to disruption efforts is to provide assessments to foreign government partners that lay the groundwork for the CIA to pursue joint operations or develop new streams of intelligence sharing. Analysts like me routinely would meet with foreign partners to share the CIA's assessments on terrorist groups and associated individuals whom the partner service might be able to collect against or disrupt. In my experience, this "intelligence diplomacy" consisted of one part sober analysis to two parts salesmanship. As with any diplomatic démarche, the briefings I delivered met with varied reactions, from a polite noncommittal response to an enthusiastic request by the partner to meet again and expand intelligence sharing. The responses reflected less the quality of CIA analysis than the partner's view of the CT threat and their tolerance for risk, but the overall effect of this largely invisible dialogue between governments was to stitch together the global counterterrorism apparatus that has paid big dividends for US national security.

Defeat: The Elusive Goal

The third objective of defeating terrorism remains the most problematic for CT analysts and operators alike. Many analysts saw this more as an exhortation than a task, and one that begs the question who specifically the United States seeks to defeat and what "victory" over the adversary looks like. To be sure, two decades of defensive antiterrorism measures and offensive counterterrorism operations, first against al-Qaeda and later against ISIS, have secured the US homeland against terrorist infiltration and attacks either directed or enabled by jihadists against US persons and interests. Similarly, in other Western countries and all but a handful of other countries, the frequency and casualties from terrorist attacks against Western and local targets plummeted from the peak levels of 2014–16.[42]

The defeat objective becomes less compelling and more elusive when the focus shifts to the wider set of allied and affiliated jihadist groups, which still represent a potent threat. As of 2021, al-Qaeda had formal affiliates and allied groupings in about ten countries, while ISIS has declared branches or networks in approximately twenty nations. Developing a precise estimate of the number of fighters affiliated with the jihadist movements worldwide is extremely difficult, and many nongovernment researchers tend toward higher estimates than intelligence community analysts would venture, but the number of jihadist fighters and their geographic footprint in 2021 far exceed the scale of the transnational network in 2001.[43] Even as al-Qaeda and ISIS's core leadership has been depleted and their propaganda no longer inspires, their local affiliates have exploited geopolitical upheaval and weak or declining central government authority in Africa, the Middle East, and Asia to gain footholds and enable attacks on local and regional targets. The fusion of local grievances with the universalist ideology, narrative themes, and operational methodologies of jihadism presents an enduring analytic problem because there will be few clear indicators when a group makes a strategic decision to focus on US or other Western targets. Suzanne Raine, a former senior British counterterrorism official, highlights this analytic challenge as an unfortunate legacy of the framework for victory over terror-ism. At what point, Raine wonders, can analysts say, "they are still there, but we are confident that they do not mean us any harm."[44]

Facing weakened but adaptive and resilient adversaries, CT analysts could inform a more strategic approach to counter the threat with tailored threat assessments that rank the level of threat for individual countries, groups, or a class of targets. Analysts at the Defense Intelligence Agency and State Department's Bureau of Diplomatic Security already have a process for threat rankings or tiered threat levels to inform decisions about protective measures for US personnel overseas, but there has been no equivalent effort to "rack and stack" threats to guide a national strategy toward a practical objective other than "defeat." The CIA produces periodic assessments that rank threats by group, but the effort has suffered from a too-narrow focus on threats to the US homeland and a scoring method that is not sensitive to shifts in terrorist tac-tics, capabilities, and targeting priorities. Stephen Tankel offers a proposal for threat rankings to guide counterterrorism mission planning for the US military that assigns for specific terrorist groups a threat level and particular mission objective ranging from defeat to dismantle, degrade, disrupt, monitor, and identify and understand.[45] CT analysis could undertake a similar policy-driven effort at the national level, although I would expand Tankel's list to include two other objectives: to deter and contain ter-rorist groups. Such an effort would rely on a typology of group characteristics and goals and more systematic methods to rank threats, link means to ends, and conduct reviews of the rankings against terrorist attack data and other measures to evaluate the rankings and measure progress. Over time, these findings would help the national security bureaucracy to distinguish between terrorist groups with different goals and capabilities and help policymakers direct more resources to the most pressing threats and adopt less ambitious approaches—such as passive monitoring—for declining ones.

CONCLUSION

The United States is now well past the twenty-year mark since the 9/11 attacks. Most counterterrorism practitioners and experts outside the government would probably agree that dramatic breakthroughs in counterterrorism intelligence have occurred in devising novel methods to collect human and technical intelligence and glean insights from massive volumes of data to enable remarkably precise kinetic and nonkinetic operations. However, there has been no equivalent breakthrough regarding a strate-gic analysis of terrorism, which today is more detailed and broad-scoped than ever before but not more sophisticated in explaining what drives terrorism and the inter-play between terrorism and counterterrorism. The heavy focus on analytic support to operations tends to limit the range of questions that analysts address and create subtle disincentives for comparative analysis and alternative approaches to CT. In my opinion, most CIA analysis underscores the utility of targeted killing and network disruptions because these operational approaches fit neatly in the familiar CT "tool kit."

Looking ahead, counterterrorism is more likely to solidify its place among the established analytic disciplines by adopting more precise definitions of the problem, better ways to measure the adversary's strength and weakness, and better collaboration with analysts from other disciplines. First, regarding the definitions, intelligence community analysts have taken a rigorous approach to define the organizational components that make up al-Qaeda and ISIS, drawing clear distinctions between ISIS branches and networks based on their function and relations with core leaders, for example. Unfortunately, the intelligence and policy communities often have not applied the same rigor to characterize unaffiliated persons who espouse support for al-Qaeda and ISIS and often fall back on the terms "extremist" and "radicalized" to describe such individuals, in particular those based in the West. These terms remain ill-defined, lack a rigorous pedigree, and have no foundation in international law. Loose definitions muddle the analysis of what drives terrorism, misrepresent the scale of the challenge, and obscure efforts to evaluate how best to counter it.[46]

Second, counterterrorism analysts could advance their discipline by developing better measures of terrorist success and failure, consistent with the scientific methods applied in other disciplines. In general, counterterrorism analysts do not rely on a comparative approach to evaluate a single group or network, and insights derived from effective counterterrorism operations are not applied in a systematic way across the wider target set. A well-regarded assessment from 2016 outlined measures to suppress (vice defeat) the transnational jihadist movement based on historic case studies. However, the metrics and variables highlighted in that study were not adopted by other CT analysts to evaluate current and prospective approaches. As with the threat ranking model, a structured approach to examine terrorist failures, vulnerabilities, and setbacks of terrorist groups would illuminate key variables that apply across multiple groups and networks and allow more comparative analytics. Such an approach would also highlight how the adversary might adapt to overcome setbacks and whether terrorist capabilities have degraded to the point that some costly antiterrorism measures could be dropped.

Finally, in addition to the selected approaches and methods outlined above, CT analysts could advance their discipline by integrating terrorism analysis with regional and country-level political, military, economic, and other types of analysis to address the strategic questions, and not treat terrorism or terrorist groups as a stand-alone phenomenon. For example, after the Arab uprisings in 2011, I prepared several CIA current intelligence articles and National Intelligence Council–coordinated products in collaboration with political analysts responsible for the Near East region; they were assessing the political and security implications of the turmoil in Egypt, Libya, Syria, Tunisia, and Yemen, and I reviewed terrorist group reactions and plans. Invariably, political analysts would write a section on political developments, and I would cover the terrorism and security issues in a separate section. We would deliver sequential briefings to policymakers and liaison partners using this same bifurcated approach. While more comprehensive, this stovepipe approach failed to meet the customer's needs for an integrated analysis that addressed the interplay between state and non-state actors and, ironically, meant that my efforts were better integrated and aligned with those of my operational colleagues in the CTMC than with my fellow analysts in the DA. A more useful approach would have been for me to write, for instance, a section on how terrorist groups are reading and responding to local politics, and for my political analyst counterpart to assess what this means for terrorism. In the future, one hopes that more of this kind of collaborative analysis will become the norm.

NOTES

1. Daniel Byman, "The Intelligence War on Terrorism," *Intelligence and National Security* 29, no. 6 (2014): 837–63.

2. Anonymous author (1985), "The Predicament of the Terrorism Analyst," *Studies in Intelligence* 29 (Winter 1985), declassified, FOIA document 0000620573, 20.

3. Author interview with Edward Mickolus, former CIA terrorism analyst, January 2, 2022.

4. Paul Pillar, *Terrorism and US Foreign Policy*, updated ed. (Washington, DC: Brookings Institution Press, 2003), xxii.

5. Daniel Byman, "Strategic Surprise and the September 11 Attacks," *Annual Review of Political Science* 8 (June 15, 2005): 145–70, https://doi.org/10.1146/annurev.polisci.8.082103 .104927. See also the National Commission on Terrorist Attacks in the United States (2004), "The 9/11 Commission Report," 265, https://govinfo.library.unt.edu/911/report/index.htm.

6. Based on the author's recollection of CTC analytic cadre in 2001. The "9/11 Commission Report," 342, refers to CTC's "30- to 40-person analytic group" as of 9/11, but the high-end number includes a small cadre of analysts directed to the CTC just weeks before September 2001. A 9/11 Commission staff report, "The Performance of the Intelligence Community," Staff Statement No. 11, notes that September 10, 2001, was the arrival date for the team leader of the CTC's new, 10-member strategic assessments branch established in July 2001.

7. Interview with Dennis Pluchinsky, former counterterrorism analyst with the Department of State, January 2022.

8. Alex P. Schmid, "Frameworks for Conceptualising Terrorism," *Terrorism and Political Violence* 16, no. 2 (2004): 197–22.

9. Barak Mendelsohn, "Sobering Thoughts about the Study of Terrorism," September 2, 2020, Political Science at Haverford College blog, https://pols.sites.haverford.edu/professors corner/sobering-thoughts-about-the-study-of-terrorism/.

10. Bruce Hoffman's biography, https://gufaculty360.georgetown.edu/s/contact/003360 00014RVAcAAO/bruce-hoffman.

11. John W. Bodnar, *Warning Analysis for the Information Age : Rethinking the Intelligence Process* (Bethesda, MD: Joint Military Intelligence College, Center for Strategic Intelligence Research, 2003), https://play.google.com/books/reader?id=punvaQnLtX8C&pg=GBS.PR14&hl=en.

12. John A. Gentry and Joseph S. Gordon, *Strategic Warning Intelligence: History, Challenges, and Prospects* (Washington, DC: Georgetown University Press, 2018), chap. 5.

13. Terry Bishop (1966–2017), obituary, https://www.legacy.com/us/obituaries/theday/name/terry-bishop-obituary?id=14125899.

14. Martha Crenshaw, "The Causes of Terrorism," *Comparative Politics* 13, no. 4 (July 1981): 379–99.

15. Robert Draper, *To Start a War: How the Bush Administration Took America into Iraq* (New York: Penguin Press, 2020). See also David Frum, "The Enduring Lessons of the 'Axis of Evil' Speech," *Atlantic*, January 29, 2022; and Robert Kagan, "It Wasn't Hubris That Drove America into Afghanistan, It Was Fear," *Washington Post*, January 26, 2021.

16. Carter Malkasian, "How the Good War Went Bad: America's Slow-Motion Failure in Afghanistan," *Foreign Affairs*, March–April 2020.

17. Office of the Director of National Intelligence, "Annual Threat Assessment of the US Intelligence Community," February 7, 2022, https://www.armed-services.senate.gov/imo/media/doc/Annual%20Threat%20Assessment.pdf.

18. Richard A. Posner, *Countering Terrorism: Blurred Focus, Halting Steps* (New York: Rowman & Littlefield, 2007), 6.

19. Gregory F. Treverton, "The Intelligence of Counterterrorism," in *The Long Shadow of 9/11: America's Response to Terrorism*, ed. Brian Michael Jenkins and John Paul Godges (Santa Monica, CA: RAND Corporation, 2011), 161–68.

20. Susan Hassler, "Cement, Speeches, Terrorism, and Stray Cats," in *More Stories from Langley: Another Glimpse Inside the CIA*, ed. Edward Mickolus (Lincoln: University of Nebraska Press, 2020), 147–58.

21. Vernon Loeb, "Where the CIA Wages Its New World War," *Washington Post*, September 9, 1998, https://www.washingtonpost.com/archive/politics/1998/09/09/where-the-cia-wages-its-new-world-war/d1982bbc-1f2e-4559-9ea0-c3366f561b23.

22. 9/11 Review Commission, "FBI: Protecting the Homeland in the 21st Century: Report of the Congressionally Directed 9/11 Review Commission to the Director of the Federal Bureau of Investigation, by Commissioners Bruce Hoffman, Edwin Meese III, and Timothy J Roemer," March 2015, 38–52, 85, https://www.hsdl.org/?abstract&did=763412. Also, the legal authorities granted the FBI under various statutes—such as the Foreign Intelligence Surveillance Act, USA Patriot Act, and others—to collect on terrorist communications have been crucial for national-level CT analysts to gain insights into transnational jihadist networks, in addition helping the FBI to investigate terrorism cases within the United States.

23. Sean Naylor, *Relentless Strike: The Secret History of the Joint Special Operations Command* (New York: St. Martin's Press, 2015), 243.

24. Peter Bergen, *The Longest War: The Enduring Conflict between America and al-Qaeda* (New York: Free Press, 2011), 405.

25. A tearline is a sanitized version of an intelligence report that can figuratively be "torn off" and then shared with a foreign security service without revealing intelligence sources or methods.

26. For a critical appraisal of the 9/11 Commission report and recommendations from a perceptive observer outside the intelligence community, see Richard A. Posner, *Preventing Surprise Attacks: Intelligence Reform in the Wake of 9/11* (New York: Rowman & Littlefield, 2005).

27. Paul R. Pillar, "Good Literature and Bad History: The 9/11 Commission's Tale of Strategic Intelligence," *Intelligence and National Security* 21, no. 6 (2006): 1022–44.

28. Author's recollection of remarks by Fran Moore, chief of analysis in the Counterterrorism Center, before an analyst conference in 2006.

29. In addition to the CSG, other interagency bodies that have produced warning analysis since before 9/11 to the present include the Interagency Intelligence Committee on Terrorism, now administratively housed under the director of national intelligence's National Counterterrorism Center. See National Counterterrorism Center, "Information Sharing Five Years Since 9/11: A Report Card," September 2006, https://www.hsdl.org/?view&did=471770.

30. Michael V. Hayden, *Playing to the Edge: American Intelligence in the Age of Terror* (New York: Penguin, 2015), 33.

31. Christopher J. Fuller, *See It/Shoot It: The Secret History of the CIA's Lethal Drone Program*, Published to University Press Scholarship Online: September 2017, doi:10.12987 /yale/9780300218541.001.0001.

32. Author's recollection of a conversation with CTC Director Cofer Black in 1999.

33. John Sipher and Bernadette Doerr, "Dear CIA: Whither the Re-Org?" blog post, July 14, 2016, https://medium.com/@bernadette.doerr.

34. *Country Reports on Terrorism, 2008*, US Department of State, released April 2008, 129–31.

35. Walter Pincus, "Missile Strike Carried Out with Yemeni Cooperation," *Washington Post*, November 6, 2002, https://www.washingtonpost.com/archive/politics/2002/11/06/missile -strike-carried-out-with-yemeni-cooperation/db580142-c920-4fec-95cf-24c90b29b8de/.

36. Pincus.

37. "US Kills Al-Qaeda Suspects in Yemen," *USA Today*, November 5, 2002, http://usa today30.usatoday.com/news/world/2002-11-04-yemen-explosion_x.htm.

38. Gabriel Koehler-Derrick, "False Foundation: AQAP, Tribes and Ungoverned Space in Yemen," US Military Academy Combating Terrorism Center, September 2011, 31, https://www .ctc.usma.edu/wp-content/uploads/2011/10/CTC_False_Foundation2.pdf. See also the case study of the US strike in Yemen by Karl P. Mueller, Jasen J. Castillo, Forrest E. Morgan, Negeen Pegahi, and Brian Rosen, *Striking First: Preemptive and Preventive Attack in US National Security Policy* (Santa Monica, CA: RAND, 2006): 241–55.

39. National Commission on Terrorist Attacks in the United States, *The 9/11 Commission Report*, 152–53; see also "Overview of the Enemy," 9/11 Commission Staff Statement Number 15, https://govinfo.library.unt.edu/911/staff_statements/staff_statement_15.pdf.

40. For a fuller treatment of the dynamics of responses to US counterterrorism and counterinsurgency operations, seek David Killcullen, *The Accidental Guerrilla: Fighting Small Wars in the Midst of a Big One* (Oxford: Oxford University Press, 2011).

41. Petter Nesser, "Military Interventions, Jihadi Networks, and Terrorist Entrepreneurs: How the Islamic State Terror Wave Rose So High in Europe," *CTC Sentinel* 12, no. 3 (March 2019), https://ctc.usma.edu/military-interventions-jihadi-networks-terrorist-entrepreneurs -islamic-state-terror-wave-rose-high-europe/.

42. New America, "Terrorism in America 19 Years after 9/11," compiled by David Sterman, Peter Bergen, and Melissa Salyk-Virk, last updated September 11, 2020, https://www.newamerica.org/international-security/reports/terrorism-america-19-years-after-911/.

43. Bruce Hoffman, "How Has the Terrorism Threat Changed Twenty Years after 9/11?" Council on Foreign Relations brief, August 12, 2021, https://www.cfr.org/in-brief/how-has-terrorism-threat-changed-twenty-years-after-911; Center for Strategic and International Studies, "The Evolution of the Salafi-Jihadist Threat: Current and Future Challenges from the Islamic State, al-Qaeda, and Other Groups," November 2018, https://www.csis.org/analysis/evolution-salafi-jihadist-threat.

44. Suzanne Raine, "A View from the CT Foxhole: Suzanne Raine, Former Head of the United Kingdom's Joint Terrorism Analysis Centre," *CTC Sentinel* 12, no. 7 (August 2019).

45. Stephen Tankel, "Making the US Military's Counterterrorism Mission Sustainable," *War on the Rocks*, September 28, 2020, https://warontherocks.com/2020/09/making-the-u-s-militarys-counterterrorism-mission-sustainable/.

46. Ric Coolsaet, "Theorizing Radicalization and Violent Extremism," from *Making Sense of Radicalization and Violent Extremism: Interviews and Conversations*, edited by Mitjac Sardoc (London: Routledge, 2022), 107–19. See also an interview with Fionnuala Ní Aoláin, *Counter-Terrorism after 9/11*, September 21, 2021; and Alex Schmid, "Radicalisation, De-Radicalisation, Counter-Radicalisation: A Conceptual Discussion and Literature Review," Interagency Intelligence Committee on Terrorism Research Paper, International Centre for Counter-Terrorism–The Hague, March 2013.

9

CYBER ANALYSIS: IDENTIFYING MALICIOUS TECHNOLOGY AND ACTORS

Steve Stigall

INTRODUCTION: CYBER ANALYSIS AND THE CIA'S ROLE

Since the 1990s, a new analytic discipline has emerged that shares the stage with those covered earlier in this volume.[1] The cyber analyst identifies and assesses foreign threats to Western computer systems and critical infrastructures that depend on them. Given the essentiality and interconnectedness of computers and information technologies in a modern state, the cyber issue increasingly cuts across all intelligence disciplines and processes and touches on a wide range of policymaker interests. These various "cyber accounts" have become specialized and differentiated over time. Wherever there are computers—or really any device with an Internet protocol address—one may find hackers, whether a criminal lone wolf, or cyber mercenaries, or pirates working for a foreign sponsor. There, too, will be the intelligence community and CIA cyber analysts.

The cyber analysis discipline to the layperson may resemble a hybrid between those of a military analyst and a science, technology, and weapons (ST&W) analyst.[2] Of course, the cyber analyst tracks and assesses cyber "weapons" and their actual or potential use, so superficially the field shares a concern about technology advances to produce weapons. In other respects, especially warning, the cyber discipline also shares some of the same challenges that counterterrorism analysts face (discussed later in this chapter). But over the past two decades, cyber has become a distinct area.[3] While many senior policymakers may not know much about cyber, they now know they depend on it and must understand the threats and their implications.

By happy accident, I was in at the beginning of the discipline. While the CIA had tracked Soviet computer science for some years, looking at foreign computer hackers emerged out of a response to a single question posed to the CIA in the mid-1990s by the US Army. After Operation Desert Storm, there was much speculation about the degree to which future conflicts would revolve around precision-guided weapons, and the electronic (and often automated) communications systems that would make their use possible. The Defense Department (DoD), to its credit, saw that a new kind of threat might compromise the security and effectiveness of its growing dependence on electronic and networked communications systems. Specifically, DoD was concerned that a hacker could shut down a simulator training system—or, worse, introduce false data into it, which would skew the results of the simulated combat. Thus was born one of the US government's first concerns about computer hackers, and the military asked the CIA if hackers were something it should worry about. At that time, there were few computer science analysts. As a former Soviet defense technology analyst, the military's question about hackers ended up with me. Our response to this tasking led to a wider consideration of the computer hacking threat to the US government in general and to our computer-dependent critical infrastructures. This early effort drove the gradual development of a discipline.

The CIA's role in the cyber threat environment has expanded but also is limited by its focus on foreign cyber threats. These include any foreign individual or group, whether sponsored by a hostile government or not, that attempts to gain unauthorized access to classified or otherwise critical US computer systems. The motive for gaining unauthorized access may be to steal, alter, damage, or destroy the data on those systems. Typically, foreign groups that get our attention do so by targeting national-level, US government computer systems. Because many US critical infrastructures are privately owned and operated, other US government agencies are largely responsible for dealing with these threats. However, special legal collection mechanisms are used to provide CIA cyber analysts with information regarding threats to these.[4]

The CIA's role in identifying and characterizing foreign cyber threats is a fundamentally defensive endeavor. Typically, in the cyber world, this refers to an organization's internal efforts to ensure that its network has up-to-date security software in place, "strong" passwords, and user compliances and practices aligned with protecting computers against unauthorized access. However, the CIA has a different role—namely, to identify external (i.e., foreign) threats to computers and cyberdependent enterprises rather than finding vulnerabilities inside them. By Executive Order 12333, signed by President Reagan in 1981, the CIA is confined to monitoring foreign threats—including its cyber analysis.

The CIA often speaks of its analysts as users of "all-source" intelligence, and in a wider, cyber context, the CIA's role is one of many that try to address the cyber challenge in a "whole of government" manner. For example, CIA analysts are not responsible for fixing the cyber vulnerabilities of other US government agencies or private sector critical infrastructures, nor even of actively countering threats to them. However, if a foreign cyber threat arises that is serious enough to warn the president about, nine times out of ten, it will be a CIA analysis that provides that warning.

Not surprisingly, most CIA analysts reside in its aptly named Directorate of Analysis. However, this is not necessarily the case for cyber analysts, because of the relatively recent creation of the Directorate for Digital Innovation (DDI). Analysts drawn to the intersection of technical analysis and operational planning are more apt to find themselves as targeting analysts in the DDI rather than writing President's Daily Briefs (PDBs) in the DA. Organizationally, for over twenty years, most cyber activities have been housed in a Mission Center. Such centers were originally conceived in the 1980s as a bureaucratic way to break down so-called stovepipes—or barriers— between analysts, operations officers, and technical specialists. When the cyber issue reached critical mass as an intelligence matter in the late 1990s, it was natural that a center would be the organizational form it would take.

The CIA's cyber center is a large enterprise, and it has many partners. As a center, it engages with all other national intelligence community members and many US government entities—including cyber center staff located around the National Capital area, at military commands, and embassies around the world. Not unexpectedly, the CIA's key partners in this include the National Security Agency (NSA), for its technical expertise and understanding of foreign telecommunications systems. This is because a computer network is in essence a telecommunications enterprise, which uses these systems to connect with each other worldwide. This connectivity to the NSA, the Defense Department, and its Combatant Commands around the world, as well as the Defense Intelligence Agency (DIA), enables CIA cyber analysts to be sensitive and responsive to foreign cyber threats to US and Allies' military networks and computer-dependent operations. In addition, the FBI, with its pool of foreign and US sources in both the criminal and counterintelligence operations, allows it to straddle multiple sides of cyber security and threats. Especially since 9/11, the FBI has been a key partner and provider of raw intelligence—properly sanitized if originally collected in a domestic criminal context—for CIA analysts. Also, the Treasury Department's financially savvy intelligence unit helps the broader intelligence community "follow the money"—which is largely in the form of digitized electrons. Finally, the Department of Energy provides modeling and networks expertise.

WHO ARE CYBER ANALYSTS?

In the cyber arena, CIA analysts bring to the table comparable backgrounds, skills, and strengths as analysts in other disciplines. This field has its share of social science and liberal arts majors; however, one will find a heavy representation of technical degrees and STEM backgrounds. This mix of skills ranges from such "conventional" academic backgrounds as physicists and engineers, to a new breed, data scientists, who typically analyze and interpret extremely large amounts of data. Today most cyber analysts will typically have a technical background, but this is not universal or even generally required. Cyber analysts also come with psychology and sociology degrees as well as foreign area studies concentrations. Naturally, today's younger analysts join the CIA with significant online experience. But like other disciplines, these are analysts who have an interest and understanding of international affairs.

My own career began in 1985 and predated cyber, and is somewhat typical of my generation. With an MA in Russian history, I joined a CIA branch that focused on the Soviet research-and-development sector. Ten years later, this experience analyzing how a foreign military-industrial complex transforms technical requirements into high-tech weapons provided me with a mental framework to see how computers and telecommunications could project destructive power, not just run consumer devices. Other analysts would also crossover from the technical-military analytical tasks of the Cold War to computer-based threats emerging from the new Information Age.

As mentioned above, the cyber analysis discipline shares some similarities to both military and ST&W analysis. However, the way this new discipline conducts its analysis is somewhat different. While military and ST&W analysts can use an adversary's research, development, and use of conventional and weapons of mass destruction to determine that actor's intentions, cyber analysts first begin by assessing intent. Why? Simply because in many cases the basic technical capability to compromise or harm a computer system is already widely proliferated around the world. Unlike military or ST&W analysts, who assess the capabilities and numbers of weapons and delivery systems, the cyber analyst is not too concerned with an adversary's stock of computers, servers, or other cyber components.

Moreover, those components are largely civil in nature, having applications in both the private sector and government and/or military entities. Even understanding the technical contours of an adversary's telecommunications system may be of limited value, especially if that adversary seeks to attack a state, using its own telecommunications system.

The cyber analyst is usually responding either to a specific attack, or compromise of a computer system, or to a potential threat that might result in such a compromise. If the former, one must first understand with as much technical detail as possible exactly what happened or is happening. Gathering and assessing the "what" behind an attack or compromise will serve to illuminate the seriousness of the compromise— and provide insight into the attacker's identity. For example, a distributed denial-of-service attack is probably the simplest of malicious cyber actions, within the reach of the stereotypical teenage hacker. But an attack that exploits how a computer boots up, or that uses a so-called zero-day exploit, is typically indicative of a more capable actor—and one that quickly gets on the cyber analyst's radar. Thus, there is some correlation between the technical and operational sophistication required for an attack and how one infers the identity and intent of the attacker.

Alternatively, a raw intelligence report that describes an adversary's *intent* to harm a US computer system, and which would have clear national security implications if carried out, will typically imply or clearly state the attackers' identity and goals. There are a range of motivations and capabilities a foreign state or nonstate actor might consider before using cyber. A state actor might wish to conduct espionage, harass an opponent, or even prepare the battlefield by disrupting an enemy's computerized military systems (see box 9.1). Foreign actors often can find cyber "weapons" attractive because they are relatively cheap to develop and use, easy to hide, and the target environment is very rich; moreover, hostile actors most likely believe that their cyber

---

BOX 9.1: THE SPECTRUM OF CYBERATTACKS

Potential cyberattacks have in fact ranged widely in purpose and effects. The variety of targets, purposes, and intended consequences suggests there are multiple dimensions to characterizing any cyberattack. The spectrum can range from behavior that is broadly accepted and practiced in the international community (military espionage) to acts that could be classed as casus belli and even war crimes (the destruction of strictly civilian water supplies):

1. Cyber activities that are intelligence espionage, probing and penetrating foreign systems to extract sensitive military information (e.g., foreign weapons' capabilities or order of battle), are internationally accepted practices that no country would want to give up.
2. Harassment of foreign virtual presence (e.g., defacement of foreign military recruiting sites).
3. Preparation of the battlefield that includes implanting code in foreign military systems that could be triggered in a crisis or war.
4. Limited, impermanent attacks against military targets (e.g., denial-of-service attacks against nonvital military networks).
5. Limited, impermanent attacks against nonmilitary/civilian targets intended to inflict significant costs and extract concessions or instill fear of greater, future attacks (e.g., hostage-ware attacks against banking systems or telephone systems). Attacks against some target sets (hospitals, health systems)—even if limited, impermanent, and intended to extract payoffs—are further up the escalatory ladder.
6. Focused, permanent attacks/sabotage against military infrastructure.
7. Acts of sabotage against dual-use infrastructure (e.g., electricity supply used for air defense systems but also for civilian use).
8. Intentionally lethal attacks against military targets (e.g., interference with weapon control systems that results in casualties).
9. Lethal acts of sabotage against civilian infrastructure (e.g., water supplies, civilian air traffic control, chemical or other industries to release toxic substances).

Sources: Many articles define and categorize types of cyber actors, the purposes of their attacks, and the methods and tools they use. A few key articles are those by Melanie Bernier, "Military Activities and Cyber Effects (MACE) Taxonomy," Defence R&D Canada, December 2013, www.semanticscholar.org/paper/Military-Activities-and-Cyber-Effects-(-MACE-)-Bernier/3cd3f81778ec2e20a0201dc7123f84dafc61ca80; *Department of the Navy Cyber Glossary: Terms and Definitions*, December 11, 2017, https://www.doncio.navy.mil/ContentView.aspx?id=9828; and Samuel Chng, Han Yu Lu, Ayush Kumar, and David Yau, "Hacker Types, Motivations and Strategies: A Comprehensive Framework," *Computers in Human Behavior Reports* 5 (2022).

TABLE 9.1. Examples of Cyber Actors and Attacks

Actors	Intended Effect	Attack Methods	Cases
Organized crime. Purpose almost always is financial gain.	*Interruption.* Attacks that install ransomware inflict loss of revenue, business disruption, damage to reputation.	*Malware.* Viruses and other computer code that infects systems to damage them, provide attacker with information, or provide remote access.	May 2021. *Ransomware attack against Colonial Pipeline* (largest fuel pipeline in the US). Attributed to DarkSide, Russian-speaking group.
Hacktivists. Actors have political or social motives.	*Modification or fabrication.* Attacks gain access to systems to degrade, disable, or distort.	*Phishing and social engineering.* Tricking legitimate users into giving away their names and passwords or installing malware.	March 2010. *Unknown hackers post the real incomes of Latvian government officials* after accessing their tax records, creating political turmoil.
Recreational hackers. Hacking for fun.	*Interruption.* Prevent normal use of systems, often with relatively crude, overwhelming attacks.	*Distributed denial of service (DDoS).* Overload systems by volume causing them to fail.	May 2013. An *unknown attacker* utilized a DDoS attack to *bring down the website of the Iranian Basij military branch* (basij.ir).
Hostile states or terrorists.	*Interception.* Theft of intellectual property, espionage.	*Hacking.* Exploit weaknesses in security to gain access to systems.	2014. *China's hackers stole more than 21 million records from* the federal government's Office of Personnel Management.

Source: All cases are drawn from "Significant Cyber Incidents since 2006," Center for Strategic and International Studies, https://csis-website-prod.s3.amazonaws.com/s3fs-public/220527_SignificantCyberIncidents.pdf?kBE7Y6ATOnePQxJbCxS8m98V2zdIqIj.

operations are not only hard to deter, counter, and attribute, but also, they thrust on the defender more costly countermeasures and a fear of escalation.

Second, he or she must identify the types—not numbers—of cyber weapons that an entity uses and their technical and operational characteristics. In the cyber context, these weapons are an array of techniques (e.g., phishing, personal identity theft) and software programs (e.g., malware or ransomware), or tools, that can penetrate and exploit, steal, or harm the data on a computer system (see table 9.1).

Third, having identified and characterized the weapons, the cyber analyst must identify what an adversary's intent is in acquiring or developing these cyber weapons. Sometimes this intent can be inferred based on the type of weapons an opponent uses or seeks. Some tools, for example, are for stealing information; others can alter or destroy it. Thus, analysts may infer malicious intent to the extent that these actors seek to acquire malicious, "weaponized" applications of those tools and skills.

Key Cyber Threats

In the geopolitical domain, military or ST&W analysts often must distinguish between state-sponsored and nonstate-sponsored military or S&T threats. Likewise, the cyber discipline also focuses on both. Because so many cyber tools and techniques are already publicly available, it is not always safe to assume that state-sponsored cyber threats are automatically more threatening than the cyberattack capabilities of non-state cyberattackers. That said, generally states will have more resources at their disposal. In this category, the intelligence community has singled out China, Russia, Iran, and North Korea as the most potent cyber threats. Each adversary poses somewhat different approaches and threats, as reflected in box 9.2. While some state

---

BOX 9.2: THE INTELLIGENCE COMMUNITY'S ASSESSMENT OF CYBER THREATS

Excerpts from DNI, February 2022:

*We assess that **China** presents the broadest, most active, and persistent cyber espionage threat to US Government and private sector networks. China's cyber pursuits . . . increase the threats of attacks against the US homeland . . . [and] suppression of US web content that Beijing views as threatening to its control . . .*

- Cyber attacks . . . would disrupt critical infrastructure services within the United States, including against oil and gas pipelines and rail systems.

China leads the world in applying surveillance and censorship to monitor its population and repress dissent, particularly among minorities. . . .

- China's cyber-espionage operations have included compromising telecommunications firms, providers of managed services and broadly used software. . . .

*We assess that **Russia** will remain a top cyber threat as it refines and employs its espionage, influence, and attack capabilities. . . . Russia views cyber disruptions as a foreign policy lever to shape other countries' decisions, as well as a deterrence and military tool.*

- Russia is particularly focused on improving its ability to target critical infrastructure, including underwater cables and industrial control systems . . .
- Russia is also using cyber operations to attack entities it sees as working to undermine its interests or threaten the stability of the Russian Government.

***Iran's** growing expertise and willingness to conduct aggressive cyber operations make it a major threat to the security of US and allied networks and data. . . . critical infrastructure owners in the United States susceptible to being targeted by Tehran. . . . Recent attacks on Israeli and US targets show that Iran is more willing . . . to target countries with stronger capabilities.*

- Iran was responsible for multiple cyberattacks between April and July 2020 against Israeli water facilities. [This] . . . reflects its growing willingness to take risks when it believes retaliation is justified.

***North Korea's** cyber program poses a sophisticated and agile espionage, cybercrime, and attack threat. Pyongyang [could] . . . conduct surprise cyber attacks, given its stealth and history of bold action.*

- Pyongyang probably [could] . . . cause temporary, limited disruptions of some critical infrastructure networks and disrupt business networks in the United States.

Cyber actors linked to North Korea have conducted espionage efforts against a range of organizations, . . . media, academia, defense companies, and governments, in multiple countries.

Source: ODNI, *Annual Threat Assessment of the US Intelligence Community*, February 2022.

actors emphasize espionage, others might prioritize disruption and damage, or criminal purposes. Some state actors bludgeon their way into computer systems. Technical finesse or operational security simply does not always seem to be a priority for them. In other cases, a state actor may want the United States to know about a capability to harm American networks as a form of deterrent to US use. The attacker who is keen to be stealthy and avoid detection is whom one should most fear. Usually, these actors reveal themselves by the tiniest of mistakes, as every keystroke leaves a footprint for analysts to find.

Cyber-Finished Intelligence

All CIA regional and functional Mission Centers produce some finished intelligence that is unique to their activities. These products are usually focused on a topic, such as proliferation or a key country or region. Nevertheless, cyber, like other disciplines, produces or contributes to National Intelligence Estimates, President's Daily Briefs, and other daily products, which go out beyond the CIA to many US civilian and military recipients. Cyber products for years have included daily highlights, which usually contain little analysis but flag potentially important raw intelligence reports that have come in over the past day or two. These may include something as basic as a foreign press report on hackers in a country or a highly sensitive report that provides warning of a potential cyberattack. Analysts have published weekly, monthly, and quarterly papers that address specific cyber issues, which may not generate a PDB. For example, I published an article some years ago that showed how a local market in a foreign country was a potential source of information about that nation's government. This was all unclassified and quite "interesting." Clearly, it did not justify a PDB item for a president. It was, however, a perfect fit for a product dedicated to keeping lower-level officials informed on a gamut of cyber-related issues.

For cyber analysts, perhaps the most important question they face is the threshold for alerting decision-makers to a cyber threat and the most appropriate audience. For a president, the bar is understandably quite high. Put bluntly, a cyberattack or other malicious activity that could compromise the functionality of a critical infrastructure sector is going to get many officials' attention, not to mention those in the private sector who manage critical infrastructure.

Like other disciplines, cyber assessments involving foreign actors in various regions of the world require coordination across other CIA Mission Centers and intelligence community agencies. Happily, there is *generally* little analytical friction among CIA cyber analysts, other agency elements, and intelligence community counterparts. At times, there may be a range of judgments regarding the seriousness of a threat or the level of confidence that intelligence community agencies harbor about a specific threat.

Differences driven by "turf" may be bureaucratically challenging at times. For example, a cyber portfolio may overlap with a country analyst who follows military or ST&W issues. Does a military analyst who covers the Chinese People's Liberation Army (PLA), in a Mission Center whose entire focus is China, also have a perspective on the PLA's cyber operations? Or should most cyber analysis on that country be solely the domain of the CIA's Directorate for Digital Intelligence? Again, different cyber analytic lanes—based on an analyst's agency, mission, and focus—may incur some friction on the edges of these lanes. When, for example, does a criminal cyber act—of FBI concern—constitute one that may be a national security threat as well? When does a foreign online activity or capability make it a military target for neutralization by CYBERCOM?

Of course, producing finished intelligence that relies on law enforcement reporting can cause friction. Before 9/11, the so-called wall protected evidence collected by law enforcement agencies for possible criminal cases. In many cases, CIA analysts were not privy to such information; but even so, we were not allowed even to use the word "evidence" in our cyber finished intelligence pieces. Thankfully, the post-9/11 intelligence reforms improved the ability of intelligence community and law enforcement analysts to correspond electronically—a technical capability lacking (other than the telephone) before 2001. Furthermore, with extensive caveating, intelligence community cyber analysts now routinely use sensitive law enforcement information in their assessments. This is information collected in either a counterintelligence or other criminal context, which is stripped of details that could either compromise the criminal investigative side of the FBI's activities or otherwise identify US persons or entities.

In contrast to some other disciplines, analytical or turf conflicts have been relatively rare. Part of this may be due to the more technical nature of cyber analysis and the personalities of those who do it. In my experience, cyber analysts faced much less bureaucratic friction with groups that did technical or military analysis than with political analysts who followed a foreign country's foreign or domestic policies. In these instances, one camp knew little of a foreign state's domestic politics and foreign policy, and the other knew less about Internet protocol addresses. Why a foreign government chose to conduct a cyber action against US interests is a policy question for political analysts. The cyber analyst does not work in a policy or political vacuum, but our first concern is to figure out what cyber operations are occurring—and who is behind it.

In this regard, the CIA's "duty to warn"—felt by all disciplines—is particularly challenging, given the speed with which cyberattacks can occur and cause damage. The moment an analyst receives a report and realizes or intuitively senses that a particular new cyber development has emerged, then there is reason to notify national decision-makers. Strategic warning can elevate policymakers' long-term awareness of the threat environment, as highlighted in box 9.2. This includes the identification and characterization of likely threat actors, intentions, and capabilities. Tactical warning, however, is far more challenging. When an attacker's weapons are electrons that move at the speed of light, a tactical warning may come *after* an attack is launched or is under way but before its full effects are felt. For the counterterrorist analyst, this kind of warning would be a deadly proposition; for the cyber analyst, it is the norm.

This "duty to warn" concept was originally developed in the CIA's Operational Directorate, when it might learn of a physical attack against a foreign individual. Frankly, there is an obvious difference between the CIA's receipt of information that could lead to the harm or even death of a foreign official, and the CIA's collection of intelligence that a foreign computer system could be facing imminent attack. In the latter case, a cyber analyst might often want to study the technical merits of a potential attack to gather insights into vulnerabilities of that foreign network. For US domestic entities, however, a more typical process would have that US company, organization, or other domestic group ask the CIA about a specific foreign threat, not the other way around.

Thus, the warning environment for the cyber analyst is unusually dynamic. Although the CIA has alerted successive administrations to perceived cyber threats since the 1990s, a more general awareness of the potential for such attacks has grown over the past decade. More than ever, policymakers responsible for cyber defense need to remain open to a changing threat picture, one not captive to the latest headline or technology fad. Considering the speed of information technology's evolution, there is almost no such thing as science fiction: if a CIA analyst can imagine a computer or information technology being weaponized and used against the United States, then some other actor, somewhere, has also probably imagined it.

WORKING WITH COLLECTORS

Any discussion of how intelligence about a given topic is collected may often be another way of asking which sources are most important for that topic. Does a military analyst lean heavily on imagery for tracking foreign bases and military operations? Is a political analyst more dependent on human source reporting to describe the intentions and priorities of foreign leaders? Thus, what sourcing would a cyber analyst find most useful? As an all-source analyst, I have written President's Daily Briefs whose "hook" was an open source media story. I have also based them on HUMINT reporting or highly sensitive signals intelligence. One might assume that because "cyber" is essentially a form of technical analysis, the full gamut of electronic collection systems is at the center of cyber analysis. However, it depends on what part of the "cyber problem" on which one focuses. More often than not, technical intelligence collection about computer systems points one to the "how," the "where," and the "what." HUMINT often can reveal the "who" and the "why" and sometimes the "when."

HUMINT

To the extent that the cyber analyst focuses on the "human in the loop," one will leverage those HUMINT collection systems that reveal the actions, communications, and expectations of people. Computers are run and software is built by people, where hackers like to brag or search out like-minded enthusiasts and actors. To identify these individuals, analysts can work with DO partners to drive collection and leverage relationships with foreign intelligence services. Such sources may have been in places and seen or heard things no American—let alone an intelligence analyst—can learn. HUMINT reports can be force multipliers. In the cyber arena, where technical capability arguably offers a more level playing field than other instruments of national "hard" power, these sources can tip the balance of intelligence awareness and estimative accuracy in the United States' favor.

SIGINT

Sometimes the cyber analyst's focus will be on the more technologically esoteric behavior of electronic systems. Electrons traveling at the speed of light are somewhat slowed, ironically, by myriad electronic speed bumps, such as gateways, servers, routers, switches, and firewalls. Each of these obstacles may be an entryway for highly esoteric collection systems to capture communications traffic that passes through them. The NSA, in both its capacity and authority to protect US government communications security as well as to collect communications from foreign governments and actors, clearly has a big role in providing cyber analysts with information.

Yet here the missions of the CIA and NSA can slightly overlap. It does not require a lot of resources to hire a hacker to break into a computer system that is connected to the Internet in some way. But how does an intelligence service access a foreign classified or otherwise closed computer system that is not connected to the Internet? The cyber collector solves some of these challenges by acquiring access to entities that themselves have access to the targeted computer system. Former directors of the NSA and CIA—Michael Hayden and George Tenet—have referred to these joint efforts as SIGINT-enabling HUMINT and HUMINT-enabling SIGINT.[5] The point is that this CIA and NSA partnership is a natural, hand-in-glove arrangement that can yield results for both agencies and their missions.

Imagery

The value of imagery is tougher to assess for the cyber analyst, aside from confirming the actual ground location of a specific foreign cyber organization or activity. Typically, imagery in the cyber context will be used to confirm or corroborate what other INTs have already reported. Yet the exceptions to this generality have produced dramatic new insights into foreign cyber actions and capabilities.

A new contribution of imagery to understanding foreign cyber threats has little to do with expensive, high-tech satellites or other collection systems typically associated with imagery collection or analysis. This concerns images appearing on social media, which are addressed in more detail below. Photos on social media may be useful to cyber analysts, as almost clinically narcissistic and nefarious cyber actors love to post photographs of themselves online, often while conducting their various illicit cyber activities. Thus, photo analysis has taken on a very new meaning in the twenty-first century.

Open Source

Perhaps it is ironic that my very first PDB was based on a rare Soviet newspaper report about their missile force, and one of the very first cyber PDBs was also based on open source information. Indeed, since the rise of the Internet (and the widespread use of computers in general), there has been a general appreciation of the rising role of unclassified, open source information available to all analysts. Cyber is no exception. The work of the online investigative group Bellingcat is illustrative of this.[6] Such groups have no monopoly on either the truth or accuracy, but they do illustrate the volume and depth of what an open source prospector can mine in the unclassified world. Similarly, open source researchers accomplished spectacular results in tracking down hackers behind a series of cyberattacks associated with the Russian attack on Georgia, in August 2008.[7]

Today, quite often CIA analysts learn of some activity through classified channels and then turn to massive amounts of open source to confirm or otherwise back up the classified materials. Cyber is no exception. In fact, today it is no secret that many sources of unprocessed unclassified data often require the use of artificial intelligence (AI)–enabled systems to make sense of it. And indeed, computers not only are good at processing such raw data but can also produce it.

The challenge for analysts, however, is that the wheat gleaned from the chaff of the mountains of data to which analysts now have access is only as good as the AI algorithms that processes it all. Almost perversely, AI's processing of these mountains of open source materials can itself become classified when the analyst uses it to reveal a hidden nugget, which has national security implications. For example, much stock is placed today in the ability of foreign social media to provide tips as to when public dissatisfaction in a country might suddenly—and unpredictably—rise to the level of national protests or even regime-threatening insurrection. The problem of course is how to identify within the huge volume of data a tipping point in public behavior. Thus, the quantity of useful information has switched during my career from a situation in which the bulk of it was classified, to the opposite today—though classified often still provides the first clue to something that we then corroborate primarily with open source information.

Still, examining the quantity of open source material about cybersecurity and threats is not the only problem for the cyber analyst. In this discipline, the real challenge is to validate a hacker's claims with technically accurate information. This demands that the analyst gets as close as possible to the actual source of a particular piece of information rather than simply relying on the first website that makes a claim or provides a data point. This often requires that the analyst "swim upstream" through other, previous media stories that also carried a claim—in order to find the "original" source. From there, they must ask, (1) What are the motivations for someone to put this information online? (2) Is what they claim technically feasible? and (3) Are they trying to deceive their audience?

Collection Challenges

The novel aspects of cyber can pose other challenges for analysts seeking to develop requirements that might rapidly change or even get their information requests the proper attention they deserve. First, it can be challenging to translate cyber requirements into easily understood English for collectors not schooled in cyber terminology. The first collection requirements for cyber drafted in the 1990s used terms that were then still new and almost unintelligible to the collectors. Analysts were just then defining exactly what was meant by "computer" or the "Internet." We decided that the term "automated electronic data processing system," while wordy, made it clear to the uninitiated what information was needed. The dynamic nature of the cyber domain, with its esoteric technical characteristics and terminology, demands that the cyber analyst be aware that many HUMINT case officers and other collectors are less well versed than themselves in this arcane field.

Second, the potential for surprise also demands rapidly evolving requirements. As one CIA cyber analyst colleague told me after 9/11, "We're always exactly one headline away from being completely wrong." This potential for surprise is exacerbated by a dynamic technology sector that was changing faster than any government bureaucracy could track. This makes the targets of cyber intelligence collection very fast-moving. Third, in the post–Cold War era, cyber was thought to be the "next big thing" in national security, until 9/11 redirected collection priorities toward counterterrorism. To our consternation, it took time for the formal collection ranking system to catch up to post-9/11 realities. So, even with notional high priorities, cyber seldom got the attention it deserved when counterterrorism overwhelmed all other priorities.

THE POLICYMAKER AND CYBER

As with other analytic disciplines, the CIA's mission is to provide senior, national-level policymakers with timely and accurate intelligence information that informs policy. In the Oval Office, it is usually a CIA assessment that is at the top of the intelligence agenda. CIA cyber assessments—even more specialized, technical ones—must be understandable to the generalist. A cyber analyst's communication skills, especially the ability to write about technical processes that are poorly understood, are critical. In written products, but especially in briefings, I would remind officials that the CIA focused on high-level threats to US government and critical infrastructure systems. At this policy level, technical jargon or slang has no place. So, although "cyber" can be a broad set of highly technical and esoteric activities, there are ways to help the layperson—even if president of the United States—to understand these. One time I helped briefers use physical props to show Oval Office attendees how terrorists avoid identification.

There are also "aha!" moments when a tricky cyber activity is suddenly comprehended by a senior policymaker. In late 2008, Defense Department computers came under a widespread and deliberate cyberattack. I was asked to brief a senior general about the CIA's view of the attack—but ended up having to give a primer on how a computer virus spreads throughout a network. When one of his deputies exclaimed, "Sir, I get it!" and then ably summarized my "tutorial," I appreciated their eureka moment. Unfortunately, the general subsequently ordered rather draconian measures to prevent further spread of the virus throughout the Defense Department—prompting me to explain to senior CIA management upon my return that I had *not* told the general to do that!

Beyond the White House as the CIA's "First Customer," the consumers of cyber intelligence fall into three broad groups: senior civilian decision-makers, the military, and law enforcement officials. Each has different missions, authorities, and perspectives, which require different types of products and handling. Moreover, law enforcement and the military also conduct their own cyber analysis and sometimes collection as well, as they too are members of the intelligence community. Law enforcement entities, such as the FBI, are focused primarily on criminal activity. For the FBI, this includes a mission to counter foreign intelligence activities conducted inside the United States. Thus, the FBI uses the CIA's foreign cyber threat intelligence as well as its own domestically collected cyber-related criminal and CI information. The Defense Department's planners and operators are primarily concerned with military aspects of the cyber tool as an instrument of national power. DIA's cyber intelligence mission also makes DoD a collector, user, and producer of finished cyber intelligence. In contrast to the analytic clashes between the CIA and DIA over Soviet military issues during the Cold War, the two agencies work mostly as partners in the cyber domain.

Also, in recent years the Defense Department has created the Cyber Command (CYBERCOM). Not surprisingly, this organization has its own cyber analysts to collect and process intelligence needed for CYBERCOM to identify foreign cyber threats—and to target foreign adversaries' cyber assets and equities. CIA cyber analysts are safest working with CYBERCOM when they provide finished intelligence that characterizes foreign cyber actors' intent and capabilities—and letting CYBERCOM determine how to "engage" them. As was revealed in the 2008 Russian cyberattacks against Georgia, CYBERCOM as a military entity will have to tread carefully when analysts determine that a foreign adversary used US infrastructure to attack foreign targets.

Civilian Policymakers

The executive branch official who uses cyber analysis has wide needs and responsibilities. These broadly include development of national cyber security policy against cyber threats, which have both domestic and foreign policy implications. Senior civilians are usually generalists—but their policy interests and political horizons vary depending on their area of responsibility.

Besides walking into the Oval Office early every morning with the President's Daily Brief, the other critical consumer of CIA cyber current intelligence is the National Security Council (NSC) staff. In the early 2000s, I was the first CIA cyber person to brief the national security adviser, which just shows how long the CIA has supported this particular customer with cyber analysis. Unfortunately, al-Qaeda and Osama bin Laden quickly overshadowed the CIA's nascent relationship with the NSC.

More recently, our relationship with the NSC has grown, but it remains a challenge. CIA cyber analysis, to be useful, must be tailored to suit the background and needs of the person in the NSC with the cyber portfolio. Is this person a technical specialist from the private sector with an understanding of the technologies and functioning of computer enterprises? Is the person an academic policy specialist, who appreciates the limits—and potential power—of any US national security activity? Perhaps the holder of the NSC's cyber portfolio is an intelligence community insider who knows how the United States acquires secrets from foreign countries. Or maybe this person, responsible for orchestrating the administration's cyber policy, is a corporate executive with the business savvy and interpersonal skill set to bring the private sector onboard to enhance not just "whole of government" but also "whole of society" in cybersecurity.

The NSC, and its development of US cyber policy, highlights the need for a US national cyber strategy that underpins it. Over the last two decades, the United States has developed, articulated, refined, and attempted to execute a national cyber strategy. It is beyond the scope of this chapter to describe or critique this strategy; needless to say, one cannot develop a national security strategy without understanding the threats that the strategy is supposed to counter.

Twenty years ago, the first US cyber strategy a president articulated was published in the shadow of 9/11. Despite the existence of what the CIA judged were capable foreign *state* cyber actors, the inescapable truth is that era was heavily influenced by a fear of the potential for cyberterrorism—including terrorists who might destroy kinetically (i.e., explosively) key telecommunications or other network nodes that ran critical infrastructures. To the extent that other administrations may view China and Russia—or even savvy mercenary cyber actors—as the dominant cyber threats to the United States, then the reigning national cyber strategy will reflect those challenges. Regardless of changing administrations and their evolving political and policy priorities, perhaps the one constant in cyber strategy and policy will be the CIA's direct intelligence support to the bodies that develop it. And not surprisingly, this will come from analysts' finished intelligence products that inform it.

While senior policymakers may focus their routine cyber requirements on the strategic threats requiring preparation of proper responses, once an attack occurs, their minds turn immediately to the question of "*Who* attacked?" Thus, *attribution* takes on an immediate significance, as well as information on the character of the attack and its consequences. Policymakers will want to fashion appropriate and usually commensurate responses. In some cases, CIA analysts may be asked to assess the attacker's reaction to a cyber response the United States might make and its consequences—intentional and otherwise. In response to the Chinese hacking of the Office of Personnel Management during the Obama administration, James Clapper recounts a Principals Meeting during which he expressed concern about the second- and third-order effects of retaliation, about which no one was confident.[8]

Cyber attribution is perhaps the most important yet also most problematic of all cyber analytic endeavors. It is made easier if an attacker uses the same techniques, approaches, and types of targets. However, a colleague once offered that "attribution is function of time." What he meant was that the more time analysts have, the greater certainty in attribution the CIA can provide. In a fast-breaking emergency, measured in hours or at most a few days, the CIA could produce a strong working hypothesis about who the attacker was. If the CIA had two weeks, analysts could make an analytically robust judgment about the adversary's identity. And on the order of four to six weeks, CIA analysis could probably convince a jury.

In an emergency, of course, time is never sufficient and is one's enemy. In early 1999, news leaked regarding a series of computer break-ins at a variety of US government and civil infrastructures. While the US government had been tracking this activity for some time, analysts had not yet produced an assessment about who was behind it. Moreover, policymakers had not pressed the CIA to address these events. Nonetheless, when the story broke, I wrote four PDBs in five days—all of which told the NSC in different ways that our government really did not know who was behind the intrusions.

A dizzying variety of technical collection systems, various HUMINT reports (if one is lucky), and even social media content may get the cyber analyst close to making a "strong judgment" about attribution. As in other analytic disciplines, reaching a high level of certainty may ironically rest on an intuitive leap, which many technically minded analysts may find difficult. More than a few times, attribution is confirmed when the attacker openly claims responsibility for an action or brags online. Finally, hackers are human, and they make mistakes and leave a cyber footprint with their keystrokes.

Law Enforcement

These agencies typically use CIA-produced cyber analysis in the context of their counterintelligence and counternarcotics efforts. In such instances, the CIA's cyber analysts face some interesting challenges in how they interact with agencies like the FBI. Such agencies have the responsibility and authority to collect criminal evidence; however, they must also protect the chain of evidence in order to prosecute legal cases in the courts.[9] At times, the FBI and other law enforcement agencies may routinely advise the CIA and other intelligence community members that some of the information they collect in a counterintelligence context directed at foreign intelligence actors should not be used by other law enforcement entities as leads in a criminal case. Still, the counterintelligence-related information about the activities of foreign intelligence officers is fair game for CIA analysts. For example, a foreign intelligence officer who hacks into a US computer system—or hires US persons to do so—may be conducting both espionage as well as theft of financial information for personal profit. An FBI report that describes and characterizes this activity would have to walk a careful line to reveal to intelligence community analysts only that part of the operation with genuine counterintelligence threats.

In fact, the burden for protecting US persons' privacy is not placed on individual analysts. Instead, a series of protective measures are taken during the processing of such information before its release to analysts. This procedure is still challenging since these foreign communications not only travel at the speed of light but also cross national borders unimpeded by any customs controls. Thus, if two criminal suspects, or perhaps foreign intelligence officers, operating overseas should converse using a telecommunications infrastructure either owned by Americans or headquartered in the United States, then the action is transferred from cyber analysts to agency lawyers.

A stark example of this, alluded to above, occurred in 2008 during the Russian attack on Georgia. CIA analysts were in constant communications with the NSA and their own operations directorate, racing to identify hackers behind at least some of the cyberattacks against Georgia. After a four-hour "hot pursuit," the chase ended abruptly. Cyber analysts immediately contacted the Agency's lawyers, who correctly advised that the CIA would stand down, and they would contact the FBI directly on how to proceed.

The bottom line here is that the law enforcement investigator is charged with collecting evidence to identify a suspect, who can be charged and tried in a court of law and who, if found guilty, may then be incarcerated. When this cycle is complete, their case is closed. However, for CIA cyber analysts, their interest continues to focus on what can be learned about future operations. Moreover, the CIA is not as concerned with the "evidentiary chain" as with protecting its sources. Thus, these are two different worlds, which overlap and sometimes clash over the use of information about foreign entities and actions that may threaten US national security.

Military Consumers

Naturally, the Defense Department has a major interest in assessing, as well as defending against, foreign cyber weapons threats. Here "military" refers mostly to the various uniformed armed services and not the civilian bureaucracy that either oversees or supports it. Military audiences for the intelligence community's cyberanalyst products are extraordinarily wide. They range from individual branches of perhaps a dozen personnel to four-star generals or admirals. These are highly disciplined individuals, and by the time they become a colonel (or captain, in the Navy or Coast Guard), they know (or think they know) exactly what they need to learn to accomplish their mission and duties. Whereas a mid-level officer in the military uses a tactical or operational-level laser pointer, the civilian Office of the Secretary of Defense (OSD) policymaker paints with a broad, necessarily strategic brush.

All analysts ought to be sensitized to the differences between the Department of Defense's OSD and the various *uniformed armed services*. While both are part of the DoD, an easy way to differentiate between the two is that OSD makes DoD-wide *policy*; the various uniformed armed services conduct actual military planning and operations. Simplistically put, although the view from the Pentagon is often different than the terrain of the warfighter, CIA cyber analysts support both. While there are no dedicated

CIA products for the military, these audiences have access to the WIRe, which goes out electronically around the world. And for decades, the secretary of defense and chairman of the Joint Chiefs of Staff have been regular recipients of both the PDB and its associated morning briefing.

Over the past decade, a huge new military player has coalesced in the cyber arena. This is the US Cyber Command (CYBERCOM), formally launched in 2010 as a combatant command within the cyberspace domain. To fulfill its mission to counter threats to DoD cyber systems and impose costs on any cyber adversary, this organization has its own cyber analysts as well as its military collection program. Here, CIA cyber analysts are in their proper lane when they provide finished intelligence that characterizes foreign cyber actors' intent and capabilities—and then let CYBERCOM determine how to "engage" them.

Overall, the CIA's support for its many consumers has been well regarded, although bad news is seldom welcomed with a smile. The areas of cyber analysis where the CIA receives the most complaints or pushback have historically dealt with assessments of a specific foreign actor's technical or operational capability. And of course, because of the technical complexities alluded to above, no issue invites analytical controversy as quickly as does the topic of attributing a cyberattack or compromise to a specific foreign actor.

As mentioned above, the cyber issue can lead to a struggle between intelligence that wishes to monitor a hacker in hopes of it leading to further significant revelations, and the military or law enforcement wanting to shut down hostile foreign cyber activity. Inevitably, there must be a weighing of the intelligence gains and losses, which is not unique to the cyber domain. In most cases, making sure that the stakeholders on both sides are aware of each other's equities is key to reducing interagency friction—along with friction between government and industry.

CONCLUSION

Over the course of my cyber career, the threat and the analytic discipline have evolved together. As the field has grown, so has the list of consumers, and they have also become more sophisticated users of cyber intelligence reporting. As a government, we have become accustomed to the idea that foreign cyber actors will constantly probe US computer systems for vulnerabilities. According to one report, the Pentagon alone thwarts 36 million attempted breaches (mostly automated) of its email systems daily. Speaking at a conference in 2018, a Pentagon official in charge of its Defense Information Systems Agency remarked, "The reality is we've got to get it right all the time, they only have to get it right once."[10] Clearly, this threat will demand that the cyber analytic discipline continue to improve its performance to meet these challenges.

Ironically, however, it is equally important, if less appreciated, how often the CIA analyst must reassure a policymaker that something is *unlikely* to happen. In the early days, one of the CIA's big successes was to dispel much of the threatening hype of most commentators who had read too many sci-fi thrillers. Pundits feared an imminent "electronic Pearl Harbor," whereby critical national computer systems could be brought down by any hacker competent enough to compromise the right networks. That kind of crippling, simultaneous telecommunications attack envisioned by such nonexperts was never probable. In fact, the Internet, not to mention the US constellation of different telecommunications providers, have proven impervious to a single attack, or even accident, which might trigger systemic and catastrophic failure. Indeed, one significant intelligence accomplishment in the cyber discipline is bounding the range of potential threats so that policymakers can focus on those that are most probable and significant.

That said, technology keeps pushing forward and changing the threat environment. For the future, the prospects of quantum computing and artificial intelligence are forcing policymakers to perceive a cyber domain that may not evolve in ways that benefit US national security. This future may not materialize soon—or, as is the case with many technologies, it is only a single breakthrough away.

For now, the bar for admission into the club of significant foreign cyber threat actor is quite high. Today's list of foreign governments that have dedicated efforts to compromise their adversaries' computers has grown, as intelligence has improved and as the technology continues to spread. Looking ahead, both Russia and China seem determined to carve out their own separate political and cultural Internets. For them, as for the United States, the cyber domain is a two-edged sword. It can be used to attack or surveil enemies, but it also creates dependencies. For example, Russia, after the Ukraine invasion and imposition of international sanctions, will discover how dependent it is on all the facets of globally derived information technologies. For China, its desire to neutralize an autonomous Taiwan, with its many information technology manufacturing centers, will likely be tempered by the risk of damaging the cyber goose that has laid golden information technology eggs for it and the world. In sum, cyber will likely become an even more important domain, requiring the CIA's cyber discipline to become even more central than it already is.

NOTES

1. Cyber threats and analysis were not even mentioned directly in the director of national intelligence's 2007 worldwide threat briefing. See https://www.dni.gov/files/documents/News room/Testimonies/20070111_testimony.pdf.

2. For an outstanding examination of how one starts a new field of technical intelligence analysis, see R. V. Jones, *Most Secret War* (London: Hamish Press, 1978). Jones was appointed

by Winston Churchill early in World War II to assess a variety of new German military research-and-development programs and weapons. He discovered to his chagrin that the field as an analytic, scientific discipline did not exist, so he created it.

3. Reflecting cyber's maturing as a distinct field, the US Joint Chiefs of Staff declared in their 2004 *National Military Strategy* that cyber was a separate "domain"—alongside land, sea, air, and space. Following suit, Secretary of Defense Robert Gates directed the reorganization of departmental cyber units, creating the new US Cyber Command in May 2010. See US Defense Department, *USCYBER COMMAND, Our History*, https://www.cybercom.mil/About/History.

4. DHS's Cybersecurity and Infrastructure Security Agency has categorized sixteen distinct private sectors operations as "critical," to include such things as energy, dams, financial, food and agriculture, and nuclear reactors. See "Identifying Critical Infrastructure during COVID-19," Cybersecurity and Infrastructure Security Agency, https://www.cisa.gov/identifying-critical-infrastructure-during-covid-19.

5. Michael V. Hayden, *Playing to the Edge: American Intelligence in the Age of Terror* (New York: Penguin Press, 2016), 145.

6. An example of the kind of reporting that is available is "Attack on Ukrainian Government Websites Linked to GRU Hackers," Bellingcat, February 23, 2022, https://www.bellingcat.com/news/2022/02/23/attack-on-ukrainan-government-websites-linked-to-russian-gru-hackers. The site credits cooperation with other independent Internet researchers in identifying a web service, which in the past had played a role in cyberattacks linked to Russian government state interests.

7. See, e.g., Jeffrey Carr, *Inside Cyber Warfare* (Sebastopol, CA: O'Reilly Media, 2009).

8. James Clapper, *Facts and Fears: Hard Truths from a Life in Intelligence* (New York: Viking Press, 2018), 296.

9. In the post-9/11 world, CIA anaysts came increasingly into contact with a wide variety of law enforcement actors, at the national, state, local, and even tribal levels. The Coast Guard, e.g., has a critical role to play in tracking seaborne narcotics shipments, and to the extent to which traffickers communicate over the Internet or other telecommunications systems, the intelligence community may be involved. Also, the New York Police Department has maintained a vast intelligence collection capacity. Because of the presence of so many foreign government representatives in New York, the CI implications of this capability is so important that intelligence community members typically maintain dedicated liaison officers embedded in the New York Police Department.

10. Frank Konkel, "Pentagon Thwarts 36 Million Email Breach Attempts Daily," *Nextgov*, January 11, 2018, https://www.nextgov.com/cybersecurity/2018/01/pentagon-thwarts-36-million-email-breach-attempts-daily/145149/.

10

NATIONAL ESTIMATES: WHERE INTELLIGENCE MEETS POLICY

Roger Z. George

During an analyst's career, the job of serving policymakers is among the most challenging. Academics and scholars in private institutions research and write about what interests them to establish their credentials in their profession. In contrast, analysts write for policymakers. This difference is huge. Academics can challenge the conventional wisdom with new theories or discoveries, taking iconoclastic—maybe even heretical—positions to distinguish themselves. They essentially serve themselves in the pursuit of "truth" or what approximates it.

Analysts, conversely, "speak truth to power," in the sense that they let the facts shape their findings, be they welcomed or disliked. Intelligence presents the evidence of what is occurring and forecast what is likely to occur to inform the decisions that elected or appointed officials must make regarding the nation's security. Intelligence must focus on real-world problems—not theories—with very tight deadlines. It is fair to say that few academics in the field of international relations have ever faced the onerous task of having to support national security policy in this way. Nor do they feel the burden of having assessed a critical problem knowing that it might be wrong, be dismissed, or otherwise complicate the policies of national leaders.

In our line of work, this intelligence–policy relationship is at the heart of what analysts do. Some have described the relationship using a sports analogy of a scout who checks out the opposing team for its strengths and weaknesses and how it operates on the playing field. A more serious analogy might be how public health experts track diseases—like COVID-19 today—and warn government officials about its spread and likely consequences; however, like intelligence, they primarily leave it to governments to determine what measures are necessary to minimize the risks to the public. Similarly, intelligence in the American tradition leaves decisions regarding policy to senior officials at the White House or in Cabinet agencies.

While current intelligence analysis can and does cause friction in the intelligence-policy relationship, national intelligence estimates (NIEs) are perhaps the art form most likely to cause major controversies between intelligence and policy. Having served as a national intelligence officer (NIO) for five years in my CIA career, I focus this chapter on this aspect of intelligence analysis, which is quite different from other disciplines covered in this volume. It also explores my experience of politicization, which often is a source of friction in the intelligence–policy relationship.

THE NATIONAL INTELLIGENCE ESTIMATE AS AN ART FORM

Compared with daily current intelligence assessments, NIEs are far less frequent because they typically address strategic issues that require more time, attention, and analytic resources.[1] The name points to two significant differences. First, "national" connotes that the assessment reflects the collective views of analysts across the intelligence community. An NIE's gravitas is further elevated by the fact that the senior leadership of all seventeen intelligence agencies is obliged to review and approve these assessments, and every NIE is disseminated under the aegis of the director of national intelligence. Second, an NIE will go beyond the known intelligence reporting or facts of a case and make an "estimate" or forecast of what might occur in the future. Depending on the NIE's topic, that future could be anywhere from a few months to several years. The art of estimating, then, rests with seasoned analysts being able to piece together what is known and unknown, lay out some basic assumptions regarding the key factors that will have an impact on a country's future or an issue's development, and then forecast one or more possible outcomes and their consequences for US national security. As Sherman Kent, a founder of the NIE format in the 1950s, famously declared, "an estimate is what we do when we do not know."

This product is more art than science. Some excellent current intelligence analysts are not ready or capable of producing well-crafted estimates. Unlike current analysis, the estimate process is not completed quickly but usually requires weeks if not months, and the paper will go through multiple drafts that can try any estimate writer's patience. An estimate is not short by current intelligence standards found in a President's Daily Brief or WIRe; indeed, short estimates can be a dozen or more pages, but complicated ones can run up to a hundred pages, if not more.

The estimative prose also must be more forward-looking—given the NIE's stated time frame—as well as "strategic" in outlook. That is, its summary findings—termed "key judgments" (KJs), which precede the longer estimate's text—must be of sufficient importance that they justify the attention of presidents and cabinet officers. The logic of the argument—setting out assumptions as transparently as possible—needs to be equally solid. Most KJs rest on major assumptions about the expected behavior of key actors or perhaps the continued importance of specific political, military, economic, or other trends. Often, the NIO will insist that there be discussion of alternative futures or a section called "What If?"—essentially examining how the estimate could prove to be wrong. Thus, the estimate writer must be open-minded enough to lay out how the future might ultimately prove to be different or shift depending on how those factors change. When writing such informed speculation, it is not easy to sound convincing. More than a few policymakers have dismissed the intelligence community's estimates as simply its "opinions" and nothing more.

The National Intelligence Council (NIC), which is responsible for preparing NIEs has, therefore, a huge challenge. Indeed, one former chairman of the NIC described the council's key assets as its NIOs. These national intelligence officers are senior experts drawn from the CIA and other intelligence agencies as well as the diplomatic or military services or outside think tanks. They are generally selected for their expertise in a specific geographic or functional area. For example, the NIO for conventional forces traditionally was a retired major general, while usually there is at least one former ambassador serving as an NIO for a region like Latin America or Africa. Other NIOs have sometimes been scholars from think tanks like the Brookings Institution or the RAND Corporation who take temporary assignments to the NIC.[2] In my experience, at least half of the dozen or so NIOs have been drawn from the senior analytical ranks at the CIA, the Defense Intelligence Agency (DIA), or the State Department's Bureau of Intelligence and Research (INR); moreover, their deputies are largely drawn from the CIA's analytic directorate. This helps, because these individuals are well known to their policy counterparts either by reputation, previous policy rotations, or through other working relationships. Indeed, these NIOs must be plugged into the policymakers and their questions that deserve to be addressed in an intelligence product as weighty and involved as a national estimate.

Within the policy world, NIOs must represent the intelligence community's views on their areas of responsibility, be it a region like Europe, in my case, or an issue like terrorism or nonproliferation.[3] Like my NIC colleagues, I attended interagency meetings focused on regional developments and was expected to brief on the latest intelligence touching on the topic of those sessions. Having served in the State Department's Policy Planning Staff the previous two years, I was on a first-name basis with most of the State Department and National Security Council (NSC) participants at those meetings. Those sessions—in addition to my periodic one-to-one meetings at the NSC, State, and Defense—provided me with great insight into the issues that were being discussed and what intelligence estimates might be useful for those decisions.

My typical day began with a review of key intelligence reports coming from a host of European capitals, foreign news stories, and a smattering of SIGINT summaries that came in through a separate and carefully controlled dissemination system. I had settled into this position after my State Department assignment—a position called a "policy rotation" that placed senior intelligence analysts in other agencies where they work as staff officers. In such positions, an intelligence officer becomes thoroughly acquainted with the workings and cultures of decision-makers. Having been at the State Department, my experience as an NIO further impressed upon me the role of interagency policy meetings and position papers that drove decisions as well as the importance accorded to diplomatic cables sent by career ambassadors.

TROUBLE WITH AN NIE

One day, an ambassadorial cable highlighted for me the importance of the work that the NIC and NIOs perform. That morning, my immediate boss, the chairman of the NIC—usually, a senior intelligence professional with considerable "downtown" experience or a former policymaker—walked into my office and announced, "Roger, you have a cable from the Ambassador regarding that draft national estimate you just finished. You better read it and we will need to respond." A knot was forming in my stomach.

So began an exercise in managing the intelligence–policy relationship that all senior intelligence officials confront on a regular basis. These moments can be as simple as briefing about the intelligence community's views on a particular topic to a skeptical staff member at the NSC or an office director at the State or Defense departments; or it could be more confrontational, such as when the intelligence community's assessments imply to a policymaker that a policy initiative or action that she supports is unlikely to succeed. That morning was shaping up to be more the latter.

Some months previously, I became convinced that a national estimate on a key friendly country was overdue. This country bordered on a regional conflict to which the president had dispatched US forces. At that moment, this nation's leader had become a key pillar for US regional policies, but his well-known charisma and pro–United States attitudes were not shared widely within his government or that country's public. As with all NIEs, the NIO selects a well-regarded senior analyst—or in some cases, a team, if the topic is extremely broad and complex—to prepare a first draft. In this case, I enlisted an analyst from the INR. Working together, we produced what was an admittedly downbeat assessment. After spending several days of coordination meetings with several dozen analysts from around the intelligence community to review and finalize the text, an agreed-on draft was disseminated to the US embassy in that country. This is a courtesy to an ambassador so he or she is not blindsided. However, the rules of the road are that the intelligence community is to use any embassy comments only to sharpen and improve the focus and analysis—but not to alter the considered views of the community's experts. That would violate what is essentially the first commandment for all analysts: thou shall not politicize intelligence!

The stern cable from the US embassy did precisely that. In a nutshell, it attacked the downbeat forecast of the intelligence assessment, claiming it should not be published. The ambassador was an influential career Foreign Service Officer with considerable experience in the region. I had met with him on numerous occasions and had great respect for him. That said, his comments seemed intemperate and appeared to have crossed the line in demanding that the estimate not be completed in its current form.

This commentary could not simply be ignored. Nor can an NIO simply ask the intelligence community's experts to go back to the drawing board and recraft the estimate to suit the wishes of the ambassador, despite his credibility within the policy and intelligence communities. Instead, my principal drafter and I sat down and reviewed the estimate and were reassured that the judgments were backed up with evidence and that other analysts around the community were solidly onboard. We presented those views to the NIC and CIA leadership. What then happened was that both the chairman of the NIC and the CIA deputy director for intelligence (DDI, as it was known then) stepped in to defend the estimate's rigor and to calm the policy waters. A cable was drafted from both officials to the ambassador, thanking him for his comments. The message assured him that the intelligence community had prepared this estimate with no intention of undermining the president's policies, but it was an important warning that needed to be heard. The ambassador relented, and the estimate was published and disseminated.

The story, however, did not end there. More than a year later, the ambassador and I had an opportunity over a lunch to discuss the estimate. By then, this diplomat had left his post and had advanced to another position, so probably he felt more at ease in explaining his views. As we both knew, the embassy had been advocating and planning the first major US presidential visit to that foreign capital, in part to bolster the international reputation of this key leader. A presidential trip might also boost this foreign leader's domestic popularity, which had been lagging. In the ambassador's view, the NIE might well have discouraged the US president from making this historic visit and thereby have upset his hopes of advancing US policy interests. In fact, the president went ahead with the trip, despite the NIE's pessimistic assessment; and a few years later, his foreign counterpart did fade from that country's political leadership. The ambassador somewhat sheepishly admitted that his own personal views were very similar to those of the intelligence community. However, he had felt obliged to ensure that nothing got in the way of the embassy's plans to host a presidential visit.

One of the obvious lessons here is that intelligence must do its job of alerting policymakers to problems, even knowing they wish it were not so or prefer that the intelligence community not remind them of those problems. The other lesson, however, was that this ambassador had sufficient respect for the product and those who produced it that he accepted it and later acknowledged that the NIE was on the mark. If intelligence had backed down and not laid out its assessment, the independence and credibility of the NIC and the NIOs would certainly have been somewhat tarnished.

POLITICIZATION, OR IRRELEVANCE?

The politicization of intelligence is not new; nor is it always blatant or even frequent. But it can occur in a variety of forms.[4] NIEs are perhaps the most obvious targets of politicization, because their findings are often perceived to be critical inputs to major decisions and carry the imprimatur of the entire intelligence community. Also, they are widely shared across the community in draft and final form, and then later they are read by many officials in the executive and congressional branches; therefore, there is a high likelihood of their key judgments being released, officially or unofficially.[5] Practically speaking, this means that policymakers also may want to criticize, use, selectively cite, or otherwise misrepresent those conclusions to bolster their own policy views. An additional reality is that to be relevant and therefore effective, NIOs and other intelligence analysts need to be at the elbow of policymakers to understand their problems and intelligence needs; yet this very closeness increases the potential for intelligence analysts to lose their objectivity or for policy advocates to press their viewpoints onto the intelligence they want to read. How, then, does the intelligence professional strike a correct balance?

A few examples from my own experience can illustrate the challenge of being either irrelevant or too close to the policy/intelligence line. In 1990, during the author's rotational assignment to the State Department, his predecessor as NIO/Europe produced a now famous NIE on the breakup of Yugoslavia. That NIE forecast the collapse of the federation of six Yugoslav republics within two years and the likelihood of major ethnic violence.[6] Those inside the CIA were aware that the estimate was exceptionally blunt and likely to draw the ire of the George H. W. Bush administration.[7] My colleagues at the Policy Planning staff were quite alarmed by it and were eager to get the attention of senior Bush administration officials.

However, the George H. W. Bush administration—although well aware of its findings—largely ignored the estimate. One exception was the then-US ambassador in Belgrade, Warren Zimmerman, who roundly criticized its forecast for fear it would discourage the White House and State Department from attempting to prevent further political disintegration of that state.[8] As he put it, "We in Belgrade were advocates not analysts, so the NIE caused me huge problems. Its message was that there was nothing we could do to change the outcome, a conclusion that made it much harder for the policy to work."[9]

National Security Adviser Brent Scowcroft also later recounted that he objected to the estimate's implication that the United States could do nothing about the breakup, as this constituted a policy view. In other words, he felt that intelligence commentary was politicized. This estimate's judgments soon leaked to the *New York Times*, allowing many political pundits to attack the Bush administration for not acting on this prescient NIE. Ironically, one can argue the estimate was largely a failure if it forecast a problem but also concluded that it was essentially futile to avert it—an implication with which the White House may well have privately agreed. Indeed, American noninvolvement in the crisis was to become an issue in the 1992 presidential campaign and confront the Clinton presidency with its own tough decisions in 1993.

I started my assignment as NIO/Europe a year after the 1990 Yugoslav estimate was produced, during the final Bush year and the presidential transition to the Clinton administration. I was attending many interagency sessions on the crisis and met often with senior NSC and State Department officials, who had the unhappy task of trying to end the conflict. In early 1992, I determined that there was a risk of a greater Balkan conflict and proposed a regional estimate with that focus. My NIC chairman was dubious that the Bush White House would welcome or needed such an estimate, but I persisted, and the NSC senior director agreed that such an estimate might indeed be valuable. (Note: The mere fact that an NSC senior director wanted an estimate is usually sufficient reason to proceed.)

My CIA drafter was an Eastern Europe specialist who had served in the region. He had tremendous credibility among his peers, and he also had a quick pen. We had a solid draft estimate in a few weeks, and coordination on most parts of the estimate went smoothly. However, there was one major dispute, which highlighted the difficulty of intelligence avoiding the pitfall of advocating policy. All agencies concurred that violence was likely to increase and spread if the international community did not take more forceful action, including the use of military force (see box 10.1). Importantly, the experts disagreed on what would be the basis for a settlement: analysts from the CIA, along with the NSA, believed a lasting settlement would require border and population shifts; however, INR analysts, joined by the military services, believed such changes would prompt more violence and dislocations.

Implicit in this analytic dispute was a worry that the intelligence community should not be promoting border changes as this was a "policy issue." Indeed, the CIA's assessment that such border and population shifts would be inevitable proved to be correct when the Dayton Accords were signed in 1995. But in 1992 it was very provocative to suggest that some of Europe's "inviolable" borders must now be changed. Where would that end? And indeed, most policymakers were opposed to contemplating a shift in borders because of the precedent it set and likely would see the CIA's position as sticking its nose into the policy tent.

BOX 10.1: EXCERPTS FROM KEY JUDGMENTS, "A BROADENING BALKAN CRISIS: CAN IT BE MANAGED?"

In the near term, nothing short of large-scale, outside military intervention—which no European country is now prepared to undertake—can end the fighting in Yugoslavia.

*   *   *   *

Over the longer-term, it may be possible to lower the current level of violence and reduce the potential for spill-over beyond Yugoslavia. That will only be possible if the international community used all available sanctions and rewards to exploit economic problems in Serbia and war weariness to bring the combatants to the negotiating table.

*   *   *   *

As to the nature of a settlement, some [intelligence community] agencies [the CIA and NSA] maintain that negotiated and internationally supervised border changes and population transfers within Yugoslavia will be required. Other agencies [INR and military services] hold that negotiated border and population shifts are generally unworkable and will result in additional violence, economic dislocation, and violations of minority and individual human rights.

*   *   *   *

Escalating violence and its potential for spill over into other Balkan states would undercut US interests in promoting democracy, economic reform, and regional cooperation.

Source: ODCI, "A Broadening Balkan Crisis: Can It Be Managed?" NIE 29/15/2, April 1992, declassified from SECRET, https://www.cia.gov/readingroom/docs/1992-04-01.pdf.

The estimate caused a temporary kerfuffle among Yugoslav watchers in the State Department and its international lawyers. However, Bosnia's steady descent into violence from 1992 to 1995 meant that the reality of border and population shifts was becoming a reality that no rational person could deny. It was only a question of how to move people and frontiers. Was this the politicization of intelligence? If so, it was a very minor case of analysts recognizing the estimate had to consider different policy approaches to give decision-makers any realistic assessment of the prospects for peace.

Throughout the histories of the CIA and the NIE, there have been numerous examples of estimative judgments that have run afoul of the political preferences of presidents from both parties. Many have become part of the public debate over presidential policies, such as the 1995 Ballistic Missile NIE or the 2007 Iran nuclear estimate (see box 10.2). In the former case, President Clinton wanted to avoid pursuing ballistic missile defenses, and in the latter case, President Bush felt it necessary to keep pressure on Iran to halt its nuclear weapons research. In the former case, critics of President Clinton judged the NIE as politicized because it was used to support the Clinton position; in the latter case, the drafters of the NIE thought the NIE demonstrated the success of President Bush's pressure on Iran but did not appreciate how the NIE might be perceived by other international players seeking a reason to lift sanctions on Iran.

BOX 10.2: EXAMPLES OF IMPORTANT AND CONTROVERSIAL NATIONAL INTELLIGENCE ESTIMATES

November 1995: Emerging Missile Threats to North America during the Next Fifteen Years
This estimate portrayed a relatively low threat that Iran, Iraq, or North Korea could develop multiple-stage ballistic missiles within that time frame, arguing that no current nuclear power had done so without elaborate testing and development. Critics of the NIE claimed its findings were politicized so that President Clinton could avoid greater antiballistic missile defenses. For example, Alaska and Hawaii were not considered as potential targets. Several inquiries—separately led by Robert Gates and Donald Rumsfeld—concluded the NIE had been prone to "mirror-imaging" and a best-case mind-set in reaching those judgments. The judgments nevertheless proved accurate.

October 2002: Iraq's Continuing Programs for Weapons of Mass Destruction
The estimate concluded that Iraq was continuing its efforts to build nuclear, chemical, and biological weapons and could have a nuclear weapon within a year or more. The NIE was used by the Bush administration to justify its decision to invade. The NIE was requested by Congress, and when proven almost entirely wrong, there were claims of "politicization" of intelligence or at least misuse of it to justify an unnecessary war. Postmortems of the NIE led to major changes in the NIE process.

January 2007: Prospects for Iraq's Stability—The Challenging Road Ahead
The NIE portrayed Iraqi society as polarized and its security forces as weak, and it forecast increasing violence from all sides. It concluded that overall security would continue to deteriorate over the next 12 to 18 months unless conditions radically changed. Importantly, it was the first NIE written on Iraq after the seriously flawed 2002 Iraq weapons of mass destruction estimate. It included more formal reviews of source reporting, a more rigorous NIE process, and clearer criteria for assessing judgments with low, medium, and high confidence. Congress requested the estimate and unclassified key judgments so it could debate the merits of the Bush administration's actions in Iraq.

November 2007: Iran's Nuclear Intentions and Capabilities
The estimate judged "with high confidence" that as early as 2003, Iran had halted its nuclear weapons program, largely due to international pressure. This was a significant departure from the 2005 NIE, which forecast continuing Iranian efforts to build a bomb. The key judgments were released publicly and caused serious problems for the Bush administration's efforts to keep pressure on Tehran, as the NIE was cited by Russia and European allies to lessen pressure on Iran. Critics of the intelligence community claimed intelligence wanted to undermine the White House efforts to get tough on Iran.

October 2021: Climate Change and International Responses
The estimate forecast increasing risks to US national security as the physical effects of climate change increase and geopolitical tensions mount over how to respond. The estimate was entirely unclassified and updated a 2008 classified NIE. Its findings were reported to Congress by the NIC, in part to inform decisions being made by the legislative and executive branches regarding US responses to global climate change. It coincided with Pentagon reports outlining how it was factoring climate change into its own defense assessments. Critics argued that the NIE did not go far enough to stress the urgency of a US strategy for combating climate change.

Other influential NIEs have also played into the politics of the day in different ways. The flawed 2002 Iraq weapons of mass destruction estimate became a lightning rod for congressional ire at the Bush administration for misrepresenting intelligence as well as at the intelligence community for allowing it to be misused. At other times, an NIE can feed into a more reasonable debate between the branches of government, as the 2007 estimate on Iraq's prospects did. Finally, an administration can sometimes want intelligence estimates released to inform Congress and the public so that it can put forward far-reaching initiatives. The 2021 NIE on global climate change fits into this category. Did this estimate run the risk of becoming a foil for an administration's policy preferences? It forecast a long-term national security problem, with which the Biden administration clearly concurred; however, skeptics of climate change in Congress might still dispute whether the intelligence community should be producing estimates on such nontraditional security topics that involve very little classified intelligence.[10]

In the policy world, NIEs are often highwire acts. Their focus on major national security issues almost guarantees that they will attract attention and criticism. NIOs expect that the views of intelligence matter, so they also anticipate reactions across the political spectrum.

UNDERSTANDING THE WORLD OF POLICY

The NIE stories given above, like others told by colleagues in this book, illustrate how the vantage points of the policy and intelligence worlds can collide, even when there may be fundamental agreement on the facts and their likely implications for the future. As most senior analysts have found, policymakers are trying to remake the world, but intelligence must describe the world as it is likely to remain.

All these examples underline how difficult it is to serve the policy community well. Every consumer is unique, and each brings a different attitude to intelligence. In my career as an analyst, as much as half of my time was spent close to the policy community. This is somewhat atypical. Most analysts focus on honing their analytical skills at Langley and then progressing up through the ranks as a junior, then a senior, analyst or as a manager of analysts. Those assignments can include moving among the Mission Centers as well as temporary assignments within other CIA directorates, to intelligence community agencies, or to overseas posts. However, it is strongly encouraged that analysts at some point in their careers seek opportunities to work more closely with policymakers.

Exposure to the policy world can take many forms. Some analysts have temporary duty assignments overseas in embassies. These assignments give analysts a general foreign area orientation to the host country but also more direct knowledge about the kinds of issues arising in that country. An added benefit for analysts is the relationship formed with the Foreign Service Officers who are writing diplomatic reports read by analysts at Langley. In other cases, analysts might take yearlong assignments to a military command, either within the continental United States (CONUS) or in regional commands; these experiences deepen a military analyst's understanding of how the US military operates as well as understanding the kind of information that warfighters use.

In my career, there were two separate policy rotations. The first—as mentioned above—was at the State Department, and the second was some six years later at the

Pentagon. These were typical rotations, and many analysts serve one- to two-year assignments within the NSC, the State and Defense departments, or other policy agencies. In the first case, I joined the secretary of state's policy planning staff (S/P) as a European specialist. It involved working with other S/P officers to develop longer-term strategies to address the secretary's diplomatic priorities. I had the advantage of having a direct line to the CIA's group of analysts following key European political and security issues and could regularly ask them to alert me to the specific issues I was following. That assignment also set me up to have the qualifications necessary to become a national intelligence officer, which followed this first policy rotation.

In turn, being NIO for Europe prepared the way for my subsequent assignment to the Pentagon, where I was similarly cast as a policy planner. This time, I was invited to head a small policy planning staff within the Office of the Assistant Secretary for International Security Affairs. In this role, an intelligence background also served me well. My principal boss, the assistant secretary, was a well-known academic who had served previously as the NIC chairman while I was an NIO. He welcomed "think-pieces" and also would make time for "intelligence roundtables" on topics ranging from NATO/Europe to Asia/China. I had a "reach-back" capability to the senior analysts at Langley, and as NIO I also knew how to reach a similar set of experts at the DIA and INR. So I tried to bring into the Pentagon whomever I thought could help inform the senior civilian leadership in the Office of the Secretary of Defense.

From these two rotational assignments, several general observations are worth noting. First, the different organizational cultures found at the State Department and Defense Department dramatically alter the way diplomats and defense planners think about their jobs and shape the kinds of intelligence they want. Scarcely any true "planning" goes on in the State Department; rather, the bureaus are responding to daily requests for policy guidance from overseas embassies. "Action officers" at each desk are working on a "need it yesterday" timeline, and so they are mostly focused on current intelligence. At the Defense Department, planning is everything. An elaborate system of weapons development and procurements taking years drives a good part of the Pentagon, where long-term assessments of foreign military weapons are critical. Likewise, war planners are interested in understanding an adversary's objectives, strategies, and tactics as well as the readiness and reliability of foreign forces. NIEs on Russian and Chinese defense modernization were always in high demand, as were briefings from CIA experts on those and other adversaries' military forces. To be sure, the action officers in the Office of the Assistant Secretary for International Security Affairs also followed the current politics in key countries, the defense debates in parliaments, and regional military-to-military relations. But they seldom had time for briefings and considered themselves experts of a sort on their accounts. If they wanted a briefing, they would naturally invite a DIA or Joint Staff intelligence briefer, with whom they would have more regular contact.

Regardless of the exact rotational assignment, CIA officers serving in them are exposed to the very different operational styles that inhabit the corridors in the NSC, Foggy Bottom, or the Pentagon. They experience the agony of coordinating policy initiatives with separate departmental offices or outside agencies that do not share their viewpoint. Or perhaps they witness how some diplomats, defense civilians, military officers, or political appointees can work bureaucratic magic to get their ideas and proposed actions in front of a president or department secretary. As I learned while serving on the Policy Planning Staff at the State Department,[11] even the language in a secretary's speech can often prove to be a clever way to announce a policy before it has ever been agreed to by other NSC principals.[12] Those analysts serving at the NSC in regional and functional directorates were also exposed to the central role of this small (several hundred professionals) staff that struggles to lead the huge interagency process and develop national security strategies for the president.

COLLECTORS MATTER TOO

One of the realities of the intelligence profession is that few policymakers have the background or inclination to understand how intelligence is collected. To be sure, they are as prone as most Americans to believing in the ability of the CIA and other collectors to ferret out "secrets" whenever they want. That myth persists. Moreover, there is seldom an appreciation for the actual costs, fragility, or riskiness of collecting some of the information they are receiving. Partly, the intelligence community is responsible for this, as it correctly guards as best it can its "sources and methods" so they will not be compromised by leaks or through detection by hostile intelligence services. So the readers of sensitive intelligence reports seldom know exactly how the information they read was collected or who was providing it. In other respects, however, policymakers can take collection for granted, not appreciating how hard or long it takes to set up reliable intelligence reporting, be it human or technical.

As an NIO, I periodically was required to delve deeply into collection methods; and in one case, I even intervened with policymakers to prevent the loss of a critical program about which they were not even aware. My NIC chairman insisted that his NIOs be well versed in the collection environment as well as the policy world. One of the most intriguing exercises he initiated during his time as NIC chairman was promulgating a broad review of intelligence capabilities against key topics by each NIO. The idea was to identify and then address key intelligence priorities and potential gaps. This was a novel experiment that had not been conducted before.[13]

The NIO had previously chaired meetings at which analysts would review and validate the national HUMINT collection priorities that could be used by Directorate of Operations (DO) collection management officers (CMOs) for tasking case officers in the field. This was also an opportunity to meet the CMOs and build a relationship that could pry open their vaults of knowledge regarding recruited sources, which might otherwise be invisible to me and other analysts.

A multicollector review—ranging from OSINT to HUMINT to SIGINT—however, was novel, and it was also more than a bit sensitive. On a regular basis, I was conducting monthly "warning" meetings that drew together the intelligence community's analysts to discuss topics put forward by their offices on the agenda for the NIC to review and monitor for possible warning issues. These meetings also were an opportunity to get to know my counterparts at INR, DIA, and NSA and thus build a network of trust. That proved especially important when asking collection offices inside the NSA and those inside the DO to reveal where they had sources or methods and, as important, where they had gaps. Coming out of the blue, this NIO probably would have gotten nowhere. As it was, my visit to the NSA to explore the world of SIGINT surfaced a great deal of hesitation about talking too explicitly with a non-NSA intelligence official. It was the good relationship between this NIO and my SINIO (SIGINT intelligence officer) counterpart that allowed him to reassure his subordinates that the information they provided would be handled carefully.

This experience made me, as an NIO, a much better advocate for collection when issues regarding programs and budgets came up for review. One case is especially relevant to the job of dealing with both collectors and policymakers, since in many ways the analyst—in this case, the NIO—was a critical link. During an ongoing conflict that had engaged the United States, and in which I became involved as an NIO, the Department of State was considering taking drastic action to express dissatisfaction with a foreign government. I became aware of a proposal to curtail some diplomatic activities in the region that would also have significantly degraded US collection activities, about which it was clear few in the State Department were aware. The intervention of the NIO and SINIO was successful in getting the attention of the undersecretary of state; he spent the time to review State's plan and modify it in such a way that avoided hamstringing a collection program that was critical to US military operations.[14]

A final observation about the importance of collection is to acknowledge that analysts are sometimes collectors. Now, to be sure, some DO managers might bridle at this statement, believing that an analyst had crossed over into the case officer's lane. But, at the DO's behest, analysts participate in analytic exchanges with liaison services, such as those conducted with the Five Eyes forum countries. Certainly, NIOs participated in those meetings at Langley as well as overseas. Such exchanges and the analytical insights gained from them will often make their way into an official cable back to CIA Headquarters for dissemination to other analysts; but those observations also are brought back by direct participants, who have gained a new perspective on their intelligence topics.

SUMMING UP

The intelligence–policy relationship must be managed. It is never static. Each president and his advisers will have occasions to criticize or dismiss the work of the intelligence community. Praise is welcomed but seldom expected. What I have learned from years of contact with numerous policymakers around the policy world is that a good relationship is hard to establish but easy to destroy. This puts a premium on using good analytical tradecraft, making the logic and argumentation as transparent as possible, and revalidating the information on which the estimator's judgments rest. Exposing one's own assumptions and judgments to outside review is also a wise step, particularly when a decision-maker is likely to challenge some assumptions or question specific findings.

As the examples given in this chapter illustrate, National Intelligence Estimates are usually focused on some of the most important policy issues—otherwise, the required time and effort would not be justified. And, if a policy is critical to the agenda of the president or his Cabinet officers, then what the estimators write will matter to them in many cases. But national estimates are not "the truth," as much as the intelligence community likes to refer to its mission as speaking "truth to power." Analysts must be humble enough to recognize that all intelligence assessments, but especially estimative products like NIEs, must extrapolate beyond the facts and can remove only part of the uncertainty surrounding the future. Hence, analysts must acknowledge that their work is imperfect, even when it is well done. At the same time, it would be very useful if every CIA analyst had the opportunity to spend time in the policy world to experience the frustration that policymakers feel when crafting effective foreign policies. Virtually every analyst who has spent time outside Langley comes back with a better sense of the kinds of intelligence that are valued. Like myself, these analysts are impressed with most policymakers' willingness to wrestle with intractable problems that we only need to describe.

The CIA has done a good job of placing many analysts in such positions as NIOs and their deputies, or in rotational assignments at the NSC and other departments, as well as serving as President's Daily Brief briefers. Thus, the challenge today is not one of relevance and closeness to policy but rather safeguarding the intelligence community's objectivity. Indeed, today the question is whether intelligence and policy are now so intertwined that it is difficult to separate where intelligence ends and policy begins. This makes for an even trickier relationship.

With each generation of policymakers and intelligence analysts, the relationship gets more complex as the range of intelligence topics broadens to include nontraditional ones like climate change and global health, which in turn expands the number of policy agencies affected by intelligence. In the latest incarnation of national policy issues, we see how the Biden administration is trying to argue that "science" and "facts" should drive public health policy; but could we say the same for intelligence driving national security policy? Or must we be more nuanced and acknowledge that intelligence can at best "inform" but not determine what policy should be? One hopes that the next generation of analysts will strive as hard as mine did to balance the goals of relevance and objectivity.

NOTES

1. The production of NIEs has fluctuated over the decades, but the number of NIEs has seldom exceeded more than two to three dozen per year. In the author's experience, he produced fewer than five per year. Other NIOs involved in more complex technical and military topics might devote close to a year to a single estimate and only be able to manage a couple such projects simultaneously.

2. Probably one of the best-known former NIOs for Russia and Eurasia was Fiona Hill, who had previously been and now has returned to the Brookings Institution as a senior researcher on Russia.

3. Within the NIC, there are roughly a dozen NIOs covering a half dozen or so regions of the world with an equal number following functional issues like economics, nonproliferation, S&T, and so on. They each have one or more deputies from a variety of agencies. Typically, the NIOs are a mix of professional intelligence officers (occasionally clandestine service officers), plus diplomats and military officers on loan from the State or Defense departments as well as nongovernment experts from academia or the private sector.

4. See Gregory Treverton, "Intelligence Analysis: Between 'Politicization' and Irrelevance," in *Analyzing Intelligence: Origins, Obstacles, and Innovations*, 1st ed., ed. Roger George and James Bruce (Washington, DC: Georgetown University Press, 2014), 91–106. Treverton lays out a typology of five categories of politicization that can range from direct pressure to a "shared mind-set" of policymakers and intelligence analysts.

5. As an NIO, the author can recall reviewing the dissemination lists of numerous NIEs that were regularly sent to more than a hundred separate offices within the executive branch departments as well as congressional oversight committees and some overseas diplomatic missions and military commands. A few sanitized NIEs might also be shared selectively with close allies, depending on the topic.

6. See Office of the Director of Central Intelligence, NIE 15-90, *Yugoslavia Transformed*, October 1990, https://www.cia/readingroom/docs/1990-10-01.pdf, approved for release in May 2006. A sanitized version was officially released more than a decade after the estimate was written and used in several case studies focused on the intelligence–policy relationship.

7. The author was told by a very senior CIA official involved in approving the Yugoslav estimate that he agonized over whether to concur with blunt language contained in it, but decided it was well documented and let it go.

8. See Thomas Shreeve, "The Intelligence Community Case Study Method Program: A National Estimate on Yugoslavia," in *Intelligence and the National Security Strategist*, ed. Roger George and Robert Kline (Lanham, MD: Rowman & Littlefield, 2006), 327–40.

9. Shreeve, 337.

10. Apparently, there was a separate classified version, which probably went into more detail on the individual actions or views of foreign actors.

11. When the author served in the Policy Planning Staff, the chief speechwriters were located on that staff, making contact with them a benefit in terms of inserting language that would advance the views of the S/P, which were not always shared within other department bureaus.

12. In the US national security process, the "principal" advisers to the president and the NSC are the secretaries of state and defense, plus the chairman of the Joint Chiefs of Staff (CJCS), as military adviser, and the director of national intelligence, as intelligence adviser. The senior committee to the NSC is called the "Principals Committee (PC)."

13. Former NIC chairman Joseph Nye describes this exercise in his chapter of *Truth to Power: A History of the US National Intelligence Council*, ed. Robert Hutchins and Gregory Treverton (Oxford: Oxford University Press, 2019), 32. Currently, the national intelligence managers (NIMs)—established by Director of National Intelligence James Clapper—have the overall responsibility for monitoring collection capabilities in their respective areas of responsibility so that NIOs are less directly involved in assessing collection priorities and gaps; however, NIOs still remain key conduits about collection when dealing with their policymaking counterparts.

14. For obvious reasons, the author cannot be more specific in detailing this episode, but it highlights that the "need to know" principle sometimes works against letting officials who need to know that their actions can have consequences.

11

CONCLUSION: BEYOND THE DISCIPLINES

Robert Levine and Roger Z. George

UNDERSTANDING THE DISCIPLINES

The preceding chapters have surveyed the broad types of analysis that have been and continue to be conducted at the Central Intelligence Agency. Collectively, the contributors of these chapters have spent hundreds of years performing analysis, working with collectors, and informing the most senior US officials about international developments that can affect America's national interests. On the surface, they are all doing essentially the same job. However, as these authors have delved more deeply into their respective disciplines, readers will have recognized that generalizations about analysis are hard to make. The core disciplines—such as political, military, economic, and science, technology, and weapons—all rely on different methods and models, rely on and work with the wide range of collectors in specific ways, and support different policymakers with specialized publications and briefings. The newer or more narrowly defined disciplines of cyber, counterintelligence, and counterterrorism, as well as leader analysis, similarly rely on different methods, collection sources, and products to satisfy both policymakers and operators. Chapter 10, on the National Intelligence Estimates and the intelligence–policy relationship, also highlights a distinct and enduring form of estimative analysis as well as the problems of politicization on topics of high policy interest.

As editors of this volume, we believe these chapters demonstrate the importance of understanding these differences as much as seeing how each discipline may confront some of the same challenges in conducting analysis, interacting with collectors, and supporting policymakers. Some commonalities are worth pointing out, without diminishing the discipline-specific varieties of analysis. Of particular interest, readers will have noticed that analysts have shared their commitment to adopting new approaches and methodologies as well as remaining self-aware of cognitive biases that can creep into their own work. Also, several chapter authors have pointed to the dual problems of having to fill collection gaps with finite resources and wrestling to get higher priorities assigned to their intelligence requirements. Other authors have highlighted some of their collection initiatives and successes, which amount to best practices in developing new sources for their disciplines. The perennial problem of warning was cited by our contributors, specifically those writing on military, economic, counterterrorism, and cyber disciplines; however, if asked, we suspect other contributors would also have acknowledged the importance of warning as the first duty of all analysts. A few contributors who have worked in disciplines outside those core ones have also mentioned the headwaters they faced within their own bureaucracies to raise their status within the CIA and the intelligence community. Collectively, these analysts provide insights into the culture of intelligence analysis.

THE ANALYTICAL CULTURE

As colleagues of these contributors, we admit that it is hard for those of us who have worked inside the CIA's analytical directorate for decades to step outside the organization to observe how its practices and priorities have been shaped by (and help define) our culture. Even senior, highly successful analysts are disinclined to identify key aspects of that culture, much less point out some of its negative features.[1] It is our obligation—both as editors and authors—to sketch out some characteristics of the Directorate of Analysis's (DA's) organizational culture that can inhibit improved analysis across the disciplines. Every occupation—be it lawyers, doctors, police, or the military profession—has its own ethos. Each has a dominant culture that rewards those who follow its commonly accepted practices, customs, and standards but (often inadvertently) constrains innovation and obscures suboptimal or defective behaviors. Intelligence analysis is no different.

Without a doubt, the dominant characteristic of the CIA's analytic culture is the overwhelming emphasis on secrecy and security. Our professional lives have been shaped by this, from extensive background investigations and polygraph tests before government service, regular reinvestigations and repolygraph tests, protocols for who "needs to know"—that is, has access to classified information—and elaborate guides on how to properly classify intelligence products. There is a separate vocabulary regarding secrecy that is foreign to nonintelligence government agencies. Acronyms like NOFORN (not releasable to foreign nationals), ORCON (originator controlled), HCS (HUMINT control system), and many more populate our processes and products. We learn to respect our colleagues' cover status and to practice prudent self-awareness of counterintelligence threats.

One of the least articulated and most profound costs of this emphasis on secrecy and security is its impact on expertise building through contact with recognized experts outside the US government. Analysts are caught between the exhortation to deepen their expertise—one that comes from policymakers and internally and can be traced through declassified documents for decades—and the severe constraints imposed on contacts by security-driven regulations.[2] "Analytic outreach" is applauded in principle but impeded in practice. Following the 9/11 Commission's findings, the director of national intelligence (DNI) directed the intelligence community to enhance the use of open source materials and outside expertise.[3] Inside the CIA, however, bureaucratic roadblocks to such contacts—including preapprovals from counterintelligence or divisions of the Directorate of Operations—have had a chilling effect. While the laudable Agency intention might have been to reduce the chances of secrets or personnel being compromised, the cost has been predictable and severe. Outside interaction dropped precipitously. Several years ago, a deputy office chief told one of the authors that analytic outreach in his office was "dead." Time will tell whether the 2023 National Intelligence Strategy's emphasis on building new contacts with academia is able to overcome the obstacles to academic outreach the authors observed and experienced.[4]

The second characteristic that plays an outsize role in shaping the culture is policy relevance. The analytic directorate was never intended to be a classified ivory tower—investigating foreign affairs for its own sake. Its purpose is to provide senior government officials with decision-making advantages. That role was never to be performed by analysts acting as mere collators of data—either secret or openly available. Rather, analysts must be attuned to the needs of policymakers, even if these are not clearly articulated by them or are beyond the short time horizons within which they operate. In most cases, this rules out exploring research questions that do not have immediate relevance but which could become future intelligence problems.

The CIA's analytic culture—like those of other professions—does not change quickly. During our careers, we saw few major shifts. The two abovementioned characteristics continue to dominate both the CIA's analytic and operational culture. How those are interpreted and implemented, of course, can change, sometimes driven by policymakers' insistence, technological advances, and intelligence failures. After the 9/11 and Iraq weapons of mass destruction (WMD) intelligence failures, the CIA was forced to share more information with other agencies, and analysts were granted more access to information regarding sources than had been the case previously. This brought the analytic directorate into much closer contact with operations. As counterterrorism and counterproliferation grew in importance to the CIA's overall mission, more and more analysts were drawn into operational activities. This closeness was enhanced in 2015, when Mission Centers placed operators and analysts in the same regional and functional units. The positive effects include better understanding of sources and more analytic relevance to the activities of the Directorate of Operations. The downside, however, has been to accentuate the "secrecy" cloak wrapped around analysts who may now have even more restrictions placed on their pursuit of academic contacts outside the Agency. Also, analysts have become even more focused on immediate impact and relevance and less on research and "sense-making" of complex international events.

IS BUILDING A GENERAL ANALYTIC DISCIPLINE DOABLE?

The most striking feature of the discipline-specific chapters, and our own experiences in the Directorate of Analysis and the National Intelligence Council, is how little seems to apply across the board to a unified "analytic discipline"—if indeed there is such a coherent thing. Rather, analysts operate within subject matter domains, each with its own questions, evidence, and analytic techniques. This is somewhat surprising at first glance. (In appendix A, the contributors have provided suggested readings in their disciplines, noting that the breadth of each field is great and that few works address how analysis is done.)

The Directorate of Analysis has invested heavily for more than twenty years in creating and staffing the Sherman Kent School for Intelligence Analysis. All new analysts go through the Career Analyst Program (CAP)—an effort that has varied in length but most recently was about three months long. Follow-on training for journeyman analysts (from all disciplines) includes explorations of structured analytic techniques, critical thinking, intelligence successes and failures, writing and presentation styles, oral briefing techniques, and the like. Any of these training courses can draw on the pool of dozens of subject matter analysts or generalists. One of the authors recalls a briefing course he cotaught for eight participants that included experienced political, economic, military, and missile analysts.

These multidisciplinary courses—both CAP and post-CAP—serve many purposes, not least of which is building understanding and contacts among attendees from different parts of the directorate. All analysts need to learn about administrative and bureaucratic procedures, such as how to properly classify each paragraph or source a publication; how to coordinate with key organizations for using sensitive information in a product or which offices must approve briefing a liaison service; and, more generally, the analyst's ethical obligations for objectivity and integrity.

The central, value-added dimension of analytic training, however, is the individual development of skills in "analytic tradecraft." This term is an odd one. Colleagues in the Directorate of Operations have tradecraft—practices that must be learned, practiced, evaluated, critiqued, and employed throughout a career as a case officer. These tradecraft skills—how to conduct a surveillance detection run; how to employ covert communications systems; how to spot, target, develop, recruit, and run an asset—have broad applicability, even if they must be tailored to each environment and situation.

What are the parallel analytic tradecraft skills that have a similar broad utility? The answer is somewhat disappointing. Analysts are told to consider multiple sides of an issue, expose assumptions, offer evidence for claims or judgments, beware of cognitive biases and take steps to avoid them, develop clear messages, and be attuned to consumer viewpoints and needs. There is nothing wrong with these admonitions. There is also surprisingly little of a concrete nature to them.

The cognitive scientist Daniel Willingham has studied whether such critical thinking skills—for that is what they are—can be taught in a general sense and whether there is transferability from a specific application to other instances.[5] His conclusion is that these principles can be taught but they do not tend to have a general effect; nor are they easily transferred. The image of the chess master who can apply his skills similarly to strategy and planning in other fields is fundamentally misleading. Likewise, as our introduction to this book suggested, we would not expect within the medical profession that best practices for a brain surgeon would be useful to a dermatologist. In fact, Willingham's core finding is that critical thinking skills can be taught and have effect in domain-specific areas. Subject matter knowledge is linked to the applicability of these skills.

The implications for intelligence analysis are clear and consistent with what we have seen in the discipline-specific chapters. Experts develop subject matter expertise and critical thinking skills together. Many of the specialized courses offered at the Sherman Kent School and other intelligence community components seem to recognize that condition and exploit it. Unlike the medical and legal professions, analysts do not have the extensive common areas of knowledge developed in years of professional education.[6] In the intelligence community, advanced courses on military, economic, or leadership analysis draw participants from those disciplines and teach critical thinking skills through discipline-specific examples.

The implications for those managing analysts and for consumers are profound, especially given the scale and scope of analytic efforts. It is futile to ask analysts to cover wide-ranging topics—there is no such thing as a "generalist expert." In the late 1970s, the analytic directorate already drew on dozens of specialties, and the diversity of fields has only grown since then.[7] This book has covered the most prominent disciplines, but there are also analysts who specialize in studying international organized crime, drug cartels, war crimes, and any number of subdisciplines within the broad ones covered in this book, as the authors of those chapters noted. To recall, a political analyst could be focused on the political parties of a specific country, but other political analysts could cover that country's religious issues, ethnic divisions, labor unions, and any of several other "political" topics.

The number of analysts fulfills the sentiment of the quotation often attributed to Stalin: "Quantity has a quality all its own." Although there are no recent, official numbers of CIA analysts, declassified documents suggest there were roughly 1,300 in the late 1980s.[8] The surge after 9/11 brought in many more. (The FBI's analytic cadre, for example, tripled from September 11, 2001, to 2011.[9]) This large analytic cadre allows for greater specialization, but it also reduces individual analysts' fields of vision. This exacerbates a problem that has been recognized and lamented for decades—namely, how to conduct true multidisciplinary analysis.

Multidisciplinary Analysis

Many of this book's contributors have suggested that they conduct multidisciplinary analysis. In their minds, it is hard to avoid writing about the political implications of some economic trend or military operation; in this sense, every analyst, regardless of their specialty, is going to draw conclusions for policymakers that go beyond their narrow field. That is what makes the CIA's analysis useful—providing the "so what" of an economic, military, or technological development.[10] However, policymakers often want more than that. In the past, senior consumers of analysis and internal managers have recognized the difficulty of producing assessments that link findings from multiple disciplines into a coherent, single product. What passes for multidisciplinary analysis is most frequently separate contributions from distinct disciplines stitched together. As one of our colleagues used to remark, "Sometimes that stitching is like that of the Frankenstein monster."

Declassified documents from the late 1970s and early 1980s (more recent, internal documents have not been released) contained biting commentary. Many critics went well beyond the late-1980 internal assessment sent to the CIA director that the analytic directorate displayed a "continuing inability to perform multi-disciplinary analysis":[11]

- A future director for analysis, Robert Gates, wrote in March 1981 that the "CIA remains primitive in the area of multi-disciplinary analysis."[12] He attributed some of this to offices organized by discipline, a situation he tried to remedy by reorganizing the directorate in the mid-1980s.
- White House officials in the 1970s and early 1980s stressed the need for long-term, in-depth studies that explored many dimensions of foreign perceptions, intentions, and capabilities—and the interactions of different areas (e.g., economic, sociological, etc.).[13]

Later internal CIA documents claimed that significant improvements had been achieved in the 1980s. A 1988 speech asserted, "In most of our analysis, we try to take a multidisciplinary approach. That is, we deliberately mix persons with almost

50 different analytical specialties—for example, in politics, economics, military affairs, and engineering—to consider major intelligence questions."[14] Gates, the 1980 critic of DA efforts, reported in 1984 that "47% of the Directorate's work was interdisciplinary to a substantial degree, nearly 40% of the papers were entirely appropriate as single disciplinary papers, . . . and some 15% showed room for improvement in this area."[15] Quite a turnaround, if in fact it were true.

Are complaints about shortfalls in multidisciplinary analysis outdated and inaccurate, or is there more to this story? We believe there is a critical definitional issue—the difference between multidisciplinary and interdisciplinary analysis. Almost all analysts contribute to multidisciplinary products. Those contributions are stitched together to provide several facets to the consumer. Done well, such products can offer rich insights.[16] In contrast, interdisciplinary analysis weaves the conceptual threads from different disciplines together. These holistic products are much harder to create and are much more valuable.[17] Rather than having chapters or sections on economics, politics, military, and technical issues, interdisciplinary works might show how the personalities of foreign leaders interact with a state's politics and economic situation to produce a situation.[18] They provide a depth of understanding and points of leverage that decision-makers cherish.

Having both served in different analytical units starting in the 1980s and evaluated a multitude of finished products in the DA's Product Evaluation Staff and Mission Production Center, the editors judge the distinction between multidisciplinary and interdisciplinary analysis to be critical. We have no doubt that the former has appeared frequently, but the latter is noticeably scarce. What can fix this gap? Analysts and their managers must develop terms of reference for such projects, which initiates an interdisciplinary perspective from the beginning of a project. As a national intelligence officer, one of the editors had the experience of hosting meetings that drew analysts from all the core disciplines together to consider how to develop a broad perspective on a target country—that is, its economic conditions, its domestic political landscape, and how its leaders viewed their personal as well as their nation's international status. In the current intelligence field, such lengthy project development meetings might be difficult to organize; however, something akin to the National Intelligence Estimate terms of reference process could be considered on a more modest scale.

ANALYSIS AND COLLECTION: AN IMPERFECT MATCH

One of the two distinguishing characteristics of all-source, national-level intelligence analysts from scholars in think tanks and the academy is the former's proximity to collectors and responsibility to enhance collection efforts. As the foregoing chapters demonstrate, wherever analysts work, they conduct research, dig up information, and frequently generate new information (e.g., through interviews or collection initiatives). CIA analysts work with some of the largest and most sophisticated information-generating systems in the world—including technical and human collection programs that violate the laws of other countries in carrying out their missions.

The contributors to this book provided several instances in which they provided collection requirements, worked with collection management officers and case officers, participated in vetting sources and information, conducted debriefings, and extracted data from technical systems to generate information. Developing a broad and deep understanding of the myriad ways information can be found or created is a core skill of intelligence analysts.

There are untold numbers of cases of successful analyst–collector cooperation. Moreover, analysts can provide windows into decision-maker interests to collectors, focusing efforts and alerting collectors to opportunities to make their raw products ever more useful. One of the authors recalls a meeting overseas with a deputy chief of station, who asked, "Can you give me a better sense of what Washington really wants to know?" The benefits can be tremendous.

The harsh truth, however, is that there are severe inhibitors to cooperative efforts. Excessive secrecy on the part of collectors is all too common.[19] Collectors have an especially critical role to play in protecting sources and methods, and analysts are not always attuned to the precariousness of collection means. Analysts facing a torrent of information spewing out of their terminals may believe they already have more information than they can handle. (The common metaphor is "drinking from a firehose.") Given that most analysts open only a small portion of the items flagged by their automated computer search systems—maybe several dozen out of hundreds of items daily—there is a kernel of truth behind this complaint. Time pressures, locations, and costs play their part in weakening the marriage of analysts and collectors. The National Security Agency is only about an hour's drive from CIA Headquarters (midday, not rush hour), but many analysts do not take the time and make the effort to know their counterparts personally. The same is also true in reverse. One of the authors brought an experienced National Security Agency manager of collection against a region of national concern to meet the DA office chief on the region. In his thirty years at the National Security Agency, he had never met a senior DA counterpart. Although some analysts get to know their collection management officers well, and perhaps work with one of the collectors, few develop numerous deep, personal contacts that can be vital to cooperation.

The consequences of a long-distance (and perhaps not fully trusting) marriage between analysts and collectors can be deleterious and unrecognized. Analysts might not understand the full capabilities of collectors and their limitations, nor competing priorities. Collectors may operate according to directives that owe their focus as much to a system's technical design and past practices as current needs. One does not need to presume malevolence to anticipate inefficiencies and missed opportunities.

THE POLICYMAKING ENVIRONMENT: GREATER COMPLEXITY AND LESS TIME

Many observers of intelligence point to a future that will be heavily influenced, if not driven, by vast increases in technical capabilities in data collection, processing, distribution, and use. At least one of our colleagues, a professional with decades of experience, has expressed the view that artificial intelligence will play the dominant role in analysis in the future.[20]

We do not doubt that significant changes are occurring and that more are on the horizon. But the fundamental task of intelligence analysis—providing curated information and insights for decision-makers who have long, packed days—will not change. It will become more important than ever as the data tsunami inadvertently sweeps up both intentional and unintentional misleading information, the world becomes ever more complex, and decision-makers' demands grow.[21] Analysis needs to be delivered more quickly, with greater detail and greater explanation, to a larger number and variety of consumers—virtually all of whom have little time to absorb new information.[22]

Complexity

As Oscar Wilde wrote, "The truth is rarely pure and never simple."[23] This is definitely the case for most intelligence problems. The problems decision-makers face and analysts must address are not only complicated and hidden by foreign denial and deception efforts. Issues that rise to the level of senior decision-makers are seldom concerned merely with foreign secrets or information that are discoverable and knowable. More commonly, these intelligence problems are mysteries—issues for which no one knows the answer. The secret-mysteries delineation is vital. It was a secret whether India planned and prepared to carry out a nuclear test in late 1995 or 1996—a secret revealed by the intelligence community and presented to US decision-makers. It was a mystery for some time whether a test would occur, given the United States' and other countries' demarches and threats of sanctions after discovery of the preparations. Indian authorities had to weigh their options, costs, and risks.

Most mysteries are complex. Complex or "wicked" problems typically involve multiple, interactive actors with independent perceptions, intentions, and capabilities; feedback loops that may exacerbate or alleviate a cycle of interactions, nonlinearity (e.g., a disproportionate relation of inputs and outputs), emergent qualities, and sheer randomness. These attributes make it exceedingly difficult to understand such types of problems thoroughly, much less forecast future conditions or behaviors. The very concept of analysis—breaking a problem into its parts, studying those parts, and premising one's understanding of the whole on understanding of the parts—is challenged by complex problems. Addressing complex mysteries calls for synthesis as much as or more than analysis. Additionally, "sense-making" is more helpful than point-predictions, which are a fool's game.

Why does all this matter? Consumers want to understand how and why an event, or a situation, occurs. Not infrequently, decision-makers want a deep enough understanding of the factors surrounding a problem so as to be able to do their own calculation about how it may develop. Complex problems do not lend themselves to well-defined causal relationships or straightforward extrapolations from the present course. Seldom can an analyst confidently explain all the drivers of an action, their interactions, or the role of chance and contingency. Moreover, analysts need to consider the unintended and long-term, second- and third-order consequences of immediate events. As Russia prepared to attack Ukraine in early 2022 the first-order questions and consequences were relatively clear—would Russia attack or just threaten to attack? If it attacked, what would its objectives be? How effective would Ukrainian resistance be? Some second-order issues would have surfaced simultaneously—would a large-scale refugee problem occur? Would neighbors support Ukraine, and in what ways? But how soon would analysts have considered the downstream effects of potential cut-offs of Ukrainian grains to parts of Africa and Asia—literally a consequence of a consequence?

Compressed Time and Space

Shakespeare's Polonius, in *Hamlet*, noted that "brevity is the soul of wit."[24] Who can argue that a short message is not desirable? But at what cost to understanding? Yet senior consumers have repeatedly told the CIA that its analytic messages must be delivered quickly—in as little space as possible—and clearly. That theme is one of the most consistent in the history of CIA analysis. The particulars found in a declassified memoranda internal to the CIA and from the White House stress:

- At the beginning of the Reagan administration, guidance from the White House called for short pieces, "One paragraph for most issues, two-to-three paragraphs at the outside should be the guide for presentation."[25]
- The President's Daily Brief (PDB) "Handbook" stated that "most articles should be about a page in length."[26]
- All products should have "first-rate summaries," and the DA had clearly fallen short of that requirement.[27]

Calls for brevity, precision, and clarity are consistently broadcast to the analytic cadre. In keeping with the lengthy PDB "Handbook," paragraphs were to be only two to three sentences in length. Most paragraphs included bullets (a maximum of three or four) that explained a judgment or, more commonly, provided evidence. These admonitions run up against the previous challenge of presenting the complexity of most problems demanding high-level decisions. How do analysts present the complexities and second- or third-order effects of a foreign action (not to mention alternative presidential decisions) in two or three paragraphs?[28] "Deep dive," in-person sessions in the Oval Office can help; but these are rare, given the time constraints, as will be mentioned next.

The tyranny of decision-makers' overcrowded schedules is hard to imagine. President George H. W. Bush released a page of his schedule to the public that illustrates this reality. Official, scheduled time slots were often only 15 minutes long, but the inked-in, actual times were as short as 3-minute blocks. A senior PDB briefer told the story of trying to find enough time for a "pull aside" for a visiting foreign dignitary. (This is a brief greet-and-handshake that involves diverting the president from a planned walk for less than a minute.) The briefer failed to find time for such a tiny deviation.[29] Even the notion of a PDB briefer is a misnomer: seldom, if ever, does that CIA officer orally brief the articles in the document. He or she "tees up" the key items and lets the president or other senior official scan through the remaining pieces "at their leisure" (another misnomer, as they have none).

The conflict that emerges from lack of time and attention, and the increasing complexity of the issues that decision-makers must tackle, is real. Fine-grained assessments in diverse subject areas—social media accounts, foreign leaders' perceptions and intentions, ethnic divisions, cryptocurrencies, explosives, and dozens of others—are required to allow decision-makers to operate effectively. But they do not have the attention bandwidth to absorb such assessments.

There is another aspect to this problem that is seldom if ever noted. How are senior analytic reviewers to evaluate what is bound to be increasingly esoteric and expertise-based judgments? The unsatisfactory answer is: with great difficulty. So, let us be frank. One of the attractions of short, reportorial pieces (e.g., one-pagers in the PDB or WIRe) is the perception of managers and reviewers that they can get their hands around the subject. Thus, PDBs are sent forward with background notes of several pages in length that explain the short article.[30] Copies of all sources are provided. Even a hard-pressed reviewer can read the provided sources and background notes and feel competent to edit the draft article. This sense of intellectual control, flawed though it is, goes all the way up to the director of national intelligence.[31]

THE US DOMESTIC CONTEXT: THE UNTOUCHABLES

Beyond the challenges of presenting complex subjects in increasingly compressed time and space, intelligence analysts have historically had to studiously avoid considering US domestic factors in their assessments. Think about this. We know that US decision-makers are influenced and often constrained in their national security planning and actions by many domestic considerations. For example, it is inconceivable to imagine that senior US officials could contemplate actions to bolster Ukraine's defense against Russian aggression without considering US public opinion, the support of Congress, the potential economic consequences to the American economy, and the drawdown of our ammunition and weapons stocks and effects on US military readiness as well as any number of additional domestic matters.

Foreign powers also consider the role of US domestic concerns in US national security, study those concerns, and play off them. It is ironic and disturbing, then, that intelligence community analysts must avoid direct reference to US domestic issues in analyzing foreign perceptions and actions. This disconnect has been recognized for decades. In his 1949 review of Sherman Kent's seminal book on US intelligence, Willmoore Kendall mocked the idea of US intelligence officers "whose 'research' must stop short at the three-mile limit even when the thread they are following runs right across it."[32] In an age of international terrorism and cyberattacks executed globally, physical boundaries constraining analysis seem more questionable, even archaic.

The rationale for these restrictions is clear, even if it is seldom spelled out. Analysts should not be seen as critiquing US policy, nor advocating actions or options. Our focus is abroad, and US domestic issues are protected by well-intentioned civil liberties.[33]

Creative analysts have found workarounds. They may not refer directly to the adverse effects of a Florida preacher burning Qur'ans in Gainesville, Florida, in 2011 and 2012 on Muslim populations and leaders, but they can cite foreign perceptions of, comments about, and reactions to the event. Similarly, military analysts have cited classified foreign assessments of US military exercises. It is nevertheless undeniable that analysts' mandated, blinkered view of influences on "our side of the hill" constrains the benefits of analysis and exacerbates their failures.[34] For example, when a policy tool like sanctions is being proposed, analysts need to be aware not only of what actions US decision-makers are contemplating but also how foreign actors might take advantage of American domestic interests that would oppose the use of sanctions. A well-documented case of South Asian nuclear tests illustrates the risks.

South Asian Nuclear Tests: Sanctions and US Domestic Politics

In May 1998, India and Pakistan each carried out nuclear tests, actions that the United States had tried to forestall with bilateral and multilateral diplomacy for years.[35] Moreover, the US Congress had mandated sanctions to deter nuclear testing—commonly referred to as the Glenn, Symington, and Pressler amendments. President Clinton had little choice but to impose these mandated sanctions on both countries after their tests.

Congress's objectives concerning proliferation and foreign policy, however, came into conflict with US business interests in both countries, and ethnic communities in the United States that had growing financial and political clout. Having failed to deter either country from testing, several congressmen focused on the downsides of the sanctions—potentially destabilizing Pakistan and, more immediately, threatening trade relationships. Within two months of the Indian tests, Congress passed, by overwhelming numbers, temporary relief from Glenn Amendment restrictions that would have prevented export financing for Pakistani wheat purchases, the third-largest overseas market. Other waivers followed shortly afterward. Within a short period, both countries had largely escaped what had appeared to be a robust deterrent and punishment screen.

Many members of Congress believed that unilateral sanctions were clumsy tools that should be used less frequently and more carefully. The reality is that sanctions use has grown. The rollbacks of sanctions after the South Asian nuclear tests demonstrated clearly the potentially decisive influence of US domestic concerns—economic and political—on foreign policy. CIA analysts were keenly aware of the intended role of sanctions in this case. However, even if they knew of the impact such export restrictions would have on domestic markets, on many politicians' constituents, and on potential US legislative actions, they clearly could not assess how this might affect Indian or Pakistani decisions.

Waiting for published or clandestinely acquired foreign commentary on US actions or domestic dimensions is problematic for at least two reasons. The first is the lag time that occurs naturally between US actions, foreign detection of those actions, foreign responses (e.g., analysis in foreign documents), and our acquisition of those foreign responses (e.g., collecting the documents by technical or human source means). The second headache for analysts is that other countries' leaders and elites frequently attribute the activities of the different parts of the US government as well as other commercial, academic, religious, and other nongovernmental organizations to a conscious, centrally controlled US plan and effort.[36] Hence, the range of US domestic actions and matters that can influence foreign actors is a vast collection challenge.

IN SEARCH OF INSIGHT?

At the end of the day, policymakers are seeking insight.[37] That can be a new perspective on a problem, or a deeper explanation of the factors behind a trend or event, or even a contrary analysis to challenge the decision-maker's own assumptions or biases. Yet both senior CIA officials and policy customers, in the past, have been vocal critics of the short, journalistic items that do little more than report the classified news. A devastating critique prepared for the director of the CIA, and seemingly endorsed by him, several decades ago was unequivocal:[38]

- The intelligence community, and the CIA in particular, operated "day-to-day as a purveyor of special information: hard, timely news, with limited inferences, little analysis, and no context within which to interpret hot flashes."
- The CIA's efforts were heavily biased toward collection, and, in particular, collection that could be presented as "news." This was paired with the observation that a common view was "the answer to hard questions will be found in collection, . . . [reinforcing] the excessive reliance on raw data vs. thought and analysis."

Senior White House officials sometimes echoed those views. Andrew Marshall, a senior aide to Henry Kissinger when he was national security adviser, told a senior CIA group in 1973 that "it is difficult to find 'real analysis' in [CIA analytic] products." A CIA meeting attendee reported that Marshall judged that "much of our analysis is wanting in interpretation, not just occasional holes, but with respect to 'whole programs.'" "[Marshall] noted that there is not much in the way of reasoning behind our intelligence statements."[39]

These criticisms from decades ago still resonate, even in the absence of more recent, declassified customer satisfaction surveys. Does an enterprise-wide emphasis on current intelligence divert collectors, analysts, and managers from what could be more useful pursuits, and is that a disservice to consumers? In 1979 the deputy director of the National Foreign Assessment Center (the predecessor of today's analytical directorate), briefing the national security adviser, suggested the answer was yes: "Demands for current intelligence continue to impinge on resources that otherwise could be applied to studied research and analysis, especially among our political and economic analysts."[40] The editors' exposure to a vast and wide range of DA publications in evaluative roles convinces us that the basic problem remains.

On the surface, it seems that current items largely would be spin-offs of analytic work that has a longer and broader perspective. A military analyst studying a foreign power's nascent nuclear weapons program might come across an item that draws her attention and might grab the attention of consumers. For example, satellite imagery might reveal unusual deployments of air defense systems around a critical nuclear production site. A current article showing the deployment (including annotated imagery with a locator map), and describing previous similar events and possible implications, could be put together.

But to what end, and at what cost? Drafting a short article and working with graphics to annotate a visual might take a couple of hours. The coordination and review process could multiply the required time by a surprisingly large number. If selected for use in the PDB, coordination and layers of review can spiral into a daylong affair or more.[41] Recall that all PDB articles must be accompanied by coordinated background notes of three to four pages in length. Generally, analysts return in the early hours of the next morning to "brief the briefers."

More critically, analysts respond to incentives. When senior managers praise the PDB as the flagship publication, when they race through their offices exclaiming, "The cupboards are bare," signaling that there were no PDBs "in the hopper" for that day, or when one 5- or 10-minute "deep dive" with the president makes an analyst's career—the implications are obvious.

This is only the tip of the iceberg. As one senior CIA officer put it, "In contrast to collection, analysis is cheap."[42] Indeed, in the single instance of declassified data on the topic, it was revealed that analysis accounted for only 6 percent of the CIA's budget.[43] The titanic effort to collect information, with its direct costs and opportunity costs, can be staggering. Case officers running human assets have a limited amount they can ask of their sources. IMINT and SIGINT assets are in constant demand. In one case, when the United States was involved in combat and a foreign power (not associated with the conflict) was making significant steps to develop WMD, one of the authors was able to get SIGINT coverage for only two hours each night—in the middle of the night—against the WMD target. And this was with the strong backing of senior National Secuirty Council (NSC) officials.

But the most telling concern is the impact on consumers. It is certainly the case that many decision-makers count on receiving their daily publications to keep them abreast of critical international developments. As noted above, however, their time and attention are severely constrained. Short, current pieces have little room to develop the context for core messages—for example, precedents and history, and comparisons with similar past cases. Interviews with senior NSC officials in about 2016 confirmed how important and valued such deeper perspectives were.

Intelligence analysis must evolve with changing international involvement and policymakers' needs. Beyond the current disciplines, we are likely to see more adaption and expansion of analytic work in the years ahead. In an August 2023 interview,

Director of National Intelligence Avril Haines suggested how the focus of intelligence analysis is changing already.[44] Haines noted that instead of daily briefings dominated by the Middle East and terrorism, as he heard as vice president, Joe Biden is regularly hearing about China's artificial intelligence research, semiconductor chip production, and the geopolitical impact of climate change.

Moreover, the 2023 National Intelligence Strategy underlines the challenges that the increasing complexity of the world represents to national security and the analysis needed to support decision-makers. The future intelligence–policy relationship will need to expand the scope of intelligence coverage and broaden interaction among key elements of the US government as well as with foreign partners, the private sector, and academia.[45] These are all, in fact, long-term trends that the contributors to this book have witnessed, participated in, and helped promote for years. We remain optimistic that the US intelligence community and the ever-evolving analytic disciplines are robust enough to face these new challenges, just as the first generation of CIA analysts faced the dangers and unknown character of the Cold War.

NOTES

1. For an insightful examination of analytical cultures, see Rob Johnston, *The Analytical Culture of the US Intelligence Community: An Ethnographic Study* (Washington, DC: Center for the Study of Intelligence, 2005). Among the many challenges he identifies, secrecy, time constraints, a focus on current production, and expertise building are prominent even today.

2. In an August 24, 1977, memorandum to his deputies, Adm. Stansfield Turner asserted that policymakers had for decades complained about "shallow" and "low-quality" analysis that was being produced and that it often was wrong as well as irrelevant to policymakers' needs. See https://www.cia.gov/readingroom/docs/CIA-RDP80M01048A001100040001-7.pdf.

3. The DNI issued in August 2013 *Intelligence Community Directive 205* on Analytic Outreach, replacing the earlier ICD issued in 2008. Such outreach is an "essential intelligence activity," designed to "leverage outside expertise as part of sound analytic tradecraft." This outreach was described as engagement with outside experts to explore new ideas and alternative perspectives, gain insights, and generate new knowledge. See https://www.dni.gov/files/documents/ICD/ICD%20205%20-%20Analytic%20Outreach.pdf.

4. The 2023 National Intelligence Strategy document is at https://www.dni.gov/files/ODNI/documents/National_Intelligence_Strategy_2023.pdf.

5. Daniel T. Willingham, *How to Teach Critical Thinking*, 2019, http://www.danielwillingham.com/uploads/5/0/0/7/5007325/willingham_2019_nsw_critical_thinking2.pdf; and "Critical Thinking: Why Is It So Hard to Teach?" *American Educator*, 2007, https://eduq.info/xmlui/bitstream/handle/11515/19710/Crit_Thinking.pdf.

6. Whatever their specialties, doctors share common knowledge of physiology, chemistry, and so on. Similarly, law students study torts, criminal procedures, and so on, no matter their future practices. As law professor Frederick Schauer notes, "It takes a squadron

of law professors and three years of law school" to inculcate legal reasoning in future law-yers. Frederick Schauer, *Thinking like a Lawyer* (Cambridge, MA: Harvard University Press, 2009), 9n14.

7. "The Directorate of Intelligence: A Brief Description, February 1977," declassified from CONFIDENTIAL, https://www.cia.gov/readingroom/docs/CIA-RDP80-00473A0006 00100010-8.pdf.

8. Two declassified numbers are especially useful. In 1977, the predecessor of the DA (the NFAC) had about 150 GS-14 analytic positions. See Quality of Intelligence Analysis, November 1977, declassified from SECRET, https://www.cia.gov/readingroom/docs/CIA -RDP83M00171R001200130001-0.pdf. In 1984, GS-14s were about 16 percent of the analysts. If we assume that the proportion of GS-14s in 1977 was close to that of 1984, in 1977 there would have been about a thousand analysts. See DDI Newsletter, January 12, 1984, declassified from SECRET, https://www.cia.gov/readingroom/docs/CIA-RDP89G00720R000100060014 -9.pdf. The number of analytic positions grew 28 percent in the ten years between 1978 and 1988, according to another document. That would push the cadre up to about 1,300 in 1988. See "The State of Analysis over the Past Ten Years, 14 October 1988," https://www.cia.gov /readingroom/docs/CIA-RDP99-00777R000302750001-7.pdf. The numbers may have been relatively static as the Cold War came to an end as part of the "peace dividend." In the middle to late 1990s, however, there were areas of growth. "Staffing for the Assessments and Information Group (AIG)—CTC's Analytic Group—Grew by 34 Percent . . . [FY96-97]." See "Inspector General Report, June 2005," declassified from TOP SECRET, https://www.cia.gov/readingroom /docs/DOC_0006184107.pdf.

9. FBI, "Intelligence Analysts," August 18, 2011, https://www.fbi.gov/news/stories /intelligence-analysts-central-to-the-mission.

10. The "so what" is an explanation of how or why an event, trend, or situation matters for foreign actors. It can cover what is next, the outlook, or alternative outcomes, or risks, opportunities, or other implications for foreign actors. Analysts are also taught to identify the implications of foreign developments for US national security.

11. "Reflections on CIA and Your Stewardship, 14 October 1980," declassified from SECRET, https://www.cia.gov/readingroom/docs/CIA-RDP05S00620R000100160003-1.pdf.

12. See "Robert Gates Memo to Director of Central Intelligence, 13 March 1981," declassified from SECRET, https://www.cia.gov/readingroom/docs/CIA-RDP95M00249R000801130002-7 .pdf. Gates also noted the "dearth of people with breadth of vision to take macro view of international affairs and see major currents at work, especially across regional boundaries."

13. "Interview of NSC/White House Staff Member, Memorandum from A. W. Marshall, 6 February 1973," declassified from SECRET, https://www.cia.gov/readingroom/docs /CIA-RDP80M01133A000800110012-6.pdf; also see "Conversation with Andrew Marshall, 4 May 1972," declassified from CONFIDENTIAL, https://www.cia.gov/readingroom/docs /CIA-RDP80M01133A000900040008-8.pdf; and "Product Improvement, Consumer Needs, 10 November 1972," declassified, https://www.cia.gov/readingroom/docs/CIA-RDP80M01133 A000900030001-6.pdf.

14. "Directorate of Intelligence Handbook," attached to "Memo from Deputy Director for Intelligence to Director of Central Intelligence, 15 November 1984," https://www.cia.gov /readingroom/docs/CIA-RDP86M00886R001700240002-9.pdf; "Since the 1981 reorganization of the DI, CIA products have shown more interdisciplinary analysis," "The State of Analysis

over the Last Ten Years, Speech at the Association of Former Intelligence Officers, 14 October 1988," https://www.cia.gov/readingroom/docs/CIA-RDP99-00777R000302750001-7.pdf.

15. "Interdisciplinary Analysis, Memo from Director of Analysis to Director of Central Intelligence, 17 October 1984," https://www.cia.gov/readingroom/docs/CIA-RDP89B00423R000100100021-1.pdf.

16. The work of Vaclav Smil illustrates the power of this approach. Vaclav Smil, *Grand Transitions: How the Modern World Was Made* (New York: Oxford University Press, 2021). Interesting, declassified products with multidisciplinary characters are a memo written just days after the Chernobyl nuclear reactor disaster and a later analysis of its consequences. See "Implications of the Chernobyl Disaster, 29 April 1986," declassified from TOP SECRET, https://www.cia.gov/readingroom/docs/19860429.pdf; and "The Chernobyl' Accident: Social and Political Implications, December 1987," declassified from SECRET, https://www.cia.gov/readingroom/docs/19871201A.pdf. There may be something about the nature of such events, including Fukushima, that promotes multidisciplinary analysis.

17. The holistic description comes from Lloyd F. Jordan, "The Case for a Holistic Intelligence," *Studies in Intelligence* 19, no. 2 (Summer 1975): 9–20, declassified from CONFIDENTIAL, https://www.cia.gov/readingroom/docs/CIA-RDP78T03194A000400010012-8.pdf.

18. A good example of this is Paul Krugman, "Wonking Out: Europe and the Economics of Blackmail," *New York Times*, August 26, 2022, https://www.nytimes.com/2022/08/26/opinion/russia-ukraine-oil-gas-prices.html. Several historians tackle their subjects with an interdisciplinary approach; see, e.g., Geoffrey Parker, *Global Crisis: War, Climate Change and Catastrophe in the Seventeenth Century* (New Haven, CT: Yale University Press, 2013). Parker's earlier *The Army of Flanders and the Spanish Road, 1567–1659. The Logistics of Spanish Victory and Defeat in the Low Countries' Wars* (Cambridge: Cambridge University Press, 1972) weaves together geography, politics, sociology, technology, economics, and military affairs brilliantly.

19. Into the 1970s, there were locked doors between Directorate of Analysis and Directorate of Operations offices at the CIA Headquarters.

20. John F. Galascione, "The End of Human Intelligence Analysis—Better Start Preparing," *Studies in Intelligence* 64, no. 3 (September 2020).

21. In 1988 the CIA claimed that the "information available to intelligence analysts probably tripled between 1977 and 1984." Similar leaps were anticipated in the future. "The State of Analysis over the Last Ten Years," Speech at the Association of Former Intelligence Officers, October 14, 1988, https://www.cia.gov/readingroom/docs/CIA-RDP99-00777R000302750001-7.pdf.

22. As with personnel, there are no current declassified numbers for DA production. But a sense is provided by a revealing declassified 1984 document from the Director of Analysis: "Production has increased to the point that it now stands at nearly the highest level in the Directorate's history. In fiscal year 1983 we published over 650 hardcover papers and more than 250 typescript memoranda disseminated to senior policymakers—a 25 percent increase in production over fiscal year 1982. Moreover, these statistics do not include current intelligence, regional monthly publications, the *Terrorist Review*, the *International Financial Situation Report*, the IEEW, and other such finished products." DDI Newsletter, January 12, 1984, declassified from SECRET, https://www.cia.gov/readingroom/docs/CIA-RDP89G00720R000100060014-9.pdf. When we add current intelligence publications such as the PDB and the National Intelligence Daily (predecessor of the WIRe), serial publications,

and others—not to mention disproportionate DA contributions to National Intelligence Estimates and other intelligence community products—the output is prodigious. "Remarks of William J. Casey, Director of Central Intelligence, to CIA Employees, 21 October 1982," 4, https://www.cia.gov/readingroom/docs/CIA-RDP83M00914R000800130005-9.pdf, has the number of National Intelligence Estimates produced in the 1960s, 1970s, and early 1980s. See "Census of NFIP Intelligence Outputs, 27 January 1981," declassified, https://www.cia.gov/readingroom/docs/CIA-RDP83M00171R000100050006-6.pdf, for indication that before 1982 there was no census of CIA analytic production.

23. Oscar Wilde, *The Importance of Being Earnest, Act I, www.gutenberg.org/files/844/844-h/844-h.htm.*

24. William Shakespeare, *Hamlet,* Act 2, Scene 2. The line is uttered by Polonius, who then goes on at length contradicting the sentiment.

25. "Memo from the Office of the Vice President, March 7, 1980, declassified from SECRET, https://www.cia.gov/readingroom/docs/CIA-RDP95M00249R000801110024-5.pdf.

26. "Interview of NSC/White House Staff Member, Memorandum from A. W. Marshall, 6 February 1973," declassified from SECRET, https://www.cia.gov/readingroom/docs/CIA-RDP80M01133A000800110012-6.pdf. In the "Frequently Asked Questions" section of the *Handbook,* on the matter of length, it is stated, "Your piece should be as long as it needs to be and as short as it can be. Most pieces are a page and one-quarter or less. Some approximate two pages. On occasion, when there is a compelling reason pieces may exceed two pages."

27. "Interview of NSC/White House Staff Member, Memorandum from A. W. Marshall, 6 February 1973," declassified from SECRET, https://www.cia.gov/readingroom/docs/CIA-RDP80M01133A000800110012-6.pdf; and "Structure of the Intelligence Community, 24 August 1977," declassified from CONFIDENTIAL, https://www.cia.gov/readingroom/docs/CIA-RDP80M01048A001100040001-7.pdf; and "White House / NSC Intelligence Requirements, 23 March 1973," declassified, https://www.cia.gov/readingroom/docs/CIA-RDP80M01133A000900040001-5.pdf.

28. The DNI has directed that analytic products meet standards that would require yet more words. See "Intelligence Community Directive 203, Analytic Standards," https://www.dni.gov/files/documents/ICD/ICD%20203%20Analytic%20Standards.pdf.

29. Such time pressures are by no means unique to the president. The schedule of the Supreme Allied Commander Europe (SACEUR), the senior-most commander in NATO, was just as packed. Many analysts experience the ire of assistants to senior officials when their briefings go long, playing havoc with the rest of overscheduled officials' schedules.

30. "PDB Handbook," https://www.dni.gov/files/documents/FOIA/DF-2021-00227-The-PDB-handbook.pdf.

31. An example illustrates this well. A Presidential PDB briefer told one of the authors, after serving about six months, how "great it was to be an expert." The author replied, "An expert in what?" Reading short articles, background notes, and a limited package of curated sources is not expertise. The issue of the management (and review) layers is not new. A declassified 1977 document notes that "all observers of the agency comment on the excessive number of layers between the consumers and the analysts who actually examine the data." "Structure of the Intelligence Community, 24 August 1977," declassified from CONFIDENTIAL, https://www.cia.gov/readingroom/docs/CIA-RDP80M01048A001100040001-7.pdf.

32. Willmoore Kendall, "The Function of Intelligence" [a review of Sherman Kent, *Strategic Intelligence*], *World Politics* 1, no. 4 (July 1949): 542–52, at 548.

33. Sensitivities run high. In one instance, congressmen were initially enraged during an intelligence presentation on religious conversion efforts in Sub-Saharan Africa. They assumed the discussion involved US evangelical Christian groups and thought it entirely inappropriate to discuss. The briefing was focused on foreign Islamic efforts. It is worth noting that an analysis of evangelical conversion efforts might be a legitimate subject. As scholars have said, you cannot understand US policy vis-à-vis China in the 1940s, and Chinese reactions, without understanding US Christian missionaries' efforts there.

34. More remarkably, analysts in the DA were told not to look at leaked, classified US material. Although the Agency intended to avoid endorsing such leaks or confirming their accuracy, there was an obvious downside. Foreign officials could read sensitive US materials and be influenced by them, but analysts were told not to see what those foreign officials might be examining.

35. This section relies heavily on the superb study by Robert M. Hathaway, "Confrontation and Retreat: The US Congress and the South Asian Nuclear Tests," *Arms Control Today* 30, no. 1 (January–February 2000): 7–14.

36. One of the authors participated in a roundtable with journalists from a foreign country brought to the United States through a State Department program. The author posited to them that when they discussed national decision-making in their country, they recognized the disparate interests and efforts of competing factions, unintended effects, and so on. When asked if they parsed US decision-making the same way—searching out individual and bureaucratic interests—or assumed a coordinated US policy, they admitted that they generally leaned toward the latter.

37. "Structure of the Intelligence Community, 24 August 1977," declassified from CONFIDENTIAL, https://www.cia.gov/readingroom/docs/CIA-RDP80M01048A001100040001-7.pdf.

38. "Structure of the Intelligence Community, 24 August 1977."

39. "Senior Seminar Procedures, 20 February 1973," https://www.cia.gov/readingroom/docs/CIA-RDP84-00780R005600030013-6.pdf.

40. "Briefing of Dr. Brzezinski, 25 April 1979," declassified from CONFIDENTIAL, https://www.cia.gov/readingroom/docs/CIA-RDP83B00100R000100020010-3.pdf.

41. One of the authors met with scholars brought in by the director of the CIA to study the PDB. The scholars' draft study assumed "Daily" meant all articles were conceived and completed in one day. They thought PDBs were orally briefed. As the author told them, "The PDB is only partly Presidential [at that time there were more than a dozen other recipients], often not Daily [in terms of producing an article], and very seldom Briefed [at that time, not to any recipient]."

42. "Structure of the Intelligence Community, 24 August 1977," declassified from CONFIDENTIAL, https://www.cia.gov/readingroom/docs/CIA-RDP80M01048A001100040001-7.pdf.

43. Then–deputy director for intelligence Ed Proctor noted that analysis constituted only 6 percent of the CIA's budget in 1975, in response to a House Select Committee staffer's question about whether analysts could possibly process and analyze all the technical intelligence

that the National Security Agency was collecting. See CIA, "Memorandum for the Record, Subject: HSC Briefing—Kirschstein, August 25," 1075, para 12, approved for release 2004/11/04, https://www.cia.gov/readingroom/docs/CIA-RDP89B00552R000100110100-6.pdf. Given the growth in the CIA's technical and operational activities, one might imagine that this percentage has not changed greatly.

44. Warren P. Strobel, "To Battle New Threats, Spy Agencies to Share More Intelligence with Private Sector," *Wall Street Journal*, August 10, 2023, https://www.wsj.com/articles/to-battle-new-threats-spy-agencies-to-share-more-intelligence-with-private-sector-db25e36.

45. The 2023 National Intelligence Strategy document is at https://www.dni.gov/files/ODNI/documents/National_Intelligence_Strategy_2023.pdf.

Appendix A:
Suggested Further Reading on
Intelligence Analysis, by Discipline

Intelligence analysts bemoan the lack of a literature on how analysis is done—especially as narrowed by individual disciplines—but all analysts draw on a rich, diverse body of academic and professional literature. The contributors to this volume have selected key works that have influenced them and that they have used in mentoring and instructing others.

The breadth and depth of each analytic discipline necessitates prioritization, and even brutal triage, to keep these sections of selected readings to manageable lengths. The notes at the end of each chapter provide many additional sources that interested readers are encouraged to explore.

POLITICAL ANALYSIS (CHAPTER 2):
MAKING SENSE OF A COMPLEX WORLD

Several publications have received attention by those teaching intelligence analysis at the CIA—not exclusively political analysis, but including it. These works highlight the role of critical thinking and the malign influence of cognitive biases. Some of the key works are Richards J. Heuer Jr., *Psychology of Intelligence Analysis* (Langley, VA: CIA Center for the Study of Intelligence, 1999), https://www.cia.gov/static /9a5f1162fd0932c29bfed1c030edf4ae/Pyschology-of-Intelligence-Analysis.pdf; Daniel Kahneman, *Thinking, Fast and Slow* (New York: Farrar, Straus & Giroux, 2011); Philip E. Tetlock, *Expert Political Judgment: How Good Is It? How Can We Know?* (Princeton, NJ: Princeton University Press, 2005); CIA, *A Tradecraft Primer: Structured Analytic Techniques for Improving Intelligence Analysis*, March 2009, https:// www.cia.gov/static/955180a45afe3f5013772c313b16face/Tradecraft-Primer-apr09 .pdf; Robert Jervis, *Perception and Misperception in International Politics* (Princeton, NJ: Princeton University Press, 2017); and Nassim Nicholas Taleb, *The Black Swan: The Impact of the Highly Improbable*, 2nd ed. (New York: Random House, 2010). Frankly, this list could go on for some pages.

A valuable exception to the dearth of literature on how political analysis as an intelligence discipline is or should be practiced is an article by Martin Peterson, a senior analytic manager at the CIA, "The Challenge for the Political Analyst," *Studies in Intelligence* 47, no. 1 (2003), https://www.cia.gov/static/Challenge-for-Political-Analyst.pdf. There are also useful insights in articles written by Jack Davis, another senior analyst at the CIA, who taught hundreds of other analysts about the successes and failures of analysis. For a selected list of his publications, see https://www.cia.gov/static/Jack-Davis.pdf; and most can be found as links at https://www.cia.gov/search/?q=Jack%20Davis&site=CIA&output=xml_no_dtd&client=CIA&myAction=%2Fsearch&proxystylesheet=CIA&submitMethod=get&p=2.

Political analysis is scrutinized in some studies of real or perceived intelligence failures. Two useful examples are Douglas J. MacEachin, *CIA Assessments of the Soviet Union: The Record versus the Charges—An Intelligence Memorandum* (Washington, DC: CIA, 1996), https://www.cia.gov/static/CIA-Assessments-Soviet-Union.pdf; and Robert Jervis, *Why Intelligence Fails: Lessons from the Iranian Revolution and the Iraq War*, 1st ed. (Ithaca, NY: Cornell University Press, 2011). MacEachin was a director of analysis at the CIA, and Jervis had long-term associations with the Agency. Declassified CIA and National Intelligence Council studies also illustrate the end products of political analysis, but the analytic techniques are often opaque.

When one turns to the literature on political analysis writ large—not the narrower intelligence discipline—the relevant literature explodes. Analysts can find rich veins to mine in original sources (e.g., Thucydides, Machiavelli, Hobbes, Locke, Hume, and Kant); interpreters of those writers (an interesting recent book that covers many from a particular angle is Hal Brands, ed., *The New Makers of Modern Strategy: From the Ancient World to the Digital Age* (Princeton, NJ: Princeton University Press, 2023); and theorists and practitioners from more recent decades (e.g., Samuel Huntington, Kenneth Waltz, Henry Kissinger, Francis Fukuyama, Dani Rodrik, Joseph Stiglitz, John Ikenberry, and Joseph Nye, to name several).

MILITARY ANALYSIS (CHAPTER 3): PEERING OVER THE HILL

Four types of works are of great value in learning and teaching the practice of military intelligence analysis. First, a wealth of material helps identify factors, actors, and interactions worth studying as well as theories about their relationships. Much of this material has a US focus but with considerable creative effort these materials can be used to teach people how to do analysis on foreign armed forces. A fine example is Richard Betts, *Military Readiness: Concepts, Choices, Consequences* (Washington, DC: Brookings Institution Press, 1995). A more recent example, again with a US focus, is Michael O'Hanlon, *Defense 101: Understanding the Military of Today and Tomorrow* (Ithaca, NY: Cornell University Press, 2021).

A second rich vein of material consists of historical studies that explore the analytic disciplines in action. Eugenia Kiesling's *Arming against Hitler: France and the Limits of Military Planning* (Lawrence: University Press of Kansas, 1996) plays a central role in the advanced military analysis course taught for years in the intelligence community and in a prominent graduate program. Studies produced with the sponsorship of the Defense Department's Office of Net Assessment—such as the three-volume set edited by Allan R. Millett and Williamson Murray, *Military Effectiveness*, 2nd ed. (Cambridge: Cambridge University Press, 2010)—are treasure troves. A particularly valuable example that has a foreign focus is Kenneth Pollack's *Arabs at War: Military Effectiveness, 1948–1991* (Lincoln: University of Nebraska Press, 2002), and his more recent *Armies of Sand: The Past, Present, and Future of Arab Military Effectiveness* (Oxford: Oxford University Press, 2019).

Third, although declassified intelligence studies seldom show how analysis was done and many are heavily redacted to protect sources and methods, there are exceptions. A wonderful instance is National Foreign Assessment Center, *The Role of Interdiction at Sea in Soviet Naval Strategy and Operations*, May 1978, declassified from TOP SECRET, https://www.cia.gov/readingroom/docs/DOC_0005530564 .pdf. Even poor analytic products can serve a pedagogic purpose. See *Implications of Recent Soviet Military-Political Activities*, Special National Intelligence Estimate, SNIE 11-10-84/JX, May 18, 1984, declassified from TOP SECRET, https://www.cia .gov/readingroom/docs/CIA-RDP09T00367R000300330001-9.pdf.

Finally, reporting and analysis on recent conflicts—Afghanistan, against ISIS, and especially Russia's aggression against Ukraine—contains a wealth of material. Particularly useful has been work by Phillips Payson O'Brien, Lawrence Freedman, and the Institute for the Study of War; see https://www.iswresearch.org. This brief foray into the relevant literature hints at the number of works that are useful. The syllabus the author uses to teach a semester-length course on "Assessing Foreign Militaries" at the graduate level includes hundreds of required and recommended readings and is seventy-seven pages long.

ECONOMIC ANALYSIS (CHAPTER 4): "INVISIBLE HANDS" AT WORK

As noted above for all the disciplines, the fact that economic analysis can take so many forms and go in many directions (e.g., international trade, licit and illicit finance, global investment, energy resources, and socioeconomic and demographic pressures) makes it difficult to recommend a particular reading list of "essentials." Nevertheless, besides having a subscription to *The Economist* handy for its breadth of coverage, one cannot go wrong in being familiar with some relatively recent classics. The *Handbook of International Economics* is a go-to set of volumes with articles on a range of topics; volumes 1 and 2 were edited by Ron Jones and Peter Kenen (Amsterdam: Elsevier, 1984 and 1985), and volume 3 was edited by Gene Grossman and Ken Rogoff (Amsterdam: Elsevier, 1995); the series now extends to volumes 4 through 6 (published in 2014, 2022, and 2022, respectively).

In *Innovation and Growth in the Global Economy* (Cambridge, MA: MIT Press, 1993), Gene Grossman and Elhanan Helpman developed a unique approach in which innovation is viewed as a deliberate outgrowth of investments in industrial research by forward-looking, profit-seeking agents. For a range of views on a surprisingly controversial subject—international trade—see Avinash Dixit and Victor Norman, *Theory of International Trade* (New York: Cambridge University Press, 1980); Paul Krugman, *Rethinking International Trade* (Cambridge, MA: MIT Press, 1994); and Robert C. Feenstra, *Advanced International Trade: Theory and Evidence* (Princeton, NJ: Princeton University Press, 2003). A unique, policy-oriented text is *Economic Development* by Michael Todaro and Stephen Smith (published in multiple editions by Pearson/Addison-Wesley), which illustrates real-world development problems, offers coverage of advances in the field, and features a balanced presentation of opposing viewpoints on today's major policy debates.

Finally, the declassified intelligence study *Globalization of Financial Markets: Implications, Vulnerabilities, and Opportunities*, October 1986—though redacted in places—gives insight into a topic that has reverberations to this day and illustrates the structure and approach of a traditional publication format, the "intelligence assessment." Produced by the CIA's former Office of Global Issues, the study was declassified from SECRET and is available at https://www.cia.gov/readingroom/docs/CIA -RDP87T01127R001100940003-0.pdf.

SCIENCE, TECHNOLOGY, AND WEAPONS ANALYSIS (CHAPTER 5): LEVERAGING SCIENCE FOR NATIONAL SECURITY

Although guides for analyzing foreign science, technology, and weapons programs are rare, some useful resources are available on cutting-edge technologies and dependencies, historical foreign programs, various weapons systems, key proliferation networks, and postmortems that have been conducted after intelligence failures. Reviewing ratified treaties also can provide insights into programs monitored and prohibited under multinational and bilateral arms control agreements. Because of the breadth and diversity of the science, technology, and weapons (ST&W) discipline, most works tend to focus on specific technical fields rather than cover ST&W issues broadly.

Rare earth elements—used in peaceful high-technology programs as well as defense programs—exemplify how understanding potential accessibility barriers and dependencies are critical to ST&W analysis. Useful resources include Guillaume Pitron and Bianca Jacobsohn, *The Rare Metals War: The Dark Side of Clean Energy and Digital Technologies* (London: Scribe UK, 2020) as well as J. H. L. Voncken, *The Rare Earth Elements: An Introduction* (Cham, Switzerland: Springer, 2016). Similarly, cutting-edge technologies and shifting military capabilities inform assessments of foreign ST&W threats. Two examples are John D. Anderson Jr., *Hypersonic and High-Temperature Gas Dynamics*, 3rd ed. (Reston, VA: American Institute of Aeronautics and Astronautics, 2019); and Gerry Doyle and Blake Herzinger, *Carrier Killer: China's Anti-Ship Ballistic Missiles and Theater of Operations in the Early 21st Century* (Warwick, UK: Helion, 2022).

We gain insights from studies of historical biological warfare programs, such as Peter Williams and David Wallace, *Unit 731: Japan's Secret Biological Warfare in World War II* (New York: Free Press, 1989); Ken Alibek and Stephen Handelman, *Biohazard: The Chilling True Story of the Largest Covert Biological Weapons Program in the World—Told from Inside by the Man Who Ran It* (New York: Random House, 1999); Anthony Rimmington, *The Soviet Union's Invisible Weapons of Mass Destruction: Biopreparat's Covert Biological Warfare Programme* (Cham, Switzerland: Springer Nature, 2021); Anthony Rimmington, *The Soviet Union's Agricultural Biowarfare Programme: Ploughshares to Swords* (Cham, Switzerland: Springer Nature, 2021). Useful insights into the evolution of programs and effects are captured by Robert Harris and Jeremy Paxman, *A Higher Form of Killing: The Secret Story of Chemical and Biological Warfare* (New York: Noonday Press, 1982); and Jonathan B. Tucker, *War of Nerves: Chemical Warfare from World War I to Al-Qaeda* (New York: Anchor Books, 2006).

Understanding proliferation mechanisms and risks are illustrated by James E. Doyle, *Nuclear Safeguards, Security, and Nonproliferation: Achieving Security with Technology and Policy*, 2nd ed. (Cambridge, MA: Elsevier/Butterworth-Heinemann, 2019). One of the best-known cases of nuclear proliferation—the A. Q. Khan network—is covered by Gordon Corera, *Shopping for Bombs: Nuclear Proliferation, Global Insecurity, and the Rise and Fall of the A. Q. Khan Network* (New York: Oxford University Press, 2006); Naval Postgraduate School, *The A. Q. Khan Network: Causes and Implications* (Scotts Valley, CA: CreateSpace, 2016); and a dossier by the International Institute for Strategic Studies, *Nuclear Black Markets: Pakistan, A. Q. Khan and the Rise of Proliferation Networks—A Net Assessment* (London: International Institute for Strategic Studies, 2007).

Postmortems on intelligence failures often include useful insights into potential analytic perils. These include the Iraq weapons of mass destruction case, detailed by the Commission on the Intelligence Capabilities of the United States Regarding

Weapons of Mass Destruction, *Report of the Commission: Official Government Edition* (Washington, DC: US Government Printing Office, 2005); and Robert Jervis, *Why Intelligence Fails: Lessons from the Iranian Revolution and the Iraq War* (Ithaca, NY: Cornell University Press, 2010).

A study of ST&W-related treaties that monitor or ban weapons programs highlights critical technologies. See, for example, the Chemical Weapons Convention, https://www.opcw.org/chemical-weapons-convention; the New START Treaty, https://www.state.gov/new-start/; the Treaty on the Non-Proliferation of Nuclear Weapons, https://www.iaea.org/publications/documents/treaties/npt; and the Convention on the Prohibition of the Development, Production, and Stockpiling of Bacteriological (Biological) and Toxin Weapons and on Their Destruction, https://treaties.unoda.org/t/bwc.

LEADERSHIP ANALYSIS (CHAPTER 6): THE WORLDWIDE WHO'S WHO

As discussed at the beginning of chapter 6, the world is awash with pop culture books that discuss one purported leadership concept or another. A small percentage may have some value to a new analyst, but a better introduction to leader analysis would be a broad academic overview of classic leadership topics selected by an expert, such as J. Thomas Wren, *The Leader's Companion: Insights on Leadership through the Ages* (New York: Free Press, 1995). Biographies and autobiographies of specific leaders have obvious value within the context of their own country or culture. They must, however, be taken with multiple grains of self-serving salt, as both authors and subjects often look to reframe history or settle political scores.

Analysts also go beyond studying individual leaders by reading books that dive deep into the common experiences and mind-sets of individuals who lead similar groups. A counterterrorism leader analyst would reference works like that by John G. Horgan, *The Psychology of Terrorism*, 2nd ed. (Abingdon-on-Thames, UK: Routledge, 2014). A leader analyst who covers a country led by a pioneering businessperson might think outside the box and find useful insights in a book like that by Walter Isaacson, *The Innovators: How a Group of Hackers, Geniuses, and Geeks Created the Digital Revolution*, reprint ed. (New York: Simon & Schuster, 2015). Going beyond individual leaders also drives analysts to read topical scholarly works like that by Donelson Forsyth, *Group Dynamics*, 7th ed. (Boston: Cengage Learning, 2018). Other academics who could be consulted usefully, and a few of their works, are David Patrick Houghton, *Political Psychology: Situation, Individuals, and Cases*, 2nd ed. (Abingdon-on-Thames, UK: Routledge, 2015) and David Patrick Houghton, *The Decision Point: Six Cases in US Foreign Policy Decision Making* (Oxford: Oxford

University Press, 2013); Robert Jervis, *Perception and Misperception in International Politics* (Princeton, NJ: Princeton University Press, 2017); Margaret G. Hermann, *Political Psychology: Contemporary Problems and Issues* (Hoboken, NJ: Jossey Bass, 2004); and Kenneth B. Dekleva, "Leadership Analysis and Political Psychology in the 21st Century," *Journal of the American Academy of Psychiatry and the Law* 46, no. 3 (2018): 359–63.

Finally, who better to explain leader analysis to a new initiate than a successful former leader analyst like Jerrold Post, who was behind the leadership profiles cited in this chapter that so impressed President Carter? Post wrote multiple remarkable works, with two notable examples being *Leaders and Their Followers in a Dangerous World: The Psychology of Political Behavior* (Ithaca, NY: Cornell University Press, 2004); and *The Psychological Assessment of Political Leaders: With Profiles of Saddam Hussein and Bill Clinton* (Ann Arbor: University of Michigan Press, 2003).

COUNTERINTELLIGENCE ANALYSIS (CHAPTER 7): CATCHING SPIES AND COUNTERING FOES

Despite Roy Godson's apt description of counterintelligence analysis as the queen on the intelligence chessboard, and its "potential to be a powerful multiplier," precious little academic study has focused on it. Still, a rich, if mixed, literature on US counterintelligence itself, with occasional analytic vignettes, can be found in these works, including Godson's excellent historical survey in *Dirty Tricks or Trump Cards: US Covert Action and Counterintelligence* (New Brunswick, NJ: Transaction, 2001). Both practitioners and academics have addressed the discipline, and perhaps the best of the studies have been produced by writers with experience in both worlds. These include James M. Olson, *To Catch a Spy: The Art of Counterintelligence* (Washington, DC: Georgetown University Press, 2019); Michael J. Sulick, *American Spies: Espionage against the United States from the Cold War to the Present* (Washington, DC: Georgetown University Press, 2013); and selections by Jennifer E. Sims and Burton Gerber, eds., *Vaults, Mirrors, and Masks: Rediscovering US Counterintelligence* (Washington, DC: Georgetown University Press, 2009). Counterintelligence as a human spy versus spy activity is well told by Milt Bearden and James Risen, *The Main Enemy: The Inside Story of the CIA's Final Showdown with the KGB* (New York: Ballantine Books, 2003), while remarkable analytic exploitation of technical counterintelligence is given by John Earl Haynes and Harvey Klehr, *VENONA: Decoding Soviet Espionage in America* (New Haven, CT: Yale University Press, 1999). Counterintelligence conducted by authoritarian regimes is addressed by Blake W. Mobley and Carl A. Wege, *The Fragile Dictator: Counterintelligence Pathologies in Authoritarian States* (Lanham, MD: Lexington Books, 2023); and Victor Cherkashin with Gregory Feifer, *Spy*

Handler: Memoir of a KGB Officer—The True Story of the Man Who Recruited Robert Hanssen and Aldrich Ames (New York: Basic Books, 2005). Representative examples of counterespionage analysis of important spy cases are found in the literature cited in the notes to the chapter. The abundant, though generally ill-informed literature, on the CIA's controversial counterintelligence chief James J. Angleton can be skipped—instead, read the definitive account by David Robarge, "Moles, Defectors, and Deceptions: James Angleton and CIA Counterintelligence," *Journal of Intelligence History* 3, no. 2 (Winter 2003): 21–49.

COUNTERTERRORISM ANALYSIS (CHAPTER 8): PREEMPTING THREATS

Practitioners of counterterrorism (CT) analysis for intelligence purposes can draw insights from a substantial body of scholarship and journalistic coverage of terrorism and insurgency, even if the literature on the specialized tradecraft of CT intelligence analysis is limited. Several of the classic works on terrorism written before 9/11 compare favorably with what followed. Bruce Hoffman's *Inside Terrorism*, 3rd ed. (New York: Columbia University Press, 2017; orig. pub. 1998) offers still-useful insights into categories of terrorist groups, the role of the media, and tactical aspects of terrorism that preoccupy analysts today; Paul Pillar's *Terrorism and US Foreign Policy*, 1st ed. (Washington, DC: Brookings Institution Press, 2001), outlines the enduring challenges for governments in responding to terrorism and includes timeless lessons for CT analysis.

Since the 9/11 attacks, the highest-profile resource that spotlights the role of intelligence analysis and its relation to policymaking has been the report of the National Commission on Terrorist Attacks upon the United States, *The 9/11 Commission Report* (Washington, DC: US Government Printing Office, 2004). Daniel Byman's article, "The Intelligence War on Terrorism," *Intelligence and National Security* 29, no. 6 (2014): 837–63, provides a comprehensive and balanced overview of challenges of intelligence collection and analysis of terrorism, as does Gregory Treverton's chapter, "The Intelligence of Counterterrorism," in *The Long Shadow of 9/11: America's Response to Terrorism*, ed. Brian Michael Jenkins and John Paul Godges (Santa Monica, CA: RAND Corporation, 2011), https://www.jstor.org/stable/10.7249/mg1107rc.22.

There is a body of declassified material on counterterrorism, but little of it illuminates analytic techniques. Moreover, a large amount dates from the 1980s and has a focus on state-sponsored terrorism. See, for example, Directorate of Analysis, "Terrorism as a Political Weapon: Four Middle Eastern Case Studies," April 23, 1985, declassified from SECRET, https://www.cia.gov/readingroom/docs/CIA-RDP

85T01058R000406200001-4.pdf; other declassified CT analysis from this period can be found on the CIA's website (www.cia.gov/readingroom) by searching under the keyword "terror." One declassified, lightly redacted study of a terrorist group is Directorate of Intelligence, "The Abu Nidal Terror Network: Organization, State Sponsors, and Commercial Enterprise," July 1987, declassified from SECRET, https://www.cia.gov/readingroom/docs/THE%20ABU%20NIDAL%20TERROR%20NETW%5.B14950297%5D.pdf. More recent illustrative examples of analysis of threats and other contemporary challenges of terrorism include the CIA's August 2001 warning of al-Qaeda's threat to attack inside the United States, which was declassified for the 9/11 Commission and is retrievable from the National Security Archive, https://nsarchive2.gwu.edu/NSAEBB/NSAEBB116/pdb8-6-2001.pdf. For a broader analysis of global threats and the impact of CT responses, see the declassified key judgments of the National Intelligence Estimate, *Trends in Global Terrorism: Implications for the United States*, April 2006, https://www.dni.gov/files/documents/Newsroom/Press%20Releases/2006%20Press%20Releases/Declassified_NIE_Key_Judgments.pdf.

Two of the leading academic journals for terrorism studies that predate 9/11 are *Studies in Conflict and Terrorism* (published since 1977) and *Terrorism and Political Violence* (published since 1989). In 2007, the Terrorism Research Initiative, associated with the Institute of Security and Global Affairs of Leiden University's campus in The Hague, began publication of an open-access journal, *Perspectives on Terrorism*, which has a strong representation of European researchers. Also in 2007, the US Military Academy at West Point launched publication of the *CTC Sentinel*, an online journal with a strong emphasis on informing counterterrorism policymakers and practitioners.

CYBER ANALYSIS (CHAPTER 9): IDENTIFYING MALICIOUS TECHNOLOGY AND ACTORS

As a new analytic discipline, it is not surprising that the literature on cyber is evolving rapidly. The field is associated with computer science, but the kind of academic work that might guide us in other disciplines is yet to develop in this one. Nevertheless, there is no shortage of titles about the ever-growing role of, and increasing dependence on, cyber systems in modern societies. Most of these works address cyber as a specific technology or as an infrastructure critical to those societies. This includes studies of criminal online activities such as hacking. The challenge is to find authors who address cyber as an instrument of national power, especially in its potential roles in intelligence analysis and collection, and development of national security strategy. Former senior National Security Council staff member Richard Clarke's *The Fifth Domain: Defending Our Country, Our Companies, and Ourselves in the Age of Cyber*

Threats (New York: Penguin, 2019) is his latest book treatment on the subject. Joseph Menn's *Fatal System Error: The Hunt for the New Crime Lords Who Are Bringing Down the Internet* (New York: PublicAffairs, 2010) is the latest edition of Menn's characterization of the nexus of national security and cybercrime. Fred Kaplan, *Dark Territory: The Secret History of Cyber War* (New York: Simon & Schuster, 2017), is a unique attempt to fuse national security strategy, covert intelligence operations, and cyber. In this vein, Stuart Starr's chapter, "Toward a Preliminary Theory of Cyber Power," in *Cyber Power and National Security*, ed. Franklin D. Kramer, Stuart H. Starr, and Larry K. Wentz (Washington, DC: National Defense University Press, 2010), offers a foundation for the still-emerging field of dedicated cyber strategy. In a broader context, historical examinations of the impact of new technologies on military operations and national security suggest parallels for the development of cyber. See, for example, Williamson Murray and Allan R. Millett, eds., *Military Innovation in the Interwar Period* (Cambridge: Cambridge University Press, 1996).

NATIONAL ESTIMATES (CHAPTER 10): WHERE INTELLIGENCE MEETS POLICY

The early practitioners of estimative intelligence have produced some foundational studies. For those, see Sherman Kent, *Strategic Intelligence for an American World Policy* (Princeton, NJ: Princeton Legacy Library, 1966); and Harold P. Ford, *Estimative Intelligence: Purpose and Problems of National Intelligence Estimating* (Lanham, MD: University of America Press, 1993). Equally useful are the collected essays of Sherman Kent, which are included by Donald P. Steury, ed., *Sherman Kent and the Board of National Estimates: Collected Essays* (Washington, DC: Center for the Study of Intelligence, 1994), https://www.cia.gov/static/sherman-kent-and-the-board -of-national-estimates-collected-essays.pdf. More recently, former chairmen of the National Intelligence Council have discussed their roles in shaping National Intelligence Estimates. For that discussion, see Robert Hutchings and Gregory Treverton, eds., *Truth to Power: A History of the US National Intelligence Council* (Oxford: Oxford University Press, 2019). Academic critiques of estimates are also useful in pointing out the major challenges that analysts face in preparing national estimates. Some of the most insightful include these: Klaus Knorr, "Failures in National Intelligence Estimates: The Case of the Cuban Missiles," *World Politics* 16, no. 3 (1964): 455–67; Willis C. Armstrong et al., "The Hazards of Single-Outcome Forecasting," *Studies in Intelligence* 28, no. 3 (1984): 57–70; Robert Jervis, *Why Intelligence Fails: Lessons from the Iranian Revolution and the Iraq War* (Ithaca, NY: Cornell University Press, 2010); Greg Treverton, "CIA Support to Policymakers: The 2007 National Intelligence Estimate on Iran's Nuclear Intentions and Capabilities," *Intelligence and*

National Security 36, no. 2 (2013): 164–75; and Jeffrey A. Friedman and Richard Zeck-hauser, "Assessing Uncertainty in Intelligence," *Intelligence and National Security* 27, no. 6 (2012): 824–47.

The literature on the intelligence–policy relationship has been examined by intelligence practitioners as well as academics over the years. Books and memoirs by former senior intelligence officials often recount their experiences working with presidents and their advisers and the frictions that can exist. Christopher Andrew's massive history of American intelligence is full of clashes between intelligence and policy: Christopher Andrew, *For the President's Eyes Only: Secret Intelligence and the American Presidency from Washington to Bush* (New York: Harper Perennial, 1996). Former CIA careerist and National Intelligence Council vice chairman Harold Ford's more modest monograph, *CIA and the Vietnam Policymakers: Three Episodes 1962–1968* (Washington, DC: Center for the Study of Intelligence, 1991), analyzes the challenges intelligence analysts faced in providing negative assessments to White House and Defense Department officials committed to victory in Vietnam. Two outstanding academic treatments of the intelligence–policy relationship as well as politicization were written by Robert Jervis, "Why Intelligence and Policymakers Clash," *Political Science Quarterly* 125, no. 2 (Summer 2010): 185–204; and Joshua Rovner, *Fixing the Facts: National Security and the Politics of Intelligence* (Ithaca, NY: Cornell University Press, 2011). The former vice chairmen of the National Intelligence Council, Gregory Treverton, also crafted an excellent chapter on politicization: "Intelligence Analysis: Between Politicization and Irrelevance," in *Analyzing Intelligence: Origins, Obstacles, and Innovations*," ed. Roger Z. George and James Bruce (Washington, DC: Georgetown University Press, 2008), 91–106. Finally, readers can also find more recent examples of the sometimes productive as well as tense intelligence–policy relationship in former CIA director Michael Hayden's memoir, *Playing to the Edge: American Intelligence in the Age of Terror* (New York: Penguin Press, 2016); and former director of national intelligence James Clapper's book, *Facts and Fears: Hard Truths from a Life in Intelli*gence (New York: Viking Press, 2018).

Appendix B:
Glossary of Intelligence Analysis Terms

actionable intelligence. Intelligence that can lead to quick decisions or actions is often termed "actionable" to connote that it is highly valued as being timely and detailed enough to give decision-makers a decision advantage in being able to act quickly in ways that can mitigate risks or take advantage of opportunities.

all-source analysis. All-source analysis is based on the best reporting available from all sources, including HUMINT (human intelligence), IMINT (imagery intelligence), SIGINT (signals intelligence), and open sources. All-source analysts are those experts able to access both classified and unclassified sources, who are not working solely with a single source of information, which is what imagery or SIGINT analysts perform.

alternative analysis. Alternative analysis is the term often applied to a range of structured analytic techniques used to challenge conventional thinking on an analytic problem. The word "alternative" is used to underline the importance of using various techniques—such as devil's advocacy, Team A / Team B analysis, or analysis of competing hypotheses—to surface "alternative" interpretations of available information.

analysis. In intelligence, analysis is a cognitive and empirical activity combining reasoning and evidence in order to produce judgments, insights, and forecasts intended to enhance understanding and reduce uncertainty for national security policymakers. Analysts prepare "finished" assessments spanning current intelligence or more strategic research issues addressing the information requirements of government officials. Analysis includes understanding and tasking collection, assessing and using open source and classified information, generating and evaluating hypotheses about events or developments, and identifying their implications for US security policies.

analysis of competing hypotheses. Analysis of competing hypotheses is a technique for identifying alternative explanations (hypotheses) for a development and evaluating all available evidence to help disconfirm, rather than confirm, these explanations. The process arrays all the data against multiple hypotheses and determines which pieces of evidence are consistent or inconsistent with each hypothesis.

Analysts can quickly see that data often support multiple hypotheses and only a few will stand out as the ones that disprove a specific explanation.

analytic assumptions. An assumption is any hypothesis that analysts have accepted to be true and that forms the basis of their assessments. The use of assumptions is part of the analytic process, but it is often difficult for analysts to identify these hypotheses in advance. Implicit assumptions can drive an analytic argument without their ever being articulated or examined.

analytical tradecraft. Analytical tradecraft is the term used to describe the principles and tools used by analysts to instill rigor in their thinking and prevent cognitive biases from skewing their analytic judgments. Through the use of so-called structured analytic techniques, analysts make their argumentation and logic more transparent and subject to further investigation. The term "tradecraft" originated with the Directorate of Operations term for techniques used to avoid counterintelligence detection and to successfully recruit and run agents.

anchoring bias. A form of cognitive bias, anchoring occurs when a previous analysis of a target acts to prevent analysts from reassessing their judgments and allows for only incremental change in their forecasts. In essence, the initial judgment acts as an anchor, making the final estimate closer to the original one than should be the case, given the new information available to analysts.

basic intelligence. Basic intelligence is the fundamental and factual reference material on a country or issue, which forms the foundation on which analysts can base current and estimative analysis. Examples would include economic statistics, topographic and geographic information, and documentary information on a country's form of government, rules of law, and electoral procedures and patterns. The CIA's "World Fact Book" is a product containing basic information on major countries of the world.

caveat. A caveat is a term used within the analytic community to suggest analysts are qualifying their judgments because of a problem in sourcing or in interpreting available information regarding an intelligence topic. Caveats include the use of qualifying statements, such as "we assess" or "we estimate," which indicate that analysts are reaching judgments, not stating facts.

clandestine. In intelligence terms, clandestine refers to the manner of acquiring information on a target in such a way as to conceal the collection operation itself as well as the identity of the source. It differs from covert in that a covert operation is observable but the United States is able to plausibly deny it had conducted the operation.

classified intelligence. Classified intelligence information requires special, expensive, or risky methods to collect, either by technical systems or humans, which must be protected. The risk of compromising these sources and methods is given a security classification (confidential, secret, or top secret). Classified intelligence is then shared only with those individuals who have a "need to know" this information. Analysts use this information in written assessments, and they carefully mark these reports with the classification according to the information used.

cognitive bias. Cognitive biases are mental errors caused by unconscious and simplified information-processing strategies. The human mind's natural tendency to develop patterns of thinking, or "mind-sets," often distorts, exaggerates, or dismisses new information in ways that produce errors in judgment or thinking. Forms of cognitive bias can include mirror-imaging, anchoring bias, confirmation bias, and hindsight bias, to name a few.

collection gap. Analysts identify gaps in their knowledge on a subject, and these collection shortfalls become "requirements" for future collection efforts. Identifying important collection gaps not only aids collectors but also sensitizes analysts to the need to qualify or "caveat" their judgments or set more modest levels of "confidence" in reaching their analytic conclusions.

collector. The organizations that operate a variety of technical systems or espionage units. They are part of the US intelligence community and are tasked by analysts through the development of complex sets of "collection requirements." For example, the National Security Agency is the principal SIGINT collector, while the CIA's Directorate of Operations is the principal HUMINT collector.

COMINT. Communications intelligence is information gathered from the electronic gathering of foreign communications of individuals or organizations that can include telephone, fax, and Internet systems that can indicate the plans, intentions, and capabilities of foreign actors. It is part of the SIGINT technical collection system.

competitive analysis. Competitive analysis refers to the explicit use of competing sets of analysts or analytic units to reach judgments on the same intelligence subject. The goal is to determine whether competing analysis will uncover different sets of assumptions, using evidence or contrasting perspectives, that would enhance analysts' understanding of an important topic. Historically, the CIA and the Defense Intelligence Agency provided competing analysis of Soviet military developments, often based on different assumptions about Soviet behavior.

confirmation bias. Confirmation bias is the human tendency to search for or interpret information in a way that confirms a preconception. Analysts will often seek out or give more weight to evidence that confirms a current hypothesis or the "conventional wisdom" while dismissing or devaluing disconfirming information.

coordination process. Many analysts or units often review an assessment because it may discuss aspects covered by more than one expert. The lead analyst or unit will coordinate its product with other experts across the CIA or even with experts in other analytic agencies. This coordination process produces a "corporate" product that reflects the collective views of an agency or the entire intelligence community rather than the individual view of the principal drafter. Coordination is sometimes blamed for watering down judgments to a lowest common denominator. Conversely, coordination ensures analytical accountability because many analysts and mangers have checked sourcing, language precision, and the quality of a product.

counterespionage. As part of a counterintelligence effort, counterespionage seeks to penetrate foreign intelligence entities to assess their capabilities, exploit their vulnerabilities, and disrupt their hostile activities aimed at the United States.

counterintelligence. The gathering and analysis of information as well as the activities conducted to counter hostile foreign intelligence efforts to penetrate US national security and intelligence systems. It requires identifying foreign intelligence threats and countering or neutralizing them.

current analysis. Current analysis is reporting on development of immediate interest that is disseminated daily or even more frequently, allowing for little time for evaluation or further research. Current analysis appears in the daily publications like the President's Daily Brief (PDB) or the Worldwide Intelligence Report (WIRe) as well as other departmental intelligence publications.

Deputies Committee (DC). A subgroup of the National Security Council made up of the deputy secretaries of state, defense, homeland security, treasury, with the vice chairman of the Joint Chiefs of Staff and deputy director of national intelligence as military and intelligence advisers. Additional deputy Cabinet officers will be invited if issues related to their departments are to be discussed. The Deputies Committee reviews the work of lower-level interagency policy committees and forwards any policy issues and recommendations to the Principals Committee. The DC is also responsible for monitoring the implementation of presidential decisions made after National Security Council and DC discussions.

devil's advocacy. Devil's advocacy is an analytic technique designed to challenge a consensus view held on an intelligence topic by developing a contrary case. Such a "contrarian" analysis focuses on questioning the key assumptions or the evidence used by analysts holding to the conventional wisdom. Designed more as a test of current thinking than a true alternative to it, devil's advocacy has been used by some intelligence agencies on those issues said to be "life or death" matters.

director of national intelligence. The director of national intelligence (DNI) serves as the head of the US intelligence community. The DNI also acts as the principal adviser to the president and the National Security Council for intelligence matters related to national security. He also oversees and directs the implementation of the National Intelligence Program.

Directorate of Analysis (DA). Formerly known as the Directorate of Intelligence, the Directorate of Analysis is the major branch of the CIA in which all-source analysis is conducted on both regional and functional topics. Within the CIA, there are individual Mission Centers responsible for China, Europe/Russia, Asia, Africa, Latin America, the Near East, and South Asia as well as centers responsible for analyzing transnational issues, weapons developments, proliferation, and arms control subjects. Both DA and DO officers serve in those centers.

Directorate of Operations (DO). Formerly known as the National Clandestine Service, the DO now is responsible for directing all HUMINT operations across the US government, including the FBI and Department of Defense, for conducting foreign intelligence collection and covert action abroad. The deputy director of the DO reports to the director of the Central Intelligence Agency. As such the DO is the principal "collection" manager—like the National Security Agency, for SIGINT—for human intelligence.

ELINT. Electronic intelligence is gathered from a variety of technical collectors that reveals the existence and characteristics of foreign electronic systems such as radars, air defense systems, and other military electronic systems. It assists traffic analysis that identifies the location, frequency, and strength of electronic warfare systems.

estimative intelligence. Finished intelligence assessments that are focused on longer-term and inherently unknowable events are termed "estimative" to convey that analytic judgments rest on incomplete or sometimes nonexistent evidence. Assessing the future actions, behavior, or military potential of known adversaries are by definition estimative. The best-known form of estimative intelligence is the National Intelligence Estimate, which is produced by the National Intelligence Council.

finished analysis. Finished analysis refers to the written assessments produced by all-source analysts, who evaluate raw intelligence reporting and prepare reports that are then disseminated to other US government agencies. Examples of finished intelligence include the President's Daily Brief, the National Intelligence Daily (now called the WIRe), and the Defense Intelligence Agency's Defense Intelligence Digest. Finished analysis also includes longer-term assessments such as Intelligence Assessments and NIEs.

FISINT. Foreign instrumentation signals intelligence is part of the SIGINT technical collection system, which primarily monitors foreign military and scientific testing and tracking systems. TELINT (telemetry intelligence) is one such category of missile test data used for monitoring foreign military activities, which contributes to national technical means (NTM).

forecast. A forecast is an intelligence judgment concerning the future. In analysis, such estimative or predictive statements aim to reduce or bound uncertainty about a developing or uncertain situation and highlight the implications for policymakers. Forecasts are accompanied by probability statements ranging, for example, from highly likely to very unlikely or by specifying numerical "odds" that an event or outcome will or will not happen.

GEOINT (geospatial intelligence). GEOINT is derived from exploitation and analysis of imagery and geospatial information describing and visually depicting physical features and geographically referenced activities on the Earth.

groupthink. Groupthink is a concept that refers to faulty group decision-making, which prevents consideration of all alternatives in the pursuit of unanimity. Groupthink occurs when small groups are highly cohesive and must reach decisions under severe time pressures. The psychologist Irving Janis developed this notion in studying US decision-making during the Vietnam War. It is often misapplied to analytic failures, where there might have been cognitive errors.

HUMINT (human intelligence). HUMINT consists of collection activities to gain access to people (agents or liaison services), locations, or things (e.g., information systems) to obtain sensitive information that has implications for US security interests. Examples would be information collected clandestinely by agents, obtained from foreign intelligence services of other governments ("liaison"), or more openly by diplomats and military attachés and other US government officials. HUMINT is particularly valuable for analysts when assessing the plans and intentions of governments or nonstate actors.

IMINT (imagery intelligence). Previously referred to as PHOTINT (photo intelligence), imagery intelligence is derived from the images collected from a variety of platforms, ranging from handheld cameras to space-based and other overhead technical imaging systems controlled by the US government. Imagery analysts study specific intelligence targets through the use of imaging systems and issue reports based principally on those collected images. The National Geospatial Intelligence Agency processes and analyzes IMINT and geospatial data for use by all-source analysts and other US government agencies.

intelligence community. As of 2024, the intelligence community includes these seventeen agencies or key elements of them: Air Force Intelligence, Army Intelligence, the Central Intelligence Agency, Coast Guard Intelligence, the Defense Intelligence Agency (DIA), the Department of Energy, the Department of Homeland Security (DHS), the State Department's Bureau of Intelligence and Research (INR), the Department of the Treasury, the Drug Enforcement Agency (DEA), the Federal Bureau of Investigation (FBI), Marine Corp Intelligence, the National Geospatial Intelligence Agency (NGA), the National Reconnaissance Office (NRO), the National Security Agency (NSA), Navy Intelligence, and Space Force Intelligence. The director of national intelligence (DNI) heads the intelligence community.

intelligence cycle. The intelligence cycle comprises the multistep process of setting intelligence requirements, collecting and processing information, analyzing and producing finished intelligence, and disseminating it to policymakers, who may then provide feedback on what further intelligence they will need or pose questions about the intelligence provided.

intelligence failure. Although there is no commonly accepted definition, this failure occurs when there is a systemic or organizational inability to collect correct and accurate information in a timely fashion or interpret this information properly and analyze it in a timely way in order to alert policymakers to a major new development. Typically, an intelligence failure is characterized by collection and analysis problems, along with insufficient attention to bringing a warning to policymakers so they can respond appropriately.

interagency process. Analysts participate in many "interagency" meetings, where they present their intelligence assessments for use in policy discussions among the National Security Council, State Department, and Defense Department. Working-level "interagency" meetings are often held before more senior-level meetings where decisions will be made. Typically, analysts support discussions at the working level and participate in those meetings. For Deputies Committee (deputy secretary level) or Principals Committee (secretary-level) meetings, analysts will provide briefing papers or prepare senior intelligence community leaders such as the DNI or CIA director, who will represent the community in those discussions.

level of confidence. Analysts must determine how confident they are in reaching analytic judgments based on the quality of the information available and the complexity of the issue. Assigning a "low" level of confidence to a judgment may result from collection gaps, contradictory information, or the presence of deception and denial. "High" confidence may result from having very sensitive HUMINT or extremely precise technical intelligence on a military plan or a weapons system that is corroborated from multiple, independent sources.

MASINT (measurement and signatures intelligence). Measurement and signature intelligence is technically derived intelligence data other than standard imagery and SIGINT. It employs a broad group of disciplines including nuclear, optical, radio frequency, acoustics, seismic, and materials sciences. Examples of MASINT are the detection of low-yield nuclear tests by seismic sensors or by collecting and analyzing the composition of air and water samples.

mind-set. A mind-set is a type of cognitive filter or lens through which information is evaluated and weighed by the analyst. Beliefs, assumptions, concepts, and information retrieved from memory form a mind-set or mental model that guides perception and processing of new information. Typically, a mind-set rests on a series of assumptions about the way the target of the analyst's investigation behaves. Closely related to mind-set is a "mental model," which connotes a more highly developed set of ideas about a specific subject. Mind-sets and mental models form quickly and become hard to change, particularly when they prove useful in forecasting future trends; once proven successful, analysts accept them uncritically despite changes in the environment that would suggest they have become outdated or inaccurate.

mirror imaging. Mirror imaging is a cognitive error that occurs when analysts presume that a foreign actor will behave much as they would in the same situation. In this sense, the analysts see their image when they observe the foreign actor. Often analysts have developed a strong expertise on a subject and believe there is a logical way to develop a weapons system, conduct a coup, or reach a decision. They will, then, presume that a foreign actor would go about these tasks as they would. Classic examples include analytic views that assumed risk-averse Soviet behavior in the Cuban missile crisis or similar Arab reluctance to start a war with Israel in 1973.

National Counterintelligence and Security Center (NCSC). The NCSC oversees the counterintelligence activities conducted by the CIA, FBI, and the Department of Defense and oversees and coordinates the programs and priorities on behalf of the DNI. It also conducts damage assessments of American counterintelligence cases.

National Counterproliferation Center (NCPC). The NCPC was established in 2005 within the Office of the Director of National Intelligence. It coordinates intelligence support to stem the proliferation of weapons of mass destruction and related delivery systems. It also develops long-term strategies for better collection and analysis on future threats from weapons of mass destruction.

National Counterterrorism Center (NCTC). The NCTC was established in 2005 as part of the Intelligence Reform and Terrorism Prevention Act of 2004. The NCTC integrates all intelligence—both foreign and domestic—within the US government pertaining to terrorism and counterterrorism. It conducts strategic operational planning and also produces intelligence analysis for key policy agencies. It is part of the Office of the Director of National Intelligence.

National Intelligence Council (NIC). The NIC is responsible for producing National Intelligence Estimates for the US government and for evaluating community-wide collection and production of intelligence by the intelligence community. The NIC is made up of roughly a dozen senior intelligence officers, known as national intelligence officers.

National Intelligence Estimate (NIE). An NIE is usually a strategic assessment of the capabilities, vulnerabilities, and probable courses of action of foreign nations or nonstate actors produced at the national level as a composite of the views of analysts throughout the US intelligence community. It is prepared under the auspices of the National Intelligence Council, and one or more national intelligence officers will guide the drafting of the estimate. Analysts throughout the intelligence community participate in preparing and approving the text. The NIE is then presented to the heads of the US intelligence community and officially released by the director of national intelligence as the community's most authoritative statement on an intelligence subject.

national intelligence officer (NIO). A NIO is a senior expert on either a regional area (e.g., Europe, Asia, Africa, or the Middle East) or a functional area (e.g., weapons of mass destruction, transnational threats, or conventional military) who directs the production of NIEs on those topics. They guide and evaluate the quality of analysis in their substantive areas. NIOs represent intelligence community analysts at interagency meetings and interact regularly with senior policy officials to ensure intelligence production is directed at policy issues of importance.

National Intelligence Priorities Framework (NIPF). An elaborate framework for prioritizing intelligence collection and analysis priorities according to the target country and intelligence topic. The NIPF assigns a numerical priority (1–5), according to the importance senior officials attach to the topic, and those priorities are used to allocate and justify intelligence community resources and programs.

National Security Council (NSC). Established by the 1947 National Security Act, this body is chaired by the president and includes the vice president and the secretaries of defense, state, and the Treasury as well as the national security adviser. The chairman of the Joint Chiefs of Staff and the director of national intelligence participate as the president's senior military and intelligence advisers. The NSC directs the work of lower-level committees: the principals, deputies, and interagency policy committees.

Office of Strategic Services (OSS). The intelligence organization established during World War II, which later became the basis for the CIA. The OSS conducted overseas collection and covert action as well as maintained a research and analysis capability. It was led by William "Wild Bill" Donovan.

opportunity analysis. CIA analysts occasionally produce assessments of how foreign actors could respond to potential courses of action that policymakers might consider to address an international development. These assessments are not policy recommendations or endorsements. Rather, they sketch out the positive and negative consequences of potential US military, diplomatic, economic, or other measures designed to take advantage of a foreign entity's vulnerabilities or to maximize US influence over it. It is incumbent on CIA analysts to have a good grasp of US national elements of power and to maintain their objectivity in weighing the pros and cons of each potential course of action.

order of battle. In military analysis, the order of battle identifies military units, their command structure, and the strength and disposition of personnel, equipment, and units of an organized military force on the battlefield.

OSINT (open source intelligence). Open source intelligence involves collecting information from unclassified, publicly available sources and analyzing its significance to the US government. Open sources would include newspapers, magazines, radio, television, and computer-based information in many foreign languages; public data found in government reports, press releases, and speeches; and professional and academic journals and conference proceedings. Increasingly, open source has focused on exploiting the Internet world of websites and bloggers. The Open Source Center is the intelligence community's primary organization responsible for the collection and analysis of open source information.

policy support. Used to describe intelligence reporting and analysis that is provided specifically to inform policy decisions and improve information used to conduct or evaluate policy options. It does not imply intelligence advocating any particular policy agenda.

politicization. There is no generally accepted definition of politicization, but it commonly refers to the intentional biasing of intelligence analysis to suit a particular set of political goals or agendas. Analysts can be prone to politicization if they allow their personal views to influence their analytic judgments; likewise, policymakers can "politicize" intelligence by pressuring analysts to tailor their judgments to suit a policy agenda or by misrepresenting analysis as supporting their preferred policies.

President's Daily Brief (PDB). The President's Daily Brief is a compilation of current intelligence items of high significance to national policy concerns provided daily by the Director of National Intelligence. It is produced principally by the Central Intelligence Agency, with contributions from the Defense Intelligence Agency and the State Department's Bureau of Intelligence and Research. A PDB briefer delivers it to the president, and other briefers provide it to a select group of senior officials designated by the president as recipients. The PDB is constantly being refined to suit the individual needs of each president's preference for format, presentation style, and length.

Principals Committee (PC). The group of senior Cabinet officials advising the president on national security matters. The secretaries of state, defense, treasury, and homeland security, along with the director of national intelligence and chairman of the Joint Chiefs of Staff, form the core group, to which are often added other

Cabinet officials when issues within their areas of responsibilities are discussed. The PC is customarily chaired by the national security adviser, and its recommendations are then provided to the president directly or brought to the National Security Council, at which the president and principals meet.

Red Team analysis. This structured analytical technique is aimed at countering cultural bias and the "mirror-imaging" problem by constructing a team of analysts who will consciously try to "think like the enemy" rather than like American intelligence analysts. "Red Team" analysts study and then role play the key decision-makers in a foreign government or perhaps a terrorist cell. They adopt the same decision-making styles, goals, or methods that an adversary might use in accomplishing their objectives. The Red Team assessments provide US policymakers with an unconventional look at how their opponents might perceive a situation or react to US policy actions.

scenarios analysis (or scenarios development). This structured analytic technique is designed to generate multiple hypotheses about a future trend or development through the use of group-designed exercises that create alternative futures. Scenario exercises bring together experts from diverse fields and invite them to brainstorm on key factors that will shape future trends. After determining the key factors (often called "drivers"), the exercise designs three or more different futures by combining these drivers in different ways. The technique has been used extensively in private industry and other business consulting firms but is now regularly employed by intelligence and other national security agencies.

SIGINT (signals intelligence). Interception and analysis of a target's use of technical signals and communications systems. It encompasses COMINT (communications intelligence) as well as ELINT (electronic intelligence systems) and FISINT (foreign instrumentation or telemetry). The National Security Agency is the principal SIGINT collector in the US government.

situation reporting. Situational reporting (commonly called "sit-reps") is analysis that is rapidly disseminated to give policymakers the most up-to-date information for a quickly developing story. "Sit-reps" typically focus on what the facts are and any immediate implications of the event. Reporting on coups, deaths of world leaders, military clashes, and sudden breakdowns in civil order or diplomatic negotiations would be the most likely topics of such reporting.

sources and methods. Sources and methods are those technical and human means of gathering information clandestinely on intelligence topics. A source can be a satellite imaging system operating high above a foreign country, a diplomat's reporting from an embassy, or a source's clandestine meeting with a case officer to report on a high-level meeting of his government. Analysts must "source" their reports and assessments by demonstrating they have a variety of reporting, preferably from very different kinds of sources and collection disciplines, and assess the validity and credibility of the reporting. Such scrutiny reduces the chances of deception or fabrication of reporting if it came from a single source.

strategic analysis. Unlike situational reporting or current analysis, strategic analysis focuses less on events than on long-term trends. It is usually performed only on subjects of enduring interest to the United States. For example, strategic analysis of foreign ballistic missile developments or of the Chinese military would be of enduring interest to policymakers, regardless of their immediate policy agendas. Strategic analysis is inherently "estimative," as there is little detailed information on trends beyond a year or more.

structured analytic techniques (SATs). Structured analytic techniques are used to provide more rigor to analytic judgments and to make them more transparent and testable. Various structured analytic techniques—such as devil's advocacy, Team A / Team B analysis, analysis of competing hypotheses, and scenarios analysis—attempt to record the logic employed by analysts in reaching judgments. By structuring the analysis according to a set of principles (e.g., listing key assumptions, evaluating the quality of information, examining multiple hypotheses, identifying collection gaps, and detecting possible deception and denial), analysts can establish more systematically their levels of confidence in judgments reached. Moreover, they can also track changes in their judgments over time and revisit conclusions that new evidence might appear to challenge.

target analysis. Analysis is conducted in direct support of collection, covert action, and other operations often aimed at terrorism or proliferation targets. Such analysis focuses on understanding, monitoring, and targeting specific individuals, organizations, or networks and uses specialized tools for exploiting large volumes of data collected on such targets. Unlike traditional forms of analysis prepared for policymakers, target analysis directly supports the military, law enforcement, or other operators to interdict or eliminate hostile targets.

Team A / Team B analysis. This structured analytic technique uses separate analytic teams that contrast two or more strongly held views or competing hypotheses about an intelligence topic. Each team will develop its assessments using the available evidence after laying out their key assumptions about the topic. The value comes in arraying the two competing views side by side, which highlights how different premises cause analysts to reach different conclusions.

TECHINT. TECHINT are technical intelligence collection systems—including IMINT, GEOINT, SIGINT, COMINT, ELINT, FISINT, and MASINT. They are used in combination with HUMINT intelligence to observe and monitor foreign government and nonstate actor actions and behavior. They comprise the largest portion of the US intelligence community's budget and programs.

weapons of mass destruction (WMD). Commonly considered to be nuclear, chemical, biological, or radiological weapons that can cause mass casualties. In some cases, cyber capabilities might also qualify if it has mass effects.

Worldwide Intelligence Report (WIRe). The Worldwide Intelligence Report (electronic) has replaced the National Intelligence Daily (NID) as the CIA's current publication circulated throughout the US government to senior policy officials. This is now a more web-based publication that has an electronic dissemination within Washington and overseas. It can be updated frequently throughout the day rather than operate as a once-a-day publication like the NID.

Contributors

Cynthia "Cindy" S. Barkanic retired in early 2020 after more than thirty-seven years at the CIA. She served as a senior economic analyst and was promoted to the Senior Intelligence Service in 2016. Her regions of research and analysis were the Middle East, North Africa, and South Asia. She is currently a consultant to the CIA. She also is the founder of CSB Coaching Insights LLC, which provides coaching, assessment, and support to fine-tune the leadership skills of managers at all levels, in the intelligence field and beyond. She received her master's in public affairs from Princeton University, with a concentration in economics and quantitative analysis.

James B. Bruce entered the CIA as a Soviet specialist in 1982 and retired as a senior intelligence officer twenty-four years later. Much of his career spanned counterintelligence and foreign deception of US intelligence. He worked as a counterintelligence analyst in the Directorate of Operations and as chief of counterintelligence training in the Counterintelligence Center. He also served as deputy national intelligence officer for science and technology and as a senior staff member on the Iraq WMD Commission, focusing on human and technical collection issues. He also coedited, with Roger George, *Analyzing Intelligence: National Security Practitioners' Perspectives*, 2nd ed. (Georgetown University Press, 2014).

Jane P. Fletcher retired after more than thirty-two years of public service, including twenty-nine years at the CIA, where she primarily focused on combating threats from weapons of mass destruction. In her last assignment, she served as the deputy national intelligence manager for counterproliferation as well as the National Counterproliferation Center senior strategist. She also previously served as the Weapons Intelligence, Nonproliferation, and Arms Control Center senior scientist, the first-ever Senior Analytic Service program manager, and deputy director and acting director of the Kent Center for Analytic Tradecraft at the Sherman Kent School for Intelligence Analysis. In recognition of her efforts, she was named the CIA's 1996 Scientist of the Year and promoted to the Senior Intelligence Service.

Roger Z. George had a thirty-year career as a political-military analyst at the CIA, where he also served as a national intelligence officer as well as a policy planner in the Department of State and Department of Defense. He has taught intelligence and national security at the National War College, Georgetown University, and Occidental College. He received his PhD from the Fletcher School of Law and Diplomacy and published *Intelligence for the National Security Enterprise: An Introduction* (Georgetown University Press, 2019). He also coedited *The National Security Enterprise: Navigating the Labyrinth,* 2nd ed. (Georgetown University Press, 2016).

Robert Levine retired from the CIA in December 2018 after thirty-three years in the US intelligence community. He served as a senior military analyst and ran the internal analytic quality evaluation program for the CIA's Directorate of Analysis. He taught intelligence and national security policy at the National War College, within the intelligence community, and at Mercyhurst College. He received his PhD from the RAND Graduate Institute and published "Principles of Intelligence Analysis," in *Studies in Intelligence.* He is currently a lecturer at Johns Hopkins University.

Blake W. Mobley served as a counterintelligence officer at the CIA supporting clandestine operations and senior US policymakers. Specializing in nonstate actors, he conducted counterintelligence analysis at a major station abroad. In the private sector, he managed security and counterintelligence operations in both the biotechnology and renewable energy sectors. He received a PhD from Georgetown University, an MPP from Harvard University, and a BA from Stanford University. He is the author of *Terrorism and Counterintelligence: How Terrorist Groups Elude Detection* (Columbia University Press, 2012), in addition to contributing to other books and articles on counterintelligence.

Clark Shannon retired from the CIA in 2021 after more than three decades of service as a senior analyst and manager in the CIA's Directorate of Analysis. His primary focus was on counterterrorism. He also served multiple CIA assignments overseas and rotational assignments at the US Department of State in Washington and at the CIA's Sherman Kent School for Intelligence Analysis. He received degrees from the Fletcher School for Law and Diplomacy and Trinity University in Texas.

Steve Stigall joined the CIA in 1985, when he began his career as a military analyst on Soviet strategic and naval forces. He was one of the first intelligence analysts assigned to track foreign cyber threats and was the lead drafter of two National Intelligence Estimates. He has written dozens of President's Daily Brief articles and other current intelligence assessments on cyber. Throughout his career, he has been assigned to numerous military commands and has served in both the Afghan and Iraqi war zones. He has also taught as an "officer-in-residence" at the US Air Force Academy and as the CIA's representative at the National War College. Most recently, he was on the faculty of the National Intelligence University. He is a member of the CIA's Senior Analytic Service. He received his BA in history and political science from Webster University in Saint Louis and his MA in Russian history from Indiana University.

Jeffrey Waggett was the first leadership analyst hired by the CIA with an academic degree in leadership studies. As a senior China leadership analyst, he frequently contributed to the President's Daily Brief, wrote numerous leadership profiles and assessments, and briefed all levels of civilian and military officials. He served as a CIA White House briefer in the aftermath of the September 11, 2001, terrorist attacks. Over his long career, he has provided a broad range of analytic support to CIA activities across two war zones, in most CIA directorates, and for the Office of the Director of National Intelligence. He received his BA in leadership studies from the University of Richmond and his MA in security studies from Georgetown University. He is currently serving as a speechwriter for senior US government officials.

Adam Wasserman retired in 2017 after thirty-five years in the CIA's Directorate of Intelligence. He began his career as a Soviet military analyst and subsequently was a manager and analyst on political topics dealing with the former USSR, Southeast Asia, Iraq, and Afghanistan. He served in rotation assignments at a US embassy, on the State Department's Policy Planning Staff, and as director for Iraq at the National Security Council. He taught at the Air War College and at the Sherman Kent School for Intelligence Analysis. He received an MA in political philosophy from the University of Chicago and a master's in international affairs from the Fletcher School of Law and Diplomacy. He is a member of the Senior Analytic Service. Since retiring, he has consulted with the National Intelligence Council and recently contributed to *Global Trends 2040*, a long-range forecasting project.

Index